HEIDEGGER TOWARD THE TURN

SUNY series in
Contemporary Continental Philosophy

Dennis J. Schmidt, editor

HEIDEGGER TOWARD THE TURN

ESSAYS ON THE WORK OF THE 1930s

edited by
James Risser

STATE UNIVERSITY OF NEW YORK PRESS

Chapter 3 reprinted from John D. Caputo, "Heidegger's Revolution: The Politics of the Myths of Being," from *Demythologizing Heidegger* (Bloomington: Indiana University Press, 1993) with the permission of Indiana University Press. Copyright 1993 by John D. Caputo.

Chapter 7 is a translation from the German of Hans-Georg Gadamer, *Denken und Dichten bei Heidegger und Hölderlin* (Tübingen: J.C.B. Mohr (Paul Siebeck). Reprinted by permission of J.C.B. Mohr and Hans-Georg Gadamer.

Chapter 12 reprinted from Reiner Schürmann, "Ultimate Double Binds," in *Graduate Faculty Philosophy Journal* (New York: New School for Social Research). Reprinted by permission of New School for Social Research and Reiner Schürmann.

Production by Ruth Fisher
Marketing by Anne M. Valentine

Published by
State University of New York Press, Albany

© 1999 State University of New York

All rights reserved

Printed in the United States of America

No part of this book may be used or reproduced in any manner whatsoever without written permission. No part of this book may be stored in a retrieval system or transmitted in any form or by any means including electronic, electrostatic, magnetic tape, mechanical, photocopying, recording, or otherwise without the prior permission in writing of the publisher.

For information, address the State University of New York Press, State University Plaza, Albany, NY 12246

Library of Congress Cataloging-in-Publication Data

Heidegger toward the turn : essays on the work of the 1930s / edited by James Risser.
    p. cm. — (SUNY series in contemporary continental philosophy)
    Includes bibliographical references and index.
    ISBN 0-7914-4301-9 (alk. paper). — ISBN 0-7914-4302-7 (pbk. : alk. paper)
    1. Heidegger, Martin, 1889–1976. I. Risser, James, 1946– . II. Series.
B3279.H49H35254   1999
193—dc21
                                                         99-26111
                                                                CIP

10 9 8 7 6 5 4 3 2 1

CONTENTS

Acknowledgments/ vii

Abbreviations/ ix

Introduction/
James Risser 1

I. On Truth

Chapter 1. Interrupting Truth/
John Sallis 19

Chapter 2. Tuned to Accord: On Heidegger's Concept of Truth/
Rodolphe Gasché 31

II. Metaphysics and the History of Being

Chapter 3. Heidegger's Revolution: An Introduction to *An Introduction to Metaphysics*/
John D. Caputo 53

Chapter 4. Heidegger and 'The' Greeks: History, Catastrophe, and Community/
Dennis J. Schmidt 75

III. The Work of Art

Chapter 5. The Greatness of the Work of Art/
Robert Bernasconi 95

Chapter 6. Heidegger's Freiburg Version of the Origin of the Work of Art/
Françoise Dastur 119

IV. Reading Hölderlin

Chapter 7. Thinking and Poetizing in Heidegger and in Hölderlin's "Andenken"/
Hans-Georg Gadamer — 145

Chapter 8. Heidegger, Hölderlin, and Sophoclean Tragedy/
Véronique M. Fóti — 163

Chapter 9. Heidegger's Turn to *Germanien*—a Sigetic Venture/
Wilhelm S. Wurzer — 187

V. Heidegger and Ethics

Chapter 10. The Question of Ethics in Heidegger's Account of Authenticity/
Charles E. Scott — 211

Chapter 11. Heidegger on Values/
Jacques Taminiaux — 225

VI. Reading the *Beiträge*

Chapter 12. Ultimate Double Binds/
Reiner Schürmann — 243

Chapter 13. Contributions to Life/
David Farrell Krell — 269

VII. Thinking the "Da" of Dasein

Chapter 14. Empty Time and Indifference to Being/
Michel Haar — 295

Chapter 15. *Heimat:* Heidegger on the Threshold/
Will McNeill — 319

Bibliography/ — 351

Notes on Contributors/ — 357

General Index/ — 361

ACKNOWLEDGMENTS

I would like to thank the editors of:

J.C.B. Mohr (Paul Siebeck), Tübingen, for permission to translate and reprint Hans-Georg Gadamer's article "Denken und Dichten bei Heidegger und Hölderlin" published in *Gesammelte Werke* Band 10: *Hermeneutik im Rückblick* (1995).

Graduate Faculty Philosophy Journal for permission to reprint Reiner Schürmann's "Ultimate Double Binds," which appeared in an earlier version in the journal.

Obsidiance, Paris, for permission to translate and reprint Michel Haar's article, "Le temps vide et l'indifference a l'etre," published in *Exercises de la patience*, 2 (1986), pp. 17–36.

I would also like to thank Douglas Brick for his translation of the Michel Haar article, "Le temps vide et l'indifference a l'etre," and Richard Palmer for his translation of Hans-Georg Gadamer's article, "Denken und Dichten bei Heidegger und Hölderlin."

Finally I would like to thank Dennis Schmidt for his guidance in this project, Catherine LePiane for her assistance in preparing the manuscript for publication, and my wife Jean whose patience knows no bounds.

ABBREVIATIONS

Gesamtausgabe Volumes

GA 2   *Sein und Zeit* (1927). Edited by Friedrich-Wilhelm von Hermann. 1977.

GA 3   *Kant und das Problem der Metaphysik* (1929). Edited by Friedrich-Wilhelm von Herrmann. 1991.

GA 4   *Erläuterungen zu Hölderlins Dichtung* (1936–1968). Edited by Friedrich-Wilhelm von Herrmann. 1981.

GA 5   *Holzwege* (1935–1946). Edited by Friedrich-Wilhelm von Herrmann. 1977.

GA 9   *Wegmarken* (1919–1961). Edited by Friedrich-Wilhelm von Herrmann. 1976.

GA 13   *Aus der Erfahrung des Denkens.* Edited by Hermann Heidegger. 1983.

GA 24   *Die Grundprobleme der Phänomenologie.* (Sommersemester 1927). Edited by Friedrich-Wilhelm von Herrmann. 1975.

GA 26   *Metaphysische Anfangsgründe der Logik im Ausgang von Leibniz* (Sommersemester 1930). Edited by Klaus Held. 1978.

GA 29/30   *Die Grundbegriffe der Metaphysik: Welt-Endlichkeit-Einsamkeit* (Wintersemester 1929/30). Edited by Friedrich-Wilhelm von Herrmann. 1983.

GA 31   *Vom Wesen der menschlichen Freiheit: Einleitung in die Philosophie* (Sommersemester 1930). Edited by Hartmut Tietjen. 1982.

GA 32	*Hegels Phänomenologie des Geistes* (Wintersemester 1930/31). Edited by Ingtraud Görland. 1980.
GA 33	*Aristoteles: Metaphysik IX 1–3* (Sommersemester 1931). Edited by Heinrich Hüni. 1981.
GA 34	*Vom Wesen der Wahrheit. Zu Platons Höhlengleichnis und Theätet* (Wintersemester 1931/32). Edited by Hermann Mörchen. 1988.
GA 39	*Hölderlins Hymnen "Germanien" und "der Rhein"* (Wintersemester 1934/35). Edited by Susanne Ziegler. 1980.
GA 40	*Einführung in die Metaphysik* (Sommersemester 1935). Edited by Petra Jaeger. 1983.
GA 41	*Die Frage nach dem Ding. Zu Kants Lehre von den transzendentalen Grundsätzen* (Wintersemester 1935/36). Edited by Petra Jaeger. 1984.
GA 42	*Schelling: Vom Wesen der menschlichen Freiheit* (Sommersemester 1936). Edited by Ingrid Schüssler. 1988.
GA 43	*Nietzsche: Der Wille zur Macht als Kunst* (Wintersemester 1936/37). Edited by Bernd Heimbüchel. 1985.
GA 44	*Nietzsches metaphysische Grundstellung im abendländische Denken: Die ewige Wiederkehr des Gleichen* (Sommersemester 1937). Edited by Marion Heinz. 1986.
GA 45	*Grundfragen der Philosophie. Ausgewählte »Probleme« der »Logik«* (Wintersemester 1937/38). Edited by Friedrich-Wilhelm von Herrmann. 1984.
GA 47	*Nietzsches Lehre vom Willen zur Macht als Erkenntnis* (Sommersemester 1939). Edited by Eberhard Hanser. 1989.
GA 48	*Nietzsche: Der europäische Nihilismus* (II. Trimester 1940). Edited by Petra Jaeger. 1986.
GA 51	*Grundbegriffe* (Sommersemester 1941). Edited by Petra Jaeger. 1981.
GA 52	*Hölderlins Hymne »Andenken«* (Wintersemester 1941/42). Edited by Curd Ochwadt. 1982.

GA 53	*Hölderlins Hymne »Der Ister«* (Sommersemester 1942). Edited by Walter Biemel. 1984.
GA 54	*Parmenides* (Wintersemester 1942/43). Edited by Manfred S. Frings. 1982.
GA 55	*Heraklit. 1. Der Anfang des abendländischen Denkens* (Heraklit) (Sommersemester 1943). *2. Logik. Heraklits Lehre vom Logos* (Sommersemester 1944). Edited by Manfred S. Frings. 1979.
GA 65	*Beiträge zur Philosophie.* (Vom Ereignis) (1936–1938). Edited by Friedrich-Wilhelm von Herrmann. 1989.

Other Works by Heidegger

BP	*The Basic Problems of Phenomenology.* Translated by Albert Hofstadter. Bloomington: Indiana University Press, 1982.
OA	*De l'origine de l'oeuvre d'art. Premiere version 1935.* Edited by E. Martineau. Paris: Authentica, 1987.
D	*Denkerfahrungen.* Edited by Hermann Heidegger. Frankfurt: Klostermann, 1983.
EM	*Einführung in die Metaphysik.* Tübingen: Niemeyer, 1966.
IM	———. *An Introduction to Metaphysics.* Translated by Ralph Mannheim. New Haven: Yale University Press, 1959.
EHD	*Erläuterungen zu Hölderlins Dichtung.* 4th edition. Frankfurt: Klostermann, 1971.
FS	*Frühe Schriften.* Frankfurt: Klostermann, 1974.
G	*Gelassenheit.* Pfullingen: Neske, 1985.
BW	*Heidegger: Basic Writings.* Edited by David F. Krell. New York: Harper & Row, 1977.
HW	*Holzwege.* Frankfurt: Klostermann, 1972.
NI, NII	*Nietzsche* (1936–1946). 2 vols. Pfullingen: Neske, 1961.

Ni	———. *Nietzsche Vol. 1. The Will to Power as Art.* Translated by David F. Krell. New York: Harper & Row, 1979.
PLT	*Poetry Language Thought.* Translated by Albert Hofstadter. New York: Harper & Row, 1971.
SG	*Der Satz Vom Grund.* Pfullingen: Neske, 1978.
SZ	*Sein und Zeit.* 9th ed. Tübingen: Max Niemeyer, 1960.
BT	———. *Being and Time.* Translated by J. Macquarrie and E. Robinson. New York: Harper & Row, 1962.
SU	*Die Selbstbehauptung der Deutschen Universität (1933)* and *Das Rektorat 1933/1934* (1945). Edited by Herrmann Heidegger. Frankfurt: Klostermann, 1983.
SA	———. "The Self Assertion of the German University." Translated by Karsten Harries. *Review of Metaphysics* 38.3 (1985): 467–502.
QT	*The Question Concerning Technology and Other Essays.* Translated by W. Lovitt. New York: Harper & Row, 1977.
US	*Unterwegs zur Sprache.* Pfullingen: Neske, 1977.
VS	*Vier Seminare.* Frankfurt: Klostermann, 1977.
VA	*Vorträge und Aufsätze.* Pfullingen: Neske, 1954.
W	*Wegmarken.* Edited by Friedrich-Wilhelm von Herrmann. Frankfurt: Klostermann, 1976.

INTRODUCTION

"Heidegger toward the turn." What does this mean? At its simplest, it designates a certain chronological period in Heidegger's life that beings immediately after the publication of *Being and Time* in 1927 and can be said to end with the work of Nietzsche that consumes Heidegger around the outbreak of World War II in Germany. Such simplicity, if not artificiality, in marking a period of philosophical development chronologically, just as easily allows us to indicate the period at its outset by the year 1929, when Heidegger returned to Freiburg from Marburg on the occasion of his appointment to the Chair of Philosophy that was left vacant by Husserl's retirement. In that year Heidegger saw the publication of his first works since *Being and Time: Kant and the Problem of Metaphysics*[1] and *The Essence of Reasons*[2] (written for a *Festschrift* for Edmund Husserl on his seventieth birthday), works that purportedly demonstrate a movement forward in the thought of being. To ask further about this movement forward on the basis of subsequent writings in the decade of the thirties, one may be surprised to see that Heidegger actually published very little. His inaugural lecture given at Freiburg University, "What Is Metaphysics?," appeared in 1930;[3] his rectorate address to the University, "The Self-Assertion of the German University," was published in 1933;[4] and his 1936 lecture, "Hölderlin and the Essence of Poetry," was presented in Rome and published the following year.[5]

This is not to suggest that this was a period of inactivity for Heidegger. One has only to look at the number of works composed during this period, but not published until later, to see that, on the contrary, it was a period of intense philosophical activity: "On the Essence of Truth" (1930, published in 1943),[6] *An Introduction to Metaphysics* (1935, published in 1953),[7] "The Origin of the Work of Art" (1935, published in 1950),[8] *What Is a Thing* (1935–36, published in 1962),[9] »Die Zeit des Weltbildes« (1938, published in 1950),

»Wie wenn am Feiertage . . . « (1939, published in 1951), and most of the lectures on Nietzsche (1936–41) that appeared in the two-volume edition published in 1961. An even more complete picture of Heidegger's philosophical work during this time is obtained through the lecture courses that he gave at Freiburg and the other writings that are now being published in the *Gesamtausgabe*,[10] including Vol. 39: *Hölderlins Hymnen »Germanien« und »Der Rhein«* (1934–35) and Vol. 65: *Beiträge zur Philosophie (Vom Ereignis)* (1936–38). Looked at thematically, the variety of topics covered by these writings indicate that Heidegger's path of thinking toward the turn cannot be reduced to a singular expression. Nevertheless we can proceed from a general expression of the character of this thinking in order to see precisely what is indicated by the phrase "toward the turn." In the most general terms, Heidegger's thinking during this period was engaged in a thinking on the question of the meaning of being that seemingly "turns" from the problematic of the existential analytic of Dasein to the thinking of being as such. This statement, given Heidegger's self-interpretation of his work from this period, cannot be interpreted to mean that Heidegger changes the standpoint in his thinking. The turn is not a matter of abandoning the standpoint of Dasein in order to take up the standpoint of being itself. In the "Letter on Humanism" (1947), written as a response to Sartre and to the misunderstanding of his own philosophy as a metaphysics of subjectivity where the projection of being is read as an accomplishment of subjectivity, Heidegger tries to make clear that the understanding of being can only be thought in the context of the existential analytic "as the ecstatic relation to the clearing of being."[11] The issue of a turn in thinking pertains to the adequacy of the articulation of this thought within the transcendental framework in which *Being and Time* was cast.

What Heidegger realizes soon after the publication of *Being and Time* is that the being event cannot be read simply from Dasein as the place of the understanding of being.[12] But this is not to say that Heidegger abandons Dasein, since the thinking of being never escapes the question of human being who speaks being. His realization produced a shift in emphasis from an analysis of the being of Dasein to an analysis of the event of being itself that occurs in the "there" (Da) of Dasein. Thus Heidegger writes:

> The adequate execution and completion of this other thinking that abandons subjectivity is surely made more difficult by the fact that in the publication of *Being and Time* the third

division of the first part, "Time and Being," was held back ... Here everything is reversed. The section in question was held back because thinking failed in the adequate saying of this turning *[Kehre]* and did not succeed with the help of the language of metaphysics. The lecture "On the Essence of Truth," thought out and delivered in 1930 but not printed until 1943, provides a certain insight into the thinking of the turning from "Being and Time" to "Time and Being." This turning is not a change in standpoint from *Being and Time*, but in it the thinking that was sought first arrives at the location of that dimension out of which *Being and Time* is experienced, that is to say, experienced from the fundamental experience of the oblivion of Being.[13]

Heidegger repeats the general tone of these remarks in his letter to William Richardson (1962). The thinking of the *Kehre*, Heidegger tells us, is a change in his thought, but the change is not a consequence of a change in standpoint "much less of abandoning the fundamental issue of *Being and Time*. The thinking of the *Kehre* results from the fact that I stayed with the matter-for-thought [of] "Being and Time," sc. by inquiring into that perspective which already in *Being and Time* (p. 39) was designated as "Time and Being."[14] From these comments in the letter to Richardson we know that a certain insight into the being event is now to be gained as a result of his lecture on the essence of truth (1930), viz., that in the "there" of Dasein being forms a clearing. Within this, however, the real insight is not so much that the being event is the event of truth as disclosure, but that the disclosure of being is "simultaneously and intrinsically" the concealing of being as a whole. Or, expressed differently: at the heart of the being event is the self-withdrawal in truth as unconcealment. This insight does nothing to alter the fact that for Heidegger the oblivion of being remains the constant theme.

If it is the case then that Heidegger is not changing his standpoint, but that in his thinking he is trying to break free of the metaphysics that held his own thinking on the oblivion of being captive, how might we indicate, in a positive expression, what is meant by the phrase "toward the turn"? Let us say that "toward the turn" captures those turnings in Heidegger's thinking before the question of language comes to the forefront in which he attempts to stay with what has always been for him the constant matter to be thought. If we then look directly at the principal writings from this period, "toward the turn" means at once not simply a turn from an analysis of Dasein to thinking of being; but, in its positive multiplicity: a focus on the question of truth, an expansion of the task of the destruction of metaphysics, and an attempt to re-think the question of history out of the turmoil of the 1930s.

First and foremost, then, Heidegger turns the question of the meaning of being in the direction of the question of the truth of being. One must say "foremost" not only because through this question Heidegger is really asking about the metaphysics of metaphysics, about going back into the ground of metaphysics in which the matter of the oblivion of being is to be thought. The oblivion of being pertains to the staying away of the ground—an abyssal ground—that is now expressed in the lecture on the essence of truth as the non-essence of untruth. To say it once more, concealment belongs to the essence of unconcealment. Accordingly, even the question of being as we witness it in the history of metaphysics—a topic that soon comes to the forefront of Heidegger's thinking in the 1930s—falls prey to a fundamental errancy. Metaphysics according to Heidegger has thought the nature of beings while being itself is covered over in oblivion. But the turning of the question from the meaning of being to the *truth* of being is also foremost because it then pervades Heidegger's writings throughout the 1930s and beyond,[15] and becomes the explicit topic in a number of lecture courses, including "The Basic Questions of Philosophy" (1937–1938) and "Parmenides" (1942–1943).

With the emphasis now on the question of truth of being, Heidegger begins to confront the understanding of being in metaphysics even more directly than he had in *Being and Time* and even in *Kant and the Problem of Metaphysics* (1929), in which he had, by his own confession, relapsed into the standpoint of the transcendental question. In *An Introduction to Metaphysics* (1935) Heidegger explicitly exposes the emptiness of the concept of being as it has traditionally been grasped with the history of metaphysics. What emerges from this destruction is the renewed consideration of the question of being as a historical question that now includes a reexamination of the understanding of being as it was first articulated by the early Greeks. Most decisively, however, the historical character of the being question is not restricted to its self-understanding within the tradition of Western metaphysics; for Heidegger, the historical density of the West is bound up with the manner of asking and answering this question. This means that, in posing the question of being, Heidegger is not concerned with setting up an ontology in a traditional style, but with something totally different: "to restore man's historical existence—and that always includes our own future existence in the totality of the history allotted to us—to the domain of being."[16] Heidegger sees the Western world as a consequence of the way being reveals itself, and thus to ask the question of being is at once to inquire into the hidden ground of our historical existence. What is at stake in the being question, in the question of truth of being, is not an esoteric matter, but the comprehension of a people and how such people are historically and culturally fulfilled.

When Heidegger turns his attention to art and poetry around this same time—a time that follows his distressing experience with politics—one would quite naturally expect to see the same issue presented there as well. This is indeed the case, for even the most cursory reading of these texts must be able to see that what lies behind these reflections is more than a matter of a thinker broadening his interests to include questions of aesthetics and poetics. In the Addendum to "The Origin of the Work of Art," Heidegger describes his essay as moving "deliberately, yet tacitly" on the path of the question of how being comes-to-presence. The determination of art is also to be thought from the perspective of the question of the truth of being. But again, this question is now the question of historical destiny. As Heidegger sees it, whenever art happens, a thrust enters history; and history means here "the transporting of a people into its appointed task as entrance into that people's endowment."[17] In other essays, Heidegger will turn to the work of Hölderlin in particular as a way of encountering the very ground of the historical world of a people. In this poetry Heidegger can sense the urgency of the question, that he himself feels, of a future yet to come—the question of home and homeland.

Of course between 1930 ("Essence of Truth") and 1935 ("Origin of the Work of Art") there occurred the events of 1933–34 in which Heidegger, after joining the Nazi party, was appointed rector of the university—a position from which he then resigned in April 1934. This period of Heidegger's life that lead to the most profound crisis in his life—when he had to face the possible loss of his teaching position as well as that of his personal library and home—has generated controversy that has overshadowed his philosophical work and gone beyond simple philosophical differences.[18] The controversy came to public attention principally with the publication of the Victor Farias book on Heidegger, which appeared to sensationalize Heidegger's involvement with National Socialism. Even with the more balanced treatment of Heidegger's "political life" given by Hugo Ott in his book on Heidegger, the fact remains that Heidegger not only supported the National Socialist movement, but actually linked his philosophical project to its purer goals (if one can even say such a thing). The fact that Heidegger never felt personally responsible for contributing to the moral failure of the National Socialist movement only appeared to vindicate his harshest critics.

The nagging question in all this, a question that cannot be decided here, is whether it is the ideology that invades philosophy—a position that would go so far as to retrace the disposition toward the cultural elitism of National Socialism in Heidegger's work as early as *Being and Time* if not before—or whether a philosophy attentive to the growing crisis of western civilization is momentarily fed by the possibilities of a spiritual awakening promised in the National Socialist movement. To say the least, the growing awareness of what exactly Heidegger did during this time has certainly provided the opportunity for a critical re-reading and reassessment of much of Heidegger's work from this period, as several of the essays in this volume demonstrate. To their credit, the authors of these essays take seriously the assertion that even Habermas, one of Heidegger's harshest critics, would not deny, viz., that Heidegger's political conduct "cannot and should not serve the purpose of a global depreciation of this thought."

Notwithstanding the fact that Heidegger in 1933 supported National Socialism, there is little doubt that after 1935 Heidegger saw the National Socialist movement as a ruined revolution, one that could no longer approximate the call to destiny found within the growing spiritual crisis of the West. Heidegger's own personal struggles aside, what he feels is to be thought in such a time of spiritual exigency is not the calculation of solutions, but the "neediness" of the time as such. Over the course of the subsequent years—certainly all through the 1940s—the urgency of the "saving" (*Rettung*) does not diminish as Heidegger continues to turn to the poets, who like himself faced a "destitute time." Now, in a technological era the danger, from which the saving comes, grows ever deeper. Here the question of the truth of being is the question of *ereignis* as the granting of an epoch in the history of being. And here in this epoch where being is most withdrawn, where Heidegger sees his beloved Freiburg in ruins, his home occupied, and the fate of the Western world clouded by those darkest of days, Heidegger can proclaim that "only a God can save us now."[19] Such a proclamation is, once again, an expression of that constant matter of thought from which Heidegger himself could not escape its errancy—the oblivion of being.

In light of the political crisis and its subsequent developments, the turn in Heidegger's thinking can be expressed yet somewhat differently, not to change the basic sense of the turning, but to highlight the way in which the crisis engaged the matter of thinking for Heidegger. The turn from the existential analytic of Dasein to the thinking of being is a turn to the history of metaphysics understood as a history of a fall (from being). Concomitantly, the event of truth and untruth, of the self-withdrawal of truth, is an event of a people who are now confronted with a decision regarding their common historical fate.

The essays that comprise this volume are all concerned with aspects of Heidegger's work during the 1930s. In "Interrupting Truth," John Sallis points to the pervasiveness of the question of truth in Heidegger's thinking and to the way in which this question decisively affects Heidegger's thinking during the 1930s. The decisive effect on Heidegger's thinking is pursued through the specific indication on the question of truth given in the *Contributions to Philosophy*. Here, Sallis insists, Heidegger claims that the transition from truth as correctness to the essence of truth, that transition from the metaphysical determination of truth to the essence of truth as the truth of being, is always interrupted. The question for Sallis then is to determine how this interruption occurs. Sallis insists that what releases the interruption is a certain transformation to which the phenomenon of truth is submitted in those texts of the 1930s that take up the question of the essence of truth. The transformation is reflected in the methodological character of the texts which stand in marked contrast to *Being and Time*. According to Sallis, these discourses on truth are no longer oriented to self-showing; rather, they are haunted by a sub-discourse on untruth, a reserve of concealment that withholds the essence of truth from the demand for self-showing and thus limits the possibility of a phenomenological discourse on the essence of truth.

Rodolphe Gasché also pursues the question of truth in Heidegger through a close reading of the essay of 1930, "The Essence of Truth." What is most important for Gasché is what is entailed by the identification of the traditional criterion of truth as an accordance. Following Heidegger, Gasché points out that, on the face of things, the meaning of accordance is problematic since what are in accordance are two dissimilar things—the matter and the statement about the matter. In Heidegger's analysis this difficulty is resolved by noting that a more originary accordance is required, an accordance which presupposes an open region in which things first stand. The accordance is understood then as a presenting comportment where the statement directs us toward something that itself instructs the statement as to what and how the thing is. Again, following Heidegger, Gasché then shows how Heidegger relates this presenting comportment to freedom as the letting things be. But this phenomenon, Gasché rightly shows, is for Heidegger at once the event of disclosure. The accord is found to be derivative upon Being's concealedness. In the end the question of truth for Heidegger is a matter of thinking a non-conceptualizable accord that is not an accord.

The question of Heidegger's politics as it relates to Heidegger's thinking is taken up by John Caputo in his "Heidegger's Revolution: An Introduction to *An Introduction to Metaphysics*." In his direct manner, Caputo argues that, in the *Introduction to Metaphysics*, Heidegger, while wanting to extol the greatness of the "movement," did not at the same time conceal his disdain for the way in which the Party ideologues were mindlessly misleading the movement. They identified the greatness of the movement with Max Schmelling instead of Sophocles. The party ideologues were simply not thinkers: they did not see that the success of the revolution is tied to philosophy. Caputo examines in detail Heidegger's claim that the revolutionary movement is inseparable from a radical and fundamental questioning. What we learn from the *Introduction to Metaphysics*, according to Caputo, is that great philosophy, as radical questioning, is inherently revolutionary, and that the character of this revolution is not to secure a new foundation for culture but to engage in the task of making things more difficult. For Heidegger, then, to be up to the revolution, the German nation must be capable of entering the struggle with Being, of entering into the *polemos* where no standardization of the spirit is possible. The National Socialist revolution must be a repetition of the great Greek beginning in which the great tragedians and artists grapple with Being itself in the forging of the first beginning. In this movement of Being setting-into-work, the revolution cannot really be about culture and values, but simply about how history happens as the issue of Being itself. In view of such an understanding, Caputo thinks that the party members were right in keeping their distance from Heidegger. But this also becomes Caputo's criticism of Heidegger. What if, Caputo asks, Heidegger had turned the question of Being loose on National Socialism, instead of putting it into the service of National Socialism? What if Heidegger's radical questioning of grounds were applied to the grounds of National Socialism itself? Even more radical still, Caputo thinks that Heidegger's radical questioning needs to be applied to Heidegger himself, to turn Heidegger against Heidegger by Heidegger himself. In doing so, we begin to really ask the questions of history, destiny, and new beginnings.

The question that Caputo suggests at the end of his essay, the question of Heidegger's privileging of the Greeks, is taken up by Dennis Schmidt in his essay, "Heidegger and 'the' Greeks: History, Catastrophe and Community." According to Schmidt, the question of how we are to think history, for Heidegger, especially as we see this question raised in the texts between 1929 and 1946, is inseparable not only from a consideration of the way in which the Greeks, standing at the beginning of a certain history, are able to enter into that history. The question is also inseparable from a consideration of the real question for Heidegger, viz., the question of who "we" are today. In this latter question is the truth of history that, as Schmidt presents it, is inseparable from the themes of withdrawal, distress, the ineluctability of language, and the crisis of our singularity. The attempt to answer the question of who "we" are today, then,—the question that is at the heart of the political (and Heidegger's political decision)—is at once the question of whether the Greeks can still speak to us today. Schmidt shows that the answer to this question is found in the way in which Heidegger translates a number of Greek words, primarily *deinon* and *techne*. But in this translation, Heidegger realizes that "the" Greeks have not yet appeared and the task becomes of rewriting Greek thought as the manner of standing within the question of who we are today.

Heidegger's essay, "The Origin of the Work of Art," along with the recently published earlier versions of the lectures that formed the basis for the published essay, is taken up in both Robert Bernasconi's and Françoise Dastur's articles. Robert Bernasconi probes the significance of Heidegger's claim in the published essay that only great art is under consideration. As Bernasconi sees it, the question of great art is essentially the question of a non-metaphysical conception of art in which aesthetics is put radically into question. In comparing the various versions of the essay and in analyzing the connection between great art and aesthetics that Heidegger lays out in the first lecture course on Nietzsche, Bernasconi is able to show, among other things, that by the time Heidegger writes the Frankfurt version in late 1936 (the published version that appears in *Holzwege*), the non-metaphysical conception of art is decisively linked with the political situation of the 1930s. According to Bernasconi, Heidegger's question shifts from one of determining the nature of great art to whether there is great art any longer; it shifts from whether art is an origin to whether art can be an origin again, whether art can contribute to the decision of the public to become a *Volk* living from the earth. Bernasconi shows furthermore that this question stays with Heidegger well into the 1950's when, in the essay, "The Question Concerning Technology," Heidegger attempts to mark the difference between the artwork and equipment, and ultimately discusses how art provides an essential confrontation with technology, where the question of the people is no longer the issue.

In "Heidegger's Freiburg Version of the Origin of the Work of Art," Françoise Dastur provides a detailed analysis of the difference between the published Frankfurt version of the essay that appears in *Holzwege* and the version given in 1935, first published in France in 1987. Her analysis focuses on what she sees as at least seven key notions that undergo a transformation or modification in the one version to the other. She shows us, for example, how the concept of work becomes the leading concept in the earlier version because Heidegger is engaged here in his first attempt at thinking the non-representational character of art. She also shows us how the concept of world in the earlier version is overtly tied to the issue of a historical people, and how the character of truth in art is much more subtly developed in the Frankfurt version.

In "Poetizing and Thinking," an enlarged version of a paper initially presented at a meeting of the Martin Heidegger Gesellschaft, Hans-Georg Gadamer explores Heidegger's encounter with Hölderlin within the context of his own philosophical concerns. That "nearest and distance" between poetizing and thinking relates fundamentally to the power of the word to speak. And this, Gadamer insists, is what is at the heart of the truth of the word. But authentic speaking always involves searching for the word. This linguistic need *(Sprachnot)*, which rests within the experience of thinking for Heidegger is also something that Heidegger encountered in Hölderlin. Gadamer goes on to show how this *Sprachnot* is allowed to present itself in Hölderlin's *Andenken*, and then complements his analysis by introducing another poet of the most extreme *Sprachnot* and for whom there occurred a real encounter between a thinker and a poet, viz., Paul Celan. In the poetry of Celan the *Sprachnot* often leads to verbal violence, but when successful, the word is able to speak as a new "counterword." In the end, the thinker and the poet both face the unending task of going beyond ourselves, which is precisely what is captured by the power of the word.

Introduction 11

In "Heidegger, Hölderlin, and Sophoclean Tragedy," Veronique Foti links Heidegger's confrontation with National Socialism after 1934 not simply with his reading of the poet Hölderlin, but with his reading of Hölderlin's retrieval of Greek tragedy. According to Foti, at issue for Heidegger in this reading is the thematization and clarification of the essential historical configuration of planetary technicity that, unfolding from Greece, has now devolved upon Germany. Precisely because he sees an essential historical bond linking planetary technicity to Greek *techne*, and, through *poiesis*, to poetry, Heidegger turns to Hölderlin as a translator and theoretician of Greek tragedy. In particular, Foti proceeds first of all to analyze Heidegger's two main discussions of Sophocles's *Antigone* with respect to their cryptopolitical import. Then, secondly, she problematizes his distorting appropriation of Hölderlin's "unwilling deconstruction" of the speculative matrix of tragedy. And finally, she returns to the issue of the implications of Heidegger's tragic thought of historicity.

In the course of her analysis, Foti makes it clear that Heidegger in fact never really considers the questions of tragedy, viz., the questions of justice, law and duty, but continues to develop everything at the ontological level where the tragic conflict is played out within the modalities of homelessness and homecoming. In this context, Heidegger's thought, unlike Hölderlin's, remains essentially speculative, and, in the end, is shown to be insensitive to the destructive potential for irrational excess. What the reading of tragedy should produce is a re-examination of ethical praxis which asks about our concrete dwelling in the world.

In "Heidegger's Turn to *Germanien*—a Sigetic Venture," Wilhelm Wurzer also confronts Heidegger's interpretation of Hölderlin. For Wurzer what is at issue in Heidegger's reading of Hölderlin's *Germanien* is a particular instance of the way in which the later Heidegger attempts to encounter philosophy and its history with respect to philosophy's new beginning, a "time yet to come." The turn to the poetic word is decisive for this encounter, for in the poet's word is found the language that opens a historical terrain in which thinking moves beyond being merely the "disputations of metaphysical self-certainty."

But in the end one has to ask what Heidegger's reading of *Germanien* actually accomplishes. For Wurzer the founding of being, which tarries in the way-making power of the word, necessarily engages in a rethinking of the political and the ethical, and it does so in the most appropriate manner. *Germanien* is not a blue-print for a new Germany but poses the question of who one is within a "pledge" to drift away from particular political spacings. Heidegger's reading of *Germanien* is a movement into thought where we can sift apart for the first time the political dream of identity that is thought within the matrix of historical understanding. But to suspend the political in this manner is also to suspend the question of responsibility insofar as it disengages from a derivative concept of praxis and explores possibilities of a nonprincipial economy of responsibility.

Both Charles Scott and Jacques Taminiaux are concerned with the question of ethics in Heidegger's philosophy. Although Scott deals primarily with the question of ethics in *Being and Time*, the orientation and the direction of his analysis reflect the issues of the 1930s. The specific question for Scott is how ethics is put in question in *Being and Time*, where the question of ethics becomes translated into the question of the proper way for Dasein to be with regard to its being. Scott's claim is that in terms of this question of authenticity, ethics undergoes a distinctive interruption. If it is the case that ethical thought is part of everyday fallen lives, then the turn to authenticity is a turning away from ethics as we know it. The voice of conscience then serves to make everyday values and standards uncertain. Such a connection between ethics and authenticity rests on the fact that for Heidegger, Dasein's call to itself is a call to a being whose meaning is mortal temporality and not to a being with an intrinsic meaning. Accordingly, authenticity is not about self-realization, but the disclosure of human-being-in-question without the possibility of resolving the question. Affirming mortal temporality, as the way to be of Dasein's coming-to-itself, pertains to the opening of difference in its being relative to the status of its life.

In the first part of "Heidegger on Values," Taminiaux explores the main features of Heidegger's treatment of values in the framework of his meditation on the history of being as the history of Western metaphysics. Specifically, Taminiaux points out how for Heidegger the metaphysics of values has come to pass from the development of two important determinations within the history of metaphysics. As preparatory for a metaphysics of values, there occurred first of all Plato's transformation of aletheia into correctness. Then, secondly, modern philosophy brings everything under the notion of subjectivity, which is carried to its summit in Nietzsche's notion of the will-to-power. In this later development, being is accordingly absorbed in and reduced to the renewed perspectives that the will-to-power constantly projects.

In the remainder of his paper, Taminiaux problematizes Heidegger's analysis of values by posing a number of questions (some of which are then briefly attended to). What, he asks, does Heidegger have to say about values before the turn (and the development of the question of values within the framework of the history of being)? A reading of *Being and Time* shows that, even before the turn, posing the question of values for Heidegger meant confronting the work of Plato and Nietzsche. More importantly, Taminiaux asks whether the question of values can be taken up solely from the viewpoint of ontology. Can the question of values really be posed, in other words, outside the question of responsibility? For Taminiaux the answer would seem to be no.

Reiner Schürmann's "Ultimate Double Binds" begins with the question, "What has Heidegger done with—and to—philosophy?" Schürmann poses this question in view of the fact that the later Heidegger claims to establish philosophy on entirely new grounds while at the same time he also claims to put an end to it. This seemingly contradictory position can be accounted for if one considers what is entailed in Heidegger's understanding of being as time. On the one hand, to name being at all is to undertake that quest for ultimacy—to establish the law of laws—that is the hallmark of every philosophical project. On the other hand, Heidegger undercuts every attempt at legislation, the positing of simplicity that is essential to any law. Under the framework of what he calls legislation-transgression, Schürmann analyzes, principally through a reading of the *Beiträge*, the way in which the counter-law, a law in discord with itself, is operative in Heidegger's philosophy. Consequently, Schürmann thinks that what we find in the *Beiträge* is the articulation of the originality of being in which ultimacy is rethought. Such rethinking, wherein we find a complex notion of differing in the thematics of nothingness and singularity (nothingness singularizes being into an event), is for Schürmann an attempt to think the law of laws as a normative double bind. In the double bind is the step back from epochal institutions that have held and continue to hold normative power. Schürmann's response then to the question of what has Heidegger done with and to philosophy is that Heidegger establishes philosophy on new grounds in an attempt to phase out the traditional motive of seeking simple ultimates.

In "Contributions to Life," David Farrell Krell examines only two of the two hundred and eighty-one sections of Heidegger's *Beiträge zur Philosophie*. The sections under discussion are the two that deal with life in Part IV, "*Der Sprung*," of the *Beiträge*. Krell reads the two sections on life as a peculiar interruption—an interruption mirrored by Krell in his own text by a second text on Freud's Schreber Case and Mann's *Magic Mountain*—of the movement within the text that can be characterized as the leap, the movement from "the nothing" to "being unto death." For Krell the interruption underscores the importance of life for the history of being and remains to be appropriated by thought at the "other commencement" of thinking. Accordingly, life, which here is not to be confused with the biological but pertains primarily to the phenomenon of closure and disclosure, must be allowed to interrupt the leap (or fissure) of thinking and being. "Daimon life" would then name the region of beings for which revealing and concealing, growth and decline would come to the fore and into question.

In "Empty Time and the Indifference to Being" Michel Haar provides a detailed reading and interpretation of Heidegger's analysis of boredom (as the phenomenon of indifference) found in the 1929–30 lecture course, *Die Grundbegriffe der Metaphysik: Welt—Endlichkeit—Einsamkeit*. The analysis begins by explaining how the phenomenon of indifference is not the absence of mood (*Stimmung*), but a particular mood in which we encounter a relation to time and to our being. The question then becomes one of understanding how the mood of boredom differs from anxiety. In this comparison, Haar first lays out the essential traits of indifference, as it is described in relation to everydayness in *Being and Time*, then analyzes the three circles of boredom from the 1929–30 lecture course. Haar concludes that the emptiness of boredom, although it is like anxiety in that it reveals beings in their totality as disappearing, is not the same as the nothingness of anxiety. With respect to the former, the disclosive dimension of the mood pertains principally to time, whereas the mood of anxiety is disclosive principally of being. What he convincingly shows then is how it is that, *within* the empty time of profound boredom (the third circle of boredom), the possibility of reappropriating time is revealed to us, i.e., profound boredom allows us to rediscover all possible time. There is, according to Haar, a replenishment of time at the depths of its own abyss, not unlike what we find in the related notion which marks the contemporary age for Heidegger, viz., the possibility of saving from within the danger (of modern technicity).

In "*Heimat:* Heidegger on the Threshold," McNeill undertakes to problematize the claim that Heidegger's defense of National Socialism can be explained by his belief in a soil-like rootedness comprising the identity of the German people. According to McNeill, what needs to be determined in this context is Heidegger's understanding of home/*Heimat*. For McNeill the question of home is second to none in Heidegger's work. Hence, Heidegger's concerns during the 1930s, as in the question of nationalism, are to be interpreted from the perspective of this question. McNeill prepares the ground for this analysis by demonstrating how the question of home is given priority already in *Being and Time* where the question is formulated in terms of Dasein's dwelling. McNeill notes that for Heidegger the disclosure of Dasein's dwelling occurs in the "unhomeliness" of anxiety, which stands at the threshold of the home. Accordingly, the question of home in Heidegger's thinking centers around this relational configuration of home and unhomeliness. When Heidegger then turns to the work of Hölderlin in the 1930s, it is because of the way in which the poet is the one who leads us to that threshold. For Hölderlin, to be at the threshold is to be at the historical determination of the national. But in Heidegger's hands, the poet's message is not simply one of nationalism or of the political as such. It pertains rather to a non-metaphysical thinking of the home that is marked by essential confrontation and strife. Dwelling in the polis, as we see from a reading of *Introduction to Metaphysics*, is to be exposed to risk. Dwelling, in other words, is the becoming homely of a being unhomely.

Notes

1. *Kant und das Problem der Metaphysik*, (Frankfurt: Klostermann, 1929). English translation by Richard Taft, *Kant and the Problem of Metaphysics*, (Bloomington: Indiana University Press, 1990).
2. "Vom Wesen des Grundes," in *Ergänzungsband zum Jahrbuch für Philosophie and phänomenologische Forschung*, (Halle, 1929), pp. 71–100. English translation by Terrence Malick, *The Essence of Reasons*, (Evanston: Northwestern University Press, 1969).
3. *Was ist Metaphysik?* (Bonn: Friedrich Cohen, 1929).
4. *Die Selbstbehauptung der deutschen Universität*, (Breslau: Korn Verlag, 1933). English translation by Karsten Harries, "The Self-Assertion of the German University," *Review of Metaphysics* 38 (March 1985): 467–502.
5. *Hölderlin und das Wesen der Dichtung*, (München: Langen und Müller, 1937). English translation by Douglas Scott, "Hölderlin and the Essence of Poetry," in *Existence and Being*, ed. Werner Brock, (Chicago: Henry Regnery, 1949).
6. *Vom Wesen der Wahrheit*, (Frankfurt: Klostermann, 1943). English translation by John Sallis, "The Essence of Truth," in *Heidegger: Basic Writings*, ed. by David F. Krell, (New York: Harper & Row, 1977).
7. *Einführung in die Metaphysik*, (Tübingen: Niemeyer, 1953). English translation by Ralph Manheim, *An Introduction to Metaphysics*, (New Haven: Yale University Press, 1959).

8. "Der Ursprung des Kunstwerkes," *Holzwege*, (Frankfurt: Klostermann, 1950). English translation by Albert Hofstadter, "The Origin of the Work of Art," *Poetry, Language, Thought*, (New York: Harper & Row, 1971).

9. *Die Frage nach dem Ding*, (Tübingen: Niemeyer, 1962). English translation by W. B. Barton, Jr. and Vera Deutsch, *What Is a Thing?* (Chicago: Henry Regnery, 1967).

10. See the Appendix for a list of published volumes of the *Gesamtausgabe* that deal with the period in question.

11. "Letter on Humanism" *Heidegger: Basic Writings*, p. 207.

12. See *Sein und Zeit*, Gesamtausgabe vol. 2 (Frankfurt: Klostermann, 1977), p. 11, note b.

13. Heidegger, "Letter on Humanism" in *Martin Heidegger Basic Writings*, p. 207–208.

14. William Richardson, "Letter to Father Richardson," *Heidegger: Through Phenomenology to Thought* (The Hague: Martinus Nijhoff, 1967), p. xvi.

15. Such a claim can be made following the work of Walter Beimal, who claims that the core of Heidegger's thinking pertains to the question of truth and the question of being that are in the end the same question. In his *Martin Heidegger: An Illustrated Study*, translated by J. L. Mehta (New York: Harcourt, Brace, Jovanovich, 1976), Beimal takes the development of Heidegger's thinking to be sustained through the following works: "On the Essence of Truth" (1930), "The Origin of the work of Art" (1935), "Letter on Humanism" (1946), "The Question Concerning Technology" (1953), "The Nature of Language" (1957), "The End of Philosophy and the Task of Thinking" (1964).

16. *Einführung des Metaphysik*, p. 32. *An Introduction to Metaphysics*, p. 34.

17. "The Origin of the Work of Art," p. 77.

18. See for example, "Symposium on Heidegger and Nazism" in *Critical Inquiry* (Winter 1989), Vol. 15, 2: 407–488; *Martin Heidegger and National Socialism: Questions and Answers*, ed. Gunther Neske and Emil Kettering (New York: Paragon Press, 1990); "Heidegger and the Political," *Graduate Faculty Philosophy Journal* Vol. 14, 2–Vol. 15, 1.

19. This is the title of the interview that Heidegger gave in 1966. It was published in *Der Spiegel* May 31, 1976.

I. On Truth

Chapter 1

Interrupting Truth

John Sallis

Das Wesen der Wahrheit ist die Un-wahrheit.
—Heidegger, *Beiträge zur Philosophie*

The question of truth cannot be merely one among several questions to be taken up by a thinking secure in itself. It can never have been—however much it may have seemed to be—a question to be addressed by a thinking already established from the outset, already fully determined as philosophical thinking. On the contrary, the development of the question of truth belongs to the very determination of philosophy, to its most classical determination, for example, as ἐπιστήμη τῆς ἀληθείας.[1] It is not as though philosophy is first delimited as such and then brought to bear on the question of truth; rather, the way in which the question of truth is addressed, the way in which truth is determined as such, determines the very project of philosophy, even if, in turn, that project must already have been broached in the determination of truth. In the formulation developed in Heidegger's 1937–1938 course, *Basic Questions of Philosophy*, the question of truth is that by which philosophy is first brought to itself, gathered to itself, concentrated in its proper simplicity. (GA 45, 13)

The trajectory of Heidegger's thought cannot, then, but have been determined in large measure by the question of truth. Thus it is that Heidegger's thinking of the history of metaphysics thematizes this history as that of the determination of truth: from the Platonic determination of truth as correctness (ὀρθότης) or correspondence (ὁμοίωοίς) to the utter inversion that this determination undergoes in Nietzsche's definition of truth as *"the kind of error* without which a certain kind of living being could not live."[2] What is called for by the end that such inversion marks is a thinking of truth that is more originary, a recovery of truth within a dimension of origin that remained concealed in the history of metaphysics, that concealment belonging even to the very condition of the possibility of metaphysics, a concealment that will (prove to) have made metaphysics possible precisely by holding in reserve a truth that otherwise could not but interrupt metaphysics, an interrupting truth. The task of thinking at the end of metaphysics is, then, to translate the truth of metaphysics back into the interruptive truth, the ἀλήθεια, that in this manner precedes metaphysics.

The question of truth remains, then, always in play in Heidegger's work, from the courses of the Marburg period such as *Logic: The Question concerning Truth* (1926–27, GA 21) up through such very late texts as "The End of Philosophy and the Task of Thinking" (1964)[3] and the Zähringen Seminar (1973, GA 15). Yet it is during the 1930s, more precisely, during the period 1927–1943, that the question of truth assumes the greatest urgency in Heidegger's thought and comes to determine most powerfully and most transparently the itinerary of that thought. Within the methodological structure of *Being and Time* (1927), the analysis of truth (§44) serves as a pivot, gathering up the entire series of preparatory analyses of Dasein (Division One), concentrating the results of those analyses in such a way as to prepare for the more originary project disclosive of temporality as the meaning *(Sinn)* of the Being of Dasein (Division Two). In the attempt—later identified as having been undertaken from 1930 on[4]—to deploy the question of *Being and Time* in a more originary way, to shape its *Fragestellung* more originarily, the question of truth becomes still more prominent, entitling in fact a number of the discourses that engage most directly in the move—or rather, the break—to the more originary. The lecture that was eventually to be published as "On the Essence of Truth" (1943, in GA 9) was first presented in 1930 under the title "Philosophizing and Believing: The Essence of Truth"; it was repeated several times and revised quite extensively, and indeed one can discern in the difference between the 1930 lecture and the 1943 published text certain of the most decisive moves in the transformation that Heidegger's thought undergoes, in that more originary deployment to which it submits its questioning. There is, in addition, the 1937–1938 course cited above, which belongs to the very years in which Heidegger composed *Contributions to Philosophy (Beiträge zur Philosophie)*. The latter, which remained unpublished until 1989, contains an extended series of discourses (GA 65, §§204–237) grouped under the title "The Essence of Truth"; among these discourses one finds some of the most decisive moves inscribed with a radicality that borders on the abysmal. During the same period there is also the series of texts in which Heidegger reflects on the transformation that he takes the essence of truth to have undergone in Plato's thought: the course entitled *On the Essence of Truth* (1931–1932, GA 34), in which Heidegger presents his reading of the *Republic*; the course *Parmenides* (1942–1943, GA 54), in which he extends (and complicates somewhat) that reading; and, finally, the published work, *Plato's Doctrine of Truth* (written in 1940, first published in 1942, now in GA 9).

I shall not undertake here to follow this itinerary as a whole. Rather, I shall focus on *a single decisive indication* that the *Contributions* gives regarding the question of truth; then, circling back to the analysis of truth in *Being and Time* and drawing out a single strand of the development to which Heidegger's work in the 1930s submits that analysis, I shall attempt to broach some understanding of the interruption announced by the indication from the *Contributions,* even though that interruption could not but produce also a certain break in Heidegger's very delimitation of understanding.

The indication on which I want to focus is given in a section of the *Contributions* (§226) entitled "The Clearing of Concealment and ἀλήθεια *(Die Lichtung der Verbergung und die* ἀλήθεια*).* This section is divided into four untitled subsections. The first stresses the need for questioning to engage concealment itself and not merely to think it as something superseded *(aufgehoben)* by revealment *(Entbergung)* and clearing *(Lichtung).* Heidegger enforces this demand by writing: *Wahrheit als die Lichtung für die Verbergung.* He broaches even "the captious formulation: truth is untruth"; and, though insisting that this formulation can too easily be misinterpreted, he grants that it serves "to indicate the strangeness *[das Befremdliche]* involved in the new projection of essence."

The indication on which I want to focus draws what appears to be a consequence of this strangeness of the essence of truth. It is given in the second subsection:

> But the previous attempts in *Being and Time* and the subsequent writings to carry *this* essence of truth through, as the ground of Da-sein itself, in opposition to the correctness of

representation and assertion, had to remain insufficient, because it was still carried through by *opposition* [*aus der Abwehr*] and so was still oriented to what it opposed, thus making it impossible to know the essence of truth by way of its ground [*von Grund aus*], the ground as which it itself essentially unfolds [*west*]. For this to succeed it is necessary no longer to hold back the saying of the essence of Being and to put aside the opinion that, in spite of the insight into the necessity of the advancing project [*des vorspringenden Entwurfts*], it is in the end still possible to clear a way step by step from the previous [view] to the truth of Being. But this must always fail. (GA 65, 351–52)

The passage indicates the insufficiency of an attempted transition, the transition *from* truth as the correctness of representation and assertion *to* that essence of truth that would be the ground of Dasein itself and that can also be called the truth of Being. This is the transition that was ventured by the analysis of truth in *Being and Time*. Now Heidegger insists that it remained oriented to the metaphysical determination of truth, even if by opposition; and thus circulating still within the opposition, it could not advance to the essence of truth as unfolding ground. Or rather, its attempt to advance step by step from the metaphysical determination of truth to that essence of truth that would be the truth of Being cannot but be interrupted.

How does this interruption occur? What is it that comes to interrupt the move from truth to truth (if in this dimension one can still appeal to the classical question τί ἐστι . . . ?)? From what kind of advance must one have returned in order to identify what appeared to be a transition as indeed an interruption?

In *Being and Time* a certain orientation to the traditional concept of truth is quite evident from the outset. Heidegger identifies three theses constitutive of the traditional concept, and his discussion of these theses serves to introduce his own effort at undercutting them, his attempt to move to a more originary concept of truth, from which (it could subsequently be shown) the traditional concept would have arisen. Thus, the point of departure of the analysis of truth is one of opposition, though indeed an opposition that aims not at rejection but at a move to the more originary. What Heidegger's analysis opposes in the traditional concept of truth is its distance from the originary phenomenon of truth. His analysis would move across that distance and recover the more originary phenomenon from which the traditional concept would have arisen. Beneath that concept, nearer to the origin, his analysis would bring to light the originary phenomenon that the traditional concept of truth would prove hitherto to have concealed.

Heidegger begins with the three theses:

> Three theses characterize the traditional conception of truth and the view of how it was first defined: 1. The "locus" of truth is assertion (judgment). 2. The essence of truth lies in the "correspondence" of the judgment with its object. 3. Aristotle, the father of logic, both assigned truth to the judgment as its originary locus and also launched the definition of truth as "correspondence." (SZ 214)

From the outset the analysis is thus both phenomenological and de(con)structive. By means of phenomenological analysis it is to undercut the first two theses, to show that truth has a more originary locus than assertion and that correspondence between judgment and its object is grounded in a more originary phenomenon. The effect of carrying this analysis through and of engaging in the movement that it makes possible will be to clear away what has blocked access to the originary sources from which the essence of truth was first determined by the Greeks. Thus, the analysis would loosen up the "hardened tradition" (SZ 22), breaking apart the ossified concept passed on by tradition, interrupting that truth in the interest of recovering a truth nearer the origin. In the end it is to be a matter of recovering the force of an elemental word: ἀλήθεια.

Neither the word nor the concept as such is the primary object of the analysis of truth. Rather, it is a *phenomenological* analysis in the sense, first of all, determined in the Introduction to *Being and Time* (see SZ §7). That determination prescribes that the analysis must be one that proceeds in reference to the *way truth shows itself;* that is, it must be an analysis that attends to the process within which truth comes to show itself *as truth* and that thematizes what, within such a process of self-showing, truth shows itself to be. This is why Heidegger begins by asking: "When does truth become phenomenally explicit in knowledge itself?" He answers: "It does so when knowing demonstrates itself *[sich . . . ausweist] as true*" (SZ 217). Truth shows itself as truth in the context of demonstration. Such is, then, the phenomenal context to which the analysis must attend: it is a matter of thematizing what truth shows itself to be when in the course of demonstration it comes to show itself as truth.

The analysis involves two phases, two distinct movements toward the more originary. The first begins at the level of the traditional theory of truth, though the effect of the analysis is to subvert that theory for the sake of a more originary determination of truth. For this phase of the analysis Heidegger requires less than two pages (SZ 217–18). The second phase carries out the movement from the more originary determination of what the traditional concept took to be truth *to* a more originary phenomenon that, while making truth in its traditional sense possible, would, on the other hand, have been largely passed over by the tradition. For this phase of the analysis Heidegger requires only a few sentences (SZ 220).

Let me review once more the remarkable analysis with which Heidegger begins and which constitutes the first phase of the analysis as a whole. It is remarkable for its simplicity, for the directness with which it brings the decisive breakthrough of Husserl's phenomenology into play precisely in analyzing the things themselves and with a certain independence of Husserl's specific formulations.[5]

Heidegger begins with the situation in which a person, with his back to the wall, makes the true assertion: "The picture on the wall is hanging askew." The demonstration occurs when the person turns around and perceives the picture hanging askew on the wall. Then it is that the assertion comes to be demonstrated, that it proves to be true; its truth becomes manifest as truth. It is a question, then, of what exactly occurs in such demonstration. Just how does truth show itself in the demonstration? One could say that it shows itself as a kind of agreement. One could say even that it shows itself as a kind of agreement between knowledge (i.e., the assertion) and the thing known (i.e., the thing about which the assertion is made). To this extent the traditional concept can be declared correct. And yet, the question remains: Just what kind of agreement is this? In what sense can knowledge be said to agree with things? How can there be agreement between terms as disparate as knowledge and things?

Heidegger asks: To what is the speaker related when he initially makes the assertion? Can one say that the asserting relates to a representation of the picture, to a mental image of the real picture, a picture of the picture? Heidegger says: to insert such a representation is "to falsify the phenomenal state of affairs" (SZ 218). With these words he brings into play that decisive breakthrough that Husserl carried out in the *Logical Investigations* under the title *intentionality*: the character of consciousness as consciousness *of* requires that all such mediating representations, all images that would stand between an act that means something and that which is meant be expelled. Hence, when it is asserted that the picture on the wall is hanging askew, this asserting relates, not to a picture of the picture, but to the picture itself, to the thing itself. What one means in the assertion is the real picture itself and nothing else: "The asserting is a Being toward the thing itself" (SZ 218).

What happens, then, when the person turns around and actually perceives the picture? What comes to be demonstrated? Heidegger answers: "Nothing else than *that* it *is* the very being that was meant in the assertion" (SZ 218). Hence, the correspondence that comes to be demonstrated is not an agreement of a representation (something psychic) with the thing itself (something physical) but rather an agreement between what is meant and the thing itself; more precisely, it is an agreement between the thing itself *as* meant and the thing itself as perceived, as it shows itself concretely. In Heidegger's words, what occurs is that "that about which the assertion is made, namely the being itself, shows itself *as that very same being*. *Confirmation* signifies the self-showing of the being in its sameness" (SZ 218). In Husserl's terms, it is a matter of identification through intentional fulfillment.

What, then, does the demonstration serve to demonstrate about the assertion? Heidegger answers: "What comes up for confirmation is that the assertive Being toward that of which something is asserted is a pointing-out *[Aufzeigen]* of the being, that such Being-toward uncovers *[entdeckt]* the being toward which it is. What gets demonstrated is the Being-uncovering *[Entdeckend-sein]* of the assertion" (SZ 218). In other words, what is demonstrated is that the assertion points out that about which it is made, that it uncovers that being; what is demonstrated is that the asserting is an uncovering, a pointing-out, of the thing itself.

How, then, is truth manifest? In such demonstration of the truth of assertion, how does truth show itself as such? What character does it show itself to have? Heidegger answers:

> To say that an assertion is true signifies that it uncovers the being in itself. It asserts, it points out, it lets the being be seen (ἀπόφανσις) in its uncoveredness. The Being-true (truth) of the assertion must be understood as Being-uncovering *[entdeckend-sein]*. (SZ 218)

The truth of the assertion lies in its character as uncovering, and in demonstration it comes to show itself as such, as being-uncovering.

Thus, Heidegger's analysis—or rather, the first of its two phases—proceeds in a way exemplary of phenomenology: the preconceptions that obscure the phenomena are set aside, and the analysis attends simply to the self-showing in which truth comes to show itself as such. The result is essentially a reinscription of the classical Husserlian analysis within the project of fundamental ontology.

The second phase of the analysis is different. For it does not simply undertake to clear away the traditional misconceptions so as to let the phenomenon be thematized in its self-showing, bringing thus to a self-showing the same phenomenon that was inadequately thematized in the traditional concept of truth; rather, in its second phase the analysis ventures a transition to another level, one that was not in play in the traditional concept of truth; it ventures a *move from* the phenomenon of truth as correspondence or being-uncovered *to another phenomenon* that can also be called *truth*. The second phase of the analysis is thus a regress to what Heidegger calls the originary *(ursprünglich)* phenomenon of truth, or even the *most originary* phenomenon of truth. Not that the analysis simply ceases in this phase to be phenomenological: it begins to gather up the entire complex of phenomenological analyses that the First Division of *Being and Time* has carried out and to bring the resources of those analyses into play in relation to the question of truth. And yet, however thoroughly inscribed within its phenomenological context, this move has a character that cannot but appear quite traditional, at least as long as it is carried out this side of the redeterminations that would have been produced by the never-published Third Division: it is a move from truth as being-uncovering to the ground of the possibility of such truth.

Heidegger does not actually carry out the move but only, identifying the ground to which the analysis moves, refers to previous analyses (specifically, that of the worldhood of the world) as having in effect already carried it out. Recalling those analyses , one could say—to give the very briefest indication—that in order for Dasein to comport itself to things in a way that uncovers them (as in assertion), world must already be disclosed. For at least two reasons: because world is that within which things can be intended, meant, as in assertion; and because world is that from out of which things can show themselves in such a way that a demonstration of an assertion becomes possible. Hence: "That beings within the world come to be uncovered *is grounded* in the disclosedness of world *[die Entdecktheit des innerweltlichen Seienden* gründet *in der Erschlossenheit der Welt]*" (SZ 220). Truth—that is, being-uncovering as a mode of intentional comportment in which, as in assertion, beings can be uncovered—is possible only on the basis of *disclosedness*.

Near the beginning of the short passage that announces this move, Heidegger proposes a peculiar extension of the word *truth*, a doubling in the direction of ground: "Being-true as Being-uncovering is a way of Being of Dasein. What makes this very uncovering possible must necessarily be called 'true' in a still more originary sense" (SZ 220). Thus it is that Heidegger calls disclosedness *truth*, not only *more* originary but indeed *most* originary: disclosedness is "the most originary phenomenon of truth" (SZ 220–21).

But what about this doubling of truth? What is the necessity—redoubled in Heidegger's formulation: ". . . must necessarily be called 'true' . . . "—that compels Heidegger to extend the word *truth* to that which makes truth possible? Or does the redoubling formulation betray some uncertainty regarding the move, as if Heidegger were attempting in the formulation to reinforce a move whose force, whose necessity, might otherwise seem insufficient? For is it indeed necessary that the ground be called by the same name as that which it would make possible? In other instances is it even the case that the ground is called by the same name as that which it grounds? Or is the difference between ground and grounded not usually marked linguistically in a more emphatic way than merely by employment of the comparative and superlative degrees? Is the difference between ground and grounded only a matter of degree? Or does its presentation as a matter of degree perhaps serve to mask the difference, to make ground and grounded seem more homogeneous than they may be? Does the doubling and the appeal to its necessity have the effect of concealing the complexity—or even the impossibility—of the transition from the traditional or phenomenological concept of truth to the other phenomenon, which *Being and Time* calls disclosedness, which in the 1930s will be called the truth of Being, but which finally will not be called truth at all but only ἀλήθεια? Is this effect, this facilitating of the transition, not carried even further when Heidegger goes on in *Being and Time* to round out the analysis of truth by showing how the traditional concept must have arisen from the originary phenomenon of truth? For then it turns out that—once one gathers up the results of the preparatory analysis of Dasein—one not only can move directly from the traditional concept of truth to that most originary phenomenon that is its ground and that is also called truth; but also one can proceed back from originary truth to the traditional concept, proceeding step by step, completing the circle. Even if Dasein is not only in the truth but also in the untruth. Even if it is essential to Dasein not only to uncover but also to conceal, to cover up and close off. Fundamental ontology will have broken through all that kept even the originary phenomenon of truth itself covered up in the history of metaphysics.

The simple doubling to which the name *truth* is submitted and its enforcement of a certain homogeneity between the traditional concept of truth and the originary phenomenon have the effect of constraining the analysis within an opposition; it is thus that the attempt in *Being and Time* to address the question of truth remained, as the *Contributions* charges, "still oriented to what it opposed." Thus, too, was it "impossible to know the essence of truth by way of its ground, the ground as which it itself essentially unfolds," for the phenomenon constitutive of the ground or essence of truth continued to be thematized too exclusively by its opposition—that is, *within* its opposition—to the traditional concept of truth as redetermined in the phenomenological analysis.

Yet, how is it that the simple opposition comes to be broken apart, broken off, and the originary phenomenon so twisted free of it that every attempt to clear a way leading step by step from the traditional concept of truth back to the originary phenomenon must, as the *Contributions* insists, "always fail." What comes to interrupt that move that seemed so assured—though no less decisive—in *Being and Time*?

What releases the interruption is a certain transformation—or, more precisely, a decentering, a dislocation—to which the phenomenon of truth is submitted in those texts of the 1930s that take up the question of the essence of truth. The transformation is reflected in the methodological character of these texts in contrast to that of *Being and Time*. Both the 1930 lecture and the 1943 published text that evolved from it begin by considering what one ordinarily understands by truth and by discussing what is commonly meant by the word *truth*. It is from this point that the essence of truth is then unfolded through its series of ever more originary determinations: correspondence, openness of comportment, freedom, letting-be. What is striking, especially in the point of departure, is that the phenomenological injunction is not sounded: Heidegger does not proceed by analyzing a situation in which truth comes to show itself as truth but rather begins with what is commonly meant by the word *truth* and proceeds by way of a series of analyses that, though too complex to analyze here,[6] are manifestly not phenomenological in the direct way exemplified in *Being and Time*. Even if one insists that these texts remain phenomenological in a sense such as that which Heidegger later adumbrates retrospectively,[7] it is clear that a decisive methodological shift has reoriented the discourses on truth broached after *Being and Time:* they are no longer simply oriented to self-showing.

Even before Heidegger begins to consider what is commonly meant by the word *truth*, the discourse of "On the Essence of Truth" is interrupted by the demands and attacks of common sense, its demand for the actual truth and its attack on all such questions as that of the essence of truth. The discourse on the question of truth has hardly begun when common sense—Heidegger will call it also sophistry—interrupts with its suspicion that the question of the essence of truth is "the most inessential and superfluous that could be asked" (GA 9, 177). Nonetheless, a certain unfolding of the essence of truth does ensue, and it produces a double series of redeterminations, redetermining both *essence* and *truth*. This discourse is haunted by a sub-discourse on untruth, which keeps returning throughout the series of redeterminations: at first it is only a remainder that truth has an opposite, untruth, and that the discourse on truth will eventually have to be rounded out by a discourse on this opposite. One is reminded of the way that untruth is brought in at the end of the analysis of truth in *Being and Time* (Dasein is both in the truth and—as *verfallen*—also in the untruth); or rather, one would be so reminded were it not for the almost compulsive repetition of the subdiscourse and, most decisively, the dislocation that takes place at what would be the center of "On the Essence of Truth." For it turns out that the discourse on untruth is anything but a mere rounding out of the prior discourse on truth. Its effect is, rather, to interrupt that discourse by inscribing untruth within truth, by—as the 1930 lecture expresses it—letting the nonessence into the essence. In the 1943 published text the interruption is still more decisive: not only does untruth, concealment, belong to the essence of truth, but within that essence untruth is *older* than what would have been called truth (see GA 9, 193–94). In the word *older* Heidegger would say—but in a way that could also unsay—an ordering that would exceed all the words by which it has been named in the history of metaphysics. It is this excess, this reserve of concealment, that withholds the essence of truth from the demand for self-showing and that limits the possibility of a phenomenological discourse on the essence of truth. It limits also—and finally interrupts—every progression by which one would attempt to move step by step—that is, by reiterated appeal to evidence, to self-showing—from the traditional concept of truth to that essence of truth to which the still older untruth would—essentially, one would have said—belong. Indeed, as the concluding Note in the later editions of "On the Essence of Truth" indicates,[8] this very movement is what is enacted by that text, the movement now thought as that from the essence of truth to the truth of essence, the movement enacted in the text before finally being said in the nonproposition enunciated in the Note: "The essence of truth is the truth of essence." It is little wonder, then, that this text proves to be anything but a step-by-step progression; indeed its interruption is even such that, in a note later written in his copy of the text, Heidegger identifies the move from section 5 ("The Essence of Truth") to section 6 ("Untruth as Concealment") as a *leap,* as *"der Sprung in die (im Ereignis wesende) Kehre."*

Contributions to Philosophy says the same when it declares, even if with caution: "The essence of truth is un-truth." Not only does this saying "bring nearer the strangeness of the strange essence of truth" (GA 65: 356), but also in saying this strangeness, it bespeaks the very interrupting of truth.

Notes

1. Aristotle, *Metaphysics* 993b20.
2. Nietzsche, *Der Wille zur Macht,* ed. Peter Gast and Elizabeth Förster-Nietzsche (Stuttgart: Alfred Kröner, 1959), §493.
3. In *Zur Sache des Denkens* (Tübingen: Max Niemeyer, 1969).
4. Ibid., 61.
5. In *History of the Concept of Time* Heidegger takes up the same problems within a more specifically Husserlian context. Here, too, he insists, as in *Being and Time,* on the complexity of what is required by the phenomenological injunction "to the matters themselves" (*"zu den Sachen selbst"):* "We must free ourselves from the prejudice that, because phenomenology calls upon us to apprehend the matters themselves, these matters must be apprehended all at once, without any preparation. Rather, the movement toward the matters themselves is a long and involved process which, before anything else, has to remove the prejudices that obscure them" (GA 20: 36–37). The simplicity of the analysis in *Being and Time* is not simply in opposition to the complexity that characterizes this long and involved process; rather, it is precisely through its peculiar simplicity that the analysis, breaking up the ossified concept, removing the obscuring prejudices, opens up the complexity of the question of truth.
6. I have discussed these analyses in detail in "Deformatives: Essentially Other Than Truth," *Reading Heidegger: Commemorations* (Bloomington: Indiana University Press, 1991), 29–46.
7. See *Zur Sache des Denkens,* 81–90.
8. Beginning with the second edition (1949).

Chapter 2

Tuned to Accord: On Heidegger's Concept of Truth

Rodolphe Gasché

Common sense, as well as an old and venerable tradition of thinking, are in full accord about the essence of truth: truth consists in accordance. Whether it is ordinary, everyday, or philosophical consciousness that makes a statement or a proposition about the truth of a matter, in each case the criterion for truth is agreement, concordance, accordance. Both common sense and technical philosophy speak in one voice of this accord of truth between itself and what thus is said to be its essence. Indeed, it is a truth about truth that is "immediately evident to everyone" or, more precisely, obvious and universally valid (BW 121). Yet, the universality and the "obviousness which this concept of truth seems to have but which is hardly attended to as regards its essential grounds" (BW 121) are, according to Heidegger, the result of a protective, self-securing isolation of this determination of truth from "the interpretation of the essence of the Being of all beings, which always includes a corresponding interpretation of the essence of man" (BW 121). Although in "On the Essence of Truth," Heidegger claims that between common sense—and with it, the tradition of thinking that is not only in accord with it, but even provides a ground for the latter's understanding of truth—and philosophy (in a strict sense), there is no transition, no possible communication; he does not wish to refute common sense and what has "long been called 'philosophy'." "Philosophy," Heidegger writes, "can never refute common sense, for the latter is deaf to the language of philosophy. Nor may it even wish to do so, since common sense is blind to what philosophy sets before its essential vision," (BW 118). But what *is* possible, is to lift the common-sensical and "philosophical" concept of truth as accordance above its isolation, and to relate it to an interpretation of the whole—the Being of all beings. In short, what is possible for thought is a one-way approach to the common-sensical concept of truth as accordance, by which this concept, without common sense's knowledge, becomes grounded in the order of Being. It is this approach that Heidegger provides in "On the Essence of Truth."

The traditional criterion for the truth, then, is accordance. *Accordance* here renders *Übereinstimmung*, which in turn translates the Greek *homoiosis* or *orthothes*, and the Latin *adaequatio*. In everyday speech, one says: *es stimmt*, "it is in accord," or simply, "it is true." Truth, consequently, is "what accords, the accordant *(was stimmt, das Stimmende)*" (BW 119). Such *stimmen* is at least dual, and refers to the *Übereinstimmung*—or, as Heidegger also says, to *Einstimmigkeit*, that is unison, unanimity, consonance, agreement, and so on—that comes of, on the one hand, "a matter with what is supposed in advance regarding it and on the other . . . of what is meant in the statement with the matter" (BW 119). Layman and philosopher alike agree that truth is what accords. All have come to the agreement, univocally, that this definition of truth is in accord. Heidegger undoubtedly knows that *stimmen* also has the meaning of casting a vote, of having a voice, of exercising a political franchise. Indeed, the usual (and metaphysical) concept of truth has juridical and political connotations. The character of being in accord is based on a unanimous casting of votes, on all voices ringing in unison. Truth as accord is the result of an egalitarian leveling of voices which celebrate the consonance—that is, absence of heterogeneity—between either matter and meaning, or matter and proposition. In short, the essence of the universally valid and self-evident concept of truth as accordance is justice in the sense of *Gerechtigkeit*: what is in accord is nothing less than 'correct' *(richtig)* and right *(recht)*.[1]

Having argued that accordance is dual, Heidegger also reminds us of the hierarchical relation of ontological and logical dependence between the two modes of the common concept of truth. Indeed, propositional truth *(Satzwahrheit)* rests, by right, on material truth, on the ontic truth of what is *(Sachwahrheit)*, that is, on the accordance of things to their idea or concept. This duality and hierarchy of accordance—in full agreement with classical philosophical exigencies, yet forgotten by positivist theories that restrict truth to propositional statements—is already a hint provided by Heidegger of a complication in the very idea of unison which is characteristic of truth. As we shall see, this complication arises from the determination of accordance as correctness. Heidegger writes: "Both concepts of the essence of *veritas* have continually in view a conforming to *(Sichrichten nach)* ... and hence think truth as correctness *(Richtigkeit)*" (BW 120). Correctness, as a criterion of truth in the ordinary sense, presupposes that, in the unison between proposition and thing, the proposition and the thing must be *directed, oriented, turned toward* one another. Conformity is not possible without a *conforming to*. Nothing could be more banal that the discovery of this directedness, one may object. But after scrutinizing this apparently self-evident and unquestioned implication of truth as correct accordance and consonance, Heidegger will in fact be led to relativize and foreground the traditional concept of truth. What, then, is this directedness at the heart of accordance and correctness? To answer the question, we must follow Heidegger through his discussion of the ways in which the two modes of accordance—material and propositional truth—relate to one another.

Material truth, Heidegger notes, is a function of the Christian theological belief that things have been created by God in conformity with the idea that He conceived of them. If a thing can be said to conform to its idea in the divine intellect—if it is *idee-gerecht*, that is, correct *(richtig)*, just and justified—it can be said to be true. The same conformity must also be expected from the human intellect as an *ens creatum*. It achieves such conformity in accomplishing "in its propositions the correspondence of what is thought to the matter, which in its turn must be in conformity with the *idea*. If all beings are 'created', the possibility of the truth of human knowledge is grounded in the fact that matter and proposition measure up to the idea, and therefore are fitted to each other *(aufeinander zugerichtet)* on the basis of the unity of the divine plan of creation" (BW 120). The directedness which is at the heart of the conformity of matter and proposition to the idea is thus a function of a prior destination of one for the other, a prior fitting of matter and proposition to their divine conception. Without such original directedness of matter and proposition to the idea within the unity of the divine plan of creation, no proposition could hope to achieve any accordance whatsoever. Heidegger remarks: "Throughout, *veritas* essentially implies *convenientia*, the coming of beings themselves, as created, into agreement with the Creator, an 'accord' with regard to the way they are determined in the order of creation *(ein 'Stimmen' nach der Bestimmung der Schöpfungsordnung)*" (BW 121). Consequently, accordance *(Stimmen, Übereinstimmung, Einstimmigkeit)*, whether of material or propositional truth, is grounded in the "being destined for one another" *(Bestimmung)* of matter and idea, matter and proposition, according to the divine plan. There is no possible accordance without a prior "being directed to one another" of the items that make up the accord, and without the end in view that such a destination represents. And furthermore, no correctedness is possible without a certain justness, rectitude, righteousness, by which justice is done—in the last judgment—to the goals or ends *(Bestimmung)* of the divine creation and its order.

It is essential to remark here that this theological account of the "being fitted for one another" of matter and idea, matter and proposition, continues to hold true for all secular notions of truth, as long as they are based on accordance. Any concept of truth constituted by *Übereinstimmung*, or simply by *Stimmen*, presupposes directedness toward one another of what is to accord, within the horizon not so much of the telos of a plan of creation, as of a world order in general. Furthermore, when secularization has reached its climax, the possibility of a universal planification, or ordering into a plan of all objects, underlies truth as accordance. In a radically secularized world, truth as accordance presupposes, indeed, the ontological possibility of a universal subjectability to ends, not just to a particular end or to multiple ends, but the possibility of absolutely everything lending itself to ends. In short, all accordance rests on destination, or, in general terms, on what one might call destinability. All *Stimmen* as *Übereinstimmen* presupposes *Bestimmung* by an order, or more generally, by the possibility of yielding to order. The prefix *Be-* of *Bestimmung* confers the directedness toward an end upon the consonant agreement of the *Stimmen* through which truth rings.

With these developments, which correspond to Chapter I of "On the Essence of Truth," Heidegger seems to have rounded out his discussion of the traditional concept of truth—of ordinary and metaphysical truth. This conception of truth is called a particular *(diese)* "definition *(Bestimmung)* of the essence of truth" (BW 121). Is this to say that truth, understood as accordance, is an interested determination of truth in which truth becomes subjected to an end? And if so, does this mean that there are other possible determinations of truth's essence? How, then, should we understand 'determination' or 'destination' in this case? Finally, could what Heidegger says here about the usual conception of truth mean that there might possibly be a determination of truth that is not a determination of it, and in which truth is not suspended from an end, but without, for all that, being undetermined *(unbestimmt)*? Is there a determination of truth that would altogether escape the logic of *Bestimmung* in the double sense of determination and destination?

In the following chapter, Heidegger inquires into "the inner possibility of accordance." It is the *first* of three steps by which the usual determination of the essence of truth as *Übereinstimmung,* or more simply as *Stimmen,* becomes interrogated as to its conditions of possibility, and foregrounded in a more elementary conception of truth. Yet, has not Heidegger with his reference to the *ens creata* and the divine plan—to the *Bestimmung* in the perspective of the order of creation—already answered that question? Have not metaphysics and theology put to rest the question of the possibility of the determination of truth as accord, by arguing that that determination is based on the mutual destination for one another of matter and idea, matter and proposition, within the horizon of the divine plan? What both disciplines (which, according to Heidegger, are ultimately one and the same) establish is that accordance is a function of matter and idea, and matter and proposition, being fitted to each other on the basis of a *Bestimmung* (determination/ destination) by the divine order of the creation. What Heidegger seeks to clarify, however, is the *inner possibility* of such being-fitted-to, and hence of accordance. This is a quest that is eminently *philosophical,* as opposed to the metaphysical and theological determination of the essence of truth. It is a quest that perhaps no longer seeks to *determine* the essence of truth, if determination is also, and always, a determination by an end.

Before embarking on an analysis of Heidegger's inquiry into the inner possibility of truth as accordance and correctness, let me stress the unbridgeable gap that remains, between the metaphysical and theological account of truth, and the philosophical attempt to question its inner possibility. As Heidegger notes at the beginning of the essay, common sense—and both metaphysics and theology are of that order—is deaf to the language of philosophy. Common sense cannot be refuted, but without its becoming aware of it, it can be foregrounded. As a consequence of this linear approach, everything that has been said about the relation of *Stimmen* and *Bestimmung* with respect to the common concept of truth, because it is still 'unphilosophical,' will be marked by a certain heterogeneity compared to the truly philosophical elaborations on the inner possibility of *stimmen.* A certain discrepancy, perhaps a discord *(Verstimmung),* between common sense and the philosophical treatment of *stimmen* as accordance will distinguish Heidegger's text. In order to inquire into the inner possibilities of accord, Heidegger's approach has to be out of tune with metaphysic's statements on accord; more precisely, it has to sustain the discord in such a manner that the philosophical foregrounding of the metaphysical statements of accordance becomes possible. Otherwise, the metaphysical determination of truth would be replaced by just another determination.

Let us recall that Heidegger's insistence on investigating the inner possibility of accordance arises from the obviousness in which this possibility is being held both by ordinary thinking and metaphysics, but especially by that sort of thinking which restricts truth to propositional truth. Although this kind of thought can lay claim to a venerable tradition, its determination of truth as the accordance of statement with matter turns the question of the meaning of 'accordance' into a pressing issue. This question is all the more urgent, since what are said to be in accordance are entirely dissimilar things—namely, matter and proposition. How can there be accord between things as heterogeneous as matter and proposition, and, if accord occurs, what, then, is the meaning of such according?

A relation of accordance between such things as matter and proposition, Heidegger remarks, is only conceivable as a relation of presentation, in which the presenting statement expatiates upon the matter *as* presented. Presentation *(Vor-stellung)* is not representation *(Vorstellung)*. As "that perceiving which does not take beings in passively, but which can actively give to itself what is present as such in its outward appearance *(eidos)* by gazing up at it," presentation is *noein*,[2] and has to be demarcated from all philosophical and psychological theories of representation. But to let "a thing stand opposed as object," as is the case with presentation, presupposes an open region, a domain of relatedness and opposedness, which a presenting statement must traverse before meeting the object that stands against it.

In turning to this region, a region unthematized not only by the dominant brand of thinking that limits truth to propositional truth, but by the theological and metaphysical explications of the possibility and reason for accordance, Heidegger embarks on a philosophical analysis, strictly speaking. This open region, without which no presentative statement could possibly relate and be in accord with a presented thing, "is not first created by the presenting but rather is only entered into and taken over as a domain of relatedness" (BW 123–24). As Birault has remarked, it is "the openness of an opening that no intentional relation could institute and

Tuned to Accord: On Heidegger's Concept of Truth   37

that all our comportments presuppose."³ The presentative traversal of the openness of the open region in question is "the accomplishment of that bearing *(Verhältnis)* which originally and always comes to prevail as a comportment *(Verhalten)*" (BW 124).

This presenting comportment is one of many possible modifications of comportment, which Heidegger defines as the open relatedness *(offenständiger Bezug)* in general of man or *Dasein* "to something opened up *as such (ein Offenbares als ein solches)*" (BW 124). But within this openness to beings that characterizes comportment in general, a presenting comportment relates only—like all other forms of comportment, "according to the particular perspective that guides them" (BW 123)—to the particular way in which a thing is *(wie es als dieses ist)*. Indeed, things do appear in the mere openedness of their appearance to comportment; they appear always as these particular things (as *what* they are) according to the perspective that all comportment brings with it, and that determines *how* things are. As for the presenting proposition: things become presented in it "with regard to what they are and how they are" (BW 124). In the openness of a presenting comportment, what is presents itself as it is *(selbst vorstellig wird)* to presenting statement *(vorstellendes Aussagen)*. The latter, Heidegger continues, "subordinates itself to the directive *(Weisung)* that it speak of beings *such as (so-wie)* they are. In following such a directive, the statement conforms *(richtet es sich)* to beings. Speech that directs itself accordingly is correct (true) *(richtig)*" (BW 124).

To sum up: all presentative statement, and with it, the possibility of truth as accordance, presupposes—to the extent that it is first and foremost a comportment (an *act* of relating)—an open region in which it can stand open, not merely to what shows itself pure and simple, but to the particular way in which things take their stand. Such a presentative statement can achieve accordance only if it conforms to the directive which things that present themselves as such give to the presenting proposition. This, then, is the point where the *inner* possibility of accordance comes into view. Accordance as a presenting comportment rests on the statement's being directed toward something that in itself (and from itself) instructs the statement as to what and how it (the thing) is.

In short, by focusing on the open region as a domain of relatedness, accordance *(stimmen)* presupposes—and this is its inner possibility—that a concordance occurs between the being *directed toward (richten)* of the statement and the *indicating* or *ordering (Weisung)* by the thing that is to be presented. Truth as accordance thus requires the possibility of a *more originary accord* than the one between statement and the thing as it is. Truth will not occur if the directional traits of *richten* and *weisen* do not accord. These traits are the particular modifications of the general traits that characterize comportment as such—as a holding oneself in *(sich halten)* an open in which one holds on to *(sich an . . . halten)* something that presents itself by itself *(das selbst vorstellig wird)*—and that obtain for presenting comportment. Without the possibility of their "synthesis," there can be no accord between a statement and the thing it presents.

The inner possibility of accordance is thus the synthesis of the more fundamental accord of the trait that causes the proposition to respond to the particular way in which a thing is, and the equally particular trait by which a thing indicates what and how it is. But precisely because this inner possibility of adequation rests on the more originary accord of *specific* (and actually very determined) directional traits, another question arises as to the ground of this inner possibility. What are the *general* conditions, of the being-fitted-to-one-another of *richten* and *weisen*, without which a statement could not hope to secure the accord between itself and what it represents? Heidegger will answer this by elaborating on the *second* step in which the traditional characterization of the essence of truth as accordance becomes foregrounded. He asks: "Whence does the presentative statement receive the directive to conform to the object and to accord by way of correctness? Why is this accord involved in determining *(warum bestimmt dieses Stimmen mit)* the essence of truth? How can something like the accomplishment of a pregiven directedness occur? And how can the initiation into an accord *(Einweisung in ein Stimmen)* occur?" (BW 125)[4] We recall that the inner possibility of accordance established the minimal synthetic conditions for a comporting statement to adequately relate to something *opened up as such* in the specific mode of its whatness. The minimal synthesis was that of the directedness *(sich richten)* of the statement and the pregiveness of a direction *(Vorgabe einer Richte)* by the thing to be represented. The new question centers around the *donation* and the *reception* of the directive to conform to the object. The answer to this question ought to yield the *ground*, that is also the *essence*, of what enables as its inner possibility, something like accordance.

If statement as comportment is possible only to the extent that "standing in the open region, it adheres to something opened up as such" in its very specificity (BW 124), the ground for the enabling possibility of accordance resides in the being free, of stating comportment, "for what is opened up in an open region *(zum*

Offenbaren eines Offenen)" (BW 125). In other words, in order to be given a directive, stating comportment must already have "entered freely into an open region for something opened up which prevails there and which binds every presenting." Statement must have freed itself for a binding directedness "by being free for what is opened up in an open region." No directive can occur, and no directed response to it can take place, without a being free for being given a directedness. What Heidegger calls freedom here is the being *free for* what is *opened up* in the open region of comportment. It is thus the enabling countertrait to the trait of directing oneself to what gives directedness in the open region as a domain of relatedness. To *yield to* a directive is possible only if one is *open,* or *free for* in the sense of being bound by what is opened up as such. Conversely, it must be said (although Heidegger does not make this move explicitly), that for a thing (i.e., something opened up in an open region of comportment) to point out its mode of presentation, the thing must be drawn to, must be free for, being said as it is. It is the enabling countertrait to the trait of pointing out by which a thing gives its directives to statement. Such being-free-for, and the corresponding being-drawn-to-being-said, are the two countertraits that relate to *richten* and *weisen* and that represent the ground or essence of (correct) accordance. This double being-free-for, or more precisely, the finely tuned accord of these two freedoms which are directed against one another, and which embrace one another in the open region, is the essence of truth as correspondence. Truth as accord is grounded in a *stimmen* of these two counter-vectorial traits, traits more originary than those that make up the synthesis of the inner possibility of accordance. As the ground of truth as correspondence, it is a *stimmen* more originary as well than that which makes up its inner possibility.

In the chapter entitled "The Essence of Freedom," Heidegger sets out to further refine the notion of freedom, that is, of being *free for what presents itself* in the open of an open region, a freedom he characterizes as "letting beings be." (BW 127). Freedom, as the ground of truth as correspondence or accordance, can serve only as "the ground of the inner possibility of correctness... because it receives its own essence from the more original essence of uniquely essential truth *(der einzig wesentlichen Wahrheit)*" (BW 127). The twice-double accord of the directional and counter-directional traits, making truth as accordance possible and also grounding it, will consequently depend on a gift that it receives from that more originary and unique truth.[5] By inquiring into how freedom, as the ground of the inner possibility of truth as accordance, receives its own essence from a more originary conception, if not happening, of truth—of a truth that does not primarily reside in correspondence, and that escapes (at least to some extent) the logic of *Bestimmung* in its double meaning of definition and destination since the very meaning of these terms depends on its occurrence—we shall encounter the *third* step by which the classical notion of truth will be foregrounded.

Freedom, as the ground of the possibility of truth as correctness, is the being free for what is opened up in an open region *(das Offenbare eines Offenen)*. Such freedom lets beings be the beings they are, because it responds to the things that *present themselves* in the open region of comportment. Yet in this response and 'subsequent' letting-be, the freedom in question shows itself to be engaged "with the open region and its openness *(das Offene und dessen Offenheit)* into which every being comes to stand, bringing that openness, as it were, along with itself" (BW 127). In other words, for accordance to be possible—i.e., for a proposition to be able to direct itself according to the directive given by the thing to the thing—the proposition must not only be free for what presents itself in specificity (for its *was sein* and *so sein*), but it must also, and primarily, relate to the open region itself in which (and as which) the presencing of the thing occurs. For there to be an accord between statement and matter, statement (as a modification of comportment, that is, an open relatedness, *offenständiger Bezug*) must from the start be open or free, not so much for what is in the open as for the openedness of the open itself. It must from the start be free to accommodate, not the thing in its specificity itself, but the openedness of that which is opened up in the open. Without being bound by the openness of the opened up, a statement could not possibly hope to come into accord with what presences itself as such in an open region. An open relatedness, comportment is engaged with disclosedness, first and foremost. But Heidegger writes:

> To engage oneself with the disclosedness of beings is not to lose oneself in them; rather, such engagement withdraws *(entfaltet sich in einem Zurücktreten vor)* in the face of beings in order that they might reveal themselves with respect to what and how they are and in order that presentative correspondence might take its standard from them. As this letting-be it exposes itself *(setzt sich aus)* to beings as such and transposes *(versetzt)* all comportment into the open region. Letting-be, i.e., freedom, is intrinsically exposing *(aus-setzend)*, ek-sistent. Considered in regard to the essence of truth, the

essence of freedom manifests itself as exposure to the disclosedness of beings. (BW 128)

Qua open relatedness, all stating comportment is thus necessarily engaged with the disclosedness of beings. It is grounded in the freedom that, as letting-be *(Seinlassen)*, is an engagement with *(Sicheinlassen auf)* the openness of the open. But at the same time, and according to the same 'logic' of letting-be, this freedom for the openness of the open is also freedom for what is disclosed in the open. It withdraws *(Zurücktreten vor)*, in order to expose itself to what is disclosed as such. In this free retreat, engagement with the openness of the open makes room for the beings that take their stand in this open. It makes room for beings in their disclosedness, so that they can show themselves in themselves and from themselves. An ever more refined accord thus seems to characterize the third step of the foregrounding of truth as accordance. Provisionally, I construe it as the accord between the traits of letting-be, withdrawing, on the one hand, and, on the other, as an indication of disclosure as such (of things in what and how they are).

Yet before further elaborating on this latter accord (which, after those seen at the heart of the inner possibility and the ground of truth as correctness, is an ever more original essence of truth), it may be appropriate to reflect for a moment on the status of this as yet uncompleted new accord. Heidegger's terminology—inner possibility, ground or essence, and now "the more original essence of uniquely essential truth"—would seem to aim at deeper and deeper syntheses. One can expect this more original essence and the accord that constitutes it to be the ultimate condition of truth as accordance. The question that thus arises concerns the criteria by which it becomes decided that *the* final condition has been established; that is, what distinguishes the more original essence and its accord from the accord that makes up the inner possibility and the ground of truth as correctness? Freedom for what is opened up in its singularity, as the ground of the inner possibility of accordance, seems to be (in conformity with established rules of thinking), a deeper, fundamental and enabling reason. Yet what can be the meaning of a 'more originary essence' than essence, of a more fundamental foundation, supposing, as one must, that Heidegger does not indulge in a *regressus ad infinitum*? It certainly cannot be an essence, ground, or foundation in the traditional sense. Heidegger suggests as much when he claims that freedom as the ground of truth has its own essence in uniquely essential truth, i.e. in the far from ordinary concept of truth as unconcealment.

But the accord exhibited in the third step of foregrounding is not another still deeper synthesis since, while it does exhibit the *fundamental* implications inherent in the very determination of statement as comportment, that is, of an open relatedness in an open region, it does nothing more than formulate the *hidden implications* under which the inner possibility, and the ground of truth as accordance, become meaningful in the first place. It does not add a new possibility or ground to the previous one, but recasts them in terms of an engagement with the openness of the open that the very conditions of accordance require. Presentative concordance can take its standards from beings, and beings can present themselves on their own terms, only if such comportment is in its freedom for what is opened up in the open region, freedom for the open region and its openness or for the self-revealing of things. This engagement with disclosedness is not a more profound ground for accordance, but the framework without which the inner possibility of truth as correctness, and its ground in freedom, could not be what they are. Yet this accord, which can be shown to resonate through the accords that make up the inner possibility and the very ground of truth as correspondence, is certainly not a condition of possibility or ground any more. It is an accord, by contrast, which is required in order to speak of inner possibility and ground in the first place, and of accord and accordance as well. But there is perhaps still another reason why this latter accord is dissimilar to those that constitute inner possibilities and essences.

Heidegger hints at such a dissimilarity when, toward the end of chapter IV, he notes that if truth is primarily freedom, that is, engagement with disclosedness, then covering up, concealment, distortion, are equally primordial possibilities of truth. In short, if, as we have seen, the more originary essence of freedom as the essence of truth harbors an accord, then it must also be inhabited by a certain dis(ac)cord. We shall thus have to pursue our analysis of the more refined accord, which we have seen orchestrating both the inner possibility and the ground of truth. This ever more refined accord must accord, it would seem, with a trait that accounts in an essential manner for the possibility of covering up, that is, un-truth.

At the beginning of the chapter entitled "The Essence of Truth," Heidegger claims that freedom, as disclosive letting beings be, is "engagement in the disclosure of being as a whole as such *(des Seienden im Ganzen als einem solchen)*" (BW 130-31).

Similarly, the last paragraphs of the previous chapter had contended that the experience of unconcealment is that of Being as a whole. (BW 129) The exposure to the disclosedness of beings, in which freedom as letting beings be is rooted, is exposure to, and disclosure of, what all beings qua beings imply, that is, Being as a whole, the openedness as disclosed openedness as such. Now Heidegger writes that any comportment, to the extent that it is open *(offenständiges Verhalten)*, "flourishes *(schwingt)* in letting beings be" (BW 130). It flourishes thus in the essence of freedom as a disclosure of beings in their Being, and consequently, in the disclosure of Being as a whole and as such. Each and every mode of comportment to beings, Heidegger holds, is "already attuned (by freedom) to being as a whole *(hat die Freiheit alles Verhalten schon auf das Seiende im Ganzen abgestimmt)*" (BW 131). The ever more refined and more essential accord (between disclosive letting-be, and the corresponding showing itself as such of beings) that enables us to more originarily think the possibility of truth as accordance and its ground thus appears to derive its more fundamental status from the fact that it articulates the most universal condition for every mode of open comportment, as a comportment to a particular being. The condition that it sets forth is that each and every particular mode of comportment has to be attuned to Being as a whole, that every comportment must flourish according to the tune of Being, so to speak. Such attuning is called "being attuned (attunement) *[Gestimmtheit (Stimmung)]*." Attunement, which as Heidegger remarks, is not a psychological mood, "draws up *(hebt hinein)* into beings as a whole" (BW 131).

Attunement explains why no relation to a thing can ever be free of a historical understanding relation to the whole of the open in which this thing takes its stand, and why all relation to the thing is thus originally and always an open comportment. Consequently, although stating does nothing but assert the accord between what is said of a thing and the thing as it presents itself, it is a comportment that is attuned "in a way that discloses beings as a whole." The limited accord achieved in propositional truth presupposes that a universal accord (a being attuned to beings as a whole and as such to the disclosedness of Being) flourishes in it. No accordance, then, without such a universal accord achieved in the (always historical) attunement of comportment to Being in its disclosedness. No *Übereinstimmung* without *Gestimmtheit*, no *stimmen* without the *Stimmung* that, prior to all modifications of comportment and all modes in which a thing can present itself as such, secures the openedness of the disclosedness of Being as a whole within which beings can relate to one another.[6]

Heidegger writes: "Letting beings be, which is an attuning, a bringing into accord, prevails throughout and anticipates all the open comportment that flourishes in it (*Das stimmende Seinlassen von Seiendem greift durch alles in ihm schwingende offenständinge Verhalten hindurch und greift ihm vor*). Man's comportment is brought into definite accord *(durchstimmt)* throughout by the openedness of being as a whole" (BW 131–32). The universal attunement in question strikes (as one strikes an accord) or stretches (as one stretches an octave, for instance) through the open comportment that swings, vibrates, oscillates in it (according to the rhythm of the accord). It anticipates *(greift ihm vor)* all comportment, Heidegger notes, and thus emphasizes the antecedence of the attunement in question. Through it, all of man's comportments have always already been attuned *(abgestimmt)* to the openedness of Being as a whole which pervades it *(durchstimmt)* from the start.

Now, if the openedness of Being as a whole is the being-attuned or attunement in which all open comportment, and in particular, stating comportment, flourishes, then it is not only what precedes all possible accordance (and the latter's inner possibility and ground), but it is also what precedes it as an ever more refined accord. In the attempt to foreground truth as accordance and to assess its dependence on a destination according to the order of creation *Übereinstimmung* and *Bestimmung)* in the inner possibility and the ground of truth as correctness, Heidegger himself did not construe these enabling conditions in terms of an accord of the vectorial traits discussed above. However, when dealing with the openedness of the open, and with truth in the essential sense of *aletheia* (that is, with the final presuppositions or implications of the traditional concept of truth), he has recourse to terms—*Gestimmtheit, Stimmung*—that not only mean being-attuned, or mood, but that also echo 'accord.' With the fundamental being attuned of all comportment to Being as a whole, with this disclosedness, openness as such, and upon which something as narrow as the accordance of proposition and matter rests, a background melody, or rather a rhythm, comes into sight that is indistinguishable from the openedness of Being as a whole. "From the point of view of everyday calculations and preoccupations this 'as a whole' appears to be incalculable and incomprehensible. It cannot be understood on the basis of the beings opened up in any given case, whether they belong to nature or to history," Heidegger writes; and he adds: "Although it ceaselessly brings everything into definite accord *(ständig alles stimmend)*, still it remains indefinite, indeterminable *(das Unbestimmte, Unbestimmbare)*" (BW 132).

From the point of view of everyday thinking, science, and metaphysics, such attuning that allows for accord and accordance must remain indeterminable. For a thinking engaged in determination, that which makes accordance possible must necessarily escape determination. To speak of the whole that attunes as something indeterminate or indeterminable is to speak of it metaphysically, which is to succumb, if we follow Heidegger, to a most common and unconsidering manner. But, if that which ceaselessly brings everything into accord by attuning it to Being as a whole and as such also appears undetermined and indeterminable, the reason for this may be that what brings into accord cannot in itself be an accord anymore in the usual sense. Perhaps it itself no longer accords. Or, perhaps it accords without according (itself). But because this originary attuning is undetermined or indeterminable, it is not, therefore, a fleeting unfathomable, or vague concept. Indeed, what ceaselessly *accords* everything can achieve such a task only with the help of very precise and definite means. We must therefore try to grasp with all the possible rigor—and that means, by its constitutive traits—the necessarily indeterminable, and perhaps no longer simply accorded, accord on which accordance depends.

As already noted, being-attuned as something indeterminable, "coincides for the most part *(fällt . . . zusammen)* with what is most fleeting and most unconsidered" (BW 132). The two reasons advanced—the inability of metaphysics and common understanding to think of it otherwise, and the specific ontological status of being-attuned—bring about this collapse of what accords ceaselessly into the indeterminable and the most common. By becoming determined as the indeterminable, what ceaselessly accords everything becomes concealed. But this concealment is a self-concealment. As that which lies at the origin of all accord, what ceaselessly accords must withdraw from what it brings harmoniously together. It achieves such withdrawal as the undetermined and indeterminable, both of which are inevitable counterconcepts to determining thought within the latter's sphere. If originary attunement is lost in the indeterminable, it is because it loses itself in allowing for the possibility of accord and accordance in the sphere of the determinable. The indeterminable is in that very sphere the proxy, the phantom image, of originary attunement in which image it is lost as well. Heidegger can thus claim that "what brings into accord is not nothing [not something trifle, trivial, fleeting, etc.] but rather a concealing as a whole." He explains: "Precisely because letting-be always lets beings be in a particular comportment which relates to them and thus discloses them, it conceals beings as a whole. Letting-be is intrinsically at the same time a concealing" (BW 132).

In order to achieve accordance between a particular statement and a particular matter, that without which a particular being could not reveal itself in its very particularity, namely its appearing as such (Being as such as a whole), must withdraw in order for the particularity of a being to show itself in and from itself. The withdrawal of Being as a whole is coeval with the actualization of Being as such in letting-be. The dissimulation of what makes it possible for a particular being to present itself as such, in what it is and how it is, is the necessary condition for the very presence of that being itself.[7] This necessary dissimulation in letting-be, the inevitable withdrawal of Being as a whole in the coming into their own rights of singular beings, also affects the accordance on which truth as correctness rests. Accordance and accord also are always singular, and thus their being-attuned to Being as a whole must necessarily become dissimulated too. What is opened up as a singular accord obfuscates the openedness, the being-open, by which it becomes accorded. As a result, what ceaselessly accords everything must necessarily comport the trait not only of withdrawal, concealment, retreat, but also of a certain discord. What ceaselessly accords puts out of accord. The necessary eclipse of the according whole of Being as such in letting a particular being be is also, and inevitably, the event of discord, of the war among beings.[8] The ultimate accord, which attunes all human comportment to seek accordance between itself and what it lets be, can thus only be an accord very much unlike those which we have seen to render possible and to ground truth as correctness. It must be an accord whose constituting trait cannot but comport with the countertrait of discord. But how are we to think the unity or economy of such a complex? Can it still have the nature of an accord?

In the following chapter, "Untruth of Concealing," Heidegger argues that "concealment of beings as a whole, untruth proper, is older than every openness of this or that thing. It is also older than letting-be itself which in disclosing already holds concealed and comports itself toward concealing" (BW 132). Older than letting-be is "the concealing of what is concealed *(die Verbergung des Verborgenen)* as a whole, of beings as such, i.e., the mystery *(Geheimnis).*" (BW 132) What Heidegger calls "the one mystery," is not just the exact counterpart of disclosedness or the openness of the open. Being as a whole and as such attunes and accords everything ceaselessly. But this same being in its openness is wrenched from concealedness; it is 'derivative' upon Being's concealedness. The concealing of this concealedness—the mystery—is older than all letting-be, and thus also implies that it does not comport with the disclosure of disclosedness in a symmetrical fashion. It does not harmoniously accord with it in a unitary synthesis. The concealing of concealedness, indeed, refers what ceaselessly accords, Being as a whole, not to a definite or determined trait that would be the bipolar correspondent to the according trait (and which could lend itself to entering into accord with the according trait), but to an abyssal trait. The mystery names the inner limit, not only of truth as correspondence, but of truth as *aletheia* as well.

All disclosing letting-be, with the inescapable dissimilation of Being as a whole that goes with it, is itself 'dependant' on the concealing of what is concealed.[9] This concealing is, as Heidegger puts it, "the fundamental occurrence *(Grundgeschehen)*" (BW 134) on which letting-be and the withdrawal of Being that accompany it hinge. Although it is the ineluctable abyss, or blind spot, that accompanies truth as *aletheia* (and by extension truth as *adaequatio* or *homoiosis*), it is also older than truth, not only because singular accordance presupposes the withdrawal of Being as a whole to which it must be attuned, but because the disclosing of Being as a whole itself entails that it be wrenched from concealedness. The concealing of what is concealed—of Being as a whole—is the dissymmetric (and abyssal) counter-trait, to which Being as a whole relates as it ceaselessly accords. The ultimate synthesis, then—the third, but perhaps *fourth,* fifth, sixth, etc., step in Heidegger's attempt to foreground truth as accordance—is no longer an accord, strictly speaking. It is certainly not the accord of the accord and discord. Rather, in it the accord comes to stand in a relation to its limit. That which attunes and accords ceaselessly is not inhabited by discord. There is no *Verstimmung* intrinsically linked up with the enabling accord of *Gestimmtheit*. The dissymmetry of this ultimate synthesis precludes the possibility that any simple opposite of *Stimmung* could enter into a relation to it. This dissymmetry also precludes the possibility that the *Stimmung* is limited by thought in terms of a (linguistic, etymological) derivative of the term in question.

Heidegger recognizes as much when he shows the limit of accord to be the mystery of the concealing of the concealed—*Geheimnis*. Neither a name nor a concept can hope to designate this strange arrangement. *Stimmung* and *Geheimnis* are names in a Heideggerian sense. For the economy of their interrelatedness, however, Heidegger could not find a name. That is why he left it unnamed. But name and concept do not exhaust the linguistic means for thinking and spelling out the disposition of the traits that make up the ultimate accord that is no longer an accord. To think and spell this out, it is perhaps necessary to turn around, and take up once again Heidegger's analysis, whose very premises lead him to search for names for both the fundamental occurrences of concealing, and what rests on it—*aletheia*. To think this unnameable and non-conceptualizable accord that is not an accord, it would perhaps be necessary to displace the whole style of Heidegger's analysis. But that would perhaps also mean to no longer be able to maintain the distinction between metaphysics and ordinary thinking, on the one hand, and philosophy, on the other. Such a displacement would involve shaking up the manner in which Heidegger conceived of the relations that exist between these types of thinking. And finally, a question, modalized by probability as well: Would such an undertaking, if possible and successful (if that could still mean something here), still be thinking? Would the spelled-out accord, which is no longer an accord, be an accord that has been thought?

Notes

1. For how justice, as universal egalitarian leveling, becomes revealed at the end of metaphysics as the essence of truth, see Reiner Schürmann, *Heidegger on Being and Acting: From Principles to Anarchy*, trans. C. M. Gros (Bloomington: Indiana University Press, 1987), p. 192–193.

2. Martin Heidegger, *Nietzsche*, Vol. III: *The Will to Power as Knowledge and as Metaphysics*, trans. F. A. Capuzzi et al. (New York: Harper and Row, 1987), p. 219.

3. Henri Birault. *Heidegger et l'experience de la pensée* (Paris: Gallimard, 1978), p. 467.

4. It must be noted here that in "The Essence of Truth," the chain of *stimmen* (*Übereinstimmen, einstimmen, bestimmen*, etc.) intersects with the chain of *weisen* (*anweisen, einweisen*, etc.), as well as with the chain of *richten* (*sich richten nach, die Richte, Richtigkeit*, etc.). Heidegger does not think these different chains together in a "conceptual" knot by means of which the enabling conditions of accordance would have become articulated in a most economic torsion. As far as the question of *Bestimmung* is concerned, Heidegger does not achieve anything comparable to the notions of *Gestell* or *Ereignis*. The most he will venture to do is to think *Bestimmung* in the direction of a more originary *Gestimmtheit*, or to make some use of hyphenation to demarcate metaphysical *Bestimmung* from one that is open to the *Stimme des Sein* (See in this context Martin Heidegger, *Was is das—die Philosophie?* [Pfullingen: Neske, 1956]). What is the reason for such hesitance? Is it because the Heideggerian gathering presupposes (linguistic, etymological) homogeneity, and thus does not permit inclusion of heterogeneous chains (such as *stimmen, richten, weisen*) in *one* terminological construct?

5. This twice-double accord is not chiasmatic, strictly speaking, since the two accords that seem to produce the crisscross effect are not homogeneous. The accord that constitutes the inner possibility of accordance, and the one that grounds it, occur on very distinct levels of thought.

6. In Chapter IV, Heidegger had already shown that engagement with disclosedness is the more essential ground not only of the traditional concept of truth as accordance, but also of history. Engagement with disclosedness (as opposed to the freedom for something opened up as such in its singularity) takes place, Heidegger writes, as "a distinctive relatedness to a being as a whole *(zu einem Seienden im Ganzen als einem solchen)* which first founds all history" (BW, 129, slightly modified). Engagement with beings as such, as a whole, occurs in a particular way each time, and is constitutive of the very manner in which a people relates to "its essential possibilities" that are conserved *(ver-wahrt)* in such disclosure (BW, 130). The more essential ground of truth as accordance (of *Übereinstimmung,* and its subsequent function of logical determination, of *Bestimmung*) is thus as well the ground for the *Bestimmung* of a historical mankind, that is, for its vocation, its teleology, its *Geschick*. Heidegger's attempt to foreground the classical conception of truth thus lays the groundwork for accounting for the (modern) distinction of logical and historical determination, and the exchanges between both. Heidegger's developments towards what we have seen to amount to a 'fundamental' theory of accord lead in such a direction.

7. See Birault, p. 496.

8. This eclipse is also the reason for the inevitable plurality of, and hence discord between, the goals or ends *(Bestimmungen)* to which all particular truth claims *(Übereinstimmungen)* must yield.

9. Heidegger touches here on the limits of phenomenology, on what one could call a constitutive blind spot of a philosophy of appearing as such.

II. Metaphysics and the History of Being

Chapter 3

Heidegger's Revolution: An Introduction to *An Introduction to Metaphysics*

John D. Caputo

Heidegger thought he could be *the* philosopher of the new *Reich*, the one who could provide it with a truly philosophical voice, with genuine spiritual leadership. By showing the origin of the "movement" in the primordial Greek beginning he would make plain to all the spiritual authority of National Socialism as the true future and destiny of Germany, of Europe, of the West. Such a philosophical vocation was not to be assumed lightly. It did not belong to just anybody, but only to a National Socialist thinker—to one who was of a "new mind"—who could think radically, metaphysically, historically. It belonged to him. This was Heidegger's vocation.[1]

By the time of the 1935 lecture course *An Introduction to Metaphysics,* it was quite clear to Heidegger that the Party was inclined to pass up the opportunity to have the greatest German philosopher since Nietzsche as its intellectual leader.[2] The ideological control of the Party had fallen into lesser hands, to smaller minds. The party members were baffled by the connection that Heidegger was making between the meaning of the revolution and the question of Being. They were troubled by all his talk about the Nothing which seemed to them so much nihilism. They were worried about Heidegger's call for a radical questioning which would expose everyone and everything to the insecurity of the abyss. That did not seem to them an effective way to run a revolution. As deeply as Heidegger was committed to the *Führer* and to the new order, they really were not comfortable with him and did not understand the way he spoke. Besides, he had made quite a mess of things as Rector at Freiburg the one time he did have real administrative authority. The best way that Heidegger could serve the movement, they had concluded, was to stay at his post as a professor, where they could count on his loyalty to the national revolution—even though they were not sure what the revolution meant to him—and to let them run the Party.

That is why Heidegger makes no attempt in *An Introduction to Metaphysics* to conceal his disdain—born no doubt of considerable disappointment—for these Party ideologues and for the direction in which they were (mis)leading, seducing *(verführen)* the movement and maybe even the *Führer* himself.[3] In Heidegger's mind, the movement was being taken over by its least worthy, its most spiritually benighted elements, by people who do not understand that the greatness of Germany's future must be linked with the great Greek beginning. They mindlessly identify the greatness of the movement with Max Schmelling[4] instead of with Sophocles; they mistake the truly gathering power of the *logos* with mass rallies (GA 40, 41; IM 38);[5] they confuse the aboriginal power of historical destiny with the superficiality of subjectivistic "values." These Party hacks do not think; they do not know how to question. The philosophical works that these people are peddling—and this is the phrase that (rightly) stuck in the young Habermas' throat—"have nothing whatever to do with the inner truth and greatness of the movement [Party?]" (GA 40, 208; IM 199).[6] For this inner truth and greatness is spiritual, metaphysical, historical; it has do with the need to think, to question, to philosophize in a true and great manner. That is what Heidegger was offering them and that is what they, at their peril, were refusing.

The ideologues who had gained control of the Party do not understand that the success of the revolution is tied to philosophy. If the nation is to be renewed from the ground up, this can only proceed from a *Grund-frage,* from questioning into the ground, from a radical and fundamental questioning which would make the ground tremble. A revolutionary renewal of the nation must be keyed to radical, revolutionary thinking. The power of the revolution must be keyed to the "hidden power" (GA 40, 3; IM 1) of the question of Being. Great nations ask great questions; nations of the highest rank ask the question which is first in rank. A radical revolution requires that we let the very ground tremble by letting the "why" pull the ground out from under beings as a whole and then by letting this why "recoil" *(Rückstoss)* upon ourselves so that we too tremble and waver in insecurity, we who ask this question. The power of the nation is a function of the "power of the spirit" *(Kraft des Geistes)* to raise the most "originary" *(ürsprünglich)* of questions, to put the "why" to things, to make the "leap" *(Sprung)* which thrusts away, leaps away *(Absprung)* from all the safety and security *(Geborgenheit)* of life (GA 40, 7–8; IM 5–6). Security is the death of philosophy—whether this security comes from faith or from somewhere else. Philosophy occurs only where there is daring *(Wagen:* GA 40, 10; IM 8).

Philosophy is radical questioning, and questioning is not something that can be housed safely in a university that is reduced to career training and producing state functionaries.[7] If you try to master philosophical questioning like a skill and put it to work for you, then what you do will not be philosophy. If you try to make philosophy catch up to the times and be timely, you will destroy it. If you try to use it, you will find that it is useless. The worst thing the Party can do is to try to use philosophy like a tool for its own purposes, to treat it in a purely utilitarian fashion.

Heidegger is by no means suggesting that the question of Being has nothing to do with the greatness of the national purpose, with the great destiny of the people, but only that the Party hacks have gotten the thing backwards. That is why he adds: "But what is useless can still be a force *(Macht),* and perhaps the only real one *(erst recht)*" (GA 40, 10; IM 8). If you try to use philosophy to produce an echo *(Wiederklang)* in the times, you will miss the genuine "harmony" *(Einklang)* of philosophy with what is really happening in the history of a people, indeed, you will miss its capacity to ring this in *(Vorklang)* in advance, to announce in advance a great breakthrough, to produce something new, to create new spaces for the spirit. Put in Derridean terms, philosophy is *glas,* a tolling that tolls in advance a great breakthrough, to produce something new, to create new spaces for the spirit, a new order, which is at the heart of the etymological link between *glas* and *classicus*: philosophy announces, indeed, it creates an order of rank. The question which is first in the order of rank *(dem Range nach)* will bring forth a new order of the highest rank, a new *classicus* which will repeat the classical Greek order (GA 40, 4; IM 2).

By giving ourselves over to radical questioning, i.e., to philosophy, the inherently revolutionary power of philosophy will give something to us and hence to the revolution. Great philosophy, as radical questioning, is inherently revolutionary, for it creates a new space, a revolutionarily new and other beginning. We must not attempt to use philosophy for the revolution, but we must let the revolutionary power of philosophy use us:

> It is absolutely right and in order to say that "You can't do [start] *(angangen)* anything with philosophy." It is only wrong to suppose that this is the last word on philosophy. For the rejoinder imposes itself: granted that *we* cannot do anything with philosophy, might not philosophy, if we let ourselves be engaged with it, do something with us? (GA 40, 14; IM 12)

We must not apply philosophy to the times, but let philosophical questioning open up a new space of time *(Zeitspielraum)*, a new age, a new order, "another beginning" (GA 40, 42; IM 39).

But philosophy will do this for us only if we recognize its unique nature, for philosophy is one of the few truly "autonomous" *(eigenständig)* and truly creative *(schöpferisch)* possibilities that have been granted to human Dasein (a possibility which is also now a necessity) (GA 40, 11; IM 9). Philosophy will effect renewal only if we give it its head, if we let it loose in radical questioning, if we admit ourselves *(einlassen)* into it. But it is an appreciation of the uniqueness of philosophical questioning, and above all of the question of Being, that is lacking to those elements in the Party who have now gained power. Their misunderstandings of philosophy—and there are two of them—could not be more perverse.

(1) Because philosophy goes to the very ground and essence *(Grund)* of things, these people expect philosophy to provide a grounding *(Grundlegung)* for a historical people, something upon which we can build up the culture *(die Kultur aufbauen)*. And they complain when it does not, e.g., now they are complaining that metaphysics did nothing to prepare for the revolution! (Would that were so!) But that is to expect too much of philosophy, Heidegger says. It is to mistake philosophy for a tool you can use to build something. It is to misunderstand the uniqueness of philosophy: philosophy belongs to a special creative few who, by giving themselves over to radical questioning, will produce a profound transformation *(Verwandlung)*, who will then change things all around *(Umsetzung)*, who will create a new space which the many can later on comfortably fill up as if it had been there all along as a matter of course *(selbstverständlich)*. But this creative work cannot be expected to produce direct and immediate results, and further-

more it will not happen by an *Aufbauen* but rather by opening up a kind of knowledge *(Wissen)* which will "light a fire under *(feuern)*, which will threaten *(bedrohen)*, which will necessitate all questioning and valuing *(Schätzen)*" (GA 40, 12; IM 10).

Now all that sounded to the Party a lot more like an *Abbauen* of the culture than an *Aufbauen*. We can see why the Party was worried about this. Heidegger's idea of getting the movement underway was to threaten and question everything, a notion which did not, evidently, capture the Party's fancy. The people who were running the Party expected philosophy to give everybody a *Grundlegung* and Heidegger was offering them an *Abbauen,* and they could not see how that would help at all. That was the gist of their differences. They were not divided from Heidegger by their shared devotion to the success of the revolution but by their differing conception of the role that philosophy, especially Heidegger's philosophy, was to play in the revolution's success. Heidegger was telling them that the revolution would succeed only if they entrusted themselves to the groundlessness of radical questioning, to the truly revolutionary power of philosophy to make revolutionaries out of those who gave themselves over to it *(einlassen)*. But it was beyond the Party members as to how throwing themselves into an abyss was going to bring about the new order. Such a conception of philosophy seemed to them a lot more likely to endanger the revolution than to secure it.

One of the more interesting results of the work of Farias and Ott is the account they give of the perception of Heidegger within the Party and the Party's reasons for keeping him out of power. Although not a Nazi report itself, the response of the faculty at Munich to a Nazi Minister's proposal of Heidegger for a chair there is typical: the faculty was wary of a tendency in Heidegger's philosophy to "dissolve into an aporetic of endless questioning"; it suspected him of scepticism and worried that this endless questioning of Being would lead to paralysis.[8] Farias thinks that the Party hierarchy regarded him as a very radical revolutionary, "a rebel against compromise with the need to respect the rhythm of political development," a threat to the Party's attempt to consolidate power.[9] Krieck and his circle considered his question of Being to be nihilistic, not only because he talked about the Nothing *(Nichts)*, but because of the restlessness of a questioning which never came to end. They thought his influence was subversive.[10] One of the most interesting critiques comes from one Walter Jaensch, whose philosopher brother (Erich) was an early and strident opponent of Heidegger. Farias writes:

> [W.] Jaensch emphasized the danger of Heidegger's "revolutionary ardor." Heidegger had joined National Socialism simply because of his innate penchant for revolution, period. "Well-informed sources say that he fears the day when revolution among us would cease. It is certain that this 'pure revolutionary' would then no longer be on our side, but would be a turncoat."[11]

The radicality of Heidegger's thought, of the question of Being, its capacity to recoil on whatever or whoever tried to enlist it in their service, its capacity to pull the ground out from under things, made the Party more than a little nervous about Heidegger.

It is in this light that we should view Heidegger's formulation of the charge of nihilism made against his thought:

> Moreover, he who takes the nothing seriously is allying himself with nothingness. He is patently promoting the spirit of negation and serving the cause of disintegration *(Zerstörung)* ... What disregards the fundamental law of thought and also destroys the will to build *(Aufbauenwillen)* and faith is pure nihilism. (GA 40, 26; IM 23)

At the end of the lectures, he warns his students that, without the question of Being, the Germans will stagger around:

> We stagger *(taumeln)* even when we assure one another that we are no longer staggering, even when, as in recent years, people do their best to show that this inquiry about Being brings only confusion, that its effect is destructive *(zerstörend),* that it is nihilism. [One must be very naive to suppose that this misinterpretation of the question of Being, renewed since the appearance of existentialism, is new.] [The sentence in square brackets was added in 1953.] (GA 40, 211–12; IM 202–03)

In other words, the Nazis had the same sort of objection to Heidegger that most people have against "deconstruction" and "postmodernism" today, that this thinking is nihilistic, that it could never eventuate in building anything but only in tearing things down. It is demoralizing and debilitating, negative and nihilistic. It might have been useful in un-building and deconstructing the Weimar state, but it was of questionable worth for building the Third Reich. Heidegger looked so radical and revolutionary to Party members that they were worried that he would not even be content with a National Socialist revolution.

That was what Heidegger was up against in trying to assert his right to be the philosopher of the new Reich. He would try to demonstrate the revolutionary potential of the question of Being in *An Introduction to Metaphysics*. He would show them that asking the question of Being was the great gift of the German spirit and that it went to the heart of the greatness of the German nation. He would warn them that failing to measure up to this question, his question, would only reproduce the failure which occurred in the nineteenth century when Germany failed to measure up to the greatness of German Idealist thinking.

(2) The second misunderstanding of philosophy concedes that we ought not to expect philosophy to supply a *Grundlegung* or an *Aufbauen* of the culture, which would be to demand too much; but it does expect that philosophy "could still contribute to the facilitation of its construction *[Erleichterung ihres Aufbaues]*" (GA 40, 12–13; IM 10).[12] Philosophy draws a world-map *(Weltkarte)* which marks off the various regions of beings and that should provide a very useful orientation for us when we set out on our various purposes. Philosophy can also put the house of the sciences in order by reflecting on their foundations and presuppositions, thereby relieving science of a lot of work. Philosophy, in short, can make things easier.

But the truth is, Heidegger says, that "philosophy by its very nature never makes things easier, but only more difficult *(schwerer)*." That is only partly because of the well-known penchant of philosophers themselves for saying even the simplest things in a difficult and forbidding language. The real explanation for this, Heidegger says, is that "making difficulty for historical Dasein *(Erschwerung des geschichtlichen Daseins)* and hence fundamentally for Being pure and simple *(Seins schlechthin)* is really the genuine meaning of philosophical activity." "Making things difficult," Heidegger continues, "gives the weight *(Gewicht)* (the Being) back to things, to beings." To take things lightly, to make life easy *(Erleichterung)* is to rob things of their weight, to expose them and oneself to the unbearable lightness of Being, to let things float away in ontological weightlessness. (Were it not for the fact that the Nazis invaded his country, we would wager that Milan Kundera must have had *An Introduction to Metaphysics* on his shelf.[13]) "Making things difficult," Heidegger adds, "is one of the essential, fundamental conditions for the origin of everything great..." By greatness Heidegger hastens to add he means "before all else the destiny

(Schicksal) of a historical people *(geschichtlichen Volkes)* and of its works" (GA 40, 9; IM 11). The Party leaders do not see the tie between greatness and difficulty, and between difficulty and questioning. (And not only the Party leaders, but most philosophy professors also miss the connections, assuming as they do that their job primarily consists in presenting a certain amount of material clearly so as to facilitate understanding.)

This misunderstanding amounts to a perversion *(Verkehrung)*, a perverse reversal of philosophy from *Erschwerung* to *Erleichterung*, from intensifying the difficulty to making things easier. But this is a perversion of a deeper truth. Philosophy may have nothing to do with facilitating the "culture business—it is not the sort of thing that gets a leading role in the works of popular culture or makes the rounds of the talk shows—but it does make possible a truly "historical existence." It makes historical existence *great* and it does this because greatness and difficulty go hand in hand. Philosophy is a kind of primordial historicizing just because it is primordial trouble making. Philosophical questioning gives historical existence depth and weight by making both Dasein and Sein itself more difficult.

What sort of difficulty does philosophy produce? What does Heidegger mean? What is the horizon within which we are to think difficulty? This much at least is clear. Philosophy is groundbreaking, path-making, originary; it creates historical openings where previously there was only closure, habituation, and stagnation. It is driven by a deep energy which can energize an entire people *(Volk)*. It is driven by a relentless questioning, a merciless will to know which cuts through the banalities of culture to the deep structure, the *Wesen,* of that people's historical destiny. Above all else, difficulty means questioning, the difficulty of really asking questions rather than just repeating formulae. Without the ground-breaking work of philosophy a people will drift aimlessly, frivolously, consumed by consumerism, overrun by the rule of the masses, the indifferent, by the measureless et cetera of the always the same—just as in American and Russia (GA 40, 49; IM 46) where they have no philosophy—and in Weimar Germany, where they caved in to the easy life, where life really was a Cabaret. Without the hardness and comfortlessness of philosophy, a historical people will lack all aim, indeed will remain only a soft, comfort-seeking culture and never become historical, never acquire a destiny. Without the groundbreaking work of philosophy, the Party itself will be misled into mistaking the essence of the revolution, and confusing the inner truth and greatness of a historical-epochal movement with the banalities of mass rallies and prize fighters.

So Heidegger will set the Party straight about the true meaning of the Revolution which is now in danger of being perverted by the manifest spiritual shortcomings of these ideologues. He will show them that the Revolution has nothing to do with Max Schmelling and everything to do with Sophocles, that it has nothing to do with the "crude scribblers" who speak in Nietzsche's name but with the profound void of Being (GA 40, 39–40; IM 36), which is the meaning of nihilism spoken by Nietzsche himself. He will warn them that by its degradation of spirit into calculative intelligence, National Socialism is putting itself in league with Russian Marxism and American positivism. Hence he warns them of a triple threat:

> The spirit falsified into intelligence thus falls to the level of a tool in the service of others, a tool the manipulation of which can be taught and learned. Whether this use of intelligence relates to the regulation and domination of the material conditions of production (as in Marxism) or in general to the intelligent ordering and explanation of everything that is present and already posited at any time (as in positivism), or whether it is applied to the organization and regulation of a nation's vital resources and race *(Lebensmasse und Rasse eines Volkes)*—in any case the spirit as intelligence becomes the impotent superstructure for something else, which because it is without spirit or even opposed to spirit is taken for actual reality.

The biological racism of these ideologues misses the truly spiritual character of the movement. Heidegger does not condemn the cultivation of the body and the sword but he demands that these practices be ordered by a spiritual principle:

> For all true power and beauty of the body, all the sureness and boldness of the sword, all authenticity and inventiveness of the understanding, are grounded in the spirit ... It [the spirit] is the sustaining, dominating [principle] ... (GA 40, 51; IM 47)[14]

Volk means something spiritual, something linguistic, and something "metaphysical" (in the language of 1935); it is not to be crudely reduced to something physical and biological.

Heidegger wants to show them that the revolution is all about "another beginning" *(anderen Anfang)*, by which is meant not a simple imitation of the first beginning, but a "retrieval" *(Wieder-*

holung), beginning again *more originarily,* "with all of the strangeness, darkness, and insecurity that attend a true beginning" (GA 41, 42; IM 39). He takes it upon himself to show them that the struggle—the *Kampf*—in which the party is engaged is not related to boxing matches but to Heraclitus' *polemos,* which he translates as *Kampf,* for *polemos* is the father of all things. In *An Introduction to Metaphysics,* Heidegger tries to refute the charge of nihilism by demonstrating that it is only be entering into the aboriginal struggle with Being—what he called the *Kampf um das Sein* (GA 40, 114; IM 107)—that the German nation could be up to its destiny and the Revolution could be true to itself. The question of Being, far from Being a vacuous abstraction or a nihilistic wallowing in the void, will alone raise the people and the Party to the heights of their power, of their spirit, and will save the nation and the movement from their own worst tendencies.

Polemos is not war in the human sense, nor a strife between gods and men, but rather that aboriginal struggle *(Kampf)* which first sets out the differences between things and sets up the order of rank among gods and men, men and slaves (GA 40, 66; IM 62). There is no levelled off mass man here, no standardization of the spirit here (GA 40, 50; IM 46) not in Heraclitus, for struggle and strife create the differential order of rank:

> Because Being as logos is basic gathering, not mass and turmoil in which everything has as much or as little value as everything else, rank and domination are implicit in being. If being is to disclose itself, it must itself have and maintain a rank. That is why Heraclitus spoke of the many as dogs and donkeys. This attitude was an essential part of Greek Dasein. Nowadays a little too much fuss is sometimes made over the polis. If one is going to concern oneself with the polis, this aspect should not be forgotten. (GA 40, 141; IM 133)

The best *polis* maintains an order of rank and does not disperse into democratic diffusion and turmoil. Struggle *(Kampf)* is the *logos* which collects things together, snatching them away from the dissemination of democracy and ordering them hierarchically. Being and the true are for the strong because Being and the true are hidden and superior:

> What has the higher rank is the stronger. Therefore being, the *logos* as gathering and harmony, is not easily accessible

and not accessible to all in the same form; unlike the harmony that is mere compromise, destruction of tension, flattening, it is hidden...

The true is not for every man but only for the strong. (GA 40, 141; IM 133)

This aboriginal struggle *(polemos)* which brings forth beings (the beings which contend with one another) is then carried on and sustained *(getragen)* by the great creators, the poets, the thinkers and statesmen. Their role, in Heidegger's view, is to throw up certain temporary blocks or barriers which contain for a fleeting moment the enormous power of the Overwhelming. Their poetry, their deeds, their thought, in short their works, capture this enormous something new, a new order of things, which then soon enough, all too soon, is simply passed along to the "many" who use it, look at it, copy it. The great world epiphany which irrupted with the struggle between the world-creators and Being, which, being great, can only last for a short time, all too soon degenerates into the peace and tranquility of mere visibility. The Being of things is all too soon gone out of them. As soon as this great *Kampf* ceases, as soon as men cease to surpass themselves and grow stronger, as soon as the creators vanish, then the *Verfall* has set in (GA 40, 68; IM 63). What does not grow stronger, dies.

We can see what worried Jaensch and Heidegger's other Nazi critics. It belongs to the very "logic" of the "great" that the time of irruption and struggle can last for only a short period, after which it seems, by an inevitable momentum, to suffer a *Verfall* which lies "in the very essence of the beginning itself":

> Since it is a beginning the beginning must in a sense leave itself behind... A beginning can never directly preserve its full momentum; the only possible way to preserve its force is to repeat, to draw once again *(wieder-holen)* more deeply than ever from its source. And it is only by a thoughtful repetition that we can deal appropriately with the beginning and the breakdown of the truth. (GA 40, 199–200; IM 191)

Once things stabilize they fall in decline and require still another revolutionary struggle and retrieval. Now that is not a bad way to foment a revolution, some Nazis thought, but it is no way to consolidate it. Heidegger was not advocating an an-archical view, because his attitude was uncompromisingly hier-archical: these renewals came from the top down, from the creators, while the dogs and donkeys stayed on their leash. But his view did seem to imply permanent struggle *(Kampf)*, ceaseless repetition and renewal, an endless succession of revolutions. That is why Jaensch feared that Heidegger would soon enough turn on the Nazi Revolution once it has succeeded. The question of Being issued in a politics which was always oriented towards a *new* order, but it seems unable to accommodate itself to the thought of the stable continuance of such an order once it was brought about. Presumably, on this accounting, even if the later Heidegger's "other beginning" were actually effected, it would soon enough go into decline and we would be back to waiting for still another beginning and still another god to save us from this now eclipsed beginning.

In any case, one sees Heidegger's revolutionary program: the National Socialist revolution must be the repetition of the great Greek beginning in which the great tragedians, statesmen and artists grapple with Being itself in the forging of the first beginning. The *Kampf* in which this great revolution is engaged stands or falls on the basis of its capacity to repeat its original Greek model, the Heraclitean *polemos,* which is its primogenitor, its father *(pater)*.

In the final lectures of the course, Heidegger offers a striking interpretation of the choral song from *Antigone*, which gives remarkable voice to his views. *Kampf* must be thought in terms of "the poetic stamping of the *Kampf* between Being and appearance" as provided by Sophocles (GA 40, 115; IM 108), not in terms of the boxing career of Max Schmelling. The Greeks were engaged in a great battle between Being and appearance *(Kampf zwischen Sein und Schein)* in wresting Being from beings, bringing beings from concealment to unconcealment—in their temples, tragedies, and Olympic contests *(Wettkamp)* (GA 40, 113; IM 105–106). Sophocles' Oedipus embodies Greek Dasein because he is driven by a fundamental "passion for the disclosure of Being, that is, the struggle for Being itself" *[Kampf um das Sein selbst]*, a drive against which he himself heroically shatters—which is the token of his greatness (GA 40, 114; IM 107). He had an eye too many, Hölderlin said, which is "the fundamental condition of all great questioning and knowing and also their only metaphysical ground," Heidegger adds.

The passion of Oedipus is what knowledge *(Wissen)* meant in the great age of Greece. It had nothing to do with placid professors disinterestedly seeking objective science. Knowing was a matter for philosophers, not for school teachers (GA 40, 129; IM 121). It meant war, struggle, *polemos* with the power of Being.

Nothing shows this more clearly than the choral song from *Antigone*. Sophocles determines the Being of Greek Dasein in terms of *deinon*. *Deinon* means, on the one hand, the terrible *(das Furchbare)*, the overwhelming power *(überwaltigendes Walten)* of what fills us with terror; it means Being as terrifying *physis*. On the other hand, *deinon* names man as the most violent one, the wielder of power *(to deinataton, das Gewalt-tätige)*, the one who enters into mortal combat with the Overwhelming. *Deinon* as a whole names the *Kampf* between Being and man.

But Heidegger wants to translate *deinon* as *unheimlich*, uncanny, unfamiliar, not-at-home, not in order to attenuate the sense of power, but to accentuate it. The most uncanny one *(Unheimlichste)* means the one who has been cast out from everything homelike and familiar, from everything "safe and unendangered" *[ungefährdeten]* (GA 40, 160; IM 151). The strange and uncanny one forsakes safety for the sake of danger, leaves the safety of home in order to embrace the danger of the battle for Being. We see here the earlier, even mirror-like reversal of the later Hölderlinian formula: where the danger is, the saving grows. Here Heidegger adopts exactly the opposite position, one inspired not by Hölderlin but by Ernst Jünger: it is the safety of the home that is dangerous, and only real danger will save us, will make us strong and great.

The violence of the violent one is his violent knowledge *(Wissen)*—which is how Heidegger translates *techne*—by means of which he can do battle with Being, with *physis*: breaking out upon stormy seas, breaking into the earth with plows, snaring animals in his nets (all of which is just what Heidegger later on meant by the *Gestell*). Still this is not a course the violent one has chosen for himself but one into which he has been cast by the Overwhelming; it is the fate which has been enjoined upon him by *dike*. Nor is he finally successful, for the violent one in the end must shatter in death against the Overwhelming. There is no mastery of death (GA 40, 167; IM 158). But this is clearly not to be construed by Heidegger as a lesson in *Gelassenheit* but rather as a call to heroism. In the heroic shattering against the Overwhelming, the uncanny one asserts his order of rank, the superior power of his knowledge which, if it must crash against Being, shows the uncanny one to be first and highest and strongest among beings and peoples. In this succumbing to Being, Greek Dasein asserts its preeminence among beings. In their loss is their victory.

For it is in doing battle with Being that the violent and uncanny one shows his true power *(machanoen, techne)*, the power that has been entrusted to him to bring Being into the work of art, to subdue the overwhelming power of Being as *physis* just long enough to let it shine there (IM 159) before it overwhelms and destroys us. The greatness of the violent one does not consist in his power to subdue *physis,* for that is beyond man, but in having the heart and the courage *(tolma)* to dare to enter into this mortal—and ultimately losing—*Kampf* with Being and its succession of victories and defeats:

> Thus the *deinon* as the overpowering *(dike)* and the *deinon* as the violent *(techne)* confront one another ... In this confrontation *techne* bursts forth against *dike*, which in turn, as the Enjoining *(Fug)*, the commanding order, disposes *(verfügt)* of all *techne* ... The knower sails into the very middle of the dominant order; he tears it open and violently carries Being into the being; yet he can never master the overpowering ... Every violent curbing of the powerful is either victory or defeat. Both, each in its different way, fling him out of home and ... unfold the dangerousness of achieved or lost being ... This violent one stands at all times in venture *(tolma)*. In venturing to master Being, he must risk the assault of non-being, *me kalon* ... (GA 40, 169–70; IM 160–61)

Disaster *(Verderb)* is not something that befalls man if he slips up; it is built right into the conflict between man and Being: Violence against the preponderant power of Being *must* shatter against Being if Being rules in its essence as *physis,* as emergent power (GA 40, 171; IM 162).

It is necessary *(notwendig)* for man to be "thrown" *(geworfen)* into such a needy condition, such a state of affliction *(Not)*, because man is needed and used *(brauchen)* by Being itself as *physis* for the display of its overwhelming power. So it is only when human Dasein pushes itself to the most extreme condition of need and affliction that *physis* as such comes to appear *and* that man himself is brought to the full power of his own essence.

Now we can finally locate what Sophocles means by "the uncanny one": "to be posited by the Overwhelming as the breach in which the Overwhelming bursts into appearance, in order that this breach should itself shatter against Being (GA 40, 172; IM 163). Man is forced beyond himself and towards Being precisely in order to bring Being into the work—into city and temple, statue and poem. Precisely in this shattering against the Overwhelming, man himself achieves his greatest eminence. The violent one despises all help, all compromise, all petty satisfactions and security, because he has surrendered himself up to Being to serve as that breach in which Being itself will shine with power and glory.

Here then is the message that Heidegger bears from Sophocles to the National Socialists: the greatness of National Socialist works, of their cities and armies, of their universities and their artworks, can never be realized unless they see that such works are the setting-into-work *(Ins-Werk-setzen)* of the Overwhelming itself, that such works bring Being itself to a stand, give it a place, and unless the National Socialists see that the Being of man is to-be-posited, set-up *(Gesetz-sein)* by Being itself for this work of setting into work. This has nothing to do with "culture" or "values" but with how *history* happens as the issue of Being itself. The Greeks did not decide to turn out culture for the next few millenia of the West but to inaugurate history by responding with violence to the violence of Being (GA 40, 172–73; IM 164). The danger is that the Germans will take the side of the chorus itself, which expresses, in the song's final lines, the opinion of the lowest and most common elements of the city, who want nothing to do with such exceptionality, with such un-homeliness, and who prefer the undisturbed peace and tranquility, the safety of lives without violence.

The National Socialists, evidently, were not at all sure about this. It was not at all clear to them how much good Heraclitus and Sophocles could do for the revolution, or what difference it would make whether you backed up National Socialist claims with value-theory or with the overwhelming power of *physis*. One gets an insight into the Party's judgment on Heidegger from a dossier kept on Heidegger by the Party and uncovered by Jacques Le Rider in the archives of Quai d'Orsay. In response to a 1938 questionnaire on authors whose works were being taught in Germany, a Freiburg Party bureaucrat says of Heidegger that he is politically reliable and even important because he was such a famous academic. But he also thinks that Heidegger is rather a puzzle, that he does not have his "feet on the ground," seems "cut off from the world," and that his thought is a little too "individualistic."[15] The document shows us that four years after the resignation of the rectorate Heidegger was still a member in good standing in the Party but that the Party was largely baffled by his person and even more so by his thought. The Nazis thought that Heidegger served a purpose in his post at Freiburg, that they could rely on his political loyalty, but they did not have the slightest inclination to let either Heidegger personally or his thought be a guiding force in the new *Reich*.

Part of my argument is that the National Socialists were right to keep to their distance from Heidegger. I do not mean that they were right to question his "tactical abilities" as an administrator, as the Quai d'Orsay dossier says, although they certainly were. Nor do I mean that they had reason to be wary of his political sympathies, for they did not, although that is how Heidegger tried to make it out after the war. Everything that we have learned about Heidegger the man from Farias and Ott, and from the publication of the *Gesamtausgabe* war lectures, confirms that Heidegger was a loyal supporter of the Third Reich right up to the end of the war.

But it seems to me that they were quite right to be troubled about all this talk about the questionability of Being, the groundless abyss beneath whatever we call a ground, the Nothing which "nothings," which withdraws and leaves us empty. They were right about his thought, more so than he himself was, although they barely understood a word he said. They had their doubts that the issues Heidegger was raising would be of any use at all in consolidating the revolution. Insisting upon the radical questionability of everything, making everything tremble, was not a bad way to rouse the revolutionary spirit but it was not way to establish the new order. It was a very useful way to make trouble for the powers that be, the prevailing structures. But it was no way to consolidate one's gains, for one of the characteristics of the question of Being was what Heidegger called its *Rückstoss,* its "recoil" upon itself, so that whatever emerged from the question would itself be put into question and nothing would be left standing, not if you let the question loose, not if you let it provoke the trembling and insecurity of which it was capable.

On this point, the Party members had a better sense of the political impact of Heidegger's question than did Heidegger. For if Heidegger had turned this question loose *on* National Socialism, instead of putting it into the service *of* National Socialism, what would have been left standing? Heidegger tried to persuade the Party that the greatness of German Dasein lay in its philosophical resources, and that the greatness of philosophy lay in its power of revolutionary questioning, but the Nazis were worried that such an irruptive force could just as easily become questioning *of* the revolution. Heidegger tried to persuade them that a revolution from the ground up required a questioning of the ground, but they could not see why this questioning could not be turned against the grounds of the National Socialist revolution itself. Heidegger wanted the revolution to be fired by revolutionary questioning; they were worried that this might result in questioning the revolution.

And they were right. Consider the questions that would have issued from such an irruption, from letting the power of Heidegger's questioning turn on Heidegger's politics. Would not such a politics begin to "waver and oscillate" *(schwanken)* in instability? Would not Heidegger's words recoil on his National Socialism, that every being is "half being, half nonbeing, which is also why *we can belong wholly (ganz) to nothing,* not even to ourselves" (GA 40, 31; IM 28)—and if not to anything, then not to National Socialism either? Suppose we let the little appendage—the *und nicht vielmehr Nichts,* "and not rather nothing" (GA 40, 24 ff; IM 22 ff)—recoil upon everything that went into Heidegger's National Socialism: Why should we think in terms of the great *and not rather of the small?* Why should we be preoccupied with great beginnings and great things— and not rather with the little things that are all around us, each of which *is* and contains all the wonder of the *is rather than not?* And does not Heidegger do this, *too?* Even in this text, are not some of the most powerful passages dedicated precisely to the piece of chalk, the high school, the mountain range, the early Romanesque door (GA 40, 38; IM 35)?

And if we break the grip of the great, then what power would the great Greek beginning have over us? Or the idea that beginnings are great instead of small? Or that the Greeks are to be thought in terms of greatness? Or that the Greeks are *the* beginning? Are not Jews and Christians part of the beginning? And why stop with Greeks? Did the Greeks drop from the sky? Why not Egyptians and Mesopotamians? Why is not Sanskrit Being's primeval tongue? And why must everything since the Greeks be the loss of greatness? And if the great Greek beginning is questioned, then what remains of its metaphysico-political counterpart, the great German future? And if that is questioned, then must we not question a Party which is so single-mindedly dedicated to such a future?

But if the Greek beginning begins to waver, then what are we to think of repetition/retrieval *(Wiederholung)*? What would there be to repeat? Perhaps nothing at all, perhaps there is no beginning, nothing distinctly first that then gets repeated again and again. Perhaps there is a repetition which does not have anything to repeat? Why must repetition be the repetition of a distinct and great beginning *rather than not?* Why not a repetition which repeats *forward* instead of *backward?* Could there not be a repetition which produces what it repeats? Which produces as it repeats? And might that not all start by chance, so that a month ago we had no idea we would be involved in this repetition, that we would by now have something going, that we would be on the move?

Again: Why should we think in terms of essential destiny—and not rather of a certain uncontrolled historical proliferation and chance? Why is there destiny *rather than not?* Is not the whole idea of destiny not entirely ill-fated and dangerous? Why not think in terms of the opportunities which present themselves from time to time, little breaks and chances here and there, unforeseen Kierkegaardian "moments," little openings and possibilities instead of vast historical epochal clearings? But if we make the notion of destiny tremble, then should we not tremble at the thought of the Party of destiny, or the people of destiny?

Again: Why should we think that Being has a *Wesen* at all *rather than not?* Have we broken the grip of essentialism simply because we have shifted it from the nominative, essentialistic sense of *essentia* to the supposedly more primordial Greco-Germanic verbal sense of *An-wesen,* of coming to be and passing away? Have we made *Wesen* tremble simply because we have lifted it up a notch from the nominative to the verbal and put it in process? Why must we think in terms of *Wesen* and the *Wesentliches* at all, *and not rather* of the accidental? What is the Being of *Wesen* and *Un-wesen?* And why must we devalorize everything accidental, inessential, outside, excluded, trivialized, everything small and insignificant which may turn out in the end—who knows?—to be very important? Why is it necessary, as Heidegger thinks in *Being and Time* (§74), to drive out everything accidental and to convert it into what is historically necessary and essential? Why not learn to live with the accidental, to operate among the changeable and variable? Is that not the art of politics?

Again: why must there be *the* history of Being *and not rather* many such histories, a whole host of them, a proliferation of histories, which tell us many stories, so many that they are impossible to monitor and to organize into a grand narrative of Being's singular upsurge and decline? The notion that this is not man's history, not a story controlled by a human agency, but a history that is visited upon man, is itself a disruption of the most sedimented conceptions of history, and that is part of the power of Heidegger's thought. But why not many such histories? And why a history of Being rather than of something which is Otherwise Than Being, as Heidegger's most famous antagonist, Emmanuel Levinas, has put it? Is Justice, as Levinas describes it, Otherwise Than Being?

But if we remain faithful even to the notion of Being, what is it about Being which weds it to "our people," which makes it the specific energy and power of any people? Why does Being not belong to any and every people? To all and to none (GA 40, 38; IM 34)? Why should there be people, *Völker,* national unities at all, rather than not? Why not many peoples and peoples who have been miscegenated beyond identifiable recognition, whose identities are being gradually blurred? Heidegger thought in terms of the saving power of "our people." He thought that the greatness of the German could save us from the endless et cetera of Russian and American people. But what does thinking about Russian, German, and American give us? Stalinism, Nazism, Hiroshima. Dead bodies, dead people. Must we not be always inside and outside our people? American and not American? We are always already American (or French, or something), but we need to see how profoundly dangerous that is. Not evil, but dangerous.

Now we are back to danger. Heidegger, who always loved danger, had an eye too few for the real danger. He was oblivious of the danger of stirring up the sentiments of greatness, of people, of destiny, of the love of violence and danger. He did not see the danger in danger; he thought it was saving. The danger was that he was not making these ideas questionable, that he did not let the question of Being recoil upon them, exposing them to the little appendage, "and not rather," the little "not" that makes them tremble. Heidegger thought the question of Being belonged in the service of "people," "greatness," and "destiny." He did not have the courage or the power—although he was very interested in courage and power—to turn the question of Being on the great destiny of his people, to throw them into question and confusion. It was to the perverse credit of the Nazis that they sensed quite vividly that Heidegger's questioning could break loose in just such a disruptive volley of questions as we have just sampled and which would throw National Socialism itself into question. But Heidegger himself never saw that.

I would say, to use a military figure, that Heidegger betrayed the question of Being, that he handed it over to the enemy, enlisted it in the service *(Dienst)* of a people, that he conscripted and confined it to one people and one language (or two: Are Greek and German one or two?) He did the same thing to Greek tragedy; he made Sophocles wear a steel helmet. Let us say that our task today, like the allied armies descending on Freiburg (from which, Ott tells us, Heidegger beat a hasty retreat[16]), is to liberate the question of Being, to liberate Heraclitus and Aristotle, Aeschylus and Sophocles, from their German captors. Let us make the Germanness of Heidegger tremble, make it waver in insecurity, in order to liberate Heidegger from Heidegger, to turn Heidegger against Heidegger, and this by means of Heidegger himself. Let us make Heidegger truly the name, not of a man, but of a matter to be thought.

Notes

1. This is a constant theme in Hugo Ott, *Martin Heidegger: Unterwegs zu seiner Biographie* (Frankfurt: Campus Verlag, 1988), but see especially pp. 164–165, 190–191.

2. Ott thinks that the Party had already made up its mind on Heidegger by December 1933 and that Heidegger had by them determined to resign the Rectorate (pp. 229–230). It did not take long for Heidegger to discover that he was going nowhere in the Party (Ott, p. 240).

3. The notorious declaration of Nov. 3, 1933—"Let not propositions and 'ideas' be the rules of your Being. The *Führer* alone is the present and future German reality and its law." (*New German Critique,* No. 45 (Fall, 1988), p. 102)—may have been a warning not to heed Party ideologues but only the Führer whose true leadership Heidegger feared was being subverted.

4. Max Schmelling (b. 1905), the world heavyweight boxing champion from 1930 to 1932, had become a symbol of "Aryan superiority" by handing the black American prizefighter Joe Louis (1914–81) his first defeat in a 12-round knock-out fight in 1936, and then was knocked out by Louis in a 1938 rematch. Heidegger took the Louis-Schmelling rivalry to be a deplorable confusion of what Heraclitus meant by *polemos*.

5. All page references in parentheses in the text are to Martin Heidegger, *Gesamtausgabe,* B. 40, *Einführung in die Metaphysik* (Frankfurt: Klostermann, 1983); English translation: *An Introduction to Metaphysics,* trans. R. Mannheim (New Haven: Yale University Press, 1959). I have from time to time altered this translation, sometimes sharply.

6. Heidegger evidently said "Party" not "movement." See Harmut Buchner, "Fragmentarisches," in *Erinnerung an Martin Heidegger,* ed. Günther Neske (Pfullingen: Neske, 1977), p. 49; and Thomas Sheehan, "Heidegger and the Nazis," *The New York Review of Books* (June 16, 1988), pp. 42–43.

7. Heidegger was arguing this point about the university from the early Freiburg lectures of 1919 and 1923. See *Gesamtausgabe,* B. 56/57, *Zur Bestimmung der Philosophie* (Frankfurt: Klostermann, 1987), pp. 205–214; B. 63, *Ontologie: Hermeneutik der Faktizität* (Frankfurt: Klostermann, 1988), pp. 32–34.

8. Victor Farias, *Heidegger and Nazism,* eds. J. Margolis and T. Rockmore (Philadelphia: Temple University Press, 1989), p. 165.

9. Farias, p. 187.

10. Farias, pp. 168, 252.

11. Farias, p. 204. See also Ott, pp. 191, 243.

12. Mannheim's translation erases the occurences of *Erleichterung* and *Erschwerung* in these two paragraphs.

13. Milos Kundera, *The Unbearable Lightness of Being*, trans. M. H. Heim (New York: Harper & Row, 1984). See Winfried Franzen, "Die Sehnsucht nach Härte und Schwere," in *Heidegger und praqktische Philosophie,* eds. Otto Pöggeler and A. Gethmann-Siefert (Frankfurt: Suhrkamp, 1988), pp. 78–92.

14. Farias (pp. 220–221) tries to argue that Heidegger was not criticizing racism or biology but trying to found it on the notion of spirit. That seems to me contrived and merely polemical.

15. Jacques Le Rider, "Le dossier d'un nazi 'ordinaire,'" *Le Monde* (October 13-19, 1988), p. 12; cf. Ott, p. 254, n. 174.

16. Ott, p. 156–157, 279 ff.

Chapter 4

Heidegger and 'The' Greeks: History, Catastrophe, and Community

Dennis J. Schmidt

My intention in what follows is to discuss the general topic of "Heidegger and 'the' Greeks" and to do so with three objectives. First, I want to problematize the "the" in that topic; in other words, I want to ask about the singularity of that which Heidegger himself unproblematically designates as " 'the' Greeks." There is something haunting, perhaps even (and I say this ironically) tragic, about the blindness that might be risked in that singularity, yet paradoxically the question Heidegger puts to us today might be precisely about our captivity to that blindness. Second, I want to discuss the significance of Heidegger's conviction that it is incumbent upon us today to out Greek 'the' Greeks; in particular, I will suggest that the question of history as Heidegger poses it stakes us today to a thinking of Greeks, who finally have not yet appeared, because they belong to the withdrawal of history. But even though these "Greeks" are present under the law of a curious distance, the bond which presses us to that law rendering the Greeks a matter of our own intimacy bestows a clear specificity to the task of thinking today. I will try to show that such specificity concerns both the destiny of history itself and the still unqueried essence of *techne* as the knowledge that, according to Plato, governs every determination of the *polis*. Third, I want to raise some questions about the way in which Heidegger's confrontation with 'the' Greeks forms the special, if not only, way in which he poses the question of who "we" are today. This is a question that he first formulates out of what he characterizes as the *failure* of the metaphysical conception of *techne*. Heidegger has made us aware that only in rare moments is there the possibility of a community that is not modelled after some representation projected out of an arrested moment, be it the frozen past or merely imagined future. I believe that Heidegger takes ours to be precisely such a rare moment, since it is a time in which extreme limits are reached and so it is a time in which our blindness itself becomes evident; as such, it is the time in which we witness the possibility of forging a community that is the site of mobile, and hence real, rather than calcified and imaginary, relations. Such a community would be one that is governed by labile time and not by a representation of itself, i.e., by its self-imposed coercion.

※ ※ ※

One always wants to say that predicting the present—that means as well as asking what the past will have been and the future was to be—is the greatest difficulty of all, but that difficulty is no accident and its confession is the homage we pay to the darkness of the lived moment. When he reminds us that thinking the finiteness that we are requires that we think the conflicted temporal lines and agony of every moment, Heidegger believes that he is laying claim to being the first to have struggled against the foreclosure of history he takes to be the legacy of Greek thought. But despite Heidegger's claims to the contrary, it seems that Hegel, who Heidegger called "the last Greek,"[1] is the first to have taken that idea seriously, at least if we read him as saying that the Absolute marks the end of the representation of history and the opening of the space for such true historicity. Moreover, I would argue that, contrary Heidegger's warning, there is in fact something to be learned from confronting Hegel and Heidegger's respective understandings of the life of history, and that is something that might displace much that Heidegger believes he can rightfully say.[2] But even if Heidegger is not the first to attempt to take history seriously, it does seem fair to say that Heidegger had pressed this question of the need to think history in new directions and with an unsurpassed thematic rigor. In particular he showed that the general project of overcoming the ontotheological tradition belongs to the effort to recover history, as itself an effort to think the difficulty of that stretch we call "the present."

Heidegger reminds us that the metaphysical gesture is to annul history and face that difficulty of the present by processing it photographically[3] such that the dark and fluid present is transformed into the sole source of light and stability, and he reminds us as well that if we are to address the present honestly, that is, if we are to face the deepest difficulty of our times so that we might find their habitability, then we must overcome metaphysics as a style and strategy of thinking lacking the agility requisite to that task. Modelled after an image of an infinite and omnipresent mind, metaphysics is, according to Heidegger, the general rubric for thinking and speaking that suffers no death and undergoes no history, and as a result effaces the very difficulty that thinking is called upon to address.[4] Our actual situation, in contrast, requires that we recognize the essential feature of the difficulty in every historical present: finding a way to live in our times, a way of living up to our prior pact with the past, our implicitly made promises with the future, and in solidarity with the living. It is the difficulty of needing to live up to the burden of history while owning up to the law of finitude that governs our appearance in time at all.

Against such an effacement, Heidegger contends that our access to every present comes precisely in its withdrawal into such difficulty that marks every present as the coalescence and compression of alterity. It is that withdrawal—the self-renewing capacity of life to throw itself ever anew into darkness and the experience of heterogeneity housed in that capacity—that persisted in attracting Heidegger's attentions. Early in his career, he seemed to make an attempt to capture it under the theme of the "hermeneutics of facticity," but he gradually abandoned this desire to capture what could at best only be brought to the brink of the concept—to the point at which the concept itself is rendered suspect—and choose instead to follow its rhythms by thinking language simultaneously as the signal and survivor of that event of withdrawal.

But if we simply regard history as the movement of a unilateral retreat, of a withdrawal without rebate, then we miss the full historicity of the present, and we misunderstand its true distress because then we have already forgotten that "the concealed essence of time," the countermovement of the withdrawal of every present into its own darkness, is *"return"* (NI 28). Relentlessly, from the early texts that culminate in paragraph 74 of *Being and Time*, where we find a passage entitled "On the Basic Constitution of Historicality" in which Heidegger suggests that history is to be thought as repetition and return, through the Nietzsche volumes which culminate in their effort to reappropriate the thought of the eternal return of the same, to the suggestive hint of the very last sentence that Heidegger wrote a few days before his death and which asks about a certain withdrawal marking our present and about the prospects for return ("Today we should ask whether and how there can still be a home in the era of the technical and standardized world civilization" [D 187]), relentlessly then, Heidegger reminds us that the effort to think the ecstatic dimensions of the present, any present, leads us to the need to think its withdrawal and return *at once*.[5] "Repetition," says Heidegger, "first makes ... history ... evident" (SZ 386).[6]

Thus, if we follow Heidegger, it is not long before we come to recognize that, while history, that which is to be thought, is the rising of singular events, and, while the nature of that singularity is to be questioned and is the real stake in history, such events become visible and live as language that has happened and has taken the reality of that singularity up into itself. To ask about history is to find that death has already made its claim upon the inconceivable singularity that was, and that, consequently, one is left to ask, at the outset at least, about language that has happened. The difficulty of writing history is not so much the difficulty of recovering the oblivion of by-gone events, but of recovering language itself as repeating the crisis of the true uniqueness, the singularity at stake, in every such event. Singularity, which is the true idiom of history, is perhaps unspeakable as such. What can be spoken as redemptive of history is the idiom of the idiom itself; that, of course, is the obligation that we call poetry. The difficulty for those of us writing today is to speak again the language of the idiom that breaks the representation of history which, as the immobilization of history, renders every community, no matter how exotically plural, uninhabitable.

※ ※ ※

Now I make these admittedly far-too sweeping comments as a way of calling attention to the "fact" that the themes I propose to address—withdrawal, return, distress, the ineluctability of language and the crisis of our singularity—are not themes unique to the period and the texts in which I suggest they be examined, but are enduring themes characteristic of Heidegger's efforts to know the truth of history throughout each of the several permutations of that knowledge which is always, according to Heidegger, "knowledge that knows the hour of the happening that first forms history"

(GA 65, 395). I certainly do not intend to risk discussing that understanding through such a large sweep of texts. Rather, my special interest is in what I take to be the significant features of Heidegger's sense of history as it is articulated in the texts between 1929 and 1946—between the triumphant "What Is Metaphysics," written on the occasion of his return to the university at Freiburg, and the traumatized "Anaximander's Saying," written when Freiburg was in ruins and Heidegger was barred from the university. I want to argue that, during this period, Heidegger makes some fascinating and powerful decisions about how "we" are to think history "for us," and my intent is to pose questions about these strangely Hegelian phrases that refer to history that is "for us" and that speak of this "we" who knows about that history. This is the period in which Heidegger explicitly asks about the "we" even if it is by suggesting that "they" still know nothing about the "we": "Today the we is valued. Now is the 'time of the we' . . . We are . . . We—are. Does this statement establish the presence of a plurality of 'I's'? And what about the 'I was' and the 'we were,' what about being in the past? Has it gone away from us? Or *are* we precisely that which we were? Do we not become precisely that which we *are*?" (EM 53). Any "we" today must begin by forming itself in the face of its own prior problematization by history.

I should say from the outset that, in turning to this period and in suggesting that it is a decisive period in the development of Heidegger's concern with the question of history, my purpose is not to argue that Heidegger's thought felt and answered the impact of its day, that philosophy here comes under the sway of political concerns and present events. Heidegger's reformation of the essence of political life renders such concerns and events sufficiently problematic that I believe we would do well to ask the question of their determination first with Heidegger, rather than take for granted that we understand their full dimensions. Saying that does not exempt Heidegger's thought from submission to a political critique; it does, however, propose to submit it to the more severe scrutiny of the future that Heidegger himself begins to open, rather than the past that it seeks to overcome. In other words, I believe that Heidegger's thought is most rigorously problematized by taking it seriously, not by measuring it against the very measures it seeks to overcome, nor by ghettoizing its own political engagement. In line with that attempt, I want to ask how Heidegger suggests we think history as that which claims us.[7] As an answer I want to suggest that Heidegger's decision to feel and answer his era *as* a philosopher—if in fact that is how he does address his present—is, as Plato well knew, itself a decisive political decision.[8] Ultimately, I believe that Heidegger knew that such a choice was a political choice and that it is precisely the limitations and defensibility of this choice with which he is concerned in, for instance, the Rektoral Address as well as the lectures on Hölderlin.[9]

But this struggle with the question of the decision and choice in history "for us" has a specificity. Foremost, Heidegger in this context is committed to asking the question of his own present as the question of whether the Greeks can still speak to us today. At one point, this question of "our" contact with the Greeks, posed as a question of translation and in particular as a question of the possibility of translating the words that Heidegger takes as naming the quintessential Greekness of the Greeks, *to deinon*, leads him to make the stunning and rather dramatic comment: "Tell me what you think about translation and I will tell you who you are" (GA 53, 76).[10] Even more: in the end, Heidegger does not pose the question of whether we can speak without 'the Greeks' today, or even whether they can speak to us; rather, the question for us today, as he formulates it, is whether we can "think *more Greek* than the Greeks themselves" (GA 53, 100, emphasis added). It is the question that asks if we can still speak Greek today—a question, at least as Heidegger unfolds it, that betrays his sense that 'the Greeks' have not yet happened, and that means simply that they have not yet come to language.

So Heidegger finds it necessary to rewrite Greek thought, and to do so in detail. But, tellingly, during this period, he frequently steps back from such detailed rewritings of Greek texts and speaks collectively of 'the Greeks.' When he does that I believe that he is struggling more to invent Germany than to recover Greece, and that he is haunted by the resulting image that becomes the sole mirror in which he can see his time, and which nonetheless still has not yet appeared. Thus, shortly before posing the question, "'who are we'" (GA 39, 48), a question he seeks to answer by saying something about the "Horizon of the question of time" (GA 39, 49), Heidegger urges us to ask, "What do the Greeks still have to do with us?" (GA 39, 47), because the decision about that question is the answer to the question of the 'we.' Even if the signature of our age, the unimpeded sway of technicity, gives it a different appearance, Heidegger contends that we need to ask to what extent our age is still to be thought as bound to 'the Greeks,' and to what extent the resources for thinking our age have been transmitted by such a bond. It is a question then about the possibility of a reflection, even a question of the image of the mirror itself, of that in which a duplicate that is seen, but one that is still (perhaps) only one thing.

Heidegger begins an essay devoted to the topic of "Hegel and the Greeks" by noting that his theme might sound like "Kant and the Greeks, Leibniz and the Greeks, the medieval scholastics and the Greeks. [But though it might] sound the same, it is different." (W, 422). One must say the same about the question of "Heidegger and 'the' Greeks." I have tried to suggest that Heidegger himself might regard that as naming 'the' question of our era, the question "our" era puts to "us." I believe that if we are to take that suggestion seriously, then we should begin by asking about the questionableness of such a question, perhaps first of all about the mimetology that animates it. An outline of large questions begins to appear at this point. To what extent is Heidegger's effort to think the present age freed from the presumptions upon which that age has been cultivated still locked in the past's vision of the future? Does not the end of history, the depletion of 'the' tradition, signal the appearance of the new, of that which could in no way be comprehended by what has happened? If that is the case, then how are we to think and measure that which has no historical index other than the unanticipated future? Heidegger has taught us that the truth of history always arrives with that which breaks the law of history as the meditation and transmission of what has happened, but has the arrival of that truth itself outlived the death of history and shown itself to be both the survivor of its own destruction and the subversion of its language?

My purpose here is not to begin such a project, but to narrow it further still by trying simply to unfold the significance and unavoidable specific content of one segment of that question of Heidegger's sense of history "bonding" (GA 39, 51) us to 'the' Greeks, and to do so in one somewhat restricted slice from a much larger body of texts directly relevant to the question. My special interest now is in calling attention to one way in which that imaging of the present through 'the' Greeks tends to revolve around a rather specific axis defined by the question of *techne,* and with interrogating (but how if not with Heidegger himself?) the political meaning both of this image and of the dominant axis along which it moves.

※ ※ ※

I should begin by perhaps risking a bit of repetition and acknowledging again, but this time more clearly, that my choice of this period is determined by concerns and assumptions which I believe warrant further comment:

First, I believe that this is a period in which the question of history loomed the largest in Heidegger's thought *as* a question and that it was the most fertile period in his thought with respect to the formulation of the content of the *question* that history poses to us. Thus, one reads that "[w]e do not know our true historical time. The worldly-hour *[Weltstunde]* of our people is hidden from us" [GA 39, 50]. Furthermore, I believe that Heidegger did have a deep sense that every time we breathe and open our mouths to speak we owe a debt to history, more precisely, the debt that asks us to address our present, to ask about the way every present problematizes "us," and to find a just and appropriate attitude toward "our" times. This is the point at which Heidegger believes he is asking questions about the national and the social, about "the" people and community, about the "we" that is problematized in advance of its appearance by history.[11] It is a question that during this period penetrates even the most delicate capillaries of Heidegger's concerns. Thus, in the 1943/44 lecture course on Heraclitus, we find Heidegger urging us to hear the enigma of the language on Heraclitus's fragment 123, *physis kryptesthai philei,* and to do that he contends that "we" must ask if we have heard the "claim of thinking," " 'we'—who are we then? How do 'we' come to the point at which we can enjoin history and in particular the beginning of the essential destiny of our history?" (GA 55, 122).

Consequently, this is the period in which Heidegger raises questions about the limits of political life, for he does say, and in several ways, that, while the *polis* is the name for the relation of all relations, "the *polis* does not permit itself to be determined politically" (GA 53, 99). That does not, however, exempt other means whereby we define our political life from being a political decision. It remains then a question how "we," at the end of philosophy and history, are to determine the *polis*; it is even a question if our belonging-together can be thought any longer around the Greek model of the *polis*. And yet, since the *polis* is "the site of history" (EM 146), a confrontation with the idea of the *polis* is rendered necessary today by history itself.

Heidegger has been criticized as a human being for never addressing his own monstrous times, either "in" that present or "after," and while there is an irrelevant and overly self-righteous moralistic tone to most of those criticisms, I confess that I would not want to defend him in that regard. I would even say that it is incumbent upon those of us who choose to work in Heidegger's wake—even if with a tortured and uneasy fidelity—to be unremitting in the denunciation of every collaborative gesture that he made toward the regime of racism, domination and brutality. But I do believe that if Heidegger the man was sorely lacking in courage and conviction, "Heidegger" as a body of questions, a corpus, does put demanding questions *to us* about the ever-present singularity and distress of the present, and about the entanglements and imperatives in which we involve ourselves when we seek to speak to or out of that present.[12] Of course, the issue isn't Heidegger the singular man at all, but *our* distress, namely, that *we still have understood nothing,* that we do not know how it is that perhaps the most subtle thinking of our era could be immunized to the horror, even the simple crudeness, of its times. The banality that Heidegger hands us—"one who thinks greatly, errs greatly"—does nothing to address our distress and the endurance of such immunized thinking today. The singularity which is the true idiom of history's language sharpens the question of history, drawing it forward like "the point of a spear" (US, 105) and pointing to a determinate content. Heidegger's contention, one, despite appearances, *not* drawn from empirical observation, is that today the focal point of history is found in learning to ask the question of *techne* anew.

When the metaphysical determination of the *polis* was first defined by Plato, it was defined as a question of *techne*. At least that is the frame within which Plato has Socrates posing the question of the determination of the political: since all of activities seem to require a special knowledge, a *techne*, what, then, is the *techne* appropriate to the determination of the *polis*? Heidegger's effort to simultaneously refunction and delimit the notion and legacy of the Greek sense of *techne* is well known, but I believe that it remains inadequately acknowledged how far that effort is linked with the task of redefining the *polis*. It is with this acknowledgment in mind that we can begin to hear the full significance of Heidegger's citation of Aeschylus's Prometheus: "*techne* (which is here translated simply as "Wissen") is far weaker than necessity" (SU, 11). Heidegger retranslates that passage thereby instantly drawing that citation, and the context imported by it, into the project of thinking historical destiny, rather than *techne*, as naming the question of knowledge relevant to political life: "every knowledge about things is and remains already handed over to the higher power of destiny in the face of which such knowledge fails" (SU 11). In precisely the same respect, we would do well to recognize the kinship of this effort with Heidegger's recovery of tragic poetry for the *polis* which is itself best understood as a reversal of Plato's first decisive move in the *Republic,* namely, the decision to exile certain tragic poets.

But this is the point at which the question of *history itself* returns. Here it is significant that this question is most systematically developed during the period of fascism's momentary triumph, the time of a self-proclaimed triumph of that which Heidegger always criticized as the most stubborn remnant of metaphysical thinking: the will. It is the moment when history is arrested at the very moment of its death—at least that is how I would characterize fascism, namely, as the effort to arrest history precisely at the moment its destructive forces emerge. That is why Heidegger insists upon the "historical uniqueness of National Socialism" (GA 53, 106), and why he links the need to think that uniqueness with a certain recovery of Greek thought that has not yet happened. So, after remarking on that "uniqueness," Heidegger takes a jab at national-socialistic reappropriations of Greece and then continues by saying that *"[f]or us* it is not a matter of the 'political,' but of the essence of the *polis* and ... of the essential domain out of which it is to be determined, and that means ... according to that which must preserve the Greeks about the most *worthy* of question" (GA 53, 106–7, emphasis added).[13] The question put *to us* is whether or not Heidegger's thought opens up avenues for understanding what might be "historically unique" about such a period, and for providing suggestions for avoiding such a moment of historical arrest ever again. He is not alone in suggesting that, whatever else it was, this period can be clearly identified with the liquidation of an idea and a possibility. But I would insist that one simply cannot read Heidegger if one forgets that he was writing out of a time that from the point of view of the past had generated a time that was "without a future," in other words, if one forgets that Heidegger writes from out of the logic of the end of history, the death of history as it had been. Such a logic is most foreign to the logic of modernity, which is driven by the desire to begin *ab novo,* to be "without a past." At times, Heidegger seems to court that desire, or at least risk such courting, in his talk of a "new beginning." But his real insight is a warning about that effort to sweep away the past: hence, the tradition that cultivated and then participated in such a desire to be "without a past" has collapsed in essential ways, leaving us "without a future." Writing out of the logic of that death, Heidegger finds his thought doubly staked to the thought of death: the death that each of us bears and the death that our times mark.

So precisely at the moment of history's depletion, the juncture at which our traditions obstinately live but are no longer able to replenish themselves, freshen and grow, precisely at this time marked so thoroughly by death, we learn how necessary history is for us. We learn as well the truth of the point Nietzsche urged us to take to heart: that the "it was" stands before us as a "stone" and that it tolerates no revenge.[14] Now one understands fully the sense of Benjamin's comments about the angel of history as it is painted by Klee: "he is about to distance himself from something at which he is staring. His eyes are wide open, his mouth is open, his wings are spread... His face is turned toward the past. Where there appears to be a chain of events before *us*, he sees a *single catastrophe* which keeps piling wreckage upon wreckage and hurls it in front of his feet... a storm is blowing from paradise; it has got caught in his wings with such force that the angel can no longer close them. This storm irresistibly propels him into the future to which his back is turned, while the pile of debris grows skyward."[15] Perhaps the only preliminary comment that must be made if the presentation of this image is to be drawn closer to Heidegger's concerns is that the catastrophe spoken of here is to be thought according to its essentially Greek determination as a "countervalency" and "overturning." Catastrophe is not the by-product of history, but the revelation of the truth of history itself, namely, that the past has made possible the impossibility of its own future. But that means that catastrophe is to be thought as the arrival of the future "we" have manufactured.

Heidegger suggests that the present age can only be understood if it is thought from out of the logic that discloses its death: *"Our hour is the era of decline"* (GA 65, 397). He further contends that this death, this being in a present without a future, is not an accident, but the return and revelation of a long-standing *destiny*. A destiny defined in Greece and a catastrophe that Heidegger, in 1945, contends "broke in upon the Germans" (SU 43).

※ ※ ※

By this point it should be clear that I am groping toward asking about what appears to be two questions: one about Heidegger's sense of history, the other about the specific task to which that sense of history calls thinking that is responsive to the rigor of history itself, namely, the task of overcoming the governing, metaphysical determination of all requisite knowledge as *techne*. These apparently separate questions of history and *techne* do, however, belong together, since it is only by thinking the truth of history that the overdetermination by *techne* is overwhelmed:

again—"every knowledge about things is and remains already handed over to the higher power of destiny in the face of which such knowledge fails" (SU 11). The injunction of history "for us," itself once animated and determined by a knowing conceived as *techne*, is to address that overpowering that is historical destiny and that failure of the knowledge conceived as *techne*.

It should be said from the outset that this problematization of *techne*, as Heidegger conceives it, belongs to the question of *physis*: "Because *physis*, not *techne*, first makes *techne* as such something that is visible and that can be experienced" (GA 65, 190). But that is no surprise, since that effort to delineate the tensions between *physis* and *techne*, first thematized as such in "Origin of the Work of Art," serves as the conducting wire uniting an array of texts through, for instance, the 1939 study of Aristotle's *Physics B*, through as well the 1955 lectures on technology and beyond. Throughout, Heidegger's claim is that we will not be able to take measure of the present until we are able to conceive "the foreignness and uniqueness of that project" of thinking *physis* and the visibility of *techne* as its real achievement. The measure of our present "destitution" is that we take this project as "the most natural thing that could happen" (GA 65, 190). It should be noted that in posing the question of *techne* as a matter of its kinship with, rather than opposition to, *physis*, Heidegger attempts to translate the modern framework of the question concerning the knowledge of the subject as conceived over and against its world into an early Greek formulation. Yet here, as before, I make this point not with the intention of pursuing it now, but merely to mark the severe limitations of my own line of questioning. But that, I would remind you, is precisely the same gesture that Heidegger makes in the text in which he first develops the question of *techne* in conjunction with an effort to think the present historical juncture and the *polis*, namely, in *Introduction to Metaphysics*, where he, too, excuses himself from the full issue, quite at the outset (yet with the quiet exemption claimed by parentheses), by saying that "([i]t would take a special study to clarify what is essentially the same in *physis* and *techne*)" (EM 13).[16]

※ ※ ※

Now precisely at this moment when I risk enlarging the question beyond reason, I want to make what I hope does not seem like an utterly arbitrary move and draw these reflections to a close by focusing upon a rather peculiar manner in which the question of *techne* and destiny, the question of historical uniqueness today, emerges out of Heidegger's attempt to reflect upon what he takes to be the quintessential being of Greek Dasein: *to deinon*.[17] In the course of a lecture course on Hölderlin—who mediates virtually every significant effort to recapture "the" Greeks during this period[18]—Heidegger says that "the poet Sophocles speaks of the relation of human beings to the *polis,* and that in the context of speaking of the *deinon;* that alone points the decisive manner out of which the *polis* as the site and middle of beings will be experienced" (GA 53, 107). And in his reading of the chorus from *Antigone,* Heidegger bestows a specificity upon that experience when he argues that "[t]he *deinotation* of the *deinon,* the strangest of the strange, lies in the countervalent relation *[gegenwendigen Bezug]* of *dike* and *techne* (EM 124). Then, soon after making this remark, we read the further comment that "[t]he extreme pressure *[Andrang]* of *techne* against *dike* is, for the poet, that event through which the human being becomes strange. In such exile from home, home first exposes itself as such" (EM 127; emphasis added). Cast out of that home, "*ate*, ruin and unholiness befall him" (EM 116). But cast out of home, one is also pushed to the point at which one is open to the new and the foreign.

I call these passages to your attention not simply to thicken the matrix of terms around which Heidegger is posing the question of *techne,* adding *dike* now to *physis,* only to remind you of the web that will get dredged up shortly: *poesis, praxis,* etc. I do not want to do that and risk slowly but surely displacing the real question which I believe Heidegger is putting to us. The question, that is, about the *question* that history is putting "to us," about the way in which that question *put by history* opens up and delimits the domain in which the possibility of something like a "we," the possibility of a *polis,* first can take shape. I want to suggest that this "extreme pressure" that belongs to that "countervalent relation" is how Heidegger attempts to think the question of history put to the possibility that is "us." Today that pressure shows itself in the relation "between" (though here that notion is suspect) the "overwhelming" *(dike)* and the "powerful" *(techne)* (EM 123), a "between" that outlines the site of an essential struggle *(polemos)* out of which the present emerges. Today, at the moment of history's depletion, that struggle—which has always been the struggle of historical Dasein living in and as "the breach" (EM passim)—takes the shape of a "crisis." It is a "crisis" quite in the literal sense of the word itself: "our's" is a time of rupture and of judgment, in fact *it is around rupture and judgment that any sense of what is "our's" remains to be thought today*. It is, as Kant's examination of the situation of judgment reveals, a time in which we face unbridgeable limits, an unruly time demanding "creative transformation."

Heidegger did grant a peculiar, even ironic privilege to "his" time as the time of something "historically unique." But I would prefer to suggest that if there is something "unique" to "our" times, then it is the emergence of the enigma of "uniqueness" itself. In our times, in the time in which we witness the failure of *techne* in the face of necessity, the failure to manufacture our future, we witness as well the crisis of uniqueness itself. The crisis of history as the rising of singular events that, in their singularity, will be claimed by death, and that turn to language in their preservation, a preservation in which they provide the horizon for communities to come.

※ ※ ※

At the end of history, the point of limits reached, we find a curious *fold* that pins us to the period marking history's upsurge. That fold bends *us* back to the still hidden distress of that beginning which, as always withdrawn, has still not yet happened. This return to "the Greeks" and repetition of that which has never yet appeared is not, according to Heidegger, a "choice" today. We are rather pinned to such a return by the extremity that defines us today. Every present marks a historical extreme since every present bends all of history, with whatever force it has, back to itself. But "ours" is said to be doubly extreme by virtue of being a present as such, but also by being this specific present, namely, the present in which the forms of thinking handed down simultaneously reach their limits, the point of their untransmissability, revealing their untenability for the demands of such times.

At this moment of extreme distress—the era that Nietzsche began to think as the sign of nihilism—we are returned to the shadow of the still unthought alterity lurking in any present and every legacy. At this curious juncture of return—a period in which one senses anew the complexity voiced in Wordsworth's poetic line that calls the "child the father of the man" (a remark that is itself held strangely captive to the peculiarly Oedipal desire functioning in the effective history of another set of "Greeks")—at this period one witnesses a *reversal,* an *overturning,* of history itself, and one endures as well a blinding exile from the perceived truth of the governing imprint of our own age. I am thinking in particular of modern technicity which has won its ruling position by being the inheritor of a certain conception of *techne* that was itself articulated in response to the question of governance at all.

If we think the *exile* and *overturning* that define our "historical" juncture in their "Greek" sense, then we must say that "we" are at the moment of the *cata-stroph,* the moment in which *fate* becomes the question that beckons us and renders everything difficult. Yet, as Heidegger reminds us at the outset of *Introduction to Metaphysics,* such "rendering difficult" *(Erschwerung)* is the prelude to arrival at one's limits, at the extreme from which one first opens oneself to the encounter requisite for "the" "we," namely, the encounter of the non-domesticizability of others who "we" equally are.

Notes

1. M. Heidegger, *Einführung in die Metaphysik* (Tübingen: Niemeyer, 1966), p. 144.

2. See for instance FS, 353, as well as SZ 405 and GA 21, 257: "nothing is to be learned about temporality from Hegel." See also R. Bernasconi, *The Question of Language in Heidegger's History of Being* (New Jersey: Humanities Press, 1985), esp. ch. 1; D. Kolb, *The Critique of Pure Modernity* (Chicago: University of Chicago Press, 1986); esp. ch. 10; D. J. Schmidt, *The Ubiquity of the Finite* (Cambridge: MIT Press, 1988), esp. ch. 6.

3. So, for instance, Heidegger writes that the *Gestell* is to be thought as the "photographic negative" of *Ereignis* (VS, 104). The image here, itself drawn from a distinctive mode in which *techne* is linked with reproduction, is striking and bears further reflection in discussion of the contemporary era as under the reign of the *Gestell.*

4. If we take seriously Carl Schmitt's claim that all significant theories of political life have been secularizations of a submission to the theological imaginary, then Heidegger's efforts to dismantle such images, to show their essential uninhabitability (even, one might add, for theological inquiry), provide suggestive points of contact for an engagement between Heidegger and Schmitt. In this regard, see Heidegger's letter to Schmitt as cited by Johannes Gross in *Frankfurter Allgemeine Magazine,* Notizbuch Nr. 62.

5. For further discussion of "basic moods" which will not be pursued here, this means that we need to realize that "je freudiger die Freude, je reiner die in ihr schlummernde Trauer. Je tiefer die Trauer, je rufender die in ihr ruhende Freude" (US 235).

6. Of course such a notion is repeated with great insistence throughout Heidegger's work, often in slightly modified form, e.g., "die wahre Zeit ist Ankunft des Gewesenen" (US 57).

7. I do not believe it is necessary to defend the view that history, for Heidegger, claims us and circumscribes the horizon for our self-understanding. One could muster ample evidence for such a view simply by rallying the numerous passages that speak such as the one in *EM* (110) that reads: "Only as questioning and historical does man arrive at himself.... The Selfhood of the human being means this: man has to transform that being that discloses himself to himself into history and to bring himself to stand in that history."

8. It should go without saying that Heidegger understands the obligations of that decision differently than they are traditionally conceived—at least in part. Plato provided the first determination of the commitments of such a decision by outlining a sense of one's belonging to *techne* and one's abstinence from *praxis*. While Heidegger hestitates about the later point, he is unambiguous about regarding the obligation of the philosopher as having to push history into its extreme, not as the custodian of a provided *techne*.

9. That philosophy should be decisive for its time seems clear to Heidegger—"Philosophy always remains a knowledge that is not only able to be adjusted to its times, but rather one must say that the inverse is true: it places time under its measure" (EM 6)—the question, however, is what philosophy can be any longer. In this regard it is especially telling that those lectures contain an effort to address National Socialism, in 1942, via a dismissive criticism of national-socialistic texts on Greece. See esp. GA 53, 99f and 106–107.

10. One hears here a curious yet clear echo of both Fichte and of Jünger: the first spinning the sentence around philosophy, the second around pain. See J. G. Fichte, *Wissenschaftslehre* (Berline: de Gruyter, 1971), Bd. I, p. 434: "was für eine Philosophie man wähle, hängt sonach davon ab, was man für ein Mensch ist...", and E. Jünger, "Über den Schmerz" in *Sämtliche Werke,* Bd. VII/1 (Stuttgart: Klett-Cotta, 1980), p. 145: "Nenne mir Dein Verhältnis zum Schmerz, und ich will Dir sagen, wer Du bist!"

On the significance of translation for Heidegger, see also EM, 10–11 and SG, 162, where Heidegger suggests that the translation of Greek philosophical speech into Latin is among the most decisive events in the formation of 'the' Western tradition and culture.

11. Along with the passages already cited from GA 39, see, for instance, EM 110. Of course, it must ultimately be asked how the specific determinate of "the national" as "the German" is Heidegger's sole intent. See, for instance, GA 55, 123, where Heidegger says that "The planet is in flames. The essence of humankind is out of joint. World-historical reflection can only come from the Germans, on the condition that they find and preserve 'the German'."

12. By saying this I am not suggesting that Heidegger is "acceptable from the neck up," nor do I intend to suggest that we can divorce the person and the texts so surgically. I believe rather that there are real questions to be asked about the responsibility of writers and teachers to

the living. But I also believe, and this is the point which I am pursuing here, that the body of writing that goes under the name of "Heidegger" does offer resources for posing the question of our age that are—even if Heidegger himself had not quite anticipated them—mobilizable for progressive political thinking.

13. In light of what I have argued is the centrality of the question of *techne* as Heidegger reads the questionableness of Greek thought today, this comment, made in 1942, is fully commensurate with the disputed and still unthought comment found in the published version of *Introduction to Metaphysics* (first published in 1953, but delivered in 1935); the comment that speaks of "the inner truth and greatness of this movement (namely the encounter of technic determined on a planetary scale and contemporary humankind)..." (EM 152).

14. See "Von der Erlösung" in *Also Sprach Zarathustra, Werke,* ed. K. Schlecta, Bd. II, p. 669: "Ach, unwälzbar ist der Stein 'Es war'."

15. W. Benjamin, "Über den Bergriff der Geschichte," in *Gesammelte Schriften* (Frankfurt: Suhrkamp, 1980) Bd. I/2, pp. 697–698. Emphasis added.

16. On this question, see my "Economics of Production: Heidegger and Aristotle on *physis* and *techne*," in *Crises in Continental Philosophy,* ed. Dallery and Scott (Albany: SUNY Press, 1990).

17. One should not ignore the way in which the loud resonances with Heidegger's own key word in *Being and Time*, namely, *"Unheimlichkeit,"* provides an avenue whereby that text can be drawn forward into questions concerning the essence of the *polis* precisely along the axis of what seems to be its greatest resistance to such questioning.

18. Although to a somewhat larger extent, Hegel and Nietzsche also employ the Greeks in this way. Perhaps the most important element distinguishing Hölderlin from Hegel and Nietzsche within the framework of Heidegger's own thinking (apart from the loving fidelity of his curiously appropriating reading of Hölderlin that is the mark of a truly creative misreading) is that it is largely through Hölderlin that Heidegger arrives at a notion of the "the Germans."

III. The Work of Art

Chapter 5

The Greatness of the Work of Art

Robert Bernasconi

In the mid-1930s Heidegger indulged in a certain rhetoric of greatness. The most notorious instance of this rhetoric is the sentence from *An Introduction to Metaphysics* where Heidegger distinguishes "what is today being put about as the philosophy of National Socialism" from "the inner truth and greatness of this movement" (EM 152; IM 199).[1] More revealing—and more disturbing still—are the comments in the Rectoral Address of 1933, where Heidegger declares that there is a "will to greatness" and that the decision between it and the decline which occurs whenever things are just allowed to happen determines the fate of "the march that our people has begun into its future history" (SU 14). Other instances of the rhetoric of greatness could be multiplied,[2] but I will focus on a somewhat more discreet use of it in "The Origin of the Work of Art." The phrase in question is so familiar to everyone that it is readily overlooked. Only as one reads and rereads the text do the puzzles and enigmas to which "The Origin of the Work of Art" gives rise come to settle on the phrase "great art."

At the beginning of the second of the three lectures that constitute the essay, Heidegger observes that, compared with the work, the artist remains inconsequential in great art. Only in passing does he indicate that great art alone is what is under consideration here: "Gerade in der grossen Kunst, und von ihr allein ist hier die Rede, bleibt der Künstler gegenüber dem Werk etwas Gleichgültiges, . . . " (HW29: PLT 40). The extent and significance of this restriction is far from clear. How far does this "here" extend? Does the restriction refer to the essay as a whole? Or is it confined to the immediate context of the phrase? From where does Heidegger borrow the concept of "great art" and to what extent does he underwrite it? On the surface, the concept of "great art" belongs to aesthetics, and yet "The Origin of the Work of Art" is allegedly engaged in overcoming the aesthetic tradition. The question of whether Heidegger succeeds in twisting the concept of art free of its metaphysical heritage will prove to be all the more acute when raised with reference to the concept of great art.

Throughout Heidegger's writings, the self-evidence which accompanies inherited concepts, simply by virtue of their familiarity, is put in question. It was in those terms that Heidegger introduced the task of the destruction of the history of ontology in *Being and Time* (SZ 21; BT 43). That is why one must be cautious when Heidegger appeals to our familiarity with artworks in an attempt to resolve the problem which threatens to stop the inquiry from ever getting started. At the outset of "The Origin of the Work of Art," Heidegger observes that the question of the origin of the work of art cannot be answered with reference to the artist, because the artist is an artist only by virtue of the work. And yet the work needs the artist. Each needs the other. Furthermore, one cannot turn directly to art, as this in turn exists only in works. Heidegger suggests that we must start from actual works, because that is where art prevails, but he is well aware of the difficulty: "How are we to be certain that we are indeed basing such an examination on artworks, if we do not know beforehand what art is?" (HW 8; PLT 18). Heidegger breaks the circle, or rather he is able to embrace it, because "works of art are familiar to everyone," *(Kunstwerke sind jedermann bekannt)* (HW8; PLT 18). That is why, in order to discover what art is, he begins by posing the question of the work.

The question of the work sets the first part of the essay on a circuitous route. In outline, the question of the work becomes a question of the thingly aspect of the work. Hence, Heidegger attempts to distinguish the prevalent concepts of the thing. Because the thing is often confused with equipment, Heidegger is led to investigate what equipment is. It is only at that point, with Heidegger pursuing a trajectory which threatens to be always postponing the question of art, that, through what is presented somewhat disingenuously as sheer good fortune, something is discovered about the work: "unwittingly, in passing so to speak" *(unversehen, gleichsam beiher)* (HW24; PLT 35). This is because, contrary to the design of the inquiry, which was to proceed via the thingly aspect of the thing to the thingly aspect of the work, the apparent diversion into equipmentality proved to be a shortcut insofar as it was a work that instructed us about equipmentality. Everyone is familiar with equipment, such as a pair of shoes *(Jedermann kennt sie. . . . Jedermann weiss, was zum Schuh gehört)* (HW22; PLT 32–33). It was simply out of convenience that recourse was made to a painting of a pair of shoes. The reader is told that a pictorial representation would help with the description. Only subsequently does it emerge that the painting proved to be more than simply a convenience. The painting allows us to notice the shoe's reliability *(Verlässlichkeit)*, something which the wearer of the shoes, the peasant woman in Heidegger's example, knows without being specifically aware of it. Certainly there was no mention of reliability in *Being and Time*. There the Being of equipment was understood to be usefulness, on the basis of an analysis which relied on the obtrusiveness which arises when, for example, the shoes are worn out (HW24–25; PLT 34–35, Cf. SZ 73; BT 103). The shoe's reliability or dependability would never have been discovered without the help of the painting (HW24; PLT 35). Such is the curious itinerary of the first of the three lectures, rendered all the more circuitous when in the third lecture it is discovered that the thingly aspect of the work was rather its earthy character, so that the premise on which the inquiry set out was false (HW 57; PLT 69). One suspects that Heidegger's itinerary in the first part of "The Origin of the Work of Art" is governed in large measure by a need to redress the discussion of readiness to hand in *Being and Time,* in preparation for the revision of the concept of world, now that it is to be juxtaposed with that of the earth.

The elaborate trajectory I have just rehearsed was not part of the original outline of the essay. The discussion of Van Gogh's painting and of the different concepts of the thing in the first part of "The Origin of the Work of Art" were added to the text only when the original lecture was expanded into three lectures during 1936. The three lectures were delivered in Frankfurt in November and December 1936, and they form the basis of the edition published in 1950 in *Holzwege* with the addition of an epilogue.[3] Two earlier versions of the lecture have now been made available and this makes it possible to reread the familiar version with fresh eyes. In 1987 an unauthorized edition of the original lecture was published in France (OA). This is the version Heidegger delivered in Freiburg on 13 November 1935, a full year before the Frankfurt version. Heidegger repeated it in Zurich in January 1936. The publication of this text as "the first version" seems to have provoked the editors of the Heidegger Gesamtausgabe into releasing an undated, but clearly earlier, version under the title "Vom Ursprung des Kunstwerks. Erste Ausarbeitung" (HS).[4]

A comparison of the three versions—which I will refer to as the first draft, the Freiburg lecture and the Frankfurt lectures respectively—helps to reveal the dynamic of Heidegger's questioning and allows certain neglected features of the text to be highlighted. Furthermore, the differences between the three versions show Heidegger negotiating—or perhaps rather evading—the political realities of his time. However, even if I succeed in showing that there is an unsavory political dimension to the essay, this does not mean that the essay can simply be dismissed. It is not difficult to show that a language is contaminated, especially when that serves to restrict a text to a monotonous or monological reading, one which deprives the text of any truth it might convey. However, before judging Heidegger's political stance on the basis of such an analysis, one would need to compare Heidegger's language not just with the Nazi discourses on art of the same period, but also with other discourses on art.

To take just one example, it is not enough to show that Heidegger shares with the Nazis an enthusiasm for the word *Volk*, not least because this was already a common term in German discussions of art prior to the twentieth century. It is instructive in this context to recall Gadamer's observations in an essay written in 1966 on "The Universality of the Hermeneutical Problem." At one point in the essay, Gadamer focuses on the experience of the alienation of aesthetic consciousness which arises when one judges works of art on the basis of their aesthetic quality. He observes that the problem had already been recognized in a particularly distorted form when National Socialist politics of art, "as a means to its own ends, tried to criticize formalism be arguing that art is bound to a people."[5] Gadamer did not mention Heidegger by name, nor is there any indication there or elsewhere that he would subsume Heidegger's essay under this label, but what he went on to say would apply perfectly well to "The Origin of the Work of Art." "Despite its misuse by the National Socialists, we cannot deny that the idea of art being bound to a people involves a real insight. A genuine artistic creation stands within a particular community, and such a community is always distinguishable from the cultured society that is informed and terrorized by art criticism." The notion of the *Volk* has tended to play only a minor role in the interpretation of "The Origin of the Work of Art." Gadamer fails to mention it in his introduction to the edition of Heidegger's essay.[6] It is possible that the word has been ignored, wittingly or not, out of a certain sensitivity, an attempt to safeguard Heidegger's text from being reduced to an address to the German people, which in certain respects is exactly what it was—even when delivered to the student body at Zurich University. Far from it being the case that Heidegger retreated into a discussion of art in consequence of his political disillusionment, as used to be said on occasion, the texts on art and poetry have a strong political component.[7] Indeed, to neglect the political dimension of Heidegger's text is to risk restricting "The Origin of the Work of Art" to the realm of aesthetic alienation, instead of recognizing it as a response to aesthetic alienation.

The recently published *Beiträge zur Philosophie* confirms that Heidegger's essay belongs to the overcoming of aesthetics. In a section entitled " 'Metaphysics' and the Origin of the Work of Art" Heidegger writes that "The question [of the origin of the work of art] stands in innermost connection with the task of the overcoming of aesthetics and that means at the same time of a specific account of beings as objectively representable" (GA 65, 503). It is clear that Heidegger means "The Origin of the Work of Art" to put aesthetics radically into question, but this introduces a difficulty. Is it not possible that the concept of art is irretrievably marked by aesthetics? That Heidegger is engaged in a radical questioning of the concept of art is confirmed by *An Introduction to Metaphysics*. In the context of his statement that for us moderns the beautiful is what reposes and relaxes, such that art is a matter for pastry cooks, he says, "We must procure for the work 'art' and that which it names a new content on the basis of an original and recaptured basic position to Being" (EM 101; IM 132): "Wir müssen dem Wort 'Kunst' und dem, was es nennen will, aus einer urspruglich wiedergewonnen Grundstellung zum Sein einen neuem Gehalt verschaffen." The question is how far "The Origin of the Work of Art" accomplishes this task. When Heidegger answers the question of the origin of the work of art by designating art to be an origin, has he given the concept of art a new content? Does reliance on the familiarity of art, and specifically of great art, not imply a certain reliance on aesthetics?

The relation between great art and aesthetics is specifically explored by Heidegger in his account of the "Six Basic Developments of the History of Aesthetics" in the first of the lecture courses on Nietzsche. Heidegger offers this history in preparation for a reading of Nietzsche, but it is an indispensable accompaniment to "The Origin of the Work of Art," especially as it belongs to the same period as the Frankfurt version of the lectures. The text explores the relation between the history of the essence of aesthetics and the history of the essence of art (NI 94; Ni 79). The correlation Heidegger establishes across the six stages is an extraordinary one. Prior to metaphysics, there is great art, but there is as yet no aesthetics. Only when great art comes to an end, at the time of Plato and Aristotle, does aesthetics begin. The third stage, which corresponds to modernity, it characterized by the formation of a dominant aesthetics in terms of *aesthesis*. It is accompanied by the decline of great art. In Hegel, the fourth stage, aesthetics achieves its greatest possible height. Meanwhile, great art comes to an end. Nevertheless, the history has two further stages to run. The fifth stage is referred to Wagner and the collective artwork, which marks the dissolution of sheer feeling and which, in its effects, is the opposite of great art. Aesthetics becomes psychology in the manner of the natural sciences, and, at the same time, art history develops. Finally, aesthetics is thought to an end by Nietzsche in the physiology of art. Heidegger himself does not here directly underwrite the idea, which he attributes to Nietzsche, of art as the countermovement of nihilism, although it could be argued that he does so in "The Question concerning Technology."

It might seem that in this history, art takes an inordinate time to die and suffers many false deaths in the process, like the hero or heroine of a Victorian melodrama. In other respects, however, this story of decline is typically Heideggerian, even mirroring in its stages Heidegger's account of the history of the essence of truth (cf. HW 68; PLT 81). But in this case Heidegger seems to have been more determined than ever to have history convey a moral. Art and aesthetics are not compatible. Aesthetics prospers as art declines. Aesthetics is great when it tells what great art used to be.

Heidegger constructs this history from a framework borrowed largely from Hegel, while using the inclusion of Nietzsche to subvert the Hegelian starting-point.[8] Although Hegel is presented as the *Vollendung* or completion of aesthetics, Heidegger will later in the lecture course acknowledge that Nietzsche is its extreme form (NI 152; Ni 129). Great art is defined not on the basis of aesthetic judgments concerning the relative merits of different artistic styles but, in Hegel's phrase, as an "absolute need" (NI 100–101; Ni 84–85). Its task, in Heidegger's paraphrase of Hegel, is to be "the definite fashioner and preserver of the absolute" (NI 108; Ni 90). In Heidegger's own language, great art is "the definitive formulation and preservation of beings as a whole" (NI 106; Ni 89). But Hegel is clear that in these terms, the work performed by great art passed to religion and finally to philosophy. That is the meaning of the famous sentence, "Art is and remains for us, on the side of its highest vocation, something past."[9]

Heidegger's sketch of the history of art and aesthetics does nothing to ease the suspicion that surrounds the quest for a non-metaphysical concept of art. This is because Heidegger is hampered by the lack of a Greek concept of art. The Greek word, *techne*, is associated with the second stage of the history of art and aesthetics, not its first stage, which is where Heidegger locates great art. When, in "The Origin of the Work of Art," Heidegger appeals to *techne*, it is in the context of his observation that it is difficult to distinguish the essential features which separate the creation of works from the making of equipment, an observation which looks as if it might threaten his attempt to separate the two. To compound the difficulty he recalls the fact that the Greeks not only used the same word for both art and craft; they did not distinguish between craftsmen and artists. Indeed, both translations of *techne*, "art" and "craft," are misleading: *techne* is a form of knowing. Heidegger's redetermination of *techne* as *Wissen*, a "knowing which supports and conducts every irruption into the midst of beings" (NI 97; Ni 81), is something on which he insists in a number of different contexts. But Heidegger fails to address the question of why the Greeks, who belonged to the time of great art and who allegedly "understood something about works of art" (HW 47; PLT 59), did not leave in their language any mark of the distinction between the artwork and equipment.

Nevertheless, Heidegger does give an account of how within metaphysics the same conceptuality, the conceptuality of production—the notion of *eidos* in Plato, the notions of form and matter in Aristotle—are applied indiscriminately to works of art and to equipment. "All reflection on art and the artwork, all art theory and aesthetics since the Greeks stands until now under a remarkable fatality. With the Greeks (Plato and Aristotle) reflection on art employed the characterization of the artwork as a thing which was made, that is, a work of equipment *(Zeugwerk)*. Thereby the artwork is at first, and that means here in its actual Being, formed matter" (OA 52). Elsewhere Heidegger explains that the distinction between matter and form arose in the realm of manufacture and was subsequently transferred to that of art (NI 98; Ni 82). That metaphysics blocks our access to the work as work is an idea easily accommodated within a Heideggerian framework. What is hard to reconcile with it is the apparent lack of any recognition among the Greeks of the kind of distinction between work and equipment Heidegger seeks. In contrast to the broad conception of *techne* employed by the Greeks, he wants a highly restricted conception of great art. This does nothing to ease the suspicion that Heidegger's conception of art is trading off the very aesthetics which it is supposed to question. It seems that, at various junctures, Heidegger's discussion relies precisely on the kind of self-evidence which a thoroughgoing destruction is supposed to put in question (cf. HW 12; PLT 22).

How else is one to understand the absence from "The Origin of the Work of Art" of any sentence which would say for art what Heidegger said for religion in his lectures on Heraclitus in the summer of 1943, "There is no Greek religion at all" (GA 55, 13)? This is of particular importance given Heidegger's tendency to equate what is Greek with what is fundamental and to relegate what the Greeks lacked to the realm of the derivative and deficient. For Heidegger, religion, both as word and thing, is Roman. Why does Heidegger not say "There is no Greek art at all"? This would not commit him to saying that there is no Greek tragedy, no Greek music, no Greek dance, and so on. It would simply be an acknowledgement that the Greeks did not share the fairly recent sense that these activities have something in common which can be designated art. In fact, he seems to assume the collectivity of the fine arts, as when he refers to the way the Greeks accorded a primacy to poetry among the arts (NI 192–93; Ni 164–65). The evidence is rather that they lacked that conception of the arts which would lead one to juxtapose poetry and, for example, architecture or music. In other words, Heidegger appears to take the modern system of *les belles artes* for granted and incorporates it into his conception of art.[10]

Although Heidegger can be faulted for the way he approaches the concept of art, he is more circumspect in his approach to the artwork itself. Because metaphysics serves to obstruct access to the work as work, the question of the accessibility of the work is central to Heidegger's attempt to overcome aesthetics. It is the problem with which Heidegger begins the draft version of "The Origin of the Work of Art," just as it introduces "The Work and Truth," which is the second of the three lectures constituting the Frankfurt version. Heidegger repeats in this context the observation that the usual or inherited concepts of the thing have blocked our access to the work-being of the work. He suggests that to gain access to the work it is necessary to remove it from all relations to everything else. This presumably means that the work should not be referred to anything other than itself. For example, the work is not to be referred to the artist. This proposal is made to sound like the most natural way to proceed. Perhaps it would have been, had it been made prior to the publication of *Being and Time,* where the analysis in sections 15 to 18 showed that only when things are approached in their interconnection can one discover the relational structure which exhibits the readiness to hand of equipment. This suggests that Heidegger is being disingenuous when he of all people poses the question of the self-subsistence *(Insichselbststehen)* of the work in precisely these terms. Nevertheless, it proves to be a highly convenient way of focusing on the context in which art appears, and, importantly, given Heidegger's remarkable neglect of this aspect elsewhere in the essay, quite explicitly with reference to equipment (HW 21; PLT 32), it introduces a historico-cultural perspective. Artworks have been torn out of their own space to be exhibited in museums. Indeed, it often seems that the museum, as the place where art is exhibited, determines for the public what is and what is not art. A short essay on Raphael's *Sixtina,* written in 1955, develops the point at greater length: "Wherever this picture may yet be 'exhibited' in future, it has lost its place *(Ort).* That it might unfold its own essence incipiently, that is to say, that it might itself determine its place, remains denied to it. Transformed in its essence as artwork, the picture wanders into the alien. Presentation in a museum levels everything into the indifference of 'exhibition.' In an exhibition there are only sites, but no places" (GA 13, 120). The exhibition, the museum, corresponds in respect of location to the time of aesthetics.

Even if a work remains in its original location, as usually happens with architectural works, once the world of the work has perished, nothing can be done to restore it. As a result of the withdrawal and decay of its world, the works are no longer works. They are past (HW 30; PLT 41. Also OA 22). Although Heidegger does not say *vergangenes* but *Gewesenen,* the reference to Hegel's claim about the past character of art is clear. The self-subsistence of the work has fled. It is not simply that the art industry combines with the ordinary inherited concept of the thing to obstruct our access to the work as work, which might suggest that the work-being of the work remained concealed but intact. No amount of textual emendation, no extensive critical apparatus, can restore Sophocles's text to its own world and so let it be a work once more.

The work does not belong to the museum world, the world documented by historians, or the world of the art industry. It belongs to the world it opens up by itself. Heidegger illustrates the working of art with the following example: "The temple, in its standing there, first gives to things their look and to men their outlook on themselves." He immediately adds, "This view remains open as long as the work is a work, as long as the god has not fled from it." With the flight of the god from the temple, the self-subsistence of the work has fled with it (HW 30; PLT 41). If Heidegger had indeed visited "the remains of a Greek Temple," for example that at Paestum, he would have found not a place but a site, or in the words of *Being and Time* simply "a bit of the past . . . still in the present" (SZ 378; BT 430).

This raises the question of Heidegger's own access to the work. How did he arrive at his description of the temple? Can he account for his text at this point? He does at one point suggest that a recollection *(Erinnerung)* of the work can bring back what is past even to the point whereby such a recollection might offer the work a place from which to shape history. Nevertheless, this is to be distinguished from the case "where the work is preserved in the truth that happens by the work itself" (HW 56; PLT 68). The draft version makes clear what is at issue in this distinction. Historical recollection may enable us to experience the temple at Paestum or the cathedral at Bamburg as an 'expression' of their respective ages. They testify to the previous splendor and power of a people, but that does not mean that they are still works in Heidegger's sense. "Our 'glorious German cathedrals' can be an 'inspiration' to us. And yet—world decline and world withdrawal have broken their workbeing" (HS 7). In other words, because of world withdrawal, the Germans of the 1930s should not look to German cathedrals to *do* the work of art. Being in flight, being away *(Wegsein)* remains at hand *(vorhanden)* in the work in such a way that world decline could be said to belong to the work (HS 10). There are no immortal works of art (HW 66; PLT 70). On this view great art is from its outset always dying.

The world of the temple, like the world of Raphael's *Sixtina,* has withdrawn. This shifts attention to Heidegger's other examples, most notably the poems of Hölderlin and Van Gogh's painting of the shoes. Heidegger at one point in "The Origin of the Work of Art" establishes a clear parallel between the temple and the Van Gogh painting. "Truth happens" in both. One cannot distinguish the two cases by suggesting that Van Gogh's painting works only within the limited sphere of disclosing the equipmentality of equipment, "what equipment . . . is in truth" (HW 25; PLT 36), whereas in the case of the temple "beings as a whole are brought into unconcealment" (HW 44; PLT 56). Heidegger in the second Frankfurt lecture is quite explicit that the truth of the Van Gogh painting cannot be so restricted. Truth happens in Van Gogh's painting in such a way that "that which is as a whole—world and earth in their counterplay—attains to unconcealedness" (HW 44; PLT 56): the earth to which the shoes as equipment belong and the world of the peasant woman which protects it (HW 23; PLT 34). It would seem, therefore, that if the temple was great art in its time, the Van Gogh painting must also qualify as great art. Similarly, the role Heidegger gives to Hölderlin, particularly in the first two versions of "The Origin of the Work of Art" and in the 1934–35 lecture course, would seem to warrant a similar status for his poetry (GA 39). But how could this be reconciled with the sketch of the history of art and aesthetics given in the Nietzsche lectures where Heidegger seems to accept Hegel's claim that "art is and remains for us, on the side of its highest vocation, something past"? And, above all, if Hölderlin's poems and Van Gogh's painting were so clearly great art, what sense could one make of the questioning in which "The Origin of the Work of Art" culminates, particularly its final version? One would have to suppose that these questions were simply rhetorical, even false.[11]

All three versions of the lecture pose the question of how far and why art still exists. Contrasting the different versions, it seems that Heidegger does not proceed toward an answer so much as he succeeds in placing his initial answer in question. When in the draft, Heidegger asks if truth as "the openness of the there" must happen in the way that it arises in the origin as art, he gives a relatively unambiguous response. Because "truth is essentially earthy," then "the work, that is art, is necessary for the happening of truth" (HS 21). It hardly needs to be emphasized that this focus on the unique status of art contrasts with the recognition in both the Freiburg and Frankfurt versions that there are other ways in which truth might happen, the founding of the political state, the questions and saying of the thinker, and so on (OA 44. HW 50; PLT 61).[12] This establishes a clear difference between the draft and the subsequent versions that is not simply a matter of omissions.

Even so, it is tempting to refer this difference to an omission. What intervenes between the draft and the lectures Heidegger delivered at Freiburg and at Frankfurt is, at least on the surface, Hegel. The Freiburg version culminates in a discussion of Hegel's statements about the past character of art, and while the *Holzwege* text relegates the explicit discussion of Hegel to an Epilogue, which presumably means that it was not included in the lectures as delivered, it can be shown that Hegel's discussion of art permeates the conclusion of the main body of the text. Nothing better marks the intervention of Hegel than the definition of great art to be found in the different versions. I have already noted how in *The Will to Power as Art* Heidegger explicitly adopts the Hegelian definition, which is then adopted in the Freiburg lecture as well as the Frankfurt lectures. This is not the case in the first version of "The Origin of the Work of Art," where great art is characterized very differently. According to the draft, art is made great not only by its power of unfolding, its being an origin, but also by its related power to destroy *(Zerstörung)*. Specifically great art destroys the *Publikum* (HS 8). This constitutes the political agenda of Heidegger's discussion of art, which in the *Holzwege* version is sufficiently discreet to have allowed most readers of this essay, including myself, to have downplayed it until recently. For Heidegger, art destroys the public to form a people. In Germany in the 1930s nothing could have been more politically charged.

The crucial discussion is found in the final paragraphs of each of the three different versions. Although they use the same terms and so look remarkably similar, they point in different directions. What they share is the distinction between, on the one hand, an art which is an origin *(Urpsrung)* and as such a *Vorsprung*, and, on the other hand, an art which remains a mere supplement *(Nachtrag)*, a routine cultural phenomenon. What has to be decided, according to Heidegger, is whether art is to remain something secondary, as happens when it is conceived in terms of expression and elucidated further in terms of such concepts as embellishment, entertainment, recreation and edification, or whether art is to be an instigator of our history *(ein stiftender Vorsprung in unsere Geschichte)* (HS 22). This distinction serves as a reinscription of the distinction between great art and subsidiary forms of art, although it remains to be seen how radical a reinscription it is.

All three versions also use the language of decision, but in the draft the connection is much closer to the kind of decision to which Heidegger called the German people in the Rectoral Address, just as the idea of art as an instigator of our history echoes what he calls in the same place "the march that our people has begun into its future history." When Heidegger asks whether or not we are in the neighborhood of the essence of art as origin, it seems clear, even if he does not spell it out, that "we" means the German people. And when he says that clarity about who we are and who we are not already constitutes the decisive leap into the neighborhood of the origin, one can at least provisionally understand this as a question about whether the Germans are to be a *Publikum* or a *Volk*. The stridency of the draft means that Heidegger left relatively undeveloped any doubts he might have had about whether the German people would take the path he was laying out for them. Instead, there was a polemical tone about the draft, found also in the Hölderin lectures from the same period, and, in both cases, it was directed against the expression theory of art that he associated with Erwin G. Kolbenheyer, Oswald Spengler, and the racist ideologue, Alfred Rosenberg, and which was widely prevalent at the time (GA 39, 26–27, HS 17–18). Although nothing is spelled out, the implication is that by combatting the philosophy of art as expression, Heidegger is preparing for the time when the Germans would be ready to choose their destiny. So long as art was restricted to being a form of expression, the public might be inspired, for example by a German cathedral, but a people would never come to be founded.

The brief discussion of Hölderlin in the draft exhibits the same degree of conviction that can be found in the 1934–35 lecture course on Hölderlin. Hölderlin institutes German Being *(Seyn)* by projecting it into the most distant future (GA 39, 220). Heidegger is quite explicit about the political significance of this conviction. To side with Hölderlin is "politics" in the highest and most authentic sense, to the point that one no longer has any need to talk about the "political" (GA 39, 214). That Hölderlin is not yet a force in the history of the German people simply means that he must become one. Similarly, in the draft of "The Origin of the Work of Art," Hölderlin's poetry is introduced as "the untrodden centre" of the world and earth of the German people, where their great decisions are held in reserve (HS 15). The poems may scarcely be attended to, but they are more actual in the language of the German people than all the theatre, cinema and verse in circulation. The draft ends with a brief quotation from Hölderlin's "Die Wanderung" which, although its meaning is not explicated, is said to provide the key to what precedes it:

Schwer verlässt,
Was nahe dem Ursprung wohnet, den Ort.

Hard it is,
For what dwells near the origin, to leave its place.

How Heidegger meant these lines to be understood is not easily decided. The context suggests that the focus falls on knowing whether or not we dwell near the origin and, if we do, the manner in which we stay in proximity to the work as the only place where truth happens (HS 21).

The Freiburg lecture puts in question what the draft had presupposed by asking whether there must always be art and a work for truth to happen (OA 44). Heidegger himself acknowledges this question to be a turning point in the essay. Whereas the draft insisted that there must be a work for there to be truth, the Freiburg version says rather that if there is to be a happening of truth of the kind that one finds in art, there must be a work (OA 42). In other words, as already noted, art as a setting into work is now presented as only one of the ways in which truth happens. The result is that when in the Freiburg lecture Heidegger returns to the themes found at the end of the draft, the focus of the investigation has undergone a decisive shift. The question has now become that of whether there is great art any longer and, indeed, whether there could still be great art. That is to say, it is no longer a question of whether art is an origin, but whether it can be an origin again, and not just the accompaniment or supplement it has become. In this context, Heidegger again emphasizes the transitory character of art. Great art is never timely. An art is great if it sets into a work *the* truth which is to become the standard for a period (OA 48). That is to say, an artwork is great for a specific time, but only for a time.

The question of whether art itself is destined to remain only a supplementary announcement is posed in terms of Hegel's pronouncements of the past character of art. Heidegger agrees with Hegel that we no longer have any absolute need to present a content in the form of art, but Heidegger during the course of the lecture disputed Hegel's conviction that art is presentation (OA 52). So Heidegger says that a final decision about Hegel's judgment is still awaited. This decision, however, is not to be confused with the judgments of a critic or an art historian who might inform us about the quality and originality of certain works.[13] It is a "spiritual decision" in which a people determines who they are. Or, rather, as Heidegger is addressing the Germans, the question is that of "who *we* are." As in the draft, the role of the thinker is not clearly elaborated, but Heidegger's growing clarity about the nature of the decision now makes it possible for him to specify that a people's knowledge of what the artwork could and must be in their historical existence contributes to that decision. Presumably the thinker contributes to the people's knowledge of what the work can do, through delivering lectures like "The Origin of the Work of Art."

The Frankfurt lectures can be read as taking a stage further the transformation in the questioning which occurred between the draft and the Freiburg lecture. At the end of the Frankfurt lectures, Heidegger is quite explicit that the question of the essence of art, the question of the origin of the work of art, is to be displaced by a more genuine questioning (HW 65; PLT 78). The rhetoric of these closing pages is striking. Heidegger's questions follow after a series of assertions lasting several pages. Never had Heidegger been more assertive in his discussions on art and never was he to be so questioning. The question of what art is, such that is could properly be called an origin (HW 58; PLT 71), has changed to become the question of whether art is or is not an origin in our historical existence, the question of whether and under what conditions it can and must be an origin (HW 65; PLT 78). That is to say, even though the references to Hegel were relegated to the Epilogue, the question of the past character of great art governs the inquiry.

The question of the past character of art or, one might say, the question of the coming poets, dominates the inquiry as it becomes more enigmatic for Heidegger. As Heidegger insists in the Epilogue, he does not claim to solve the riddle of art (HW 66; PLT 79). And as he says in the Addendum, written in 1956 and first included in the Reclam edition of 1960, "What art may be is one of the questions to which no answers are given in the essay" (UK 99; PLT 86). Given the political agenda of the draft, in keeping with the explicitly acknowledged politics of the Hölderlin lectures, it is no surprise to find that this change in tone reflects a change in the relation between the thinker and the people. In the draft version, the thinker is not named. What matters is clarity about "who we are and who we are not," because such clarity is "already the decisive leap into the neighborhood of the origin" (HS 22). The question "who are we?" as a question addressed to the people had been developed in the first Hölderlin course (GA 39, 48–59). Heidegger acknowledges the time of this question as the time of the poet, the thinker, and the founder of the state insofar as they found the historical existence of a people (GA 39, 51). But the draft version of "The Origin of the Work of Art" focuses on the relation of the poet to the decision of the people. When, in the Freiburg version, Heidegger emphasizes that this decision "can only be *prepared for by long work*," it is possible to recognize this preparation as the contribution of the thinker, even though the thinker is still not named in this context. What is made clear in this version is how meditation on art since Plato and Aristotle, particularly in its form as "art theory" has proved to be an obstacle to a proper posing of the question of who we are. But only in the Frankfurt lectures, where the question of who we are is not explicitly posed, does the "we" become problematic. It becomes problematic to the extent that Heidegger seems unable to control it.

Alongside the "we of the German people is the "we" of the thinker, the one who meditates on art: "We ask about the essence of art. Why do we ask in this way? We ask in this way in order to be able to ask more genuinely whether art is or is not an origin in our historical existence, whether and under what conditions it must be an origin" (HW 65; PLT 78). In the last of these sentences, a transition is made from the "we" of Heidegger, the "we" of the thinker, to the "we" of "our historical existence" as a people. This transition to the "we" of the people is confirmed three sentences later when Heidegger asks, "Are we in our existence historically at the origin? Do we know, which means do we give heed to, the essence of the origin? Or, in our relation to art, do we still merely make appeal to a cultivated acquaintance with the past?" The specific identity of the people is made explicit when Heidegger, returning to the quotation from Hölderlin with which the draft version had also ended, acknowledges that the poet's work "still confronts the Germans as a test to be stood."

The lines from Hölderlin themselves no longer convey the same sense that they had in the draft. The context is no longer that of the question of why truth has to happen as art and the emphasis is no longer on dwelling near the origin. By the time that one reads in the Frankfurt version

> Schwer verlässt
> was nahe dem Ursprung wohnt, den Ort.

the emphasis has shifted to the oppressiveness of this departure from art as the place of origin. The earlier stridency with which Heidegger had challenged the theory that German art is an "expression" of the people (HS 18) has been replaced by a certain *Schwermut,* or melancholy, which matches the isolation that the thinker now experiences in his meditation on art. Is it a mistake to hear in this change of mood Heidegger's growing awareness of his political isolation? Does not a space open up between the thinker and the people precisely as Heidegger recognizes that he was not to be given the role in determining the direction of the Nazi Party that he had projected for himself?

In all three versions importance had been attached to a knowing which was not theoretical but the site of the decision about art. Only in the third version was this knowing specifically associated with meditation on art and thus with the thinker. The thinker's role was specified again in 1943 when Heidegger wrote, "For now there must be thinkers in advance, so that the word of the poets may be taken up" (EHD 30). The thinker prepares a space for the work, a path for the creators, and quarters for the preservers (HW 65; PLT 78). The coming preservers are a historical people (HW 62; PLT 75), whose knowing lets the work be a work and maintains its self-subsistence (HW 55; PLT 68). Although Heidegger fails to acknowledge it fully in his text, the "we" becomes as enigmatic as the work of art. Heidegger for the most part writes of the Germans as this thrown people, but the Germans in this sense are no more than a public who fail to recognize their poet. The German people that Hölderlin poetry addresses are yet to be constituted. However marked the different versions of "The Origin of the Work of Art" might be with a certain political rhetoric, which betrays Heidegger's still shocking involvement with the Nazi Party, he himself experiences the untimeliness of this thinking, a non-synchronicity between his audience as he addresses them and as they heard him—as in the famous "Become who you are." Insofar as Heidegger forced the issue and assumed the existence of the audience only the artwork could open up, he in a sense became part of the art industry, perhaps even the Nazi machine. At other times he was more sensitive: " We do not want to make Hölderlin relevant to our time but, on the contrary, we want to bring ourselves and those who are coming under the measure of the poet" (GA 39, 4).

Perhaps the enigma of whether Van Gogh's painting of the shoes is great art or not shares in the uncertainty created by the political context. It would seem that the Van Gogh painting is supplementary art, rather than great art. That is to say, it is a work, but not an origin. It expresses a world rather than instituting one. In keeping with this one might note that, although there was a time when the people in Greece who lived in the shadow of the temple relied upon the temple, the peasant woman depends on her shoes, not the painting. However, simply to see the issue in these terms is to ignore the political component of Heidegger's discussion that the present reading of "The Origin of the Work of Art" has brought to the surface. The political meaning of the Van Gogh painting for Heidegger can be seen in *An Introduction to Metaphysics,* where it is clear that he is doing more than evoking a world already in place or threatening to disappear. Heidegger described the painting in this pastoral passage: "As to what is in the picture, you are immediately alone with it as though you yourself were making your way wearily homeward with your hoe on an evening in late fall after the last potato fires have died down" (EM 27; IM 35). One is tempted to ask further about this way of "reading" paintings whereby one projects oneself into the world it represents, but more urgent is the question of whether the picture is not being evoked by Heidegger—according to the notorious phrase Heidegger apparently added to the lecture course later—as part of the encounter between global technology and modern man (EM 152; IM 199). It seems that Heidegger would have liked the painting to have been not just an expression of a culture which had had its time. He wanted it to be a still untimely work of great art, one whose preservers were awaited. In that case, the question of whether the Van Gogh painting warranted the title great art in the all important sense of helping a people determine who they are, was still undecided in 1936, so far as Heidegger was concerned. It was undecidable by the thinker at the time because the answer would come only when and if the public made their decision to become a *Volk* in the requisite sense, a *Volk* living from the earth. It was, for Heidegger at that time, no doubt also a question about the future direction of National Socialism. Hence, the melancholic mood. By the same token, it was not so much for Heidegger himself but for the people to decide. It is a question of whether or not art would again become "an essential and necessary way in which truth happens in a decisive way for our historical Dasein" (OA 54, HW 67; PLT 80).

This third version is not the last version of the closing pages of "The Origin of the Work of Art," even if one takes into account the Epilogue and the Addendum. Once one recognizes the importance of the issue of the dominance of technology and "the spiritual decline of the earth" (EM 29; IM 37–38) operative in "The Origin of the Work of Art," it quickly becomes apparent that the last two pages of "The Questioning Concerning Technology," a text known in a version dating from 1953 (VA 42–44; QT 48–49),[14] represent what was at least Heidegger's fourth attempt to write a conclusion to "The Origin of the Work of Art." Heidegger's discussion moves through at least five stages, which recapitulate, supplement and revise the essay of almost twenty years before. The discussion starts with the ambiguity of the word *techne*. In "The Origin of the Work of Art," its breadth seemed to constitute an obstacle to Heidegger's attempt to mark the difference between the artwork and equipment. In "The Question Concerning Technology," this very problem seems to provide the basis for addressing the challenge of technology. Hence, Heidegger's second step is to recall that when the arts were at their highest level, they not only bore the modest name *techne*, but were understood in terms of *poiesis* as revealing. Heidegger's third step is to understand the revealing of *poiesis* as poetical. Specific reference to *poiesis* was absent from "The Origin of the Work of Art," but the privilege given to poetry within the arts can be found in all three versions of the essay.[15] In "The Question Concerning Technology," Heidegger relates the two by looking to the fine arts in their poetic revealing to awaken anew and found our vision of and trust in that which grants (VA 43; QT 35). Heidegger turns to art not because of its power to destroy, nor because of its radical difference from the technological order. It is the proximity between art and technology, between the work and equipment, which opens the possibility that art might offer an essential meditation and a decisive confrontation with technology. The lack among the Greeks of a concept of art clearly marked off from other forms of *poiesis* is now used to advantage, although it has to be said that the reference to "the fine arts" suggests that the concept of art has still not been submitted to an adequate historical destruction.

The question of the people, the question of who we are, is no longer the issue. In a fourth step, Heidegger passes directly to the question of whether there may or may not be some rescue from the entrenchment of technology. And the decisive thought guiding the question is again Hölderlin's.

> Wo aber Gefahr ist, wächst
> Das Rettende auch.
>
> Where the danger is, that which rescues
> burgeons too.

So far as the essay's response to technology is concerned, the impact of this quotation cannot be overemphasized, particularly when placed in the context of the history of metaphysics that Heidegger had developed earlier in the essay and elsewhere.[16] Strikingly, the context is that of the end of philosophy, thought not as Hegel thought the consummation of philosophy, but more as Hegel thought the past character of art. Heidegger looks not to philosophy as such, which has in a sense exhausted its possibilities, but to the dialogue of thinking with poetizing, as evidenced by the appeal to Hölderlin.

The future of art remains a question in "The Origin of the Work of Art," just as the future of technology is left open in "The Quotation Concerning Technology." But what of art in the later essay? In the closing pages of "The Question Concerning Technology," Heidegger continued the task of withdrawing the politically charged vocabulary that had marked the draft of "The Origin of the Work of Art" and which he had already begun to sanitize in the Freiburg and Frankfurt versions.[17] He omitted all reference to the *Volk,* to decision and to "great art" as such. Heidegger found a way of continuing his confrontation with technology away from the nightmare of National Socialist politics. But meanwhile the question that "The Origin of the Work of Art" left open, the question of whether there may yet be art (UK 99; PLT 86), appears no longer to be in question.[18] The fate of technology may not have been decided, but Hölderlin's authority as "the poet" is submitted neither to the people nor apparently to any other kind of future for decision. In other words, Heidegger came to terms with his disastrous political involvement only by allowing himself to turn his back not just on politics but "on the people," a phrase which was admittedly almost always dangerous on his lips, as it usually meant for him *the* people, the Germans. In consequence, the successive rewriting of "The Origin of the Work of Art" in 1935 and 1936—through even to 1953—leaves a question as to whether the mutual isolation of the poet and the thinker in the 1950s did not mark a return to a form of aestheticism. Perhaps Heidegger should have persisted with the question "who are we?"—even, perhaps especially, in the *absence* of an answer—whereas he appears to have simply displaced the question of the German people into that of the German lanugage. A discussion of art addressed to *the* people justifiably provoked suspicion. But to reject "The Origin of the Work of Art" for a philosophy of art that excludes reference to the communities that not only spawn art, but are established by art, would seem, as Gadamer already warned, to amount to a restoration rather than an overcoming of aesthetics.

Notes

1. If we follow, not the published text of 1953, but Pöggeler's reconstruction, it would seem that the manuscript referred to "the inner truth and greatness of N.S." and that in the lecture he actually said "the inner truth and greatness of the movement." There is also reason to believe that the explanatory phrase, "namely, the encounter between global technology and modern man," was not in the manuscript, as he claimed later, although it is clear that the confrontation with technology was a, perhaps *the,* crucial political question at this time (EM 28–29; IM 37–36). On the difference between Heidegger's account of these events and the historian's reconstruction of them, see, for example, Otto Pöggeler, "Nachwort zur

zweiten Auflage," *Der Denkweg Martin Heideggers* (Pfullingen: Neske, 1983), pp. 340–42; trans. D. Magurshak and S. Barner, *Martin Heidegger's Path of Thinking* (Atlantic Highlands: Humanities Press, 1987), pp. 275–277. Also Pöggeler, "Heideggers politisches Selbstverständnis," *Heidegger und die praktische Philosophie,* ed. Annemarie Gethmann-Siefert and Otto Pöggeler (Frankfurt: Suhrkamp, 1988), p. 59 n11.

2. As an example of Heidegger's fascination for this theme, see his inscription in the copy of Burckhardt's *Grösse, Glück and Ungluück in der Weltgeschichte* that he gave to the art-historian Kurt Bauch at Christmas in 1937. Karin Schoeller-von Haslingen, "Was ist Grösse?'" *Heidegger Studies,* vol. 3/4, 1987/88, pp. 15–23. In particular Burckhardt's comments on great poets in the essay "Das Individuum und das Allgeneine (Die historische Grösse)" should be compared with certain aspects of Heidegger's discussion.

3. Heidegger's claim that parts of the epilogue were written at the same time as the lecture has been confirmed by the publication of earlier versions of the lecture. The 1950 text was revised—although most of the modifications were relatively minor—when it was published separately in 1960 in the Reclam series. At the same time, Heidegger included an Addendum which was written in 1956. The addendum tries in a certain way to rewrite the essay from the standpoint that Heidegger had attained in the 1950s. It was this text which formed the basis for the Hofstadter translation in *Poetry, Language, Thought.* The Reclam text, and not the 1950 version, served as the basis for the edition of Heidegger's *Holzwege* which appeared as volume 5 of Heidegger's *Gesamtausgabe.* Some notes were added drawn from Heidegger's copies of the third edition of *Holzwege* (1957) and the Reclam edition. The most recent version of *Holzwege* published independently of the *Gesamtausgabe* follows this text.

4. Hermann Heidegger, the editor of "Vom Ursprung des Kinstwerks. Erste Ausarbeitung" (Hereafter, HS), did not date the manuscript, but Friedrich-Willhelm von Herrmann in a note to this edition of "Zur Uberwindung der Aesthetik. Zu 'Ursprung des Kunstwerks'" has suggested that the text comes from the years 1931 and 1932. See *Heidegger Studies,* vol. 6, 1990, p. 5n. This date, if it can be sustained, is somewhat surprising on internal grounds, even though Heidegger scholars should be used by now to finding what had seemed to be late developments firmly located in earlier texts. It should be noted by dating the draft prior to the Rectoral Address of 27 May 1933, von Herrmann has refuted the interpretation associated with Pöggeler that Heidegger turned to art in response to his failure in the political arena on chronological ground and without having to argue, as I would, that the writings on art are themselves in a fundamental sense political.

5. Hans-Georg Gadamer, *Kleine Schriften* I (Tübingen: J. C. B. Mohr, 1967), pp. 102–03; trans. David E. Linge, *Philosophical Hermeneutics* (Berkeley: University of California Press, 1976), p. 5.

6. H.-G. Gadamer, "Zur Einführung," in M. Heidegger, *Der Ursprung des Kunstwerkes* (Stuttgart: Reclam, 1967), pp. 102–125. (Hereafter UK)

7. Philippe Lacoue-Labarthe recently reminded his readers that in 1933 Heidegger never said that "the beginnings of 'a *Verwindung*' of nihilism are to be found in poetic thinking." *La fiction du politique* (Paris: Christian Bourgois, 1987), p. 86; trans. Chris Turner, *Heidegger, Art and Politics* (Oxford: Basil Blackwell, 1990), p. 55. Whereas the turn to Hölderlin is dramatic in 1934 with the lecture course on the poems *Germanien* and *Der Rhein,* Heidegger's ambiguity toward National Socialism continues for some time through the turn to art and poetry. The details of that ambiguity are chartered by recent biographical studies of Heidegger.

8. For another discussion of the relation of Heidegger's "The Origin of the Work of Art" to Hegel based on Heidegger's brief sketch of the history of aesthetics and of art, see J. Taminiaux, "Le dépassement Heideggérien de l'esthétique et l'héritage de Hegel," *Recoupments* (Brussels: Ousia, 1982), pp. 175–208. Andreas Grossman insists that Heidegger's approach is opposed to that of Hegel, but he does not take into account Heidegger's sketch of the history of aesthetics that helps establish the complexity of the relation as detailed in the present chapter. See "Hegel, Heidegger, and the Question of Art Today," *Research in Phenomenology* 20, 1990, pp. 112–135.

9. G. W. F. Hegel, *Vorlesungen über die Ästhetik* I, Werke in zwanzig Bänden 13 (Frankfurt: Suhrkamp, 1970), p. 25; trans. T. M. Knox, *Aesthetics,* vol. 1 (Oxford: Oxford University Press, 1975), p. 11.

10. See W. Tatarkiewicz, "Classification of Arts in Antiquity," *Journal of the History of Ideas* 24, 1963, pp. 231–240 and P. O. Kristeller, "The Modern System of the Arts" in *Renaissance Thought and the Arts* (Princeton, N. J.: Princeton University Press, 1980), pp. 163–227.

11. The question of the status of the example of the Van Gogh painting has also been raised, though with a somewhat different resolution, by Jay Bernstein. See "Aesthetic Alienation: Heidegger, Adorno and Truth at the End of Art," *Life After Postmodernism,* ed. John Fekete (New York: St. Martin's Press, 1987), pp. 86–119.

12. The triumvirate of the poet, the thinker and the founder of the state can already be found in the Hölderlin lectures at the end of 1934, thereby raising the question as to why art was singled out in the draft. As a provisional response it can be noted that the conflict may be more apparent than real. In the relevant passage in the Hölderlin lectures, Heidegger was addressing not truth specifically, but the people, and already in this respect the poet was given a certain priority (GA 39, 51).

13. At one point in the *Beiträge zur Philosophie,* written in the years immediately following "The Origin of the Work of Art," Heidegger introduces the notion of artlessness *(Kunstlosigkeit)* to address precisely this issue (GA 65, 506). Artlessness has nothing to do with art as understood by the culture industry: "an *art-less* moment of history can be more historical and creative than times with an extensive art industry." It is only by traversing artlessness that art happens, which is seldom.

14. We have the lecture in the version delivered in Munich in November 1953. An earlier version was given as the second of a series of four

lectures delivered in Bremen in December 1949 under the title "Einblick in das was ist." The sense in which the essay on technology is a continuation of "The Origin of the Work of Art" is confirmed by a fragment in which, again drawing on Hegel, Heidegger situates his thought in the space between the "no longer of an essential relation to art" and the "not yet of an essential relation to technology." "Technik und Kunst—Ge-stell," *Kunst und Technik,* hrsg. Walter Biemel and Friedrich-Wilhelm von Herrmann (Frankfurt: Klostermann, 1989), pp. xiii–xiv.

15. In the margin of his copy of the Reclam edition of the essay, Heidegger did include a reference to *poiesis.* See *Holzwege,* Gesamtausgabe 5 (Frankfurt: Klostermann, 1977), p. 70n. Contrast Heidegger's attempt to rule out the reference from *Dichtung* to *poiesis* in 1934 (GA 39, 29).

16. I shall not discuss the role of the quotation in any more detail here. Meanwhile, see my discussion in *The Question of Language in Heidegger's History of Being* (Atlantic Highlands, New Jersey: Humanities Press, 1985), pp. 69–75.

17. Compare Habermas's description of Heidegger's tendency in the 1940s and 1950s to efface the traces of nationalism from his philosophy of the 1930s by a process of "abstraction via essentialization." Jürgen Habermas, "Heidegger—Werk und Weltanschauung," in Victor Farias, *Heidegger und der Nationalsozialismus* (Lagrane: Verdier, 1987), p. 28; trans. John McCumber, "Work and Weltanschauung: The Heidegger Controversy from a German Perspective," *Critical Inquiry,* 15, 1989, p. 449.

18. The question of whether, in the contemporary world dominated by industrial society, the work can still remain a work was posed in a 1967 lecture, but not with the same urgency as earlier. "Die Herkunft der Kunst und die Bestimmung des Denkins," *Distanz und Nähe,* ed. Petra Jaeger and Rudolf Lüthe (Würzburg: Königshausen and Neumann, 1983), p. 19.

Chapter 6

Heidegger's Freiburg Version of the Origin of the Work of Art

Françoise Dastur

In 1935, the year in which Heidegger delivered the lecture course, "Introduction to Metaphysics," he presented a lecture in Freiburg to the Society of Art Sciences (on November 13th to be exact) under the title, "Concerning the Origin of the Work of Art." He repeated the same lecture in January 1936 in Zürich where he was invited by the students of the University. He expanded this original lecture and developed it into three lectures which he presented in Frankfurt at the *Freien Deutschen Hochstift* on the 17th and 24th of November, and the 4th of December 1936. These three lectures appeared finally in *Holzwege*[1] in 1950 under the title, "The Origin of the Work of Art," with the addition of an Afterword, written in part later than 1936. In 1956, Heidegger wrote an Addendum in which he made important clarifications regarding the essay as a whole. The essay, "The Origin of the Work of Art," contains in its present form a brief introduction (about art as the origin of both the artist and the work of art), three major sections, entitled "Thing and Work," "The Work of Art," "Truth and Art," an afterword written between 1936 and 1950 and the addendum of 1956. The original lecture of 1935 was never published by Heidegger himself, but he gave it to some friends to read, among whom was Jean Beaufret, who, in turn, gave it to some of his pupils, so that one of them, Emmanuel Martineau, decided in 1987 to publish the German text with a French translation.[2]

The text of the Freiburg lecture represents not even one third of the final essay. It contains a short introduction (about the difference between "work" and "product," "origin" and "cause" and the circularity of the questioning about the origin of the work of art), and a major part which takes up this inevitable circle; the major part begins with the characterisation of what is a work in its ground or origin and back from it to the work itself. I do not intend to work out an extensive comparison between this version and the final version of "The Origin of the Work of Art." I only want to formulate some remarks as a first attempt on the way to a systematic reading of the Freiburg version.[3] Towards this more modest end, I want to put forward seven points of analysis.

The Concept of Work

The concept of work is the leading concept of the Freiburg version, in opposition to the Frankfurt version which goes to the "work" only via the question of the "thing." In the first section of the Frankfurt version, "Thing and Work," Heidegger starts from the analysis of equipment *(Zeug)* in order to differentiate thing and work, so that the way which leads from *Being and Time* to the question of the "work" is more clearly traced in 1936. In the Freiburg lecture, Heidegger asks for an immediate and seemingly arbitrary "spring" *(Sprung)* into the work-being of the work which will be roughly indicated in its essential features: *"Wir vollziehen jetzt den Sprung indem wir unvermittelt und dem Anschein nach willkurlich und in groben Hinweisen auf die Wesenszüge im Werksein des Werkes hinzeigen"* (FV 24).

What is the reason for putting the stress on the "work" in 1935? Quite simply, the analysis of everydayness in 1927 could not lead to the question of art. The word itself seems to be absent in *Being and Time* and the only reference to art is to be found in §42, where a latin fable is considered giving a "pre-ontological" testimony of the fact that the Dasein understands itself originally as concern *(Sorge)*. The only other explicit reference to art before 1935 (in the Winter Semester 1934–35, Heidegger held a course on Hölderlin: *Hölderlin Hymnen "Germanien" und "Der Rhein"*, GA 39) is found in a course from the Winter Semester 1925–26, where Heidegger occasionally refers to a picture of Franz Marc, "The Deer in the Forest" (*Logik, Die Frage nach der Wahrheit,* GA 21, 364) in dealing with the Kantian schematism. But here art is still considered in the dimension of "representation" *(Darstellung):* Heidegger writes that it is possible to consider artistic representation as a special case of schematization and consequently to say that in art the concept is represented *(dargestellt)* under the condition that we make a difference between a theoretical concept (the zoological concept of deer) and a hermeneutical concept (the deer as habitant of the forest, the in-the-forest-being of the deer). Art can then be considered the representation of a hermeneutical concept.

Art in 1935, however, can no longer be understood as representation. Heidegger writes explicitly in the Freiburg version: "But art never represents something; simply because it has nothing that it could represent, because the work creates at first what appears for the first time through it in the open" *(Allein das Kunstwerk stellt nie etwas dar; aus dem einfachen Grunde, weil es ja nichts hat, was es darstellen kann, weil das Werk dasjenige erst schafft, was erstmals durch es ins Offene tritt)* (FV 52). Therefore, it is no longer possible to say that art is an ontological representation, but an ontological effectuation. In the *Introduction to Metaphysics*, we find already the idea that *techne*, understood as knowledge *(Wissen)*, is the ability of setting-into-work the Being as a being which is always such and such *(Wissen ist das Ins-Werk-setzen-können des Seins als eines je so und so Seienden)*. The work of art is not a work because it is wrought or fabricated, but because it brings about Being in a being: *Das Werk der Kunst ist in erster Linie nicht Werk, sofrn es gewirkt, gemacht ist, sondern weil es das Sein in einem Seienden er-wirkt.*[4] For Heidegger, knowledge itself can be understood as an effectuation, a bringing about of Being, and consequently, I think that it is possible to consider this interpretation of the essence of the work along the lines of an understanding of schematism.[5] Art is *techne* in the Greek sense of knowledge—not in the modern sense of production—because it brings Being to stability and showing in the work of art as an essent, and the work of art itself is the being Being *(das seiende Sein)* which gives to everything else its limits and determination.[6] Art can no longer be understood as secondary, coming after nature, but on the contrary as initial, original *(anfänglich)*.

The Circular Structure of the Lecture

In the Introduction to the Freiburg version, Heidegger rejects two interpretations of the origin of the work of art. The first one consists in considering the artist as the origin of the work of art, whereas he is only its cause. The comparison of two words—

Ursprung and *Ursache*—says a lot. If the work of art is considered a product *(Erzeugnis)*, then the artist will be understood as its *causa efficiens*, as the "thing" which comes originally, before the product itself, as *Ur-sache*. Whereas the origin *(der Ur-sprung)* is not an original thing, but the ground *(Grund)* from which the work of art springs, what makes it possible and necessary. The second inadequate interpretation looks for the origin not in the work considered as a product but in the presence-at-hand *(die Vorhandenheit)* of the work. But today we only have access to works of art through the art business *(Kunstbetrieb)* which brings them to our disposal and makes them intelligible to us. Their exhibition in a museum or as a show for tourists transforms the quality of their presence: they are now present-at-hand *(vorhanden)* by the mere fact of becoming the objects of an artistic pleasure *(Kunstgenuss)* which is the subjective counterpart of the art business. The question of the origin of the work of art cannot be asked if we stay on the level of the "objectivity" of the work of art. But to be able to recognize that the work of art is neither a product nor an object implies that we have already an implicit knowledge of what *is* a work of art. The essence of the work of art is precisely what makes the work of art possible and necessary, i.e., its ground or origin, so that Heidegger can write: "What we look for, we must have it already and what we have we should at first look for it" (FV 24). And further in the course of the lecture, Heidegger comes back to the same idea: the pretention to avoid the circularity is a swindle (FV 37). The derivation of the essence of art from more fundamental concepts or the induction of the essence of art in comparing different works of art implies already the knowledge of this essence. We need to know what is a work of art to recognize different works of art and compare them. And we also need to have an idea of the essence of art if we want to derive it from more original concepts.

This situation is the typical hermeneutical situation and constitutes the level of the pre-comprehension of art. In *Sein und Zeit*, Heidegger shows in §32 that the explicitation of the comprehension of something implies a triple presupposition: pre-possesion *(Vorhabe)*, pre-vision *(Vorsicht)*, anticipation *(Vorgriff)*. Comprehension has to precede itself because it is necessary to project a horizon of sense into which something can be met as what it is. The structure of anticipation *(Vorstruktur)* and the structure of explicitation *(Alsstruktur)* cannot be separated, and this is the reason why trying to avoid the circle or considering it an imperfection constitutes a lack of understanding of what comprehension is. The problem is not to get out of the circle, but to enter into it "in the right manner." But what is the right manner to enter into it? To spring into it. This is the answer given by the Freiburg version, and the spring or leap consists precisely in the selection of a definite example of an art work, the example of a Greek temple, i.e., of a non-figurative work of art which consequently cannot be referred to as representation as it will be explicitly said in the Frankfurt version: "For this attempt [to make visible the happening of truth in the work] let us deliberately select a work that cannot be ranked as representational art. A building, a Greek temple portrays nothing *[bildet nichts ab]*" (HW 30, trans. 41). The Greek temple portrays nothing, is the image *(Abbild)* of nothing: it simply stands there in its pure selfsubsistence *(Insichstehen)*. By springing, we have directly sprung into the origin *(Ur-sprung* literally means primal or original spring); and the origin is the openness of the There *(die Offenheit des Da)* (FV 34), i.e., the happening or becoming of truth *(Geschehen— Werden der Wahrheit)* (FV 38).

What constitutes the origin or ground of the work of art is nothing else than the poetical institution *(Stiftung)* of an always singular There, the project of an always singular historical Dasein (FV 40–42). Art is an origin not only because it is the ground *(Grund)* of the possibility and necessity of the work of art, but principally because it is *one* origin of truth as the setting-into-work of truth *(das Ins-Werk-setzen der Wahrheit)* (FV 44). There are indeed other ways for the truth to happen: besides work, we can find political action (the foundation of a political state) and thinking and questioning; besides the artist, we find also the politician and the thinker.

With this determination of the essence of art as the becoming of truth, the lecture has reached its turning point *(Wendepunkt)*: we proceeded from the work towards its origin; now we have to go back from the origin to the work, but by taking another way. This way consists in a meditation on the initiality of the origin in connection with the essence of creation *(Schaffen)*. But creation should be understood as sustaining the openness of the ever singular There rather than as a fabrication or production. We now come back to the work and to the artist but seen as creation and creator and no longer as product and producer. The artist is then considered not as producer, but as instigator *(Anstifter)* of the struggle that takes place as work of art (FV 48). We have come back to the starting point of the lecture, but we see it in a quite other light: the work of art is not a special kind of product (an "allegorical" product), but a creation, and as such, it is the institution of history.

Art and Past

My third remark has to do with the characterization of the work of art as "has been" *(gewesen)* which is the case not only of the works of art exhibited in museums—Heidegger refers to the famous statues of Aegina in the Museum of Munich and to a sculpture from the 15th century (*"Das Bärbele,"* "the little Barbara," from Nikolaus Gerhart) of the Liebighaus in Frankfurt—but also of the works of art still standing in their original location, like the Paestum temple and the cathedral of Bamberg (all examples mentioned in the Freiburg version are Greek or Medieval art). Heidegger speaks here of the irreversibility of the withdrawal and the decay of the work *(Weltentzug und Weltzerfall)* to which they belonged (FV 22). As "having been," the works of art can be encountered only in the dimension of tradition and conservation and no more as what they were. In becoming objects of the art business, they have lost their "standing to themselves" *(Zu-sich-Stehens)*, their self-subsistence by which they were able to initiate a world. They are deprived of their origin, they have lost what Heidegger calls their "springing power" *(Sprungkraft)* (FV 46).

However, the works of art which have become objects are not exactly on the same level as the historical instrument as it is analyzed in §73 of *Being and Time*. An "antiquity" also is no more what it was, not only because it bears the markings of time, but because the world to which it belonged has disappeared, which means the Dasein who could use them is no longer existing. We can therefore only say that the Dasein "has been there" *(ist da-gewesen)*, not that it is "past," because only what can be present-at-hand or ready-at-hand can also be "past." An "antiquity" is in a strange way altogether present-at-hand and "past" *(vergangen)* (that is why Heidegger uses the quotation marks), because it is so only on the basis of a belonging to a no longer existing Dasein (SZ 380–381). However, in the Freiburg version, Heidegger speaks clearly of works of art as "having been" and not as "past"—even with the addition of quotation marks: *"Die Werke sind nicht mehr die, die sie waren; sie selbst sind es zwar, die uns da begegnen, aber sie selbst: die Gewesenen"* (FV 22). It is therefore clear that there is a more substantial relationship between Dasein and works of art than between Dasein and tools: tools are parts of the environment *(Umwelt)*, they are found inside of it. The work of art, on the contrary, has the initial capacity of creating the world, as we will see.

But if the works of art have all the character of having beenness *(Gewesenheit)* as far as they belong to the domain of tradition and conservation, it should imply that, as Hegel said, "art is for us something past" *(Ein Vergangenes)*. The Freiburg version ends up by quoting this famous Hegelian sentence. This passage will be repeated, in a more developed manner, in the Afterword (HW 66–67). Both in the 1935 and the 1950 versions of the lecture, Heidegger declares that the truth of Hegel's judgment has yet not been decided *(Die Entscheidung über Hegels Satz ist noch nicht gefallen)* (FV 54, see HW 67). It is not yet decided if art is still an essential and necessary manner in which the truth happens that is essential and decisive for our historical existence, or if it is no longer an essential and necessary manner. But how can Heidegger still escape from Hegel's conclusion if he himself considers the works of art only has having been?

In a letter about art from April 25, 1960 to Rudolph Krämer-Bardoni,[7] Heidegger comes back to this: "When in the Afterword of my essay (Holzwege, p. 66–67), I agree with Hegel's quotation which says that art is 'on the side of its highest vocation for us something past,' this is neither a agreement to Hegel's conception of art nor the affirmation that art is finished. I would rather say that the *essence* of art has become for us worth questioning. I can*not* 'remain standing near Hegel' because I have never stood near him, this is prevented by the abysmal difference in the determination of the essence of 'truth'." But if Heidegger does not agree with Hegel's conception of art, how can he agree with Hegel's statement? A careful reading of the last page of the Freiburg version can help here because it contains another sentence from Hegel which is missing in the Afterword. Heidegger points out that our entire Western thinking since the Greeks, with its established conception of being and truth, stands behind Hegel's statement on art. And all this remains today in force. That is why Hegel's sentence: "But we do not have any longer an absolute need to bring to representation a content under the form of art" *(Aber wir haben kein absolutes Berdürfnis mehr, einen Gehalt in der Form der Kunst zur Darstellung zu Bringen)* remains true. It remains true because this conception of art as representation belongs to a past period. The question is: Is this truth definitive, that is to say, is it impossible to transform the essence of art, to think art in relation to another dimension than the dimension or representation or presentation? In other terms, is it possible to think truth otherwise than Hegel, who gave us the most comprehensive reflection on the essence of art that the West possesses? Is it possible to think truth in a non-metaphysical and non-aesthetical manner, no longer as the absolute certainty of subjectivity, but as *aletheia,* non-concealment? What is at stake is a "spiritual decision" about the essence of art on the question of knowing if it can be the origin of our history or only a supplement (FV 55).

One question, nevertheless, remains unsolved: What status does Heidegger give to modern art? Has he really no interest at all for it? Besides Franz Mark, mentioned already in 1926 and Van Gogh, mentioned in the Frankfurt version, we know Heidegger's admiration for Cezanne, Braque, Paul Klee and other somewhat less famous artists of the twentieth century.[8] Rudolph Bardoni-Krämer, however, has considered that Heidegger "intentionally overlooks" the period of abstract art. To this objection, Heidegger answers in the same letter of April 1960 by saying that abstract art is not analyzed because nothing can be said about it as long as the essence of technology and the essence of truth implied by it is not sufficiently clarified, which does not imply that abstract art is a sprig *(Ableger)* of modern technology. The question about abstract art is: Where does it belong? We cannot be satisfied by its subordination to the art business. But as long as we do not take into account the transformation of the essence of truth implied by modern technology, we cannot decide on the originality or non-originality of abstract art.

The Two Essential Features of the Work of Art

As a fourth remark, I would like to come back to the central question of (re)presentation *(Darstellung)* through a reflection on the two features of the work of art analyzed by Heidegger in the Freiburg version because these two features—*Aufstellen* and *Herstellen*—are two modalities of *stellen*, of placing. If the metaphysical essence of art consists in the conception of art as (re)presentation of something suprasensible in a sensible matter submitted to a form (FV 45), it means, following the etymology of the *Dar-stellen*, that, accordingly to the metaphysical conception of art, art "places" *(stellen)* something there *(dar)*, and as such is a presentation or an exhibition—I just want to recall here that Kant translates the Latin *exhibitio* by *Darstellung*.[9] In contrast to this, Heidegger proposes to think of art as a *positio,* a *thesis,* in the sense of an institution *(stiftung)* of the There. Heidegger's definition of art is *das Ins-Werke-setzen der Wahrheit,* the setting-into-work-of truth, and we should not forget that the verb *setzen* is stronger than the verb *stellen* (which cannot be marked in the English translation).[10] The emphasis on the institutional and positional value of art brings forth a total reversal of what seems to be the "normal situation" of first nature and then art which finds in nature its location. It is the work of art which primarily gives to natural beings their visibility, so now nature comes after art. This is not only the case with architecture, but also with sculpture and poetry.[11] The statue of the god is not a picture made after him, but is the god himself, that is to say, his coming into presence and not the reproduction of an absent or remote being. Tragedy is not the telling of a story and does not speak about the battle of the gods, but in it the battle is being fought. The work of art initiates presence rather than being a (re)presentation or exhibition of something absent.

Because the work of art portrays nothing, but simply stands there, it opens a space in which everything can become visible. That is why the work of art has essentially the capacity of giving "place" to everything: the two essential features of the work of art that Heidegger analyses are two different modes of "placing": setting up *(auf-stellen)* and setting forth *(her-stellen)*.

Setting up as an essential feature of the work of art is different from the bare placing of art works in a museum or exhibition. It has the sense of dedication and praise so that in setting up the work the holy is opened up as holy. And the opening of the dimension of holiness is at the same time the setting up of a world. The work of art is therefore not set up *(aufgestellt)*, but it is essentially in itself a setting up *(Das Werk ist in sich seinem Wesen nach aufstellend)* in the sense that it opens a world (FV 28). In the Frankfurt version, Heidegger says more explicitly that this opening of a world is a "making space for" *(Einräumen)*, a liberation of the Open *(Freigeben des Freien des Offenen)* by which all things gain their dimensions (HW 34, trans. 45).

In the same way, the setting forth of the work of art should not be understood in the customary sense of fabrication *(Anfertigung)* of something out of a material, but as the pro-duction (in the literal sense of the Latin word *pro-ducere*, to bring forth) of the earth in the work of art. We consequently should not say that the work of art is set forth but rather that it is in itself a setting forth *(Das Werk ist in sich herstellend)* (FV 30). In the Freiburg version, the difference between the piece of equipment as fabricated product and the work of art remains implicit. In the Frankfurt version, Heidegger explains that the equipment takes into its service that of which it consists of, the matter, so that the material disappears into usefulness: "The material is all the better and more suitable the less it resists perishing in the equipmental being of the equipment" (HW 34, trans. 46). But matter and form are categories that are not relevant in the case of the work of art, which is not the result of a fabricating process. In the work of art, the matter does not disappear into the form but, on the contrary, shows itself for the first time. But what exactly does appear? Not a material which is waiting for a form which will make it invisible, but that which resists all attempts of penetration, that which remains undisclosed and unexplained: the earth as essentially self-secluding *(das wesenhaft Sichverschliessende)* (FV 32, HW 36). In the Freiburg version, Heidegger quotes Heraclitus's famous sentence *Physis kruptesthai philei* to underscore that the drive of the emerging and rising of all things is to keep itself secluded. What is therefore set forth in the Open through the work of art is the earth as constant self-secluding. The verb *herstellen* has also in German the meaning of restoring and restituting, so that we may be allowed to understand the setting forth of the earth as a reestablishment in the Open of that which constantly drives to seclusion. In the Frankfurt version, Heidegger uses the verb *hervor-kommen,* to come forth (HW 35, trans. 46), to emphasize the coming to appearance of earth in and through the work of art.

The setting up to world and the setting forth of earth belong together like clearing and concealing *(Lichtung und Verbergun).* The work of art in which these two processes take place is the locus of a striving between world and earth; the work of art is the striving itself and not a mere representation of it (FV 32, HW 38). As such, it is the being into which the openness takes it stand, the being which institutes and takes possession of the Open, in the sense of the Greek word *thesis,* as Heidegger says explicitly in the Frankfurt version (HW 40, trans. 61).

The Concept of World

There is a lot more to say about the striving of world and earth, but I will restrict myself, in this fifth remark, to the concept of world alone. What does it mean to say that the work of art sets up a world? In both sessions of the lecture, Heidegger declares that "the nature of world can only be indicated" (FV 28, HW 30, trans. 44) in a negative manner in order to ward off "anything that might at first distort our view of the world's nature." It is necessary indeed to prevent the misinterpretation of the phenomenon of world which has characterized the Western way of thinking since Parmenides—I refer here to a famous sentence in *Being and Time*

(SZ 100) where Heidegger declares that from Parmenides on the phenomenon of world has been leaped over *(übersprungen)*. This misinterpretation of the phenomenon of world consists in understanding the world as the mere collection of the things that are just there or as a merely imagined framework added by our representation to the sum of the given things (FV 28, HW 33, trans. 44). The world is in fact more fully in being than the tangible and perceptible things: the world reigns—*Welt waltet,* as it is said in the Freiburg version. In the Frankfurt version we find: *Welt weltet,* the world worlds, which is not a novelty, because if this expression is not to be found in the lecture course about world from the winter semester 1929–30, it is present in the essay *Vom Wesen des Grundes* published in 1929 and even before in a course from 1919.[12] But in the Freiburg version the idea of the non-objectivity of the world, that is never before us, is intensified by the idea of the reign of the world under which we stand *(Welt is nie ein Gegenstand, der vor uns steht, sondern das immer Ungegenständliche, dem wir unterstehen)* (FV 28). We are submitted to the world in the sense that we are exposed to the dispensation of the favour or disfavour of the gods. The ekstatic character[13] of human existence is now understood in relationship to the absence or presence of the gods, with reference to the dimension of holiness.

From 1927 to 1935, the concept of world was deeply transformed. In *Being and Time,* because the analysis of world starts with the analysis of equipment, we find in fact only an analysis of the environment *(Umwelt),* i.e., of the daily world, which consists in nothing else than its ontological structure of meaningfulness *(Bedeutsamkeit)* (SZ §18). There is no possibility of experiencing the world in itself on the basis of daily existence, because the world only announces itself *(meldet sich)* when the equipment is not working properly, is missing or ill-adapted. (SZ §16) The world can only be discovered in the fundamental mood of anxiety *(angst)* in the form of nothingness,[14] i.e., as a non ready-to-hand being. Moreover, in *Being and Time,* we find only an analysis of the human world, nothing is said about nature as such. This is acknowledged by Heidegger himself in a note from 1929 in *Vom Wesen des Grundes,* where he stresses that the analysis of the *Umwelt* in *Being and Time* is only a first determination of the phenomenon of world and has only a preparatory value.[15] The problem will be worked out further in the 1929–1930 lecture course already mentioned.

In the Freiburg version, the world is no longer understood as the daily *Umwelt;* on the contrary, it is immediately defined as the unity of the relations into which all the essential decisions of a people (victories, sacrifices, works) are articulated together (FV 34). We find here the Hölderlinian idea of the world as being never a world for everybody, for mankind in general, but always, on the contrary, a world for specific people, a specific historical world:[16] to a people, its world is what is imparted to it, given as a task *(Sein Welt—das ist für ein Volk jeweils das ihm Aufgegebene)* (FV 36). But to be opened to what has to be done in the future requires to be opened to what has already been given to the people in the past. We find here the same structure of historiality that was governing the existence of the single Dasein in *Being and Time*. Only a people which has a future can also have a "past"—or better, a having-beenness. To have a world for a people means nothing else than to be historial in the sense given by Heidegger to the world *Geschichtlichkeit* (See SZ §74).

But now, in 1935, historiality can no longer be thought separately; it has to be linked with the dimension of holiness—and this is another Hölderlin feature.[17] World is both the locus of the historical dimension of a definite singular mankind and the reign of holiness or of the absence of holiness, as it is the case in the modern age, which is deprived of gods, i.e., has a private relation to holiness: "The missing of gods is also a way in which the world reigns" *(Auch das Ausbleiben (der Götter) ist eine Weise wie die Welt waltet)* (FV 30). However, in 1935, the thrownness of the people is not a mere facticity that has to be reassumed by the people but what is thrown by the gods to the people. Heidegger quotes here a line from Hölderlin's poem, "Voice of the people," which says that the smiling gods throw us outside like the eagle that throws its offsprings out of the nest.[18] But if the people are thrown outside—let us say outside nature—into historiality, i.e., into the world, it does not mean that history should be an arbitrary adventure. It is just the opposite: because the opening of the world is also, as we have already seen, the coming forth of the earth, the people cannot be thrown out anywhere but precisely only into what it stands already (FV 40). We could say that the people as far as it has a world is thrown back into the earth[19]—an always specific earth in the same manner as the world is always a specific world. What is underlined in the Freiburg version in comparison to the Frankfurt version (HW 62) is the fact that the opening of a world is not the opening of a foreign dimension but the opening of what is the most proper *(das Eigenste)* to a historical people (FV 42). Historiality means now for a people to be opened to oneself and not to something foreign, exactly as in *Being and Time* it meant to inherit from oneself and not from somebody else (SZ 383). In 1935, historiality is no longer the modus of existence of an isolated Dasein, but of a collective one, of the Dasein of the people, as far as only a people can be historial *(geschichtlich ist immer nur ein Volk)* (FV 36).

We have therefore to think together, as a whole, the holy dimension of the world, the opening of the world as the setting forth of the earth and the world as the locus of the historiality of a collective singular being. We could then consider that this conception of world in the middle of the thirties is midway between the human *Umwelt* from 1927 and the world considered as the *Geviert* in the fifties. Heidegger says explicitly in *The Thing*[20] that the fourfold—earth and sky, divinities and mortals—is the worlding of world. As such it seems to me to be the unity of all the dimensions already mentioned in 1935.[21]

The Essence of Truth

Already in the Freiburg version we find a definition of art as "a way in which truth happens" (FV 34). Furthermore, in this same text, Heidegger underlines that "in art, truth first becomes" (FV 38: *In der Kunst wird erst Wahrheit*). Truth is then understood not as a state or a quality of the things but as a becoming and a happening. Heidegger defines the essence of truth in relation with the strife into which earth and world at the same time move apart and come near one another. This striving opens what Heidegger calls the There: "This openness of the There is the essence of truth. The Greeks called it *a-letheia* (unconcealedness)" *(Diese Offenheit des Da ist das Wesen der Wahrheit. Die Griechen nannten sie a-letheia <Unverborgenheit>)* (FV 34). It is therefore clear that the becoming or happening of truth is linked only to truth understood as unconcealedness and not to the traditional definition of truth as adequation between a thing and a proposition which was already determined in *Being and Time* as a non-original phenomenon (SZ §44). In the Frankfurt version, Heidegger explains even more explicitly that "it is not we who presuppose the unconcealedness of beings; rather, the unconcealedness of beings (Being) puts us into such a condition that in our representation we always remain installed within and in attendance upon unconcealedness" so that "the unconcealedness of beings has already exposed us to, placed us into that lighted realm *(das Gelichtete)* in which every being stands for us and from which it withdraws" (HW 41, trans. 52). The unconcealedness of beings is therefore not our presupposition, but rather what precedes us as this clearing into which we stand and to the light of which we are exposed. But how does this clearing happen? As the strife of what opens itself as the world and of what secludes itself as the earth so that unconcealedness includes concealedness *(weil das Wesen der Wahrheit als Unverborgenheit Ver-borgenheit einschliesst)* (FV 42). We consequently cannot conceive the clearing, the open place in the midst of beings, as "a rigid stage with a permanently raised curtain on which the play of beings runs its course" (HW 42, trans. 54). We must, on the contrary, understand that the clearing is at the same time concealment (HW 42, trans. 53).

We find already in *Being and Time* (SZ 222) the idea of Dasein as being co-originally in truth and untruth, so that the disclosedness *(Erschlossenheit)* of the Dasein as power-to-be includes also the closedness *(Verschlossenheit)* of the Dasein as fallenness and facticity. This closedness to itself, which comes from the fact that Dasein in its fallenness is lost in the world, is not total, because a total closedness would be the disappearance of Dasein itself. "Inauthentic" Dasein accomplishes its own disclosedness in a non-original manner, and beings are therefore discovered *(entdeckt)* but at the same time dissembled *(verstellt)*, because they are submitted to the public interpretation *(Auslegung)* of the "people," just as they show themselves as such in the manner of seeming-to-be *(Schein)*. Untruth in *Being and Time* has the meaning of dissimulation and seeming-to-be as happening inside the clearing. And truth itself can only be conquered over dissembling, covering-up and seeming-to-be in the sense that the discovering of beings is always an abduction *(raub)* out of concealment; this is the reason the Greeks formulated the essence of truth by means of the privative expression a-lêtheia (SZ 222). It is clear that, in 1927, *lêthê* is understood as the concealment of beings in the dissembling, covering-up and seeming-to-be of an inauthentic disclosedness, and that the struggle for truth is in the charge of Dasein itself in its authentic power-to-be.

That is exactly what we also find at first in the Freiburg version when Heidegger underlines that the untruth as dissembling and covering-up constantly belongs together to truth like the valley to the mountain *(Sie [die Unwahrheit] gehört ständig mit zur Wahrheit wie das Tal zum Berg)* (FV 34). But, immediately after, Heidegger mentions the self-seclusion and the absolutely concealed *(das Verborgene schlechthin)* which gives its limits to the Open. This is another kind of untruth that seems to be more fundamental than dissembling or covering-up in the sense that it is linked to the earth as that which gives to the Open its internal boundary. Furthermore, Heidegger writes explicitly that "truth is essentially earthy" because the earth supports *(trägt)* and binds *(bindet)* the Open (FV 42).

But the relation between the two kinds of untruth will become clear only in the Frankfurt version where Heidegger says explicitly that "concealment, however, prevails in the midst of beings in a twofold way" as far as it "can be a refusal *(Versagen)* or merely a dissembling *(Verstellen)*." Concealment as refusal is "this commencement of the clearing of what is lighted," whereas concealment as dissembling in which a being "presents itself as other than it is" "occurs within what is lighted." But "we are never fully certain whether it is the one or the other" kinds of concealment, because "concealment conceals and dissembles itself" (HW 42, trans. 53–54). The clearing happens only as this double concealment and this implies that it is never a pure light, deprived of all obscurity, but that it comes from the obscure as refusal and contains obscurity in itself as dissembling. It is therefore possible to understand the becoming or happening of truth as the event *(Ereignis)* of the simultaneity of concealing and clearing as it is suggested in the marginalia from the Reclam edition where *Geschehnis* is understood as *Ereignis* (HW, GA 5, 41–43). Because the clearing is not a mere unconcealment devoid of any concealment and because "truth is, in its essence, untruth," Heidegger uses the word "denial" *(Verweigerung)* to give a common name to the double concealment which belongs to the essence of truth as unconcealedness (HW 43, trans. 54).

It is now possible to conceive that the essence of truth understood in this manner can only result from a conflict—and from a conflict that takes place in being itself and not merely in Dasein. But the Frankfurt version makes a difference between the striving of world and earth which takes place as the work of art (HW 38, trans. 49), and the primal conflict *(Urstreit)* of lighting or clearing and concealing (HW 43, trans. 55) which constitutes the essence of truth itself. This allows us to set aside a double ambiguity that remained unresolved in the Freiburg version:

1. World and earth cannot be identified with clearing and concealing as such as it is clearly said in the Frankfurt version: "Earth juts through the world and world grounds itself on the earth only so far as truth happens as the primal conflict between clearing and concealing" (HW 44, trans. 55). The work of art as such can happen only on the ground of the primal conflict which is not to be identified with the essence of art alone.

2. The difference between the striving of earth and world as the essence of art and the conflict of clearing and concealing as the essence of truth implies that, besides art, there can be other ways

in which truth happens. In the Freiburg version, Heidegger names only two other ways, the act of the founder of a political state and the questioning and saying of the thinker (FV 44). In the Frankfurt version, two more ways are added: "the nearness of that which is not simply a being but the being that is most of all" and "the essential sacrifice" (HW 50, trans. 62). Art, politics, thinking, sacrifice, religion—but not science, which is "always the cultivation of a domain of truth already opened"[22]—are original happenings of truth. But because truth has to establish itself *(sich enrichten)* within that which is in order first to become truth (truth does not exist in itself before hand), the impulse toward the work lies in the essence of truth so that art is a distinguished possibility by which truth can happen. There is therefore a relative privilege of art over the other equally original happenings of truth which explains the sentence of the Freiburg version which says that "but where there is no art, there is a happening of truth, there is history" *(Wo dagegen Kunst ist, geschieht Wahrheit, ist Geschichte)* (FV 50).

The Heideggerian Critique of the Metaphysical Conception of Art

At the end of the Freiburg lecture, the opposition between the metaphysical and the Heideggerian conception of art is analysed under a triple aspect: a) Creation is opposed to production: *Erzeugtsein und Geschaffensein sind nicht dasselbe* (FV 48). This opposition has to do with the essence of the work of art. b) Knowledge is opposed to pleasure as far as the fundamental relation to the work of art is concerned. Heidegger writes: "That is why the fundamental relation (to the work of art) is not a pleasure, not an excitement, but a knowledge of the truth established in the work in all its references" *(Deshalb ist das Grundverhältnis nicht ein Genuss, nicht eine Erhitzung, sondern ein Wissen dieser ins Werk gesetzten Wahrheit in allen inhren Bezügen)* (FV 50). c) (Re)presentation is opposed to commencement *(Anfang)*:[23] "But the work of art never (re)presents anything for the sole reason that it has nothing that it could (re)present, because the work of art creates in the first place what appears for the first time through it in the open" *(Allein das Kunstwerk stellt nie etwas dar, aus de einfachen Grunde, weil es ja nichts hat, was es darstellen kann, weil das Werk dasjenige erst schafft, was erstmals durch es ins Offene tritt)* (FV 46). This opposition has to do with the origin of the work of art.

Looking at each aspect in more detail: (a) Is it possible to bring into a total opposition creation and production if, as Heidegger himself says, "in the domain of art a creation is always also a production" *(Jedes Geschaffene ist im Bereich der Kunst immer auch ein Erzeugtes)* (FV 48)? Heidegger adds of course immediately: "but the contrary is not true"—a production is therefore not always a creation. But if there are some productions that are also creations, it could imply that creation is a special kind of the genus production, so that it could be necessary to start from the broader concept of production in order to understand what creation is. Heidegger wants, on the contrary, to stress that this is not at all the case: "That is why it is impossible to ever conceive creation and the createdness of the work out of production and fabrication" *(Deshalb lässt sich auch vom Erzeugen und Anfertigen her nie das Schaffen und das Geschaffensein des Werkes begreifen)* (FV 48). For Heidegger, creation and production are two totally different kinds of processes in the sense that creation is not the expression of something already existing but the indication of what will be, whereas production is always reproduction of what already exists (FV 48–50).

However we find in the work itself not only the createdness of the work but also its produced-being, but precisely "veiled" by the createdness *(Das Erzeugtsein liegt zwar im Werk, wird aber gerade durch das Geschaffensein verhüllt)* (FV 50). What is the sense of this dissimulation of production under creation? Heidegger explains further: the working out of the material keeps secret *(verschweigt)* its own despair and pleasure into the self-subsistence of the work. Production remains silently "inside" creation, because, if it is required by the essence of creation, but it can never become a creation by itself. Consequently, there is not a gradual difference between production and creation—a difference in the "quality" of the craftsmanship—but a difference in the essence: from production to creation, there is also a leap *(Auch hier ist der Sprung)* (FV 50).

But what is the essence of creation? What does it mean to create? Heidegger gives an answer by defining the creator as the instigator of the strife that constitutes the work of art (FV 48). But to instigate does not mean to produce anything. On the contrary, Heidegger stresses that the becoming of truth is suffered in the poetical institution[24] *(das Werden der Wahrheit wird im dichtenden Stiften erlitten)* (FV 48). The essence of creation consists in supporting *(ertagen)*, enduring *(aushalten)* the strife of world and earth and in staying within *(innestehen)* the unfamiliar domain of the new truth. To create does not mean to make or to perform, but, on the contrary, to sustain or to undergo the happening of truth. That is why Heidegger stresses that the creator is not only the artist, but anyone who brings out one origin of the truth, one kind of the becoming of truth (FV 48). We have already seen that in the Freiburg version there are three ways for the truth to happen: besides art, truth also occurs in thought and politics. Thus, on one hand, creation seems finally to be a broader concept than art in the sense that the thinker and the politician are also creators. But, on the other hand, it seems very difficult (as we have already seen) to think the historical decision which takes place as creation as happening without any relation to art.

(b) Why cannot the relation to art be pleasure? Heidegger seems to suggest that there is pleasure only in relation to what he calls *Nachkunst,* epigonal art, or *Schein von Kunst,* semblance of art, i.e., to "inauthentic" art (FV 50); he says explicitly that there is pleasure in relation to the art business only (FV 22). But can we really leave aside the immediate artistic pleasure that we feel when dealing with art works? To this question Heidegger would probably answer that pleasure is linked only to works of art that are not "great art" because they are only expressions or results of their time and not epoch-making in the sense that they do not institute the measure of the epoch. Great art never conforms to the times; it is, on the contrary, always untimely *(die grosse Kunst ist niemals eine zeitgemässe Kunst)* (FV 48). Pleasure has to do with the given presence of artistic "objects," whereas knowledge has to do with the future, with the "authentic" work of art in the sense that it gives as such an indication not about the present but about what the future of a people can be. Pleasure is always re-active and secondary, whereas knowledge is pre-figuring and primary.

This is stressed by Heidegger in the Frankfurt version, where knowing means willing (HW 55, trans. 67). There the correct relation to the work of art is understood as preserving *(Bewahren)* and not enjoying. But preserving means standing within the openness of Being that happens in the work, and we have already seen that standing within is more "passive" than "active." Heidegger adds here that standing within is a knowing and says further that "knowing that remains a willing and willing that remains a knowing is the existing human being's entrance into and compliance with the unconcealment of being." The German text says more precisely *"Das Wissen, das ein Wollen, und das Wollen, das ein Wissen bleibt, ist das ekstatische Sichenlassen des existierenden Menschen in die Unverborgenheit des Seins";* and Heidegger points out that *Sichein-*

lassen—to engage oneself in—has here the meaning of *Entschlossenheit* (resolutedness) in *Being and Time*.

What does willing mean, then? Willing is always the willing of self-exposure to the openness of Being—a theme that comes already in a very strong manner in 1933 in *The Self-Assertion of the German University,* when Heidegger quotes a verse from the Aeschylus's Prometheus, *technê d'anagkês asthenestera makrô*— knowing, however, is far weaker than necessity—and underlines that the speech of the creative weakness of knowing is a word from the Greek *(Dieser Spruch von der schöpferischen Unkraft des Wissens ist ein Wort der Griechen).*[25] There is, on the one hand, a connection between standing within as a kind of "passivity," knowing and willing, so that knowing and willing can no longer be understood as "activities," as deliberate acts of a subject. And on the other hand, knowing is not entirely deprived of a kind of "pathos": knowing the work of art is not of course a way of having pleasure in regard to it, but it implies another "feeling," the suffering, the endurance of the strife—what will be called later *Gelassenheit*. In a marginalia to the Addendum from the 1960 Reclam edition of "The Origin of the work of art" (HW, GA 5, 70), Heidegger stresses that *Ins-Werk-Setzen* (setting into work) has to be understood as *Ins-Werk-Bringen* (bringing-into-work), *Hervor-bringen* (bringing forth), *Bringen als Lassen* (bringing as letting), *poêsis,* so that to do *(poein)* means finally to let. In the same manner, a note from 1953 added to the 1935 course, "An Introduction to Metaphysics," underlines that all willing has to be based on letting and that the relation to Being is the letting.[26]

(c) Heidegger declares that the meditation on art, i.e. aesthetics, began with Plato and Aristotle, and that, since then, all theory of art is subjected to a remarkable fate (FV 52). Because the work of art has been understood right from the start as a fabricated thing, the conception of art has always been an allegorical or symbolical conception in the sense that we think that in the work of art there is something else than the mere product—*allo agoreuein* means to say something else or something added to the mere product, and *symballein* means to bring together (FV 52). Understanding the work of art as an allegorical or symbolical product means understanding the work of art as consisting of two different parts: matter and something else—the form—or material content plus spiritual meaning. As far as art is understood as the process of bringing together matter and spirit, it is defined as (re)presentation of the suprasensible into the sensible *(Kunst ist sonach die Darstellung eines Übersinnlichen in einem geformten sinnlichen Stoff)* (FV 53). The metaphysical logic at work here is a logic of addition. In the metaphysical tradition the human being and language are understood according to the same pattern: phonetical material plus meaning for language, animal body plus soul, mind or spirit for human being. The leading idea in this metaphysical conception is that the "spiritual" element can be (re)presented in the material one. The idea of a possible presentation of what is not material or sensible is still to be found in an aesthetics of the sublime and not only in an aesthetics of the beautiful, because the sublime is still negatively defined in regard to a possible presentation of what is not presentable.[27] For Heidegger, every aesthetics is therefore unable to understand what a work of art really is. The work of art does not (re)present anything: it is neither representation of something else nor presentation of something absent. It has in fact no relationship at all to presence, but, on the contrary, it has a relationship to the becoming or happening of truth, to the coming into presence of everything. That is why Heidegger puts the stress on the initiality of the work of art: the work of art is a commencement *(Anfang)*, an institution *(Stiftung)*, a creation *(schaffen)*.

In conclusion, we can say that, for Heidegger, the work of art does not connect matter and spirit as separated domains, but initiates the conflict of world and earth, i.e., opens the free play *(Spielraum)* into which human existence becomes possible—what Heidegger calls the There. The difficulty for us is trying not to think the duality of world and earth as a new form of the ancient metaphysical duality of matter and spirit. The difference between these two dualities is a mere difference in temporality: metaphysics was and remains metaphysics of presence, but the thinking to come should be the thinking of the becoming or happening of truth, i.e., of the *Ereignis*.

Notes

1. Martin Heidegger, "Der Ursprung des Kunstwerkes," *Holzwege* (Frankfurt-am-Main: Klostermann, 1950), p. 7–68. In the most recent edition of *Holzwege,* published in 1978 as Volume 5 of Heidegger's *Gasamtausgabe,* the text of "Der Ursprung des Kunstwerkes" is given according to the modified version published in 1960 in the Reclam edition (which includes the Addendum from 1956), and includes the notes from Heidegger's hand and from his own copy of the Reclam edition, written between 1960 and 1976. The pagination of the original edition of 1950 is indicated in the

margin of volume 5 (quoted under the abbreviation HW, GA 5). The text from 1960 has been translated into English by A. Hofstadter in *Poetry, Language, Thought* (New York: Harper and Row, 1975), p. 17–87.

2. Heidegger, "De l'Origine de l'oeuvre d'art," Premiere version (1935), texte allemand inédit et traduction francaise par E. Martineau (Paris: Authentica, 1987). Cited under the abbreviation FV. This edition was published without the agreement of the German publisher and is therefore not available in bookstores. Consequently the references to the German Text will be quoted in full as far as possible. This lecture was given before I could read the authentic "first version" of The Origin of the Work of Art, a draft from the same year 1935 which will be published in *Heidegger Studies* in the fall of 1989.

3. Michel Haar and I held a common seminar on this Freiburg version in the Sorbonne in 1987. We then tried to produce a systematic reading of the text. The following remarks represent only my own commentary on some points selected by me and should be completed by the addition of Michel Haar's commentary of other equally important points.

4. Heidegger, *Einführung in die Metaphysik* (Tübingen: Niemeyer, 1953), p. 122.

5. On schematism, Kant himself says in the *Kritik der reinen Vernunft*, B 180–181, that it is "an art hidden in the depths of the human soul *(eine verborgene Kunst in den Tiefen der menschlichen Seele)*" (emphasis added), so that knowing, as the process by which a concept is associated to an intuition, is already understood as an art, a setting-into-work of the horizon or schema within which something can appear as this or that. With his doctrine of schematism, Kant shows that knowing implies for him a working process and not a pure receptivity of what is present-at-hand.

6. *Einfuhrung in die Metaphysik*, p. 122.

7. See "Ein Brief Martin Heideggers an Rudolf Bardono-Krämer Über die Kunst" in *Phänomenologische Forschungen,* Freiburg/München, Alber, 18, 1986, pp. 170–181.

8. In his Heidegger biography *Auf einem Stern zugehen* (Frankfurt, Societät-Verlag, 1983), H. W. Petzet mentions principally the names of the painter Paula Becker-Modersohn and of the sculptors Wimmer and Chillida.

9. I. Kant, *Kritik der Urteilskraft*, Einleitung, §VIII, where the *Darstellung* (exhibitio) is defined as the process of placing a corresponding intuition next to the concept *(dem Begriffe eine korrespondierende Anschauung zur Seite zu stellen).* *Darstellen* means to present in the sense of to render perceptible *(versinnlichen),* to give an intuitive presence to something, what we also call represent. That is why I have translated the word by representation or presentation according to the context or have maintained the ambiguity in writing (re)presentation. See J. Beaufret, "Kant et la notion de *Darstellung*" in *Dialogue avec Heidegger II* (Paris, E. de Minuit, 1973), p. 77–109.

10. The two German verbs *stellen* and *setzen* are translated into English by the same verb to set. Heidegger himself points out in the

Addendum (HW, GA 5, 70, trans. 82) that both *stellen* and *setzen* should be thought in the sense of the Greek *thesis,* according to the key specification *"Ins-Werk-setzen."*

11. One of the fine arts is missing here: music. Painting is not directly analyzed as it will be in the Frankfurt version, but there is at least a reference to the saying from a painter, Albrecht Dürer (FV 50), which will be reproduced in 1936 (HW 58, trans. 70). Heidegger's almost total silence on music—with the exception of one reference to Beethoven's quartets in 1936 (HW 9, trans. 19) and another one to a letter from Mozart in *Der Satz com Grund* (Pfullingen, Neske, 1971), p. 117–118—is amazing compared with the interest for music shown by many German philosophers.

12. In the lecture course from winter semester 1929–30 *(Die Grundbegriffe der Metaphysik, Welt-Endlichkeit-Einsamkeit,* GA 29–30) we find the expression *Walten der Welt* (See §74, p. 507, 510, 514, 527, 530). But in *Vom Wesen des Grundes* (Frankfurt am Main, Klostermann, 1955), an essay written in 1928, we find already the expression *Welt weltet* (p. 44: *Freiheit allein kann dem Dasein eine Welt walten und welten lassen. Welt ist nie, sondern weltet*). And in a lecture from the *Kriegsnotsemester* 1919, we find for the first time the expression *"es weltet" (Zur Bestimmung der Philosophie,* GA 56–57, p. 73).

13. The words *ektatisch* or *Ekstase* do not appear in the Freiburg version; but we find instead the words *Entrückt* (FV 36) and *Entrückung* (FV 46), which are already employed as synonyms in *Sein und Zeit* (see for example p. 339).

14. We find the expression *Nichts der Welt*—nothingness of world— in *Sein und Zeit,* p. 276 and 343. In the §40 about the fundamental disposition of anxiety, we find the expression *das Nichts, das heisst die Welt als solche* (p. 187).

15. *Vom Wesen des Grundes,* p. 36 note 55.

16. When Heidegger writes (FV 34–36): *Welt ist nie Allerweltswelt einer allgemeinen Menschheit und doch meint jede Welt immer das Seiende im Ganzen* ("World is never the world of all worlds for a general mankind and yet each world means always the totality of beings"), this reminds me of Hölderlin's philosophical essay, *Das Werden im Vergehen (Becoming in Perishing),* written around 1799. There we find the expression, *die Welt aller Welten* (the world of all worlds), and the strongly expressed idea that each finite world contains the "world of all worlds" in itself, that the infinite can only be found in the finite. Heidegger very briefly mentions Hölderlin's essay in the lecture course from the winter semester 1941/42 *Hölderlins Hymne "Andenken,"* GA 52, §41, 119–22.

17. The emerging of the dimension of holiness in relationship to world reminds me of another earlier essay from Hölderlin, *About religion,* where holiness *(das Heilige)* is understood as the experience of a more lively relation of the human being to the world than mere necessity so that a new demonstration of the existence of God can be proposed: neither ontological (based upon the cognitive experience of the subject) nor cosmological (based upon the reality of the world), but, let us say, phenomeno-

logical, i.e., based solely on the fundamental experience *(Grunderfahrung)* of the intimate relation that binds the human being to world and nature.

18. Heidegger quotes here a strophe from the first version of the poem, *Stimme des Volkes,* that says:

> *Und wie des Adlers Jungen, er wirft sie selbst,*
> *Der Vater, aus dem Neste, damit sie sich*
> *Im Felde Beute suchen, so auch*
> *Treiben uns lächelnd hinaus die Götter.*

In the final version from 1801, we find *mit richtigem Stachel* (with a right sting) instead of *lächelnd* (smiling) and *der Herrscher* (the ruler) instead of *die Götter* (the gods).

19. In the Frankfurt version (HW 35, trans. 46), we find the following passage: "That into which the work sets itself back *(Sich zurückstellt)* and which it causes to come forth *(Hervorkommen)* in this setting back of itself we called the earth." We find here the same circle: in order to go forwards we have to go backwards so that we can let be what we already exactly like the work which "lets the earth be earth." (ibid.)

20. In "The Thing," a lecture from 1950, Heidegger says explicitly that "the appropriating mirror-play of the simple onefold of earth and sky, divinities and mortals, we call the world. The world presences by worlding *[Die Welt west indem sie weltet]*." *Vorträge und Aufsätze* (Pfullingen, Neske, 1954), p. 178. English translation in *Poetry, Language, Thought,* p. 179.

21. All the dimensions of the fourfold are already present in 1935 except the sky. But we can perhaps consider that what is called in 1935 "earth" and which is understood as "the whole" *(das Ganze)* and linked to the Greek *Physis,* i.e., to the emerging and coming into light of everything, possesses a lighted side which later will be called sky. On the same page (FV 26), Heidegger underlines that *physis* has the same root as the word *phaos, phos,* meaning light.

22. There is an important difference between the status of science in 1933 and in 1936. In *The Self Assertion of the German University,* science means still questioning and thinking and is equal to philosophy as it was in 1927 when philosophy was named "the science of Being." (See *Die Selbstbehauptung der deutschen Universität,* p. 11: "All science is philosophy, no matter if it will it or not, if it knows it or not. All science remains closely bound up with this commencement of philosophy. It derives from it the strength of its essence, granted that it remains at all equal to this commencement.") However, as early as 1929, we find a text which says that philosophy no longer means science. In the lecture course from 1929–30 that was already mentioned, Heidegger writes: "Philosophy as absolute science—a high and unsurpassable ideal. It seems so. But perhaps the evaluation of philosophy in regard to the idea of science is already in itself the most fatal degradation of its inmost essence." (GA 29/30, 2–3) In opposition to philosophical thinking, science appears already in 1929 as a non-original process and this will be clearly said in 1936. But in 1933, in

his *Rektoratsrede,* Heidegger goes back in a very interesting way to his 1927 position.

23. Because Heidegger, in the Freiburg version (FV 46–48) as well as in other texts, makes a strong difference between *Anfang* and *Begninn,* I have always translated *Anfang* by commencement. We find a precise definition of both words in the lecture course from the winter semester 1934–35 *Hölderlins Hymmen "Germanien" und "Der Rhein",* GA 39, 3: *Beginn is jenes, womit etwas anhebt, Anfang das, woraus etwas entspringt* ("Beginning is that with which something starts, commencement that from which something arises"). The word *Anfang* is one key word in Heideggerian thinking and should not be dissociated from the other key word *Ursprung.*

24. The question of the essence of art as poetry *(Dichtung),* which is a central point in The Freiburg version (FV 38–42) as well as in the Frankfurt version (HW 59–65), trans. 72–81), is completely left aside here.

25. Heidegger, *Die Selbstbehauptung der deutschen Universität, Das Rektorat 1933–34,* p. 11.

26. *Einführung in die Metaphysik,* p. 16: *"Der Bezug zum Sein aber ist das Lassen. Bass alles Wollen im Lassen gründen soll, befremdet den Verstand."*

27. Kant himself defines the sublime in regard to the incapacity of nature to give a presentation *(Darstellung)* of ideas *(Kritik der Urteilskraft, Allgemeine Anmerkung zur Exposition der ästhetischen reflektierenden Urteile).* But, to my knowledge, Heidegger never said anything about the aesthetics of the sublime or about the sublime in itself, which does not imply that there is not a non-explicit re-thinking of sublimity in Heidegger's discourse on art. Concerning this, see P. Lacoue-Labarthe, "La verite sublime," in *Du Sublime* (Paris: Belin, 1988), p. 97–147.

IV. Reading Hölderlin

Chapter 7

Thinking and Poetizing in Heidegger and in Hölderlin's "Andenken"[1]

Hans-Georg Gadamer

(translated by Richard Palmer)

In the theme of our meeting, *"Dichten und Denken,"* we find quite unmistakably inscribed the fate of the West. How are we rightly to designate, for instance, what has been handed down in the great literary heritage of other high cultures? When the Buddha or a great Chinese sage utters a few simple but deeply meaningful words to his students, should we call this a poetizing *[ein Dichten]* or would it be better to call it a thinking *[ein Denken]*.[2] The path of the West, which is also the path leading to science, has forced upon us the separation and a never completely achievable unity of poetizing and thinking. Martin Heidegger has repeatedly spoken, along with the poet Friedrich Hölderlin, of two "most widely separated peaks" on which poetizing and thinking stand facing each other. There is certainly something to the idea that it is precisely the distance between the two peaks that establishes at the same time a certain nearness between them.

In any case, the topic under discussion here has been the theme of my own life since my youth. The course of my studies led me, both at the beginning as well as the end, through literature and art, and through classical philology, to philosophy. But in the most decisive things, it was from Heidegger that I have learned the most, and this applies especially to the moment when, for the first time, I heard Heidegger speak about the "origin of the artwork" in

February in 1935. This moment was like a confirmation of what I had so long been seeking in philosophy. Here, too, the theme of "poetizing and thinking" will lead us into questions which move us. In relation to these, I can only try to suggest a direction of thinking to be explored; I will leave it to the younger generations to work these indications out further.

For my own contribution here, I had in mind specifically Heidegger's encounter with Hölderlin, on the one hand, but also the more general question of whether one can expect truth from "the word." To say that a "word" can have truth does not mean to assert that the individual word as such, a single word alongside other words, can be true. Rather, "the word"[3] *[das Wort]* always already refers to a greater and more multiple unity, a unity well known in the tradition in the concept of the *verbum interius* [inner word]. Self-evidently, this broader meaning also lives on in our everyday language, as, for example, when someone says, "I would like a word with you." In this case, it does not mean one wishes to say just one word!

So if, in taking this as a starting point, I take up what I call "the truth of the word," then I am characterizing the claim of the poet, above all. For poetry is such that the word of the poem makes itself believable, and cannot be made believable or validated by anything else. Thus it is certainly erroneous, although it often happens, to try to approach the poetic word from the outside, such as when someone seeks out concretely real items and relationships in order to understand the genesis of a poetic word, or when one tries to evaluate a poetic statement by using the knowledge possessed by the sciences or scholarly disciplines, which measure the truth of what is meant in the words of the poem in terms that their scientific knowledge gives them. Granted, it is almost always the case that the poem mirrors the real world, and this worldly reality can become the theme of objective scholarly knowledge. But the fact that the word in some cases makes itself believable from itself and does not require a fulfillment from somewhere else—indeed, it does not even permit it—this is what is constitutive of the ἀλήθεια which Heidegger has translated as "unconcealment." Unconcealment involves much more than whether this or that knowledge can be designated as correct. Rather, the word can also be something that is spoken to someone, a word that by itself brings conviction. Certainly, the word that is spoken to someone is not just one word. When it applies to oneself, such as in a word of invective, or, on the other hand, in something like a title of respect, when one is given the title of "master" [of a craft or "champion" of a sport], then we suddenly realize through this example, that, like a statement, a naming can also be "true." Words are indeed not just there because they are put forward by someone who introduces them. Rather, they introduce themselves—or as Hölderlin said so well, "Words like flowers, come up *[entstehen]*." Words have a trustworthiness and self-evidence of their own, which brings it about that they call something forth, just as names do.

When I take the naming power of the word as a starting point, one can easily detect that this touches on what is most his own and most characteristic of the thinker in consequence of whom and for whose thought we gather together here. If there is something which in our century has unmistakably characterized Heidegger the thinker, it is that he sensed the naming power of words. Heidegger permitted this element to enter into the very movement of his thinking, and it was from language that, over and over again, he received direction and measure for the path of his thinking; indeed, this was the genuine impetus for his thinking.

What is naming? What is a name? Let us recollect along with Heidegger the Greek origins of our thinking and ask what ὄνομα, the Greek word for "name," actually means. Where and how does it occur in our tradition and especially in the first ventures of thinking in the history of Western thought? The word ὄνομα seems scarcely suited to shed light on the naming power of the word. In our early tradition, it was for the most part used to designate the name which one gives to a person, or which a person—whether human or a god—bears. In such usage, the name is what someone harkens to [because he or she is called by it]. In contrast to this, the formation of the grammatical concept ὄνομα in the sense of *"nomen"* is already based on a separation from being "called" *[Rufen]* and on the semantic or syntactical function which a word acquires and exercises in speech.

At this point, the concept of the λόγος, speech, necessarily thrusts itself forward. In this concept [there is the notion of a] continual "placing-together" *[Zusammenlegung]* of more meaning. It suggests [the notion of] adding up, accounting, relating, and marshalling arguments *[Begründung]*. When I speak here of the truth of the word, what I mean is still λόγος in the broadest sense and not the logical concept of judgment, and also not at all the grammatical concept of a proposition. The λόγος ἀποφαντικός to which Aristotle limited his logic and which did not include the sentence in the form of a question at all, signified a narrowing down of the way the topic was dealt with. If one wishes to ponder the nearness and distance between poetizing and thinking, however, then one must move down into a deeper dimension, a dimension in which the word displays an unrestricted power to speak. Here one must remember that to read, for the Greeks, whether the work be of poetry or of thinking, was always to speak, even if it was obliged to take that most dangerous passageway of the starkness and rigidity of writing.[4] So it is not out of place, in the end, to seek the power of saying in this power of naming, and therewith to come back to the name, which calls to someone or calls forth *[heraufruft]* something. In this connection, then, I think one ought to take into consideration what is signified by the fact that ὄνομα in its earliest usage designated persons—gods and humans—and that there is something like a respect, even veneration, that belongs to a name *[die Ehre des Names]*. An honored and respected name has a value and acceptance on its own part. In this kind of word usage, there already resides something of ἀλήθεια, namely, that one does not seek to conceal or hide anything precisely because no disgrace clings to one's name. In this sense, a name has something inviolable about it. Jokes that play with a name are bad, shameful jokes, and when someone like the despairing Ajax awakens from his madness and begins to play with his own name, this represents something like a terrible punishment or discipline he imposes on himself. Indeed, even in our own social world, one's first name still has in it something of the intimacy and value of the person. Nevertheless, in times past it was quite customary in good bourgeois household, always to call a domestic servant "Marie," even when there was a change of servants, because the master and mistress found this more convenient. But to our present-day sensibility this is already something like an offence to the value of the person.

Last names of person, and even more so, first names, are totally based on the naming function. For the most part, they possess no meaning of their own at all; in any case, such meaning as they may have plays no part in their function, if we think of it from the standpoint of name-giving, of baptism, of the choice of a name for a new pope, or the naming of Tristram Shandy. Naming, in these cases, can carry with it hopes and promises, or also a bad omen. But the name itself in its use contains no meaning of its own. Insofar as this is so, proper names are not words. What in Latin grammar we call "nomen" and what corresponds to the Greek word for "name," is a word with a meaning, and words exercise their meaning-function when they occur in a sentence—or perhaps even in the case of an individual word, such as in an invective or a form of address, which we have described earlier, where a word is in itself equivalent to a whole sentence.

Thinking and Poetizing in Heidegger and in Hölderlin 149

On the other hand, one can also ask what a word can mean purely as a "vocabulary word" *[Vokabel]*. Such words do have a meaning and are in any case more than merely separate building blocks for sentences. Every word stands in itself for a whole field of meaning that opens up within it. All assertions in which that word may occur will represent only one aspect of this realm of meaning, and this representation need not in all instances have the character of a declarative statement. However, it is always within a pragmatic situation that words exercise their function of meaning. Whether the situation is that of one person presenting an address, or of two or more in a conversation, or whatever the context may be, a word must, simply in order to exercise its function of meaning, be understandable, and if it occurs in the context of a speech, a word will serve to bring about an understanding of something that is itself not just a word.

As the right words can be lacking, one will search for the right words, and if one comes across the word, then what is meant *[das Gemeinte]*, the matter at issue *[die Sache]*, emerges. In this regard, it is meaningful to speak of "unconcealment." For certainly a phrase like "to tell the truth" is an ambiguous turn of speech, and in general one immediately thinks of the possibility that it is a lie, exactly as the Greeks did. But, again, there are cases where one would recognize with equal firmness the rightness of the assertion, its appropriateness to the matter, in the phrase, "telling the truth." The usage of the Greek term ἀλήθεια followed this second path, the path of expressing the unreservedness and frankness with which one says to another person what one thinks, without covering it up with lies, silence, or palliation. If it is through a word that that which what was at issue *[die Sache]* was raised up into the commonality of mutual understanding and then called forth, then it is at the same time in a word that it is lodged and sheltered, and it is through the word that it is disclosed; and now it can only be summoned back into memory either by the fleeting moment of self-crossing in question and answer, or on the basis of a permanent form into which it has been fixed. The truth of the said *[Gesagtes]* is thus the unconcealment of what is and which comes to stand in speaking.

But what does "what is" mean here? Surely not "that which is the case." Neither poetic speaking nor philosophical speaking has to do merely with "that which is the case." On the contrary, both have to do with something that is "there." When Aristotle sees the essence of the λόγος in the δηλοῦν, he means showing and displaying so that something is "there" when it is spoken about. In connection with his *Politics,* Aristotle distinguished the modes of understanding possessed by animals from the understanding-structure that resides in the language of words, namely, a world: a world held in common, a world governed and ordered by living together, which reaches its apex in δίχαιον, in the rightful sharing by all in the goods maintained and preserved by the community.

Here, in keeping with the context, Aristotle touches on the primal power of language and words. It is not only that the word makes nameable this or that thing, nor that the word serves as a building block in this or that statement. What is most truly mysterious about language is its power to let us see, so that something is there. This brings us back to what I call the truth of the word. In Greek thought, it seems to me, the sense of this power of words to let one see occurs first of all in Parmenides. For this he employed the terms νοεῖν and νοῦς, and it was from these that he explained ἀλήθεια as authentic unconcealment. Νοεῖν means perceiving that something is there. The word group which Parmenides draws upon in order to designate this presentness actually has its source in the sense of smell which a wild animal possesses. (Νοῦς has something to do with nose.) What it has to do with is not only the immediacy of the there but also with the indeterminacy of the "there is something." If one goes back to this point, to the point in "being" (and in nothing else) at which the perception of the "there" becomes conscious, then what one is dealing with in the truth of the word is not the unconcealment of the said the sense of showing us an existent thing, showing whether it is this or that, but rather that the "there" is and not nothing. The step to what Heidegger characterizes as metaphysical thinking under the governance of logocentrism and which he seeks to overcome, is, at that point, not yet what Parmenides had in mind at all. What is at issue at this point is not a thinking about existent things in the sense of rejecting what is false, but rather of the rejection of nothingness. This is the "completely untreadable path," the path around "being." Thinking is only in the being of the there. In the there it is uttered, and through this the being of the thing thought is there. That is what Parmenides intended. It does not appear to be so very different in Heraclitus, either, who indeed speaks expressly that the Wise is One *[Einen Weisen],* ἕν τὸ σοφόν. And perhaps it even harmonizes with Plato's αὐτὸ τὸ ἀγαθόν, that is, with what he calls "the Good itself." The issue under discussion here is not the rise of metaphysics but rather a question situated prior to it, the question of a common ground between *mythos* and *logos,* which has to do with the ἀλήθεια of the word, whether it is the word one person says to another, the word in a poem that says something to someone, or the word of the there that says something and not nothing.

I want here to bypass the whole question of *mythos* and the narrative form of language taken by the epic and the dramatic shaping of language in which the drama finds its fulfillment. For apparently it is in the lyric poem where the disturbing question of the nearness and distance of poetizing and thinking most clearly comes to language. And it appears to occur especially in the works of Hölderlin and the ways of Heidegger. Only in the correspondence between these two does the Parmenidean thesis *[Satz]* first acquire its clear evidentness. If one is to interpret and represent this inseparability of "thinking" and "being," one is not permitted the conceptual separation between being and existent beings. The poetic speaking of the thinker Parmenides overflows that of poetry in the direction of logical thinking, as if it wanted to derive predicates for "being" from existent beings. And it is not different in the case of the Heraclitean One, either, which only lets itself be thought in the transformation of the One into the Other as the One that is the Wise. Perhaps the same even holds also in Plato in relation to the Good itself, αὐτὸ τὸ ἀγαθόν, this great thing to be learned, μέγιστον μάθημα, which one is most in need of learning, and yet which one cannot learn in the way one learns other knowledge—τὰ ἀλ α μα ματα. Plato says this quite clearly in his *Seventh Letter.*

Actually, in the There of Being *[Da des Seins]*, ἀλήθεια, nothing is expressed but that Nothing simply does not exist, not that it is this and not that. In light of this, it is completely consistent for Zeno and the Eleatic School to hold that there is no Many but only the One.

Likewise it holds for a thinking that thinks Being, that its predicates are only pointers along a path—and, like all the paths of thinking, are detours on the path to the One. In the same sense, it becomes understandable that the poet, who establishes what stays, also follows many ways and detours in establishing the thing that is remembered in remembrance. In this connection, I will presently be turning to Hölderlin's poem, *"Andenken."* For Heidegger's encounter with Hölderlin stands at the centerpoint of our discussion of the nearness to and distance from each other of poetizing and thinking. Heidegger's encounter with Paul Celan is also relevant to this issue, but we will comment only briefly on this after our discussion of Hölderlin.

To what degree and through which circumstances the poetic work of Hölderlin had, in the first half of this century, become so very "contemporary" for all of us only requires a little recollection. The new access to the work of the later Hölderlin, thanks to Norbert von Hellingrath, launches a truly powerful impetus which expressed itself particularly in a movement away from *Bildungsreligion,* that is, from the educational emphasis found in German classicism and in its later rather lackluster continuations. This new impetus can be seen in two examples: One was the book on Hölderlin by Romano Guardini,[5] which was a fine interpretation of Hölderlin poetry. The standpoint Guardini took in introducing his theme is noteworthy. Hölderlin, he said, was the only great German poet whose gods one must believe in. Guardini is obviously speaking here from a standpoint that turns away from the classical *Bildungsreligion* that is found in Schiller and also in the baroque playful wisdom of *Faust: Part 2*. In Hölderlin, as Guardini saw it, a new seriousness has been brought into the question of the Divine. Something similar can also be said of Walter F. Otto, the classical philologist who, in a remarkable unburdening of himself, said he must "believe in" Dionysus or Apollo, or whatever god. Certainly the protestant pastor's home in which he grew up stands in the background of his need for faith. Compared to the other philologists, however, Otto here was certainly a good deal wiser. He had read his Schelling and knew that Shelling had called Christendom "paganism corrected"; but, for him, this meant that the Greek gods were not some kind of ghosts, spirits, demons, and devils, or mere superstition, as the fathers of the Church taught. Otto held that even if it is true that one must go beyond the heathen cults of Greece and the mythical interpretations offered in the Christian proclamation, the Greek gods represented a religious experience whose realness was not to be doubted.

For the thinker Heidegger, however, Hölderlin signified a step that went even further. Of Hölderlin, Heidegger said, "he forces us decide," and that decision had obviously been against Schelling and Hegel and for Hölderlin; that is, against the concept and for the messages from the Divine. So for Heidegger, two alternatives presented themselves to him: either the most extreme abandonment of Being in technological madness, or the premonition that "only a god can save us."[6] For this reason, Heidegger had to see Hölderlin not as a person belonging to the age of idealism but as someone belonging to a future which could usher in an overcoming of the present forgetfulness of Being. For Heidegger the consequence was that what we have in the meantime learned to call "logocentrism," and which he later developed under the slogan of the overcoming of metaphysics, compelled him to make allowance for a linguistic need *[Sprachnot]* that has been experienced in the philosophical tradition of the West only in the most extreme cases—say, in Meister Eckart or in Hegel.

Sprachnot, however, was something Heidegger also encountered in Hölderlin, something that attracted him to that poet. I have already pointed out that the high rank of Hölderlin's work was recognized only belatedly, during Heidegger's lifetime and also my own; indeed, only in the lifetime of younger people of today has it come completely to presence. What is the special quality in Hölderlin that has gained him this belated recognition? What is it that expresses itself so uniquely in his strophes and hymns? My thesis is that it is *Sprachnot*. And we find the same thing in Heidegger's thought, particularly in his late work. Of course, *Sprachnot* is more than just a lack or even a refusal *[Versagen]* of thinking or of poetizing; rather, it gives to each of these its authentic urgency. In the case of Hölderlin, also, it is not a lack in his poetry. On the contrary, *Sprachnot* gives his work its unmistakable intensity and uniqueness. To discover the right word for what one wishes to say, or for what one wishes to say to someone, remains a human goal always, and in case of success, it is a special piece of good fortune. Thus, authentic speaking always involves searching for the word. We notice this immediately, for instance, when someone reads a lecture that has been written out in advance. The listener now has an additional task: The word is not being searched for any more, and it no longer sounds as if it has just been found; thus, the listener must set it free again to be what it once was: the sought-for, and just-found word. So free and natural speaking is always granted a little forbearance. Its inexactness is compensated for by the listener, who takes on and shares in the search for the word, which is thus more easily conveyed than any word that is ever so well prepared in advance.

In 1943, which was the centennial of Hölderlin's death, a Hölderlin commemorative volume was published.[7] One of the essays in that volume was Heidegger's great and comprehensive analysis of Hölderlin's poem, *"Andenken."*[8] I, too, contributed to that volume an interpretation of Hölderlin's poem, *"Der Einzige."* In both poems a *Sprachnot* or a *Denknot* is allowed to present itself that is ultimately a *Sprachnot* of thinking as [it is] of poetizing.

The theme of *"Der Einzige"* is that only for a person who has been initiated poetically, with heart and soul, into the ancient world of heroes and gods, does the Christian message and its transmission by tradition remain immediately near and real. In this sense, the Christian era is, for Hölderlin, still so near that his whole project of conjuring up and calling back the Greek gods became an unfulfillable task, even when he began to read and interpret them in the signs and the runes formed by the rivers and mountains of his homeland. That is how things went for him, I think, as he sought to rightly name the "Only One" and to give this its proper place in the great series of his experiences of the Divine. He never completely succeeded. That was the issue that the poem, *"Der Einzige,"* dealt with and that I also posed to myself. It is a paradox that the nearest can at the same time be the farthest away. That which is nearest to me also has the greatest distance from the right word. Hölderlin experienced this paradoxical nearness, for he only sought to conjure it up in very keen reminiscences, like his "Brod und Wein," or in the sign language hidden in the landscape of his homeland.

For his contribution at that time, Heidegger chose the poem *"Andenken."* Since then, this poem has been the object of intensive discussion. Dieter Henrich has published a highly learned and insightful book on this poem,[9] a book whose main thesis pointedly contradicts Heidegger, in that from the beginning Heidegger takes the sailor to be the poet. I can agree with Henrich's point that one must look at the sequence of the poem as a sequence, which Heidegger in his explication did not do. Many scholars have worked with the poem since that time. Certainly it is one of Hölderlin's most consummately beautiful poems. Even in times when the greater part of his late poetry was regarded as merely evidence of his madness and excluded from publication, this poem was taken up by the poet's romanticist friends. Heidegger's very detailed interpretation sought at every point to release the speaking power of the words. This, in truth, is the task of every genuine listening to poetry. In listening to a poem, one is not permitted to take the word as just a sign pointing to a specific meaning; rather, one must also simultaneously perceive all that word carries with it, namely, the whole radiation and the multiplicity of directions contained in its power to mean *[Bedeutungskraft];* this intensifies the movement and direction of the meaning in its assertion and allows the volume of the poetic speaking to achieve three-dimensionality, so to speak. Thanks to the gravitational force of every single word, something other, something different, is always there with it. This is precisely what distinguishes the word that says something *[das sagenden Wort]* from the word that merely intends something *[meinenden Wort],* where one hurries from one word to the other, as in everyday speech and everyday self-orientation. Not only the poetic word but also the word in thinking can have a quite other "presence" than words in ordinary situations have. Everyone who has even once heard Heidegger speak has experienced this fact, whether his thinking moved within the artificiality of the conceptual words of the tradition or in powerful new coinages.

The poem *"Andenken"* appears to be easy to understand. In its five strophes, the third strophe stands out from the other as, in a certain sense, the real pivot of the whole poem. It is astonishing that this has not been kept enough in view in more recent interpretations. In this third strophe, the one who is speaking interrupts himself, naturally, in the course of his speech of recollection. Within this recollection, there comes this interruption:

> Es reiche aber,
> Des dunkeln Lichtes voll,
> Mir einer den duftenden Becher,
> Damit ich ruhen möge...
>
> Extend to me, however,
> Full of dark light,
> One of the fragrant cups,
> With which I would like to rest...

As in the poem as a whole, the poet—or more aptly, we might say, the poetic self-consciousness that speaks here (as Cyrus Hamlin[10] expresses it)—conjures up his sojourn in Bordeaux. His stay in Bordeaux was the first and, indeed, the only contact Hölderlin had had with life in the south [of Europe] up to that point in his life. That which he had already magically produced through his poetic eye in the *Hyperion* novel and also in many poems now confronts him for the first time in living, palpable reality: the silken ground on which brown-skinned women walk back and forth on paths in March, during the season of the equinox, with the wind full of the fragrance of coming spring, which is drawing near, heavy with golden dreams; all this rises up like dream images to a self losing itself in its recollection.

One ought to take seriously the title of the poem *"Andenken."* *Andenken* [commemoration or remembrance] is neither recollection *[Erinnerung]* nor the capacity to remember *[Gedächtnis]*, although both come into play when one speaks of commemoration or remembrance. But just as little as the capacity to remember can be seen to be the totality of all preserving in recollection, and just as little as the capacity to remember is the same as that which one remembers, in remembrance there resides a completely different kind of thing, namely, that it is a memory I want to preserve. It can be a good or a bad remembrance, but in any case it is something that is neither forgotten nor something that one just happens to remember. It is something that stays on, that remains, not as something constantly present, but always as something that is our ownmost possession, something which one thinks about and which again becomes present to one in a certain rich multiplicity.

So when Hölderlin names a poem in this way something is being emphasized. Although he dedicates a poem to remembrance in general, it is clear in this case that it deals with remembering a journey, and, indeed, this remembering is a remembrance, that is to say, it recalls something of great significance. Why, really, is this so significant?

This cannot be answered in one sentence. Rather it is in the course of the poem itself that something is called up which the poet thinks back on with joy and nostalgia. Certainly what calls up the memories is the wind, the northerly wind that the poet knows is the wind from his homeland. And it is here called the most cherished of winds. Why this is so is told to one from the beginning to the end of the whole course of the memory and of the poem. The wind recalls the ships of Bordeaux and their departure, because it is a good wind for ships to travel with. It is odd that the interpreters of this poem, above all Heidegger, cast aside this relationship with reality, although the poem from the first to the last strophe has to do with the ships and not with the poet, who, almost as a surprise, has the last word, although it is certainly an all-illuminating last word.

What is it that is so important about the ships, so important, indeed that they thrust into the background even the heroes of the dreamed world of Hyperion? Certainly it must have been a great and new experience for the Swabian poet, who as student, teacher, and household tutor possessed only a modest experience of life, when he saw the sea and sensed its great spirit *[Atem]*, no longer needing to dream it as he had had to do in his poetry. It must have given him something to ponder when he encountered bold, intrepid men who again and again go forth on dangerous ventures, risking everything instead of giving in to the magic of southern living. For that great commemorator who in poetic dreams had loved to wander within the southern landscapes of Greece, this must have been a tremendous encounter with reality. So the poet or the thinker here is overwhelmed by his memory of both: the dream heroes of Hyperion's world and this reality he experienced in Bordeaux. It is a truly Pindaric interruption which, through asking for the most forgotten place, instead finds it emphasized in a way that becomes

Thinking and Poetizing in Heidegger and in Hölderlin 157

the centerpoint of the poem. In connection with this, one may surely also want to ponder the fact that in this recollective dream that the poet conjures up, one encounters nothing of what so often becomes thematic in the later poetry of Hölderlin, namely, the blistering sun of the south and the scorching summer heat that awaken a longing for the coolness of forests. I recall, for instance, the line, *"Fast wär der Beseeler verbrannt"* [One's inspiring spirit would be almost burned up]. None of this is found in the holidays that rise up in his memory, and clearly none of this is contained in the memory of the bold and intrepid sea-farers who, in renunciation of winged war, struggle with sailless masts. What lives in his remembrance are the southern holidays with their playing of stringed instruments and their native dances.[11]

At the beginning of the poem the poet names the northeast wind of his homeland, a wind which has the task, as the poet also does, of greeting Bordeaux. There at the mouth of the Garonne River, this wind is now a wind for travel, a wind about which sailors are very happy. The speaking poet empathizes with these sailors and therewith also feels how far he himself is from home. Thus, remembrance of all the past surges up in him. After his journey home, he feels the lifelessness *[Seelosigkeit]* of the conversations he is having; he calls them thoughts that die, mortal thoughts, especially when he remembers the conversations with his friends about the fateful hopes and expectations for freeing Greece, hopes which he had conjured up in *Hyperion* between Hyperion and Bellarmin.

But where are the friends? Suddenly and immediately the topic shifts to sailors, sailors who go out from Gironde to India, sailors who, from out of all the riches of the world and with infinite efforts and dangers, bring back the beautiful. At this point the poet attaches his recollection of the venturesome seafarer whom he had encountered in his vivid personal experience in Bordeaux to the poetic dreams he is calling back to himself. There are two high forms of human existence who stand before the dreaming eye of remembrance as objective of its reflection—the warrior hero and the seafaring merchant. What the content of that reflection is, the last line of the poem tells us, and it sounds like a conclusion: *"Was bleibet aber, Stiften die Dichter"* [What is to stay, however, the poets establish]. In a rough draft of the poem, the first line of the final stanza was found to have read, "But now the friends have gone to India." This makes clear the true progression of thought in the recollection: from the poetically conjured friends to admired men experienced in lived reality. So the poet's conclusion follows from the true nature of the mission of writing poetry and from the poem. This, I think, is actually the point of the whole poem; this is how the memories of the Hyperion-world are interconnected with the memories of the real world of Bordeaux. Always it has to do with overcoming distance and with grasping and holding onto the near.

Let's have a look at this in the final strophe of the poem. It depicts the place at the mouth of the Garonne River as it flows into the sea. From there on it is called the Gironde. It is the place up to which the friends and acquaintances of departing sea-farers accompany them. This is the windy point at which the Dordogne River roars down, joins the Garonne, and then makes its exit in the sea. Whatever the exact place always was, it was the place of leave-taking, the place at which those who must remain behind gaze with the industriously fixed eyes of love at the disappearing ship, and at which those going away likewise look back at the people who must stay behind. It is one of the powers possessed by human beings, that is conjured up here, the power to overcome distances, to preserve memories, and to grasp and preserve the near. This is the reason the poem is called *"Andenken."* And one finds it perfectly natural that, in the end, this power of human beings should find fulfillment in a poem—where would it, otherwise—in what stays, endures, persists. Thus, the famous "however" in the concluding line, "What is to stay, however, the poets establish," does not wish to say that perhaps the poet has a higher initiation into the true than the others, but that he or she is able to lift up into something that stays, that power in all life which captures and fixes what passes away, which, in the give and take of remembrance, preserves the "there." That is the task of the poet. Truly, the poet is not one for whom "words just come up like flowers." He or she is the prophet in a needy time even if he or she sings of the return of the gods.

"Andenken," then, is the never to be accomplished overcoming of distance—and yet it shows, at the same time, the guarantee we have, a guarantee which lies in the constant wager of leave-taking and remembrance, and the industrious fixing on it of the eyes of love.

The poem, as it progressed, evoked what the remembrance of that lasting experience of his sojourn in Bordeaux was for his poetic self-consciousness. We ask once again: What did this experiences mean for the poet? What has he learned, such that at the end of the whole poem he concludes as a "learned one": "What is to say, however, the poets establish"? Whereas in *Hyperion* he had driven his heroes to explore distant regions, now he learns from the sea-farers that the paths and detours of fate are not to be found only in a life of high poetic dreaming. The isolated-feeling poet recognizes in this his own fate—and also his calling.

This explains the surprising, gnomic turn at the conclusion of the poem, a conclusion on which the understanding of the whole of the poem depends. The one absorbed in remembrance gets hold of himself. He has asked himself: Where is that which stays? Where is the spiritual enjoyment in holidays, where is spiritually full conversation? And he experiences what separation and departure into the uncertain distance are for those who follow the temptation of the sea and for those who preserve remembrances. It is in this that the poetry-making ego experiences itself. Yes, "many are fearful of going to the source." Here there is something like a pattern which links together separation and loyalty, departure into the distance and return home in remembrance. They wager everything and at the same time hold fast, even if they will never know the joy of return and reunion with loved ones—still the remembrance remains. This is the message of the great spirit of the sea which the poet perceives. "The sea, however, takes, and gives, memories." In his remembrance of Bordeaux the poet learns what remembrance is and that poetizing is remembrance.[12]

Although this poem does not lament the falling silent of the poet because he can never find the right word (as does *"Der Einzige"* as well as many other hymns of Hölderlin), still, at the end, Hölderlin as poet comes down strongly on the side of the heroes and the risk-takers, those who venture forth into the distance and bring back the beautiful: "you see, the spirit is not at home [with itself] . . . if it stays at its place of origin."[13]

This understanding of the poem leads us back to its decisive line: *"Mancher tragt Scheue, an die Ouelle zu gehn"* [Many a person dreads going to the place of origin]. Heidegger's interpretation of this line, it seems to me, hits the mark and rightly draws out the gnomic sense of this *"Manche."* Many a person, and indeed precisely the dreamed-of heroes, or the venturing seafarers, or the poets, belong to those named in this "many." It is a distinction, an honor, to have this dread of taking the risky paths and bypaths and then returning to the place of origin; and it is the poet's special distinction that he or she establishes what stays. He is a poet because dread hinders him. It seems to lie beyond his own naming power to name what it is. But the unnameable, that which surpasses the poet's art as well as the thinker's concepts, is precisely that which one must take risks for, must try to grasp and hold onto. It was not without justification, then, that Heidegger, later, and precisely in his critique of a "calculative" thinking which takes everything in its grasp and wishes to absorb everything, spoke of "remembrance."

Much more, of course, could be said about Heidegger's encounter with Hölderlin. I would like to add a word here about the interest Heidegger took in Paul Celan. Celan, too, was a poet of the most extreme *Sprachnot,* a situation which pressed him to the limit of an ultimate falling silent. Heidegger was in a similar state of *Sprachnot* because he wanted to overcome the thinking of metaphysics, and so he tried over and over to invert *[umzustülpen]* language, so to speak, for, language itself, to him, was the language of metaphysics. This *Sprachnot* has also led the poet Paul Celan into constant acts of verbal violence *[Gewaltsamkeiten],* in which he shatters the usual unities of meaning and demands a recoining of the meaning of words. He also wants thereby to rip the word, which finds itself trapped in fixed signifying and which thereby in effect has fallen silent, out of its customary context and cause it to speak as a new "counterword." In cases where this strategy truly succeeded, Celan was able to make such a newly created word singable and add it to song.

Similarly, Heidegger tried, through violent recoining of words, to mark out a path of thinking which was afterwards supposed to be followed. But really to follow someone in doing thinking does not mean to repeat the marks of such thinking. Such mere repetition generates no life-awakening language. *"Aber manche...."* Let us turn back to Hölderlin for a moment and recall the fact that his most accomplished creations apparently were no longer intelligible at all to his contemporaries and were withheld from publication for a century. It was a language that was all too new, a language that suddenly insisted that we leave behind the whole world of our humanism-shaped and Christianity-stamped experience and sing of the divine and of the human.

I would like to close with two lines that are familiar to everyone and which today more than ever express the situation of human beings in the world:

»Seit ein Gespräch wir sind
Und Hören können voneinander.«

Because we are a conversion
And can listen to one another.

But what kind of conversation is this? Is it the conversation of humans with the gods or of humans with humans? The poem wants to tell us that we cannot separate and distinguish in this way. What we must try to do in our given situation is to go beyond ourselves, whether it be in listening to the other person or in seeking somehow to correspond with what is completely other than human.

Notes

1. Translator's bibliographical footnote: This text based on a lecture Gadamer presented on the 26th of September, 1987, at the second colloquium of the Heidegger-Gesellschaft, in Messkirch, Germany. Some paragraphs were added by Gadamer as indicated in translator footnotes. The essay was first published privately under the title, "Von der Wahrheit des Wortes," with four other papers from the 1987 meeting (*Denken und Dichten bei Martin Heidegger,* Jahresgabe der Martin-Heidegger-Gesellschaft, 1988, pp. 7–22). Because Gadamer had written another essay with this title, he decided to rename this essay. In his *Gesammelte Werke* 10:76–83 (Tübingen: J. C. B. Mohr, 1995) Gadamer published the first half of the Messkirch essay with few changes under the title, "Denken und Dichten bei Heidegger und Hölderlin." The second half of the essay (beginning on p. 153) was omitted from *GW* 10 because it dealt principally with Hölderlin's "Andenken," and Gadamer's essay in *GW* 9:42–55 (Tübingen: J. C. B. Mohr, 1993), "Dichten un Denken im Spiegel von Hölderlins 'Andenken'," had already dealt in more detail with Hölderlin's poem. In that essay, Gadamer drew from an unpublished presentation he made in a Hölderlin colloquium at Yale in 1987. *Trans. note.*

2. Trans. note: *Dichten* and *Denken* resist translation into English. *Dichten* means to create poetry and can be translated as "to poetize," or "poetizing." *Denken* also connotes activity, here as doing thinking, and can be translated as "to think," or "thinking." The translator wishes to thank Sieglinde Keil Daniels (now of Jacksonville, Illinois) for consultation on several troublesome German words and phrases in the essay.

3. Trans. note: "Das Wort" in German carries a greater weight than "the word" in uncapitalized English. It is associated, for instance, with the Biblical reference in the Gospel of John, that "Im Anfang war das Wort" [In the beginning was the word].

4. Trans. note: This sentence was added to the 1988 text.

5. *Hölderlin: Weltbild und Frömmigkeit* (Leipzig: Jacob Hegner, 1939).

6. Trans. note: See Heidegger's 1966 interview under this title with *Der Spiegel* published May 30, 1976, shortly after his death (he requested that it not be published during his lifetime). A translation by Maria P. Alter and John D. Caputo appeared in *Philosophy Today* later that year (Winter, 1976), pp. 267–284.

7. *Hölderlin: Gedenkschrift zu seinem 100, Todestag, 7, Juni 1943,* edited by Paul Kluckhohn (Tübingen: Mohr, 1943).

8. Trans. note: Heidegger included this essay, which appears under the title of the poem, in his *Erläuterungen zu Hölderlins Dichtung* (Frankfurt: Klostermann, 1951), pp. 79–151.

9. Dieter Henrich, *Der Gang des Andenkens: Beobachtungen und Gedanken zu Hölderlins Gedicht* (Stuttgart: Klett-Cotta o.J.).

10. See Cyrus Hamlin, "Die Poetik des Gedächtnisses: Aus einem Gespräch über Hölderlins 'Andenken'," *Hölderlin-Jahrbuch* 24 (1984–1985), pp. 119–138.

11. Trans. note: This paragraph and the two preceding it were added from the earlier version.

12. Trans. note: The previous two paragraphs were added to the original text.

13. Trans. note: See "Brot und Wein," line 152: "Nemlich zu Hauß ist der Geist/Nicht im Anfang, nicht an der Quell." Here the reference would seem to be to one's homeland. Professor Gadamer suggests that it also points to the *orcus elysium,* the paradisiacal fields.

Chapter 8

Heidegger, Hölderlin, and Sophoclean Tragedy

Véronique M. Fóti

> The great ones [poets and philosophers] do not have that which they give in virtue of their own originality *(Originalität)*, but out of another origin, which sensitizes them to the "influence" of the originariness *(des Ursprünglichen)* of the other great ones ... Because Hölderlin, unlike any of his contemporaries, was granted the inner capacity to be influenced by Pindar and Sophocles, which here means to belong to the alien originary out of one's own origin, he alone was able, through historical interlocution and responsive adequation *(Zwiesprache und Entsprechung)*, to show us these poets and their poetry in a more originary light.
>
> —Heidegger, *Hölderlins Hymne, "Der Ister"*

Heidegger characterized his lecture courses of the decade following his resignation of the rectorate of Freiburg University (1934 to 1944/45) as a "confrontation" with National Socialism evident to "all who had ears to hear."[1] This characterization is puzzling at first sight, since the themes of his courses were pre-Socratic philosophy, issues in the history of metaphysics, Nietzsche, and Hölderlin's poetry—themes that seem quite remote from the political arena. By these choices, Heidegger not only contested the National Socialist appropriation of Nietzsche and Hölderlin, but he also re-problematized certain issues that had been crucial for his political engagement: the entwined issues of historiality *(Geschichtlichkeit)* and planetary technicity *(die Technik)*. One may call to mind here his admission to Karl Löwith in 1936 that his politics sprang from his understanding of historiality,[2] as well as that technicity is, in his understanding, indissociable form the history of metaphysics. His confrontation with National Socialist ideology through philosophy and poetry is characteristically displaced and encrypted.

As late as the *Spiegel* Interview of 1966, Heidegger maintained that National Socialism went "in [the] direction" of grappling with what he took to be the most crucial problem for contemporary thought, the problem of achieving a satisfactory relationship to technicity; but, he notes, the movement proved to be "too poorly equipped for thought" to fulfill its supposed promise or realize its "inner truth."[3]

For Heidegger, the history of the West is *ess*entially the history of an interpretive configuration (an epochal configuration of un-concealment) which originated in pre-Socratic Greece. In its inception, it revealed the character of manifestation to be inherently differential and therefore refractory to totalization. Since pre-Socratic thought was, in Heidegger's judgment, unable to render its guiding insight explicit, or to bring it to fruition, the latter engendered an ambiguity between differential and totalizing modalities of understanding manifestation, which Heidegger traces in terms of the relationship between *alētheia* and *orthotēs* in Plato's doctrine of truth.[4] He finds this ambiguity to be already weighted, in Plato, toward privileging archic unification or totalizing unconcealment and displacing differential presencing *(anwesen)* in favor of sheer presence *(Anwesenheit)* and present entities *(Anwesendes)*. This resolution and displacement prepare the way for the doctrines of substance and subjectivity, the modern scientific project, and the reductive totalization that characterizes planetary technicity. In the technical enframing *(Ge-stell)*, the understanding of being or manifestation at work within the Western tradition stands fully revealed; yet it remains, in this revealment, opaque to itself. The urgent task for the Heideggerian thinker is to grasp technicity for what it is, in its historical *essence*, and in its sinister yet potentially salvific power. He does not draw a distinction between the technological and the political aspects of totalization but tacitly subsumes the latter under the former.

Jacques Taminiaux points out that the issue of *technē*, which remained secondary and downgraded in Heidegger's early project of fundamental ontology, is first thrust into dramatic prominence in the Rectoral Address.[5] Germany's destinal mission is now thought, in terms of *technē*, as a creation that constitutes, in

Taminiaux's words, "the very historicality of truth"; and it will eventually be thought in terms of the *ess*ential-historical bond that links planetary technicity to Greek *technē* and to the withheld possibility of a differential modality of un-concealment. Since the salvific power of *technē* is concentrated, for Heidegger, in poetry, the responsibility for nurturing the "saving" that arises, supposedly, in the very midst of danger falls, first of all, upon Germany's destinal poets. The poet, however, can, in Heidegger's view, only institute or inaugurate a new historical configuration; it falls to the thinker, in his dialogue with the poet, to "found" it and render it firm.[6]

Within these parameters, Heidegger's privileging of Hölderlin's poetry (beginning with the 1934/35 lecture course on Hölderlin's hymns "Germanien" and "Der Rhein")[7] reflects his own preoccupation with the problematic of *technē* and *poiēsis*, with Germany's destinal relationship to ancient Greece, and with the meaning and possibility of an *ess*ential retrieval of the "unthought" of Greek thought. Since Hölderlin's own intense relationship to ancient Greece was not mediated primarily by Greek philosophy, but by its epic, lyric, and tragic poetry, Sophoclean tragedy (which preoccupied the German Idealist thinkers) becomes, for Heidegger, a particularly important focus for his meditation on *technē*. His studies of the *Antigone* and of *Oedipus Rex* in the 1935 lecture course *An Introduction to Metaphysics*, and in the 1942 lecture course on Hölderlin's hymn "Der Ister," (where the discussion of *Antigone* tends to marginalize the Hölderlinian text at issue) are not puzzling if interesting digressions, but are crucial to his questioning.[8] His encrypted confrontation with National Socialism is here played out (with a focus on the movement's inadequate grasp of essential technicity, rather than on ethics and politics) in the context of the German Idealist reading of the *Antigone* as a tragedy of historical transition *(Zeitenwende)*. Despite these explanations, it remains somewhat strange that an intellectual confrontation with a genocidal ideology and regime should proceed through Greek tragedy with its focus on the undoing of an individual; and it is also rather ironic that Sophocles, who won his first public distinction when Cimon and his fellow-commanders, acting as judges at the Greater Dionysia in 468 B.C.E., awarded him first prize with a view to his political conservatism, should be the Greek poet whose work mediates the confrontation.

Scholarly interpretation has so far focused almost exclusively on Heidegger's reading of Sophocles in *An Introduction to Metaphysics*, so that the affinities and significant differences between the two readings have not been thematized.⁹ In the absence of such thematization, their deeper import has remained largely concealed. With a view to developing this deeper import in the context of Heidegger's dialogue with Hölderlin's thought and of the problematic that structures his professed confrontation, the two readings will here be analyzed, interrogated, and brought to bear on each other.

The Power of *Technē* against Being's Overwhelming Power

To the extent that Hegel considered the *Antigone* to be the historical source and structural paradigm for his dialectical phenomenology, and hence for his understanding of history, one could regard Heidegger's reading of Sophocles, which seeks to justify the West out of its history, as Hegelian. Hegel, however, understands the *Antigone* (the exemplary tragedy for both Heidegger and German Idealism) in terms of the unsublated conflict between divine law and ethical self-consciousness, or *Sittlichkeit* and *Moralität*, whereas Heidegger divorces it from ethical engagement and human action, that is, from the entire *praxis* component of the *vita activa*, in favor of his focus on *technē* and *poiēsis*. Greek tragedy is not, for him (as it is for Martha Nussbaum, who stays closer to the plays themselves, their historical context, and the history of interpretation),¹⁰ a modality of ethical reflection questioning the ability of principles to guide human action when put to the test by complex and imprevisible situations. It is rather a meditation on the ontological role and limitations of *technē* which, through a philosophical retrieval (and hence with a claim to historical legitimation) provides a corrective to the aestheticization and glorification of technology in the writings of Ernst Jünger.¹¹

Whereas both the 1935 and 1942 readings are situated in the overarching span of this preoccupation, the former reading alone concentrates on ontological relationships of power and on the Promethean character of man. In this reading, Sophoclean tragedy is brought to bear on the question "Who is man?," asked in the context of what Heidegger understands to be the Parmenidean determination of the *ess*ence of man out of the very *ess*ence of being. This question is answerable, for Heidegger, only insofar as man creates, or, as he phrases it (with an echo of the Heraclitean *polemos*) as "confrontation":

[M]an enters into a confrontation with beings, in that he seeks to bring them into their being, that is, casts *(stellt)* them into limit and form, that is, projects something new (not yet present), that is, poetizes in an originary way, founds poetically.[12]

Man is in each case the form-giving creator; and only as such does he enter into a disclosive relationship with the being of beings.

This relationship is inherently transgressive; and Heidegger's interpretive preoccupation is with the violence and transgression involved in human creation or *poiēsis*. For this reason, he focuses both his readings on the first *stasimon* (verses 332–375), which exalts the dignity and power of man—on the more somber Sophoclean prelude, so to speak, to Renaissance humanism. He pronounces the first *stasimon* to be "the *ess*ential ground" not only of the *Antigone*, but of Sophoclean tragedy.[13] At its core is the notion of "the awe-inspiring" *(to deinon)*, introduced in the opening verse, and identified by Heidegger as the "fundamental word," not only of Greek tragedy, but of the Greek form of historical human existence *(Griechentum)* as such. Surprisingly, however, Heidegger entirely ignores the complex, echoing reiterations of *to deinon* throughout the play,[14] tacitly limiting his discussion to the choral ode. Presumably, he justifies this interpretive strategy by his view that Greek tragedy, as a "thinking poetizing" *(denkerisches Dichten)*, instructively complements the "poetizing thinking" of pre-Socratic philosophy, which is not as yet "scientific" *(wissenschaftlich)*.[15] If both await a scientifically philosophical retrieval (Heidegger's own), interpretive license may seem pardonable.

To deinon, here translated as "the awe-inspiring," also carries the connotations of being strange, out of place, or surprising.[16] For Heidegger, it is "the unhomelike" *(das Unheimische)*, which casts one out of every context of familiarity, ease, protection, or assured interpretation. This outcasting into exposure prevails over or "overwhelms" *(über-wältigt)* any order or economy of presencing.

Drawing on the inherent ambiguity of *to deinon* (as, for instance, the awe-inspiring, and the terrible), Heidegger interprets Sophocles's identification of man (the ungendered though grammatically masculine *anthrōpos* or *Mensch*) as *to deinotation*, the supremely awe-inspiring, in a twofold sense: (1) in virtue of his very disclosiveness, man is uniquely *exposed* to being as the overwhelming, whether this over-power of being is encountered through elemental forces and living beings, or through the supposedly human powers of language, understanding, passionate feeling, or skill.

These, Heidegger notes, are not properly thought of as capacities that man may exercise, but are themselves prevailed over or overwhelmed by being's over-power.[17] They are drawn into the creation of historical configurations of un-concealment, within which beings attain to their presencing. *Technē*, together with *poiēsis*, is here thought as the human enactment of power that pits itself against the over-powering sway of being's enigma. In a close parallel to his approximately contemporaneous discussion of creation in "The Origin of the Work of Art," Heidegger characterizes the key modalities of creation as poetry, *esse*ntial thinking, the founding of a state, and building or artistic formation.[18] Since these appear to establish and secure for man an intelligible domain which is, in the positive sense of *to deinon*, a marvel to behold, the way in which they veer *esse*ntially toward exposure and danger must now be brought into view.

Thrown back upon his own resourcefulness, man, Heidegger finds, becomes enraptured by his inventions to the point of entrapment in semblance *(Schein)* and of being debarred from the enigma of being *(Sein)*. Even the unrelenting frustration of human resourcefulness by death does not suffice to undo this entrapment; and its undoing is made the more difficult by the *esse*ntial proximity of semblance to the disclosure of being. *Technē*, in creating a work (especially a work of art), establishes, so to speak, a locus of manifestation or *phainesthai*. The work, however, tends immediately to insist on its own ontic privilege, to reify the world-structure within which it functions, and to support hegemonic constructs (here the technological work is more potent and danger-fraught that the work of art). Heidegger casts the tension between the work's power to open up access to being's enigma, and its power to violate and conceal that enigma, as a conflict between *technē* and *dikē*, where *dikē* is not ordinary "justice," but is understood in a more Anaximandrian sense as the overriding sway of being that exceeds the economies of phenomenal presencing and that, in each case, assigns to what presences its fitting "while." This strife in which the human work is both pro-voked (called forth) and shattered marks, in his interpretation, the heart of the tragic conflict.

The conflict between human power and being's over-powering sway is not, of course, accidental or avoidable. Rather, being as *physis*, or as "the arising that holds sway" *(aufgehendes Walten)*, must of necessity exceed and shatter the human creations that pit themselves against its enigma and pretend to univocal intelligibility and mastery. Without the work, however, and without its inevitable shattering, there could be no ontological disclosure. This emphasis on the challenge of the work, and of the work as a sort of sacrifice, has no parallel in *Being and Time*; but it does recall Heidegger's discussion of the relation of German *Dasein* to "the original Greek *esse*nce of science *(Wissenschaft)*" in the Rectoral Address.[19] He takes that *esse*nce to be expressed by a verse from Aeschylus's *Prometheus Bound*:

Τέχνη δ'ἀνάνκης ἀσθενέστερα μακρῷ (v. 514)

which he translates as "Knowing, however, is far weaker than necessity." *Technē*, as a mode of knowing *(Wissen)*, must, with "highest defiance," provoke "all the powers of the hiddenness of what is, so as to reveal, through its own inevitable failure, being's "unfathomable unalterability." In *An Introduction to Metaphysics*, the static figure of *anangkē* (necessity) as a figure of the enigma is replaced by being's historiality and temporality. Precisely by being shattered, the creative work is historicized; and being stands revealed in its temporality and historiality. The analysis presupposes that the work should have an inherent tendency to absolutize itself, on the model of political creation or metaphysical and scientific interpretation. Since, on Heidegger's own admission, self-absolutization is not characteristic of the work of art, the open possibility of a human creation that gives an abode to the enigma without violating it puts the analysis in jeopardy. This difficulty, however, is persistently glossed over.

The figure of man, the creator, is drawn with Promethean *pathos*: his necessary perdition constitutes "the most far-reaching and profound 'yes' to the over-powering."[20] Heidegger characterizes the agent or tragic protagonist as a mere "breach" or "intermediary occasion" *(Zwischenfall)* through which "the unshackled and overriding power of being" can become manifest and enter into history. Man, the creator, disappears into the created work which mesmerizes by its compelling and imprevisible singularity, while effacing the singularity of the creator.[21] Whereas Schelling saw in the perishing of the tragic hero(ine) an exaltation of human freedom, Heidegger perceives in tragedy an erasure of the face of man in favor of a revelation of being's self-concealment through the work of *technē*. Heidegger draws on Karl Reinhardt's characterization of the *Antigone* as a tragedy of semblance;[22] but he construes semblance exclusively in terms of the ontological status of human creations, to the exclusion of questions concerning singular agency or the political arena. Antigone's "work" of burying her brother's corpse can hardly be described as a creation or a work of *technē* that strives to assert itself against being's over-power. By sprinkling concealing earth over the corpse, she seeks, rather, to effect an appropriate concealment. Her thought is that in the concealed realm of Hades, the "sightless" or "unseen," the humanly sanctioned distinctions between friend or foe, patriot or traitor, are not countenanced, and that the discriminations and classifications of human sight can therefore claim no ontological privilege.[23] In the absence of any privilege, human sight reveals itself as susceptible to radical singularization.

Even if one shifts one's attention from Antigone to Creon, one is not led back to the issue of *technē*. Creon's offensive acts of exposure and concealment (exposing a corpse to the raw light of day and to the devourers of carrion, while shutting up a living woman in "a rock-hewn tomb") do not amount to works of *technē* or to meaningful challenges to the overwhelming sway of being. Both Creon and Antigone are singularized and cannot convince anyone (the chorus, Haemon, or the audience) that the principles that govern their actions have divine sanction or other authority. Rather than pitting *technē* against *dikē* in an aletheic context (as Heidegger construes it), the tragic conflict is a conflict between singularization and what Reiner Schürmann describes as the "single bind" imposed on phenomena by representations that are held to be ultimate.[24]

Homecoming to the Unhomelike

The figure of the stream as "the absconding one" *(der Schwindende)* in Hölderlin's late stream-hymns, and in particular the figure of the Ister (the upper Danube, called by the Roman name for its lower course) in its regressive movement, marks for Heidegger a conception of history that is no longer Hegelian, in that its schema is not dialectically progressive, but recursive or concerned with retrieval. Hölderlin thematizes the Ister's apparent backward flow near its source, as well as the provenance of the unnamed protagonists from the great rivers of Greece and India.[25] Perhaps it is also significant that the upper valley of the Danube (the region around Beuron, which is the locus of Hölderlin's poem) is Heidegger's own home region. Obliquely, at least, this circumstance calls attention to his role in seizing the destinal moment or *kairos* which, he believed, had arrived in Germany. The very opening verse, "Now come, oh fire!," allows him to develop the idea of the *kairos*. His discussion of the verse offers a lucid articulation of his own historical schema:

> The "now come" appears to speak from out of its present into a future. Nevertheless, it speaks first of all into what has already come to pass. "Now" indicates that something has already been decided. Precisely this, which has already "come into its own" *(sich"ereignet"hat)*, alone carries a relation to what is to come. This "now" names an event *(Ereignis)*.[26]

The itinerary of *ess*ential appropriation and the historical distention of the dwelling place that Heidegger explores through the Hölderlinian figure of the stream concern Occidental man's homecoming, out of long alienation, to his true identity as the being who responds to and safeguards being's enigma. To point out to Occidental humanity the need for and path to this homecoming is, in Heidegger's view, Germany's destinal mission (particularly that of her poets and thinkers)—however extraordinary it may be that in 1942 he could still cast the figure of Germany as Hölderlin's Germania, the "all-loving" and "defenseless" priestess and counselor.[27] For a historical people to grasp its true identity requires, for Hölderlin, a passage through what is alien without being either random or multiple; the alien is rather called for by the ownmost itself. Given the privilege that Heidegger, after the turn of 1934, accords to the poets, the relationship of the own to the alien is played out importantly in the interlocution *(Zwiesprache)* of Hölderlin as Germany's destinal poet with the poets of ancient Greece, particularly Pindar and Sophocles.

Since Heidegger takes Greek tragedy to be the "highest poetry," and since he also holds that Hölderlin's work is inspired, in its entirety (and particularly in its hymnic aspect) by the first *stasimon* of Sophocles's *Antigone* (which he describes as the "heartpiece" and "source" of Hölderlin's hymnic work),[28] he gives prominence to Sophocles over Pindar. He undertakes a second reading of the choral ode, in which he develops the complex ambiguities of the "fundamental word," *to deinon*, while seeking, at the same time, "the original and *ess*ential unity" of its opposed significations (which are taken to attest to the contrariety of truth and *ess*ential untruth). The oppositional structure in terms of which Heidegger understands *to deinon* may be diagrammed as follows:

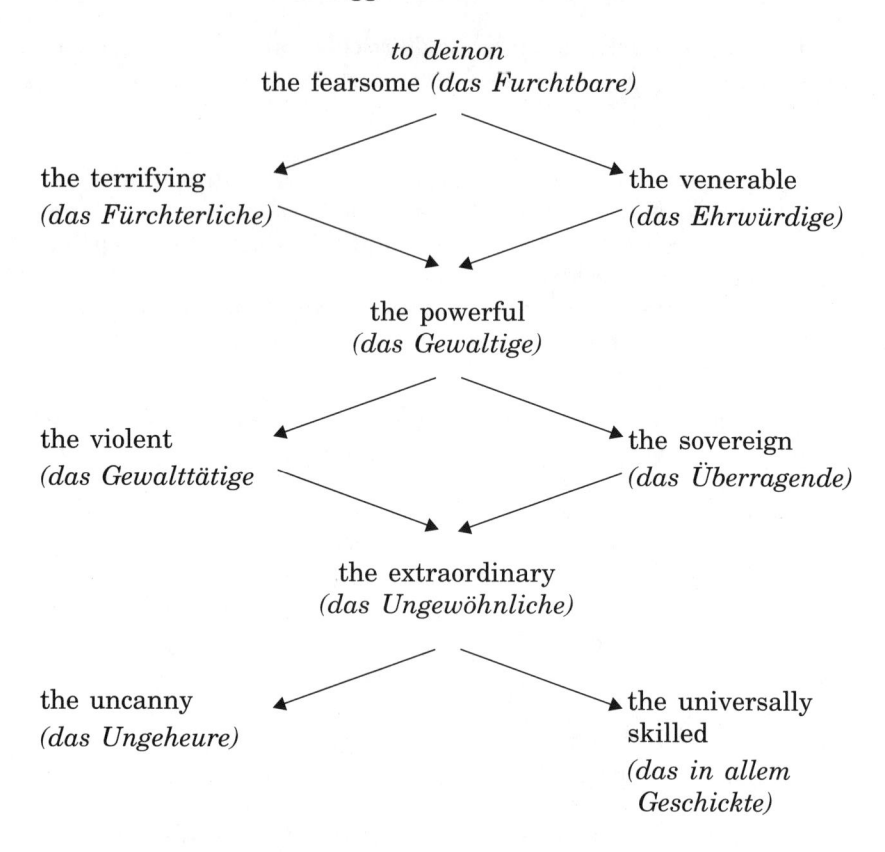

```
                        to deinon
                the fearsome (das Furchtbare)
                               ╱  ╲
   the terrifying  ◀──────          ──────▶ the venerable
   (das Fürchterliche)                      (das Ehrwürdige)
                               ╲  ╱
                        the powerful
                        (das Gewaltige)
                               ╱  ╲
   the violent    ◀──────          ──────▶ the sovereign
   (das Gewalttätige)                      (das Überragende)
                               ╲  ╱
                        the extraordinary
                        (das Ungewöhnliche)
                               ╱  ╲
   the uncanny    ◀──────          ──────▶ the universally
   (das Ungeheure)                         skilled
                                           (das in allem
                                            Geschickte)
```

Apart from rendering *to deinon* as "the fearsome," Heidegger translates it, in a more fundamental sense, as "the unhomelike" *(das Unheimische)*. He defends this translation as "more truthful" than a literally correct translation (including Hölderlin's "the uncanny"), in that it indicates, for him, what underlies the term's opposed significations as their hidden unity. "The unhomelike" is here a name for being's enigma.

Among the opposed significations of *to deinon* (for which Heidegger gives no Greek terms), "the universally skilled" needs some elucidation. Heidegger comments that the skillful mastery at issue is extraordinary *(deinon)* in that it admits nothing which exceeds its own capacities, so that it insists inflexibly on reducing all things to a common denominator, putting them into a position of mastery. *To deinon* as "the universally skilled" is evidently a figure of technicity and of its reductive posit or reductive totalization.

Although Heidegger's second reading of the *Antigone* remains focused on the first *stasimon*, he now embeds the latter in the tragedy as a whole, with particular concern for the figure of Antigone and the *ess*ential character of the *polis*. The tragic conflict is no longer played out between *technē* and *dikē*, but rather between two modalities of homelessness and homecoming; and, in keeping with this shift, the entire rhetoric has changed from a rhetoric of power to a rhetoric of alienation. Homelessness or homecoming characterize the human being which is now the locus of contrariety.

In the first, but improper, modality of homecoming, the human being seeks its abode among beings in their familiar and fully interpretable interrelationships, rejecting any concern with being's enigma as pointless and incomprehensible. Although such occlusion of being (which is characteristic of technicity) already attests to an inchoate awareness of being, it constitutes an *ess*ential homelessness that leads man inexorably "to nothingness" or to nihilistic despair. Heidegger's analysis rests here on his idiosyncratic translation of verses 360–362 of the *Antigone*, which read:

παντοπόρος · ἄπορος ἐπ' οὐδὲν ἔρχεται
τὸ μέλλον · Ἅιδα μόνον
φεῦξιν οὐκ ἐπεύξεται,

Heidegger translates:

Überall hinausfahrend unterwegs erfahrungslos ohne Ausweg kommt er zum Nichts.
Dem einzigen Andrang vermag er, dem Tod,
durch keine Flucht je zu wehren.[29]

Everywhere journeying on his way inexperienced without recourse he comes to nothingness.
Solely the rush upon him of death
he cannot ever fend off through any escape.

Even in his quotation of the Greek, Heidegger ignores the semicolon that separates παντοπόρος from ἄπορος (as he also ignores the semicolon between ὑψίπολις and ἄπολις in verse 370). The punctuation and context indicate that παντοπόρος ("all-resourceful") belongs, despite its artful juxtaposition to ἄπορος ("without recourse"), to the preceding sentence which describes man's resourcefulness as a city-dweller. A fairly literal translation of the Sophoclean verses would read as follows:

all-resourceful; without recourse he comes to nothing
that may befall him. Solely from death
he will not devise any escape.

Heidegger's transformative translation enables him to construe the verses as pointing toward nihilism (the "nothingness" toward which man is headed) as the form of alienation inherent in technicity. This alienation masks itself as a being at home in the world, notwithstanding the disruption of death.

The second modality of homecoming, by contrast, seeks its abode in being itself. It incurs therefore an estrangement from familiar patterns of world-construal and puts one at risk of losing one's home in the *polis*. Heidegger takes Antigone to exemplify this second modality of homecoming with its attendant estrangement. She reveals the "awe-inspiring" potential of the human being in that she takes as her supreme and guiding principle *(archē)* that which can in no way be governed, or harnessed to legitimize governance, and which is therefore an-archic. She is not a figure of exemplary action but, so to speak, of exemplary exposure. Greek tragedy, Heidegger remarks in this context, is not essentially a drama of human action but already "begins with perdition."[30] Antigone carries to an extreme one of the two *ess*ential human possibilities conjoined in the contrariety *(Gegenwendigkeit)* of *to deinon*: she renounces earthly concerns and attachments for the sake of an ontological passion that leads to her expulsion, not only from her native city, but, so to speak, from the lighted domain of the human lifeworld. She must abandon these for the darkness of entombment and for entering the "sightless" realm of the dead. Heidegger, however, does not develop the Sophoclean contrast between the "golden eye of day" and the darkness of Hades, but (in keeping with his tropology of homecoming), the figure of the (goddess of the) hearth, Hestia, on the basis of Sophocles's single mention of *parestios* ("sharer of the hearth") in verse 372. Antigone is, on his reading, banished from the hearth (in the sense of her home in the *polis*) because, like Hestia in the *Phaedrus* (247a2), she insists on remaining at the hearth, understood as a figure of being's enigma. Heidegger comments:

[W]hat Antigone is determined *(bestimmt)* by is that which, first of all, gives to the honoring of the dead and to the prerogative of blood its ground and necessity . . . The belonging to death and to blood which characterize the human being alone is itself determined, first of all, by the human being's relation to death itself.[31]

These remarks, with their disturbing echo of the political rhetoric of "blood" (in inevitable conjunction with death), do not succeed in showing how her commitment to giving burial to her brother Polynices is in any way mandated or called for by her homecoming to being's "hearth." Birth and death are, to be sure, the trace of the ontological mystery in moral life; but honoring the trace does not imply a willingness to sacrifice one's own life (and, as emphasized in Antigone's case, the lives of future children and generations) for the sake of burying a corpse. Such is the standpoint of Ismene (often misinterpreted as cowardice):[32] she shows herself ready to give her life out of sisterly love for Antigone (who spurns her), but not for the dead.

Antigone herself shows her awareness of the excessive character of her response to Creon's deluded pursuit of enmity beyond death: she would not have done what she did for Polynices for either husband or child, these being in a certain sense replaceable (I am accepting verses 905–912, offensive to and challenged by some interpreters, as genuine). Her passion for the family dead (or "warm heart for the cold," as Ismene calls it) is not a matter of "blood" (which a child would certainly share), or of obedience to divine law (as she earlier presents it). Neither is it a commitment to being's enigma. It is rather her singular response, inexplicable in terms of any hegemonic principles, to her particular situation as a child of the doomed house of Laius, daughter of Oedipus and Jocasta, on whom (as the elder daughter) has already fallen the womanly task of burying her parents and her other brother and on whom, as she indicates in her opening address to Ismene, the burden of shame imposed by the deeds of Oedipus, rests heavily. Whereas Ismene advocates being sensible, Antigone responds and acts eccentrically, out of her difference and her passion for those with whom birth, fate, and love have joined her and whose importance, for her, overrides both the claims of the *polis* and the claims of erotic love (which, in its generativity, and in the open-endedness of desire, is forward-looking). *Her difference cannot be subsumed under some aspect of the ontological Differing*, or her singularity construed in terms of the binary (if ambiguous) opposition between two modalities of estrangement and homecoming. Antigone envisages no homecoming but remarks (and her remark is mockingly echoed by Creon) that she is *everywhere* a stranger, among the living no less than among the dead (verses 850–852, 868, 890). For Heidegger, however, the footfall of the stranger always approaches a withheld beginning.[33]

Heidegger *essentializes* not only Antigone's action, but also the *polis*, which he elevates to the historical archetype of the political. He is careful to distinguish his own *esse*ntializing moves from contemporary claims—subservient to the structure of power—that the Greeks thought "everything" politically and were therefore "pure National Socialists" before the letter.[34] Against such historico-political opportunism, he argues that there is no approach, from the political in the modern sense, to the *polis*, but that conversely the *polis* determines the political. The thinking that accords to the *polis* the dignity of calling it into question thinks at once "more Greekly" than the Greeks and "more Germanically" than Germany's thinkers.

Heidegger, however, thinks the *polis* ontologically and aletheically, rather than in terms of pluralistic *praxis*. It constitutes, for him, the singular pivot and gathering pole *(polos)* around which beings gather to attain to their presencing *(pelein)*. As such, it is also the "stead" and "state" *(Stätte, status, Staat)* of a human-historical abiding in the midst of beings as a whole. As an aletheic configuration within the history of being, it presupposes that the human being already stand within the "opening" or disclosedness of being.

Appropriating Hölderlin's analysis of the complementary tension between Oriental Greece and Hesperian civilization, he characterizes the *polis* as the Greek accomplishment of a "sober self-grasping" that is not born of Greece's "ownmost" inspiration, but of its initial movement toward its other, the Hesperian (and specifically Germanic) gift for lucidity and order. In understanding the *polis* as the quasi-dialectical self-alienation of the Greek spirit, partaking of both the Greek and the Germanic ownmost inspirations, he projects it as the exemplary figure of the political, to be appropriated for Germany's future.

Although the *polos* that gathers un-concealment into a historical configuration of presencing is, for Heidegger, always singular, the Greek *polis* not only exhibits the bipolarity of its Oriental/Greek and Hesperian/Germanic inspirations, but is also rent by the two modalities of estrangement and homecoming. It spurs man at once toward self-exaltation in oblivion of the enigma and allows him to accomplish a true homecoming to the enigma.

Since the Greek *polis* constitutes a shelter from "the fire from heaven," it cannot tolerate a passion for the fire (the unhomelike) and will outcast one who is so impassioned. As concerns Antigone (the figure of such a passion), Heidegger disregards the fact that, as a woman, she is not a fullfledged citizen of the *polis* but is privatized from the outset (and rebels against Creon by asserting the very claims of her privatization). As a further gesture of interpretive violence, he also ignores the fact that verses 368–372 of the first *stasimon*—verses that can be seen, in retrospect, to characterize Creon as one who espouses what is ignoble "out of sheer daring,"—are spoken without reference to a specific person. By translating "the ignoble" *(to me kalon)* as "that which lacks being" *(das Unseiende)*, Heidegger further supports his appropriation of these verses for his schema of the two modalities of homecoming. He envisages a future political and spiritual configuration, born of a return to the Greek fire from out of the Hesperian/Germanic spirit of lucidity and order. Unlike the Greek *polis*, this new configuration, having accomplished not merely a necessary estrangement from its "ownmost" inspiration, but also a return from that estrangement, will be able to expose itself to the fire of ontological passion without threat to its own integrity. Through consummating this passion, it will be able to withstand the challenge of technological totalization. Heidegger goes so far as to suggest that Germany might yet outdo Greece in the latter's proper domain of "the fire from heaven" and institute a dwelling place for the gods "to which the Greek temples no longer come close."[35] He conflates the character and "law" of history with the "single history of the Germans," ignoring the multifarious complexity of history and civilizations.

What is particularly disturbing is his willingness to countenance violence and devastation as the unavoidable but in*ess*ential shadow-side of a supposedly salutary historical transition, revealed as such to an intellectual and spiritual elite:

> We stand precisely at the beginning of historiality proper, which is to say, of acting within the *ess*ential, out of being able to await the sending of the own. To be able to wait is to stand, having already jumped ahead, within the indestructible to whose neighborhood devastation belongs as does mountain to valley.[36]

The bland analogy between historical necessity and the relationship of mountain to valley recalls to any philosophically trained ear Descartes's recourse to this figure in support of his version of the *a priori* theistic argument in the Fifth Meditation. The analogy limps conspicuously, since a mountain could conceivably rise from a flat plain. To harness such a limping analogy is not to make a convincing argument, but to hide behind the reassuring front of classical Rationalism and the metaphysical tradition, even though these are otherwise criticized and repudiated. As a result, violence and devastation are legitimated by a sleight of hand, rather than analyzed or defended by arguments one could critically engage with.

Polemic Being and the Question of Singularization

In Heidegger's 1935 reading of the *Antigone, technē* is the creative human enactment of power that challenges the enigma forth into determinate, but necessarily inadequate, form. *Technē*, as oriented toward a singular creation that, in its shortfall and shattering, reveals the Differing as being's over-whelming sway, contrasts with technicity as Heidegger later thinks it, given that technicity constrains all beings to show themselves in-differently as an amorphous posit *(Bestand)* at man's disposal.[37] Heidegger, to be sure, never assimilates Greek *technē* to technicity (notwithstanding their *esse*ntial connection), since he understands the former as differential, and the latter as totalizing. However, the Promethean and tragic conception of *technē* as the creation of a unique work (especially, as indicated by the third strophe of the Sophoclean *stasimon*, a work of statecraft), is not sustained in Heidegger's thought of the 1940s and beyond.

What enables him, in the earlier reading, to sustain a connection to the tragedy is his understanding of *technē* as fundamentally a modality of knowing, given that both Antigone and Creon lay claim to a certain knowledge concerning law and justice. This understanding allows him to rejoin Reinhardt's reading of *Antigone* as a drama of being and semblance, while also effacing the Aristotelian distinction between *theōria, praxis,* and *poiēsis* as nonassimilable modalities of apprehending truth *(alētheuein)*. His non-Aristotelian understanding of knowing as an exercise of power (a creative contestation of being's over-power) brings his thought into an obscure complicity with the modern notion—datable at least to Francis Bacon—that knowledge is scientific-technological power. He sets himself apart from this equation of knowledge with power chiefly through his emphasis on the tragic moment of shattering, and on historiality as a revealment of the Differing through the violent destruction of the works of man (without which, of course, no such revealment could take place). The double blind, so to speak, which calls both for the work and for its shattering (along with the perishing of the creator), is the tragic character of finite, historicized, disclosure.

In the Ister-hymn lecture course, Heidegger's focus has shifted from *man* as the Promethean challenger to the onto-historical role of privileged *peoples*. In keeping with this shift, the *polis* is now shown as the supreme and encompassing creation which not only prescribes the meaning of the political but constitutes the site—the emplacement and disclosive structure—of a significant form of human historical existence. The tragic conflict between man the creator and being's over-power is rethought in terms of the polemic (and therefore tragic) character of being itself, explored initially through the Heraclitean and Platonic figure of *hestia* as the hearth-fire, the source of discordant illuminations, ambiguities, and reversals. As the site of un-concealment responsive to being's enigma, the *polis* itself is *esse*ntially polemic; for, although it is intrinsically aletheic, it repudiates an un-concealment of being's enigma (that which affects the circle of the hearth with strangeness) and outcasts from its own hearth one who seeks to abide in the proximity of *hestia*. A similar "polemics" characterizes *technē* in its entirety, conjoining the possibilities of aletheic revealment and in-different totalization, the poles of art and technicity and, more fundamentally, of "danger" and "saving."[38]

The polemic structure of *polis* and *technē* in their relation to the polemic character of being is not simply outlined synchronically, but is brought together with a diachronic thought of historiality inspired by Hölderlin. Instead of the creative work's being historicized by being undone, the work is thought of as intrinsically historial (bound to a historical site of disclosure), and as situated within an *essen*tial history that holds out the promise (or projects the mirage) of a surpassing retrieval of ancient Greece for the German-Occidental future, accomplished by the Heideggerian triad of creators—the poets, thinkers, and statesmen. Antigone has no place in this (tacitly gendered) triad; but she epitomizes, for Heidegger, the Greek disclosive relationship to the being of beings and stands therefore, it would seem, in a symbolic relationship to Hölderlin's Germania. This relationship is probably the reason why Heidegger neglects all the other *dramatis personae* of the tragedy, even Teiresias, to whose dramatic role Hölderlin gives special prominence.[39]

Although Heidegger's second reading of the tragedy, with its shift from man the challenger to man as a figure of exposure (symbolized, in a quite traditional way, by the stranger and outcast), is somewhat more attentive to the Sophoclean text than the first, it still evinces the creative violence of his appropriation by its fragmentation of the text, its highly idiosyncratic translations, and its unwillingness to follow out complex and pervasive textual articulations, such as the echoing tehmatizations of *to deinon* that are not confined to the first *stasimon*.[40] The underlying question—a question which cannot be pursued here—concerns the hidden exigency that constrains his thought to seek a certain esoteric "legitimation" through violently (if brilliantly) deformative readings of canonical philosophical and poetic texts, while disguising rather than countenancing the deformation. It concerns, in other words, the reason why Heidegger's thought is constrained to articulate itself through appropriations, rather than straightforwardly and in a genuinely dialogical manner.

As concerns the *Antigone*, his single-minded focus on the human being's relation, through *technē* and *poiēsis*, to being's enigma (a focus that obviates human difference) is in a strange complicity with the single-minded obsessions that constrain the thought of both Antigone and Creon, leading to their undoing. Though different in provenance and clashing in their expression, their obsessions are comparable in that they negate the complexity and fluidity of experience (a circumstance Sophocles calls attention to by his thematization of rigidity, in relation to erotic passion and Dionysian frenzy, in the fourth *stasimon*). Heidegger's single-minded focus not only effaces human singularity but valorizes (with an echo of Plato's discussions of the relationship of the philosopher to the *polis*) the estrangement from the political community experienced by one who heeds being's enigma. The human being who is *deinotaton* is not, for Heidegger, political in any meaningful sense, but is estranged either by towering "high above the *polis*" (his questionable translation of *hypsipolis*) or being "bereft of *polis*." The structure of his thinking is dichotomous in that he juxtaposes the two modalities of homecoming with their attendant estrangements (while disguising the dichotomy by the ambivalence of the key notions of homecoming, estrangement, and *hestia*), never countenancing the possibility of conjoining ontological insight with sociopolitical concern and efficacy, or with living responsively and responsibly in a world in which sentient beings are not just exposed to being, but, first of all, to each other.

If Heidegger, as Schürmann brilliantly argues, thinks "the origin of all normativity in the conflictual event" in thinking the polemic and tragic character of being, he remains unable to conjoin this thought with a recognition of the transgressive singular. His own thought remains caught up in ambiguity and does not accomplish what Schürmann describes as the subversion of hegemonic constructs and "univocally binding phantasms."[41]

It is unlikely that this failure is merely "ontic" or personal, and more likely that it is structural, tied up with the entire project of approaching the singular through a certain construal or the origin, whether as univocal or as polemic. To posit the origin as conflictual is not convertible, as Schürmann takes it to be, with a *kenōsis* or emptying out of the origin that would truly release (but not absolutize) the compelling presencing and multiplicity of the singular.

The final question to be asked here is whether Hölderlin's retrieval of Greek tragedy, with which Heidegger's thought remains engaged, offers an insight into tragic singularization that, although perhaps disregarded by Heidegger, can open up a new and significant perspective.

Hölderlin's Thought of Originary Finitude

Heidegger's reading of the first *stasimon* is indebted to Hölderlin's translation of it, which Bernhard Böschenstein characterizes as a misconstrual of the Greek text, insofar as the latter shows (particularly in the second part of Hölderlin's two-part division of the *stasimon*) "a structure open in both direction, 'now for ill, now for good', which Hölderlin has largely extirpated."[42] Like Heidegger, Hölderlin regards the juxtaposition *pantoporos; aporos* as the pivot of the ode's thought and poetic structure, so that, as Böschenstein puts it, once the negative cue 'without resource' *[aporos]* has been given, it is followed almost exclusively by further negatives, in sharp contrast to Sophocles."[43] These negatives include, as for Heidegger, the un-Sophoclean pronouncement that man "comes to nothing."

Hölderlin's concern, however, is not with the problematic of *technē* or technicity, but with singularizing differentiation. Mortality is not, for him, as it is for Schürmann, the pull of subversive singularization, in polemic relationship to the "polymorphous integrative violence" of natality.[44] It is rather the source of a "passion for death" *(Todeslust)* that draws human beings and entire peoples into the "aorgic" element, the fiery world of the dead, effacing finite differentiation. As a tragic fault or *nefas*, this passion requires a counterweight to the unthinkable, an affirmation of finitude that resists the devastating pull into the boundless. This order or logic is manifest both as poetic articulation (the calculable law or *Kalkül* that Hölderlin admires in the Greek poets and seeks to foster among the moderns), and in history, as the interrelation of the Greek and Hesperian inspirations. The parallel illuminates his own intense preoccupation, particularly during his second Homburg period, with what Gerhard Kurz calls "a formal conception and explication of aesthetic relationships, to the point of mathematical and geometrical models."[45] These relationships are not emphasized and explored for their own sakes, but for their indispensability to the incalculable and animating sense or spirit. In them, the "sign," whether human or linguistic, shows both its surpassing importance and its weakness. Lawrence Ryan speculates that, for the late Hölderlin, poetic language itself is fundamentally tragic in virtue of this paradox of strength and weakness.[46]

The stress, for Hölderlin, is not on sheer negativity, but on singularization which does not entail fragmentation but can sustain and enhance a living unity. Through the moment of rupture, the singularized constitutents acquire autonomy and, even in their weakness, resist totalization, while entering into contexts of phenomenalization. In Schürmann's terminology (which derives from Hannah Arendt's), ultimate difference reveals itself as bound to natality, rather than as introduced by the subversive trait of mortality. Schürmann himself, along with Heidegger, emphasizes mortality.

Hölderlin regards Sophocles's *Oedipus Tyrannos* and *Antigone* as tragedies of historical transition, in that they show the disintegration of previously univocal and unquestioningly accepted "truths" or constructs into a multiplicity of baffling perspectives and names—a disintegration which spells the collapse of an established hegemonic order. Oedipus, as a figure of excess, is caught up in the disruption of the Greek ideal of beauty as "the One at variance with itself," thematized by Hölderlin in *Hyperion*.[47] He cannot hold his own and suffers a devastating self-estrangement, symbolized, in the tragedy, by his capitulation to the language of servants, and by his self-blinding. Antigone, however, is a more Hesperian figure who, even in her undoing, achieves a "firm abiding before the changing time" through her singularizing self-consciousness.[48] A singularity fully conscious of itself is not bound to hegemonic constructs; its possible interrelations and contextualizations are multiple, changing, and imprevisible. Heidegger neglects this Hölderlinian emphasis on self-consciousness since any such preoccupation is, for him, part and parcel of the humanism and subjectivism of modern thought, which he criticizes.

Although, for Hölderlin, the transition from the Greek ideal to Hesperian consciousness is inevitably tragic, provoking noble individuals to excess, and casting divinity as the sheer power of annihilation, he envisages a "form of reason," developed through tragedy, that can establish itself, in "a more humane time," as an enlightened and divinely sanctioned consensus.[49] He points out that this form of reason is inherently political, mandating a "republican" political organization, in which individual autonomy does not fracture the socio-political organization.[50] The archaic ideal of the One at variance with itself (which is still valorized in *Hyperion*) cannot, by contrast, resist totalization, since the One incorporates the singular and blunts its transgressive force. Tragedy, as the transition from the One in discordance with itself (the polemic origin) to the changing contextualization of singularities is, for Hölderlin, a historical phenomenon, rather than attesting to the very character of phenomenalization. If indeed he conceives of poetic language as inherently tragic, this conception may reflect the precariousness of poetic articulation and the proximity of the Hölderlinian poet to the Greek tragic heroes as figures of excess, rather than tragedy's originary status. Hölderlin's concern for the singular that enters into changing configurations, together with his emphasis on phenomenalization rather than mortality, constitutes a significant challenge to Heidegger's thought on tragedy. Where the singular has to hold its own against absolutizing passions and claims, originary discordance is unlikely to sustain it, since it has already let it be annexed by a "polemics" of presencing, rather than allowing it to show itself as a finite origin that repudiates subsumption, but that is exposed to the fatefulness inherent in phenomenalization. In Greek tragedy, as Hölderlin perceives, the fatefulness that singularizes and renders the singular obtrusive disrupts the whole (by whatever name it may be called) that seeks to integrate subversion and difference.

Notes

1. "'Only a God Can Save Us:' The *Spiegel* Interview (1966)," trans. Wm. J. Richardson, S. J., in Thomas Sheehan, ed., *Heidegger: The Man and the Thinker* (Chicago: Precedent Publishing, Inc., 1981), 45–67 (63).

2. See Hugo Ott's discussion in *Martin Heidegger: Uterwegs zu seiner Biographie* (Frankfurt/New York: Campus Verlag, 1988), 131f. Compare also Ott's interesting treatment of Heidegger's first publication of the 1936 lecture, "Hölderlin and the *Ess*ence of Poetry," in the National Socialist periodical, *Das innere Reich*, on p. 133.

3. On the *Spiegel* Interview, see Note 1. The phrase "the inner truth and greatness of the (National Socialist) movement" is taken from

M. Heidegger, *Einführung in die Metaphysik*, 4th ed. (Tübingen: Niemeyer, 1976), 152.

4. M. Heidegger, "Platons Lehre von der Wahrheit," *Wegmarken* (Frankfurt a.M.: Klostermann, 1967), 109–144.

5. Jacques Taminiaux, "The Origin of 'The Origin of the Work of Art,'" in *Poetics, Speculation, and Judgment: The Shadow of the Work of Art from Kant to Phenomenology*, trans. and ed. by Michael Gendre (Albany: SUNY Press, 1993), 153–170. Compare M. Heidegger, *Die Selbstbehauptung der deutschen Universitat: Rede gehalten bei der feierlichen Übernahme des Rektorats der universität Freiburg im Breisgau am 27.5.1933* (Breslau: Korn, 1934). English translation by Karsten Harries, "The Self-Assertion of the German University; Address Delivered on the Solemn Assumption of the Rectorate of the University Freiburg," *Review of Metaphysics* 38 (March, 1985), 467–480.

6. See, for instance, Heidegger's lecture course on Hölderlin's hymn "Andenken," GA 52, 3.

7. M. Heidegger, *Hölderlins Hymnen "Germanien" und "Der Rhein,"* GA 39.

8. M. Heidegger, *Hölderlins Hymne "Der Ister,"* GA 53.

9. Compare Steven Davis, "The Path of a Thinking, Poetizing, Building: The Strange Uncanniness of Human Being on Earth," in Ladelle McWhorter, ed., *Heidegger and the Earth* (Kirksville, MO: The Thomas Jefferson University Press, 1992), 37–51; and William McNeill, "Porosity, Violence, and the Question of Politics," in M. Brainard, D. Jacobs, and R. Lee, eds., "Heidegger and the Political," *The Graduate Faculty Philosophy Journal* 14:2–15:1 (1991), 183–212. For a discussion of Heidegger's thematizations of *dikē* (without reference to his readings of Sophocles), see also Robert Bernasconi, *Heidegger in question: The Art of Existing* (Atlantic Highlands: Humanities Press, 1993), ch. 3.

10. Martha C. Nussbaum, *The Fragility of Goodness: Luck and Ethics in Greek Tragedy and Philosophy* (Cambridge: Cambridge University Press, 1986).

11. For a discussion, see Michael E. Zimmerman, *Heidegger's Concept of Modernity: Technology, Politics, Art* (Bloomington: Indiana University Press, 1990), chs. 4–6.

12. EM, 110. Translations from the German and Greek are the present author's.

13. EM, 62, 69; GA 53, 73.

14. See Nussbaum, *Fragility*, 72f.

15. EM, 110.

16. Compare Nussbaum, *Fragility*, 52f.

17. EM, 116–120.

18. M. Heidegger, "Der Ursprung des Kunstwerkes," *Holzwege*, 4th ed. (Frankfurt a.M.: Klostermann, 1963), 7–68. For discussion of the three versions of the essay/lecture, which have only recently become available, see J. Taminiaux, "The Origin of 'The Origin of the Work of Art,'" and R. Bernasconi, "The Greatness of the Work of Art," in *Heidegger in Question*, 99–116.

19. *Selbstbehauptung*, 7–13; SA, 471–474.
20. EM, 126.
21. EM, 125.
22. Karl Reinhardt, *Sophokles*, 3rd ed. (Frankfurt, a.M., 1947). See also his "Hölderlin und Sophokles," in A. Kelletat, ed., *Hölderlin: Beiträge zu seinem Verständnis in unserem Jahrhundert* (Tubingen, [1951], 1961).
23. Compare *Antigone*, verses 519–521. References are given to R. D. Dawe, ed., *Sophoclis Tragoediae*, vol. II; "Biblioteca Scriptorum Graecorum et Romanorum Teubneriana" (Leipzig: Teubner, 1985 [1979]).
24. Reiner Schürmann, "Ultimate Double Binds," *The Graduate Faculty Philosophy Journal* 14:2–15:1 (1991), 213–236.
25. Friedrich Hölderlin, "Der Ister," in Friedrich Beissner, ed., *Hölderlin, Sämtliche Werke, Grosse Stuttgarter Ausgabe* (Stuttgart: Kohlhammer, 1946–1957). This edition will be referred to as SA.
26. GA 53, 9.
27. See M. Heidegger, Hölderlins Hymnen "Germanien" und "Der Rhein," GA 39.
28. GA 53, 63, 73.
29. GA 53, 71–74.
30. GA 53, 128.
31. GA 53, 147.
32. Compare, for instance, Luce Irigaray's portrayal of Ismene in *Speculum of the Other Woman*, Gillian C. Gill, trans. (Ithaca: Cornell University Press, 1974), 217f.
33. See M. Heidegger, "Die Sprache im Gedicht," *Unterwegs zur Sprache*, 5th ed. (Pfullingen: Neske, 1975), 35–82. See also Véronique M. Fóti, *Heidegger and the Poets: Poiēsis, Sophia, Technē* (Atlantic Highlands: Humanities Press, 1992), ch. 2.
34. GA 53, 98.
35. GA 53, 155.
36. GA 53, 68.
37. Compare M. Heidegger, "Die Frage nach der Technik," *Vorträge und Aufsätze*, 3rd ed. (Pfullingen: Neske, 1967) vol. I, 5–36.
38. These notions are thematized in "Die Frage nach der Technik."
39. Friedrich Hölderlin, "Anmerkungen zum Oedipus," and "Anmerkungen zur Antigonae," SA 5, 195–202, and 265–272. Teiresias introduces, for Hölderlin, the *caesura* or "counter-rhythmic interruption" and is therefore crucial to the (dissimilar) poetic structure of the two tragedies.
40. See Nussbaum's discussion in *Fragility*, 62, 78f. See also her comments on reading Greek tragedy, 68f.
41. "Ultimate Double Binds," 225.
42. Bernhard Böschenstein, "Gott und Mensch in den Chorliedern der Hölderlinschen *Antigone*: Eine Skizze," in Christoph Jamme and Otto Pöggeler, eds., *Jenseits des Idealismus: Hölderlins letzte Homburger Jahre (1804–1806)* (Bonn: Bouvier, 1988), 123–138.
43. "Gott und Mensch," 125.

44. "Ultimate Double Binds," 219. Schürmann stresses, throughout his article, the dissymmetry between natality and mortality as "the singularization to come." This is an important point of his analysis; and it recalls Hölderlin's insistence (discussed by Ryan; see note 49, below) that the Hellenic/Hesperian relationship is not to be regarded as a "pretty" symmetry.

45. Gerhard Kurz, "Poetische Logik: Zu Hölderlins 'Anmerkungen' zu 'Oedipus' und 'Antigonae,'" *Jenseits des Idealismus*, 83–101 (92f).

46. Lawrence Ryan, "Hölderlins Antigone: 'Wie es vom griechischen zum hesperischen geht,'" *Jenseits des Idealismus*, 103–121 (115).

47. Hölderlin, *Hyperion*, SA.

48. "Anmerkungen zur Antigonae," 268f.

49. "Anmerkungen zur Antigonae," 270.

50. "Anmerkungen zur Antigonae," 272.

Chapter 9

Heidegger's Turn to *Germanien*— A Sigetic Venture

Wilhelm S. Wurzer

Heidegger's turn to poetry, specifically Hölderlin's, belongs necessarily to a countermetaphysical itinerary. Indeed, poetry participates in philosophy's *other* beginning, a radical departure from the specular reflexivity of a *first* beginning in which being is merely the mimetic effect of the principle of sufficient reason. Paradoxically, a creative historical surge uncovers the onto-eidetic countenance that veils metaphysics. Poetry thereby frees thinking from the "weariness" of dialectical discourse, that pale consciousness of a bi-millennial hermeneutic.

The de-cision to "step back" to philosophy's *first* language, the *logos*, reveals a linguistic order which expressly conceals the history of being *(Seyn)*. This order's renunciation of the poetic moment in philosophy is, therefore, intimately connected with the genealogy of the abandonment of being. Without poetic echoing, philosophy's possibilities consist in a mere process of argumentation. While metaphysics lets the *argument* be the conversation, the conversation turns into disputations, enframing thinking within the "noise" *(argutus)* of an antipoetic language.[1] As *other* language, poetry exceeds the disputations of metaphysical self-certainty, opening a historical terrain in which thinking, far from becoming a restful contemplation, dwells freely and dynamically.

Heidegger concedes that only poetry can heal the wound of philosophy, the tragic end of the dialectical process, the unavoidable departure of the gods. Philosophy alone cannot withstand the assault *(Angriff)* on human freedom by the contemporary political message with its heavy-handed symbolism. Nor can it cope with the singular abandoment of being operative in the political corrosion of language. For Heidegger, the vivid discourse of Nazi propaganda can only be surmounted by the poetic power of Hölderlin's words. Thus, the poem *Germanien* poses the question Germany failed to raise in the 1930s: "But do we know, *who we are*?"[2]

Can philosophy respond adequately to this question? Can it still engage in critique, in sudden changes of discursive constellations? While philosophy provides critiques of alienation, critique is itself *alienating* inasmuch as it invariably presumes to correct precisely what needs to be called into question—a negative interpretation of beings sustained without pointing to the event of being *(Seyn)*. The erosion of the power of the word cannot be discerned by a philosophy that does not attend to poetic difference in words. "The word," Heidegger writes, "has merely become an intense whipping up of a volume of sound with no regard for a sense of meaning."[3] To that extent language already marks the political extremities baring upon the fact of technology's disorder *(Ge-stell)*.

Seduced by a re-presentational grasping of beings, philosophy is helpless in confronting a general defrocking of language in an epoch that is "simultaneously a disguise for the growing emptiness" (GA 65, 123). Since the dialectical mode of constituting meaning belongs to a forgetting of being as being *(Seinsvergessenheit)*, an overcoming of nihilism is absurd. (GA 65, 129). Indeed, the abdication of goals and values becomes the condition for the possibility of "new values" based upon a mimetic repetition of the principle of exhaustion. The greatest nihilism is therefore still to come in pursuing the phantom of a pure aesthetic sensibility, and attempts to violate mimesis in the manner of "an organizational closing of one's eyes to getting rid of every human goal" (GA 65, 139). Heidegger insists that we can free ourselves from the uncanny play of falling into *Ge-stell's* disarray if we begin to listen to the unthought power of an originary promise. Notably, Hölderlin's poem *Germanien* assigns a new task to thought in the transition *(Übergang)* to this promise, the *other* beginning, signifying *how* the word is yet-to-be (genuinely historical) [GA 65, 129].

Germanien is not "Germany" but rather the state of the not-yet, the word to come, the art of *other* beginnings. In a letter to Christian Landauer (1801), Hölderlin announces his disregard for a politico-cultural reading of the state: "In the end it is indeed true that the less man experiences and knows about the state, no matter what its form may be, the greater his freedom will be."[4] In turn, *Germanien* is an open venture, a silent itinerary, a pure sigetic beginning, a strategy "to freely make use of what is one's own" *(der freie Gebrauch des Eigenen*, (HSW vi, 426).[5] To remain on familiar paths, to be swept away into common consciousness, to bypass the philosophical light shining into our window is what Hölderlin fears the most.[6] Poetry's task is to disrupt the authority of the prosaic in order to see the un-thought purity of a lighter coloration of thought. A pure interweaving of light and darkness, a sigetic chiaroscuro, the purely spoken rests altogether upon the poetic distance recognized in the difficult quest for *how* the word is yet-to-be. Hölderlin highlights the significance of this quest by digging into the expectations of spirit in the domain of a quite different questioning.

It is necessary, therefore, to focus briefly on one of Hölderlin's essays, "On the Operation of the Poetic Spirit."[7] Of particular interest is his reading of language as a poetic work of art linked to the theme of a radical disruption of spirit, a matter of the destitution of hermeneutical imitations. *Verfahrungsweise* in the essay's title, frequently translated as "operation or procedure," alludes to Hölderlin's complex unfolding of the ways in which the poetic spirit moves. In addition to "acting, behaving, proceeding," the verb, *verfahren*, may also mean "driving or traveling along," and within the mode of transport "to lose one's way," perhaps, even "to be on the wrong track." To lose one's direction, at least not to be certain of the way belongs very much to the poetic spirit's mode of operation *(Verfahrungsweise)*. However, thought's radical displacement is not a negative shift but one in which the text marks a sublime decision not to invoke, indeed, no longer to anticipate the stunning appearances of the ancient gods. Not unlike Hyperion, the poetic text strides along in variations of moods *(schreitet fort im Wechsel der Stimmungen)* [HSW, iv, 248], in which simultaneously one mood determines the other invariably bound to the law of striving forward *(Gesetz des Fortstrebens)* to purity *(das Reine)* without attaining a final destination. What is altogether pure is always already a poetic journeying, woven into the various moments of the poem's content. This means that the operation of the poetic spirit is the poem, casting hermeneutical shadows on the luminous images of Athenian gods.[8]

The poem, then, is in fact the river of "interpretations," the many infinite waves of thinking, called upon to flow into the Open, to write the word anew. What happens in the myriad avenues of manifesting spirit in language is simply a crossing over from a world of clamor to a thoroughly authentic or pure tracing of beings. The power of poetry lies, therefore, in a simultaneous intimacy and difference of the identical-differential *(harmonischentgegensezten)* forces manifesting a world of its own, "world in the world" (HSW iv, 250), a poetic state in spirit's *other* promise, *Germanien* scarcely free to be. In that terrain of journeying, spirit extends itself through being *(das Reine)* to beings *(der Rhein)* without remaining fixed in a single moment, yet always striding along *(fortschreiten)* in different tones *(Stimmungen)*, attuned to *infinite oneness* in which strife and harmony are inseparable. This poetic web of relations, the word's *own* world, a dynamic art of pure attunement, is ever open towards one and the other, bringing forth the beauty of life assumed to have gone astray.

Poetry for Hölderlin refracts the world, giving gratitude again *(den Dank wiederzubringen)* by infinitely displacing constellations of spirit and life. It demands a raising *(Erhebung)*, a lifting of oneself to "a pure re-ringing of the first life" *(zum reinen Wiederklang des ersten Lebens)* (HSW, iv, 263), the highest disruption of language. Hölderlin's poetic founding is neither a reflection of the principle of sufficient reason nor any another metaphysical grounding in lyrical form. As the *Operation* essay indicates, we are left, instead, not knowing exactly where we stand in the poetic mode of the sigetic venture. We do know, however, that language is a concealed entwining of being and beings, of the utterly pure and passionately impure. At the point of speculative sublimity, truth and illusion endure in a conflicting embrace *(widerstreitendes Verfahren)*. The word frees discourse from an abstract etherealization *(Vergeistigung)* of purity, de-signing the infinite beauty of how *Germanien* is yet-to-be.

Pointing to what is most distant and demanding, *Germanien* recedes from political haste and discourse, announcing the arrival of new gods. "The old gods are dead, the new emerge. For their arrival *Germanien* has a special message" (GA 39, 15). An innocent, young woman, Hölderlin's own image of *Germanien*, a language anterior to all languages, is hidden in the woods of silence far from the noise of urbanity and the state. While she speaks purely, traces of her origins fade in the midst of a country's early dawn. Withdrawn from ground, the poem, "upholding the abyss," speaks of a beautiful dream, unuttered, de-signing the path for things yet to come from afar. The message, the image, the poem, in short, *Germanien*, a different word, proclaims disarmament. A poetic dream

Heidegger's Turn to *Germanien*—A Sigetic Venture 191

in reason, *Germanien*, the historical power of imagination gives advice all around "to kings and peoples"—an untimely message for those seduced by the speculum of a people's army *(Volkssturm)*:

> O drink the morning breezes
> Until you are opened up
> And name what you see before you;
> No longer now the unspoken
> May remain a mystery
> Though long it has been veiled;
> For shame behooves us mortals
> And most of the time to speak thus
> Of gods indeed is wise.
> But where more superabundant than purest wellsprings
> The gold has become and the anger in Heaven earnest,
> For once between Day and Night must
> A truth be made manifest.
> Now circumscribe it threefold,
> Yet unuttered also, just as you found it,
> You who are innocent, let it remain.[9]

This stanza (and the entire poem) lies before the reader as if the hidden figure merely resolved to analyze and explain its content. But such a decision would be far from letting the poem speak and further still from letting poetry stand in its historical sphere of power *(im Machtbereich der Dichtung stehen)*. But how may a poem, in particular Hölderlin's, carry the reader away from the "great, *decisive* present" with its brutally frank speeches? How may a poem withstand the "realities" of *Dasein* immersed in the mediocrity of propaganda? Recalling an old German saying, "politics ruins the character," Heidegger, in the winter semester of 1934/35, gave special attention to a different kind of joining up *(einrucken)*, one which, as he concedes, borders on high treason: a joining up with the *other* power, arming a nation with the empire of the word. This poetic turn, a mode of stillness beyond political anticipations, reveals "things yet to come, joy-giving from the distance," quite simply, *Germanien*, the imaginal site out of which thought gives itself to think anew (HPF 401).

Heidegger proceeds in the unfamiliar course *(Verfahren)*, of *other* beginnings, underscoring that poetry is not the cultural expression or achievement of a people but rather *exposure to being (Ausgesetzheit dem Sein)* (GA 39, 36). "A poem is not a mere text charged with meaning but as a 'connected speech' *(Sprachgefüge)* it is a whirlwind which pulls us to some place or other" (GA 39, 36). No one knows exactly where or what *Germanien* is. Its disposition, a poetic whirlwind, a sigetic questioning, specifies a mysterious how in which "man is and yet is not."[10] Neither a literary phenomenon nor an aesthetic experience, poetry is "that event which has at its disposal the highest possibility of being human."[11] While it founds *(stiftet)* being through the word, it also provides an unyielding foundation *(feste Gründung)*, a "free donation" *(freie Schenkung)*, a gift *(Geschenk)*, paradoxically, man's most dangerous possession—language. "The poet is exposed to the lightning of the god" (EHD 44). In one poem, Hölderlin speaks of being struck by Apollo in a countermetaphysical distance from the optical model of Olympus. Indeed, it is the fate of the poet not only to fall from the prosaic terrain of the world but also from the overwhelming shining power of the gods. Standing *between* the splendor of vanished gods and the people, he founds in this *in-between* the enduring ground of history *(der tragende Grund der Geschichte)* (EHD 42). In effect, the poet emerges as the primordial historian, the bearer of an extraordinary gift—*das dichterische Wort* [the poetic word]— never having been realized, yet permanently guiding a historical people. By bringing the word to a people, the poet "thinks poetically out into the ground and center of being" (EHD 47).

What matters here is the intriguing question of *other* origins, a text in which the history of being opens up to the most dangerous possession, the poetic word, the silent pledge of language. Mortals take every risk in advancing toward the *how* of *other* beginnings: *how* thinking is yet-to-be in history, a post-political domain of art, a futural matter. Exceeding the dawn of dialectical reflection—the deformation of being by reason—the word disrupts the political-dialectical connection, dispelling the will in Western consciousness from its power as aesthetic imperative.

The Western aesthetic, for Heidegger, conceals the dominance of the political in philosophy's diverse discourses. He grants that the political is precisely the forgetting of the difference between being and beings, a forgetting that coincides with the control mechanisms of the metaphysical army of concepts. The pleasure derived from the reflective assault upon beings as a whole constitutes the very nature of aesthetics in general. More than a mere movement of modern genealogy, aesthetics belongs to the very history of metaphysics. In point of fact, it is the *first* beginning of philosophy, ever concealing the *other* beginning. As art of reason's management, it is what is thoroughly dialectical in the emergence of a political work. As art of the political within ontic-metaphysical relations of *Dasein*, it is the spirit of the will to power entangled in the Western history of reason. In short, it is reason's mimetic desire to dominate, to correct. Invariably discerning what is right and wrong, it masks the difference between the *political* and the *free*.

In his attempt to overcome aesthetics, Heidegger indicates the *intimacy* of art and history. And if we consider his claim that originary language is poetry as primordial essence of man's historicality, it is safe to say that art *is* history for Heidegger. This sameness, however, is not a dialectical identity but rather, what Hölderlin calls, a "unified strife" *(harmonischentgegesetztes)*. Within this strife, thinking's task is to prepare for the arrival of a pure site, a time yet to come, a historical play which lets the word be the *other* beginning of an authentic history of being. *Da-sein*, then, is historical insofar as its enduring ground is poetic conversation. We are primordially historical when we become master over the political speculum of modernity. To become master of *(Herr zu werden)* the political scene means to elevate the conflict of the word against the aesthetic politicization of beings in a poetic turn to being *(Seyn)*. This turn, "the decision about the de-cision" *(die Entscheidung uber die Entscheidung)*, is a resolve to be prepared *(Bereitschaft)* to stand in the pure realm of power, the historical domain of art. To prepare for the mastery of nihilism is not an abstract, trans-temporal operation but a historical commitment to *das Vaterland*. Here, Heidegger does not appeal to a specific national state but to the very site out of which thought gives itself purity. "This 'land of the father' is being itself" (GA 39, 121). As historical *Dasein* of a people this uncanny terrain reveals "the only authentic being" (GA 39, 121). What is possible *(das Mögliche)*, in fact, what is dis-covered in this pure terrain arises as the new power of history, the authority of a poetic nearness to thought and un-thought's own nearness to poetry.

In the poem *Germanien*, Heidegger reveals that the sigetic turn to spirit's authentic historical revolution is a message that cannot be read, a historicality without "politics," a thinking always already on the way to a countermetaphysical pledge. Hence the seminal attunement *(Grundstimmung)* of poetic difference entails "simultaneously being swept away *(entrüken)* to the gods and a stepping into *(einrücken)* the earth" (HHG 140). This distinct comportment toward language opens up a world in which being-in-the-world is bound to historical sublimity. Withdrawing from the political does not exclude the necessary founding of a state. However, such a founding is attuned to *(bestimmt)* "the three creative powers of historical Dasein—poetry, thought, and the creation of a state *(Staatsschaffen)"* (GA 39, 144). *Germanien*, therefore, signifies the arrival of a new state, the sublimity of the last god.

This poetic resolve to attune "the state," i.e., a people to the tonalities of "unmeasurable possibilities" is the authentic beginning of history. Accordingly, people and nations by themselves are too small to prepare the ways for the *other* beginning. The historical moment of the last god is open only to those great and hidden individuals who are able to grant the god who passes by the appropriate silence (GA 65, 414). Creating a state, then, is not a political operation per se but rather the sigetic resolve of thinkers who, in accordance with their de-cision to prepare for the arrival of the last god, experience the historical moment of "what comes to pass *(Ereignung)* in the turn, in which the truth of being becomes the being of truth" (GA 65, 415). The turn from an aesthetics of politics to the abyss of a purely poetic-historical site is seen by Heidegger as the "highest shape of refusal" (GA 65, 416). The refusal consists in a sigetic renunciation of the political altogether while manifesting concern for the historical power of the word. A strangely historical deed, the refusal belongs intimately to the very task of thinking. Advancing toward clearing and preparing for a different site, thinking frees philosophy from its end, the "irksome cunning" of everything small *(das Kleine)*. "But what is small desires only itself, that is, to be small" (GA 39, 146).[12] Reminiscent of Heidegger's allusion to the "public realm" *(Öffentlichkeit)* in *Being and Time*, what is called small in the Hölderlin lectures is "a levelling down of all possibilities of being."[13] Language is held a prisoner by the subtle authority of an essential *political* tendency of Dasein. The prevailing power of the inauthentic taste for the political "controls every way in which the world and Dasein get interpreted, and it is always right ... because it is insensitive to every difference of level and genuineness."[14] While poetry cannot extinguish the dominion of inauthenticity, it can keep the seductive power of political illusions under control. Indeed, it may even change the course of *Da-sein's* history by "strenghtening and enriching the seminal attunement as it begins to unfold in being opening up" (GA 39, 149).

Thus, the historical task of poetry throws *(zwingen)* beings as a whole into a new projection in which nature, history, and the gods are gathered together through the founding language *(Sagen)* of the poet. In this poetic struggle for the *other* beginning, "the poet experiences poetically a creative downfall *(Untergang)* of the prevailing truth of being" (GA 39, 150). There is no intention to overcome the flight of the gods, the destitution of western thought, the abandonment of being as if these were cultural delimitations. The staying away of being belongs to the historical truth of language, its very cleavage *(Zerklüftung,* GA 65, 236). In short, being *(Sein)* opens the poetic breast (Fr. *sein)* of history, showing the gap between the mortal and the divine, the political and the historical. While poetry names the holy beyond this gap, thinking sees this gap, the authentic-inauthentic rift, in light of a poetic naming of the holy.[15] What first emerges as an insurmountable division between the claims of political taste and the historical appropriation of the poetic word is, on Heidegger's view, "the *intimacy* with which opponents belong to each other" (HW 44/55).

The cleaving nature of language, therefore, reveals an important problematic in Heidegger's texts as a whole: the poetic resolve to withdraw from the cramped representations of the public realm and the repeated claim that inauthenticity belongs to the history of being. Does the de-cision, then, make a difference? If this conflict endures, inscribed in language itself, what are the possibilities of a *different* beginning? For Heidegger, only the few engage in the leap to a poetic site of language. "Zum Sprung kommen immer nur wenige und diese auf verschiedenen Pfaden."[16] He insists that thinking is itself the leap that is most authentic and spacious (GA 65, 237). "Out of its own leap *(eigenem Urpsrung),* thinking enters into the originary conversation with poetry" (GA 39, 151). Once again, the poetic word, invariably eluding reflection, founds *(stiftet)* that otherness in language, a "singular shining" of *Ereignis.* Yet this founding is not a permanent ground for Da-sein. On the contrary, the founding saying of the poet enables thought to traverse *(durchsteigen)* the cleaving realm of being so that *physis* and *logos* are touched simultaneously by the hands of poet and thinker alike in search of the last god.

Let us focus briefly on the rift of *physis* and *logos* in relation to the *first* and *other* beginning of language. *Physis* is not a mere idea of nature opposed to history; it entails an originary significance, embracing both nature and history prior to their separation.[17] As a distinctive region of beings, *physis* governs its own governing *(das Walten des Waltenden).*[18] Heidegger insists that *physis,* which marks the *essence* of what is held in sway, also manifests beings in their tendency to conceal being.[19]

While *logos* is an originary struggle within *physis,* what Heidegger also calls *polemos,* a setting apart, a cleft, a rift, a cleaving, being becomes what it is through a gathering of the disparate appearances of gods and mortals.[20] The *logos,* then, is the word coming to be, authentic history (EM 48). Derived from the verb *legein, logos* (in Lat. *legere*, in Ge. *legen*) denotes a laying before, a laying out, a lying there. Heidegger claims that this originary significance of *legein* illuminates the presupposed essential nature of language which the Greeks did not elucidate. Accordingly, *logos*, a "belonging-together-with-one-another *(Miteinanderzusammengehörigkeit)*, inserts itself into a poetry imaginary as *xunon* (from *xunienai*), "getting together." In these various relations, *logos* is always already *(aei)* a strife as that of day and night. Still, this governing strife emerges simultaneously as a "coming together" of the word yet-to-be a questioning of language, a *Wort-Werk (logos/ physis)*.

What about the originary essence of *logos/physis* as *Wort-Werk*? Heidegger concedes that one of several definitions for *legein* early on has been "to read, to say, to tell." Contrarily, the expressive sense of *logos* "as *ratio*, as verb, as law of the world, as logical necessity of thought, as meaning, as reason,"[21] conceals precisely what lies before us when we read or tell a story. In this regard, the story of *logos* has merely been told in *logical* aspects of its being, repeatedly obscuring the *legen, lesen, lassen* (laying, reading, letting). Surprisingly, reading, however, is a letting something be seen as it lies there. What is seen and gathered together in language, is *physis (das aufgehend-verweilende Walten*, EM 13). What lies there "does not mean a binding and linking together of representations, a manipulation of psychical occurrences where the 'problem' arises of how these bindings, as something inside, agree with something physical outside" (BT 56). Quite simply, *logos* is primordially a distinctive reading of *physis* so as always to let the *word* be the *work* yet-to-be, *Dasein's* sigetic message, its historical task. Paradoxically, then, reading is not restricted to scanning letters *(grammata)* or decoding written or spoken words; it is a gathering of *how* words will altogether be heard. What is gathered together is history *(panta)* and art *(en)*, decisively a listening to a poetic promise *(Zusage)*. This listening to *physis*, the sigetic question, takes place without interpretation, invariably flowing toward the open, what Heidegger calls *logos—die lesende Lege*, "the reading surge" (VA 224), which is simply too much for "reason" to handle. In philosophy's *first* beginning, the essence of language, *die lesende Lege* remains in oblivion in the very calm of *techne's* comfort. Without the stillness of astonishment *(thaumazein)*, the upheaval *(Gewitter)* of being gathering beings together is still left unthought. To be astonished, Heidegger claims, is to be attuned to *logos*, attending to the rule of holding sway *(physis)*, reading a promise, no doubt, of the word yet-to-be a pure work of art. Hence, *logos* is simultaneously the *first* and the *other* beginning of thinking *physis*.

Privileging the Pledge

Does Heidegger's poetic experience with language "tell us anything in the sense of giving us something we can come up with"?[22] Gerald L. Bruns contends "the upshot of Heidegger's funny words for language appears to be that they are words that play with the withholding of language, its endless deferral of itself, the way it beckons and withdraws, thus inscribing the structure of the promise, that most elusive of utterances" (E 122). While this is true, there is more: Heidegger regards the word as the power of a "new nobility," a *Befindlichkeit* that reveals the silent call of the earth, the sigetic region of a historical people. The word thus challenges the nihilism of not coming up with anything great. Indeed, the word abdicates the modern desire for "linguistic" comfort and equality. As site of authentic history, the poetic experience with language is not an uncanny wilting of the ground. A founding of being tarries in the "way-making" *(be-wegende)* power of the word. Thinking encounters a "radiant beginning," what Stefan George calls "a new way," "the darkest secret," "the moment as highest god," the song of the earth, the sigetic work of the poet. The word is the only hope after the "burning of the temple," the end of metaphysics. As pure work of art, it is free of ideological discourse and political enframing. A post-aesthetic de-framing of "essence," the poetic experience, for "those who serve the gods [and] know the earth well," comes down to the abyss *(Ab-grund)*, a "face-to-face encounter" of language and earth, a "Saying (which) gathers all things up... and does so soundlessly, as quietly as time times, space spaces, as quietly as the play of time-space is enacted."[23] In turn, the earth shines forth in poetry's sigetic call to action, illuminating a dynamic, historical economy of art: the word in "the peal of stillness," withholding human language, breaking up language, the beginning of "the true step back on the way of thinking" (WL 108).

Moreover, a countermimetic experience with language makes it possible for a historical people to turn away *(Abwendung)* from the prosaic descent into political subjectivity. A post-aesthetic radicalism, which exceeds the romantic tradition, opens the way for a poetic encounter with the earth, a sublime transformation of historical ontology. The sigetic power of the word, revealed in Heidegger's thought, is anticipated in the tone of Zarathustra's "new nobility":

> O happy silence around me! Oh, how this silence draws deep breaths of clean air! Oh, how it listens, this happy silence!
> But down there everyone talks and no one listens. You could ring in your wisdom with bells: the shopkeepers in the market place would out jingle it with pennies.
> Everyone among them talks; no one knows how to understand any more. Everything falls into the water, nothing falls into deep wells any longer.
> Everyone among them talks; nothing turns out well any more and is finished. Everyone cackles; but who still wants to sit quietly in the nest and hatch eggs?
> Everyone among them talks; everything is talked to pieces. And what even yesterday was still too hard for time itself and its tooth, today hangs, spoiled by scraping and gnawing, out of the mouths of the men of today.
> Everyone among them talks; everything is betrayed. And what was once called the secret and the secrecy of deep souls today belongs to the street trumpeters and other butterflies.
> Oh, everything human is strange, a noise on dark streets! But now it lies behind me again: my greatest danger lies behind me![24]

Nietzsche's demand for a poetic nobility is decisive for Heidegger. In this regard, attention should be drawn to Heidegger's gathering of *logos* and *physis* in a sigetic *Wort-Werk*, a privileging of what is to come into questions: the listening to the promise *(das Hören der Zusage)*.[25] "We are, then, within language and with language before all else" (WI, 112). Nevertheless, the turn to *promesse du silence* is not a reconstruction of Nietzsche's revaluation of values but rather a historical people's awakening to a new realm of the earth. Indeed, the earth, as region of pure work in the word, evokes a thinking that springs beyond Nietzsche's projection of history as will to power. Heidegger exceeds Nietzschean nihilism in letting history be the art of the word yet-to-be, invariably the *other* beginning, *physis* in language *(logos)*. In this light, earth emerges within language without regarding language as earth. In a postaesthetic economy of sigetics, the poet reveals the "elated splendor" of the word through which the earth awakens a people to the sublime abyss of its song.

The Sigetic Venture

In a recent essay, Christopher Fynsk writes: "Reflection on poetic or literary language today can no longer posit silence or stillness as a kind of *telos* or even a mere possibility; it must start from the fact of broken silence and begin to dwell with noise."[26] It is tempting to confound stillness with historical resignation or indifference. Sigetics, however, contends that the word yet-to-be is a historical site in which thought is committed to *other* beginnings of action. The sigetic venture is necessarily non-telic, and, by that token poetic *Stiftung* is not political. Indeed, the urge to politicize is fetishistic, specifically in the realm of thought *(Denken)*. The difference between *what is* and *how things ought to be* is historical not political, i.e., a sigetic tendency of the possible not the actual. While the political may be seen as the clamor of a representational now, the historical exceeds the aesthetic dominance of presence. More precisely, history, a post political domain of the word belonging to the Open, becomes the very matter of thinking. Accordingly, it explores the political dawn of dialectical thought immanent in the various unsaid phases of metaphysics. A quite different story, it sees the *first* beginning, reason's overdetermination, the film in being, the pervasive aesthetic presence of dialectical illusions. This political scene belongs distinctively to the genealogy of metaphysics, which overshadows singular possibilities of a radically different beginning. The shrewdness of managing concepts and confining imaginal modalities to strategies of *re-presentation* raises the political-dialectical connection—the will to power—to an aesthetic imperative.

The Western aesthetic cloaks the dominance of the political in philosophical discourse, quite simply, forgetting the difference between being and beings, which coincides with the control mechanisms inherent in the metaphysical army of concepts. Aesthetics, therefore, does not initially arise in modern times; it belongs to the very history of metaphysics. Indeed, it is the *first* beginning of philosophy in which *other* beginnings are metaphysically hidden. As the art of reason's management, veiling the word dialectically, aesthetics makes only the *first* beginning of philosophy prominent. As such, aesthetics is the spirit of the will to power entangled in the Western history of reason. In short, it is the political art of correctness, invariably discerning what is right and wrong, what is beautiful and unbecoming. In its "productive" desire to dominate, aesthetics masks the difference between being *political* and being *free*, thereby privileging *the* metaphysical question of ground without further questioning.

Sigetics, however, reveals the aesthetic vulgarity of *the* Greco-Western genealogy. To shelter thinking within the Open involves a "practical" strategy of de-signing, a sigetic discerning, sifting apart the political dream of identity. A historical pause, this *sigetic thea* or glance manifests in some manner the word yet-to-be. The political what-question is necessarily upset.

> Can one ask questions about the strange fact, that after several revolutions and a century or two of political apprenticeship, in spite of the newspapers, the trade unions, the parties, the intellectuals and all the energy put into educating and mobilizing people, there are still a thousand persons who stand up and twenty million who remain 'passive'—and not only passive, but who, in all good faith and with glee and without even asking themselves why frankly prefer a football match to a human and political drama? . . . Power manipulates nothing, the masses are neither mislead nor mystified. ". . . this indifference of the masses is their true, their only practice, that there is no ideal of them to imagine, nothing in this to deplore . . . a refusal to participate in the recommended ideals, however enlightened.[27]

Respectively, perhaps, one should break the windows of the political edifice altogether. This does not sanction anarchy, for anarchy is still political. The sigetic *ought*, invariably unconstraining, frees *what is* from telic judgments on the higher and lower road of thinking. The word is pure only if it is free of the will to will the world in a certain way. There is still too much self-assertion in the philosopher's urge to ask "what are we to do?" The sigetic dimension cannot presume to make anarchic or telic demands. Its silent work is not a critical representing but a pointing out, an indicating, a showing, perhaps, even an understanding in Spinoza's sense, leaving no room for merely condemning the masses or beginning politics again.

Sigetics unfolds history's *other* narrative, the silent draft, the open pages of a text.[28] While historians may not consider the *other* narrative a fitting theme, those "on the way to language" find occasion for pause for several reasons. One, history does not consist of a host of crowded facts, nor is it exhausted by the significance of programmatic and explanatory strategies. Although it may describe the phenomena of the past, it is not indissolubly linked to a definite beginning in the past, present or future. Indeed, "even a good story often no longer knows where to begin."[29] This does not open the historical narrative to *Geistesgeschichte* or some kind of higher metaphysical or mystical historicizing. Streamlining of any kind, whether empirical or metaphysical, is inadequate for the sigetic de-sign. History is not a mimetic play of subject or object in a particular terrain, but, rather, the sigetic promise of precise shadings. Earlier, Burckhardt wrote: "Real history writing requires that one live in that fine intellectual fluid which emanates to the searcher from all kinds of monuments, from art and poetry as much as from the historians proper."[30] This orientation, however, merely skirts the sigetic de-lineation of *what is* inasmuch as Burckhardt still poses the question of history from a historian's perspective, one that delimits sigetic alterity. While it guides readers safely through time, it neither makes them pause or question the absence of a new order. Burckhardt's approach must be more radically de-signed. Notwithstanding his view of history as "poetry in the highest possible degree," the word serves a metaphysical model, a coherent culture with a specific spirit. It is still the plot of *Gewaltmenschen* in the Renaissance. History for Burckhardt echoes the aesthetic-political deeds of great individuals. His style is free of a general ideological content, but not a nostalgia for form or synthesis. Sigetics, however, without a ready-made discourse, unfolds history as the question yet-to-be. The question to-be marks the pure work of questioning in language *(Wort-Werk)*.

Withdrawing from Buckhardt's celebration of superhuman subjects and, what is more, from an "absolutism of reality," sigetics tells a story not exhausted by "historical" time. While historians tend to release history from the Story of divine, moral, and cultural absolutes, they have difficulty in parting from "the absolutism of reality" a vertical helplessness of the human subject in the face of overwhelming danger. Blumenberg names the later, *Höchstspannung*, "an ongoing state of maximum excitement and suspense" which historiography *(Historie)* retains as its post-metaphysical theme.[31] Historiography strives to diminish this infrastructural "anxiety" through conventional narrative effects such as social understanding. In accord with Heidegger's sigetic venture, history, however, challenges *Höchstspannung*. The sigetic de-signing of the reality principle does not create phantoms for the poet-historian but deconstructs absolutism of reality and the counterfeiting power of metaphysical ideas. Sigetics, then, deconstructs without producing deconstructions. Unveiling the mask merely begins the narrative of *other* beginnings, the silent power of the earth, the word whose gentle blow speaks freely, necessarily. The sigetic mode of history calls for a pure work of questioning without ever becoming a complete work of art in the forms of state, society or culture. Hence, it withdraws radically from the concrete labor of politicizing, pausing to read the "extraordinary saying" of the unheard-of center, the work on the word *(Wort-Werk)*, the demonic story of the earth.

Exceeding an "either-or," history tells the story *(Geschichte)* of a work yet-to-be, a Senecean spark, a sigetic flash, a narrative pause, a disruptive de-signing of continuity and discontinuity. *Historia* and *fabula* appear to be interwoven as in the age of *Pax Romana* when the opposition between history and poetry fades. In the words of Seneca: "Let the reading of poems soothe history and let history hold it by its fables; let it be led softly and delicately."[32]

Paradoxically, history *(Geschichte)* dawns in a poetic site, prior to determining directions or securing meaningful accounts *(Historie)*. Sigetics reveals history as a pure work of antinomies, unresolved yet open for the new order of the word, a *mython mytheisthai*—telling a story beyond spatiotemporal reporting. The pure draft of the Open is not reserved for a philosophy of history. It is neither fact nor interpretation but the de-lineation of a sigetic occasion, "out-of-system" altogether. The historical context, then, is neither a particular work of art nor art in general, but a pure work invariably in progress, unreservedly a promise. Beyond describing and accounting for situations, sigetics tends to compose that peculiar texture between presence and absence, between *what is* and *how it is to be*. Hence, history reveals a novel silence, a *phuein*, a rising, a coming of how the word is yet to be sent *(geschickt)*.

Unpredictable and incomprehensible, history is the advent of necessity's *other* beginnings. Necessity cannot be represented, painted, composed, or poeticized. Often misconceived as an ontotheologic category, necessity is the pure draft of the Open, the promise of letting the question be, a pledge not to intervene dialectically, yet to disrupt the privileged presence of mimesis. Exceeding an objective causal series of events, necessity can only be what cannot be otherwise, in Stefan George's words, "wonder or dream from distant land," the new order of the word. "Where word breaks off, no thing may be."[33] Indeed, the new order is the poetic experience with necessity.

Not to withdraw *(ne-cedere)* from radical questioning does not make necessity an absolute. The necessary is what cannot be otherwise than the work in the word, the listening to the promise. The unheard-of law of parting from the political order of things occasions an "extraordinary saying" of a demonic questioning, a paradoxical historiality, a pure work of necessity in *other* beginnings. A nostalgia for action marks the rejection of sigetic de-signing and a possible falling into metaphysical narratives. Sigetic necessity is not exhausted by the economy of presence. What cannot be otherwise is not what happened already, or is happening now, or will happen tomorrow. What cannot be otherwise is *yet-to-be*. It does not present itself historically and will not present itself even as *the* question of questions. Indeed, the necessary is not a question of presence or absence, but, in advance of any question, it is precisely what comes into question as the sigetic venture, a letting-go of political, cultural and social questions altogether. Necessity is the sigetic event of the Open, the story of the pure draft of designing, a radical parting from "false necessity." Still, sigetics questions Unger's anti-necessitarian social theory with its idea of society as an artifact, as something to be imagined and made, in his words, "great and sweet."[34] The urge to reconstruct aesthetically a society free of historiographical structuring is till part of the metaphysical dream of grounding or presentifying a community. Inextricably bound up with the Open, sigetics guards against essentializing necessity. It regards time as a sigetic play *(Spiel)* in space *(Raum)*. Drawn toward a new historical *Spielraum*, its economy of apparitional questioning is the paradoxical new order which transcends the political without transcendence.

Necessity, then, is the story of how the word is yet-to-be without be-coming an actual event. While traces of utopia may surface in this story, listening to the promise is not utopian performance. A new anticipatory aesthetic, such as Bloch's metaphorical variation of Marxism, merely replicates the metaphysical hope of reason, radicalizing the economy of an open eschato-teleological presence.[35] Sigetics, on the other hand, withdraws from a sociohistorical dynamics of the subject while speaking freely of *other* beginnings. As such, it unveils a historical *Ereignis* without encouraging solidarity with ontology. Designed to be other than a particular poem, or a work of art readily linked to an economy of non-attachment, the *Wort-Werk* is purely and freely spoken—neither present nor absent—a new *Kehre* of in-finite tearing asunder *(Zerissenheit)*. Yet-to-be, the word dismantles the very ground of temporal presence, subverting temporal founding of any kind. For *to-be-yet* shall always be a coming without be-coming historically concrete or politically abstract. Only in the sigetic space of *Zerissenheit*, in the word's *Spielraum*, may the privileging of the promise reveal the necessary upheaval of the word-work, a mode of art yet-to-be without being firmly wedded to a new mimesis. A paradoxic call, a historic pause, sigetics refuses to withdraw *(ne-cedere)* from the earth, extending itself into that necessary unheard-of center between time and no-time, between Spinoza's *sub specie aeternitatis* and Heidegger's *Zeitspielraum*. Paradoxically a priori and a posteriori, the Open is there *(Da-sein)* without being present or absent. In the silent distance of Rilke's word, the Open is close to the earth, necessarily so.

Conclusion

What does sigetic promise *(Zusage)* offer with regard to an economy of responsibility? Is it bound to an ahistorical essentiality? Is it merely a postmetaphysical echo of mystical mischief? Is it a displaced resonance of a higher commodity fetishism? Sigetic promise engages neither in a conventionally action-oriented mode of thought, nor in a restful, contemplative gaze at reality. Disengaged from a derivative concept of praxis, it marks the path toward an open constellation of thought and action, initially exploring the possibilities of a non-principal economy of responsibility.[36] How thinking *ought* to be is not proposed in the context of another ethics but in light of a post-metaphysical strategy rigorously designing ways of social questioning. Hence the sigetic promise is to think the *ought* in relation to *what is*, not as a limited and limiting representation of world but as world yet to come into question. Suitably, a new emphasis on the word, a poetic experience with language exceeds a formalistic or contextually reductionistic manner of reading the text of history. Sigetics destabilizes the assertive priority of responsibility so exceedingly pronounced in contemporary discourse. Ironically, a stark concern for the good, if it were to be disappropriated from the confined space of the onto-teleolic question, is socially necessary. And certainly, after Auschwitz, it is barbaric to question the legitimacy of questioning the good. And yet, because of it, we may be tempted to embrace another ethical position, reinscribing an artificial gesture which gives metaphysical comfort to thought. Nonetheless, from this point of view, it is perhaps not poetry but ethics that cannot be done after Auschwitz.[37]

After Heidegger, *Germanien* is the event of listening to the promise of a new Germany. Hölderlin's poem continues to pose the question of the "wonder or dream from distant land," a question which reduced Heidegger to a highly problematic silence not to be confused with the sigetic venture. Hölderlin's question about *Germanien* does not answer in advance what Germany is to be. In his novel, *Hyperion*, the protagonist, experiencing the exhaustion of mimesis, wanders away from Greece and its ideals toward Germany or what is to come. But arriving on German soil, he is not exposed to the *other* beginning. Although he decides to stay in "the land of poets and thinkers," it is clear to him that Germany is not the scene of a quite different path of thought. At best, it signifies a "longing to go to another land,"[38] in Hyperion's case to seek the beauty of nature. *Germanien*, then, is not the name for Germany but a pledge to drift away from particular political spacings. This sigetic pledge is committed to a historical crossing through the question mark that invariably lies next to the imaginary texts of a new Germany. *Germanien*, conversely, is neither old nor new, but ever prepared to listen to *other* beginnings.

> The beginning still *is*. It does not lie *behind us*, as something that was long ago, but stands *before* us. As what is greatest, the beginning has passed in advance beyond all that is to come and thus also beyond us. The beginning has invaded our future. There it awaits us, a distant command bidding us catch up with its greatness.[39]

Notes

1. Argue (MF to accuse; L arguere—to make clear; argutare—to prate, also related to MLG pratten—to pout).

2. "Aber wissen wir denn, *wer wir sind?*" Martin Heidegger, *Hölderlins Hymnen, "Germanien" und "Der Rhein"* (Frankfurt am Main: Vittorio Klostermann, 1980), 49. (Unless stated otherwise, the translations from the German original in this essay are my own.)

3. "Das Wort ist nur noch der Schall und die lautstarke Aufpeitschung, bei der es auf einen 'Sinn' nicht mehr abgesehen sein kann..." Martin Heidegger, *Beiträge zur Philosophie (Vom Ereignis)* (Frankfurt am Main: Vittorio Klostermann, 1989), 123.

4. "Am Ende ist es doch wahr, je weniger der Mensch vom Staat erfährt und weis, die Form sei, wie sie will, um desto freier ist er." *Hölderlin Sämtliche Werke*, ed. Friedrich Beissner (Stuttgart: W. Kohlhammer Verlag, 1954), VI, 417. (Hereafter HSW.)

5. "Sigetic/sigetics" derived from the Greek *sigan*, "to be silent." In questioning the power of *the* question *(Fragekraft)*, sigetics, for Heidegger, notably in the *Beiträge*, is simultaneously, paradoxically, the pre- and post-aesthetic *other* beginning of thinking. It reveals the poetic power of the word and marks an *originary* thinking. Note Heidegger's saying: "Wenn uns eine Geschichte, d.h. ein Stil des Da-seins, noch geschenkt sein soll,

dann *kann* dies nur die *verborgene Geschichte der grossen Stille* sein, in der und als welche die Herrschaft des letzten Gottes das Seiende eröffnet und gestaltet" (GA 65, 34).

6. "What is truly tragic with us," Hölderlin writes, "is that quietly wrapped up in a box we disregard the state or empire *(Reich)* of the living, not that we atone for the flame which we are unable to suppress and which consumes us" (HSW, vi, 426).

7. "Über die Verfahrungsweise des Poetischen Geistes," in *Hölderlin Sämtliche Werke* (Stuttgart: W. Kohlhammer Verlag, 1961), IV, 241–265.

8. *"Das die Verfahrungsart, welche dem Gedichte seine Bedeutung gibt,"* (HSW, iv, 248).

9. Friedrich Hölderlin, *Poems and Fragments*, trans. Michael Hamburger (Ann Arbor: University of Michigan Press, 1968), 405–06. (Hereafter *HPF.*) (Translation slightly modified by W. S. W.)

10. GA 39, 36: "Der Mensch ist und ist doch nicht. Es sieht so aus wie das Seyn und ist es nicht. Und so auch die Dichtung."

11. "Die Sprache ist nicht ein verfügbares Werkzeug, sondern dasjenige Ereignis, das über die höchste Möglichkeit des Menschseins verfügt." Martin Heidegger, *Erläuterungen zu Hölderlins Dichtung* (Frankfurt am Main: Vittorio Klostermann, 1981), 38.

12. See Wilhelm Reich, *Listen, Little Man!*, trans. Ralph Manheim (New York: Farrar, Straus and Giroux, 1974).

13. Martin Heidegger, *Being and Time*, trans. J. Macquarrie and E. Robinson (New York: Harper & Row, 1962), 165.

14. Ibid., 165.

15. See Mark C. Taylor, *Altarity* (Chicago: University of Chicago Press, 1987), 35–58.

16. "Always only a few shall advance to the leap and these on different paths" (GA 65, 236).

17. See Martin Heidegger, *Die Grundbegriffe der Metaphysik* (Frankfurt am Main: Vittorio Klostermann, 1983), 39.

18. Ibid., 46.

19. "Die *physis* ist das Sein selbst, kraft dessen das Seiende erst beobachtet wird und bleibt." Martin Heidegger, *Einführung in die Metaphysik* (Tubingen: Max Niemeyer Verlag, 1966), 11.

20. *"Polemos* und *logos* sind dasselbe," (EM, 47).

21. Martin Heidegger, *Vorträge und Aufsätze* (Pfullingen: Gunther Neske, 1954), 208.

22. Gerald L. Bruns, *Heidegger's Estrangements* (New Haven and London: Yale University Press, 1989), 122. (Hereafter E.)

23. Martin Heidegger, *On the Way to Language*, trans. Peter Hertz (New York: Harper & Row, 1971), 108. (Hereafter WI.)

24. Friedrich Nietzsche, *Thus Spoke Zarathustra*, trans. Walter Kaufmann (New York: Viking Press, 1968), 296–297.

25. See John Sallis, "Flight of Spirit," in *Diacritics* 19.3–4 (1989): 25–37.

26. "Noise at the Threshold," in *Research in Phenomenology*, ed. John Sallis (Atlantic Highlands, N.J.: Humanities Press, 1990), xix, 118.

27. Jean Baudrillard, *In the Shadows of the Silent Majorities*, trans. Foss, Johnston, and Patton (New York: Semiotext(e), 1983), 14.

28. "Diese im Da-sein gegründete Geschichte ist die verborgene Geschichte der grossen Stille. In ihr allein kann noch ein Volk *sein*" (GA 65, 34).

29. Ernst Bloch, *The Utopian Function of Art and Literature*, trans. Zipes and Mecklenburg (Cambridge, MA: The MIT Press, 1989), 156. (Hereafter UF.)

30. See "Burckhardt: The Poet of Truth," in Peter Gay's *Style in History* (New York: Basic Books, Inc.), 175.

31. Hans Blumenberg, *Work on Myth*, trans. Robert M. Wallace (Cambridge, MA.: The MIT Press, 1985), 5.

32. Gerald A. Press, *The Development of the Idea of History in Antiquity* (Kingston and Montreal: McGill-Queen's University Press, 1982), 66.

33. "Kein Ding sei wo das Wort gebricht," in Stefan George's *Das Neue Reich* (Berlin: Georg Bondi, 1919), 134.

34. Roberto Mangabeira Unger, *False Necessity* (Cambridge: Cambridge University Press, 1987), 595.

35. The birth of utopia for Bloch is music, "a totally new content" (UF 125). He writes: "The music of that new dance is Beethoven's Seventh Symphony" (UF 125). Of course, he cannot elucidate how this "entirely new origin" is able to transform a mythical hope into a historical revolution. He tries by alluding to the cultural surplus in music and other works of art which may evoke the spell of archaic anticipations, the "utopian function" of hope.

36. See John Sallis, *Delimitations: Phenomenology and the End of Metaphysics* (Bloomington, Indiana University Press, 1986), esp. Part IV.

37. See Theodor W. Adorno's *Negative Dialektik* (Frankfurt am Main: Suhrkamp Verlag, 1970), 352–356.

38. "German Song," in *Friedrich Hölderlin Poems and Fragments*, trans. Michael Hamburger (Ann Arbor: University of Michigan Press, 1968), 505.

39. Martin Heidegger, "The Self-Assertion of the German University," *Review of Metaphysics* 38 (March 1985), 473.

V. Heidegger and Ethics

Chapter 10

The Question of Ethics in Heidegger's Account of Authenticity[1]

Charles E. Scott

Since dasein does not provide a basis for a metaphysically founded ethics, and since its being interrupts and ruptures meaning and values with sheer possibility and being to death, Heidegger investigates dasein's possibility of being a self that is appropriate to its being rather than a self defined by ethical norms. He uses a language of foundations and conditions for the possibility of selfhood in this discussion, as he does throughout *Being and Time*. Just as the language of wholeness and unity falls into question in the context of dasein's 'essential truth', this language, too, is broken by dasein's ability to be, its *Seinskönnen*. The term *eigentliche* now refers to specific ways in which an individual relates to its being. What is the proper way for dasein to live with regard to its being? How is it to constitute itself in its being, which interrupts the very meaning of self-constitution with its possibility of no self at all, a possibility that is dasein's and most properly so? Whereas in the previous section, *Entwurf* and *Vorlauf* interplayed to bring together the writing and the subject in question, in this section, *Bezeugung* (attestation) will interplay with *Entschlossenheit* (resoluteness) around the themes of witness and own. The chapter title is, *Die daseinsmässige Bezeugung eines eigentlichen Seinskönnens und die Entschlossenheit* ("dasein's Attestation of an Authentic Potentiality-for-being, and Resoluteness"). Section 54 has the title, *Das Problem der Bezeugung einer eigentlichen existenziellen Möglichkeit* ("The

Problem of Attesting to an Authentic Existentielle Possibility"). Our issue is, how does Heidegger put ethics in question as he establishes dasein's proper way to be vis-à-vis its being?

Selfhood, on Heidegger's account, is a way of being. The struggle for proper selfhood puts the individual at odds with its normal world in which it has its possible roles and identities set for it. To be a proper, self-authenticating self, an individual must take its fundamental cues for living from its being, not from the standards of communal normalcy. There is a double rupture involved in this process. Dasein must break from the normal, ready-made certainties that have formed it from its earliest awareness. This involves the extremely difficult process of retrieving one's understanding and of temporality, which is constitutive of dasein's being, and finding out how to be in accord with it as one lives in the patterns of life and meaning that have been developed in a trenchant, forceful ignorance of dasein's being. This direction of thought prepares us to expect some kind of natural knowledge of dasein's, some basis for correcting our erring ways of life and for guiding us to a higher fulfillment of our human nature. But instead of an immanent knowledge of human nature, we have found a nonconceptual "understanding," an alertness that takes place in dasein's temporal projecting and one that attests to mortal possibility without the possibility of circumscribing itself. The first interruption takes place as an individual finds cultural and social assurances to be without ontological foundation, to be, rather, concerned reactions that have led our Western ethos away from its own being. Heidegger finds that traditional selfhood has been formed in this reaction, and his retrieval of the West's early thoughts and questions is an effort no less revolutionary than Nietzsche's to show that *who* we can be is invested in covering over the questionableness of the ability to be a 'who' at all. From the perspective of our traditional meanings and sense of presence, the lack of a self-like basis for the self and the lack of meaning in our meanings constitutes a dismal prospect, and although Heidegger does not invoke Nietzsche at this point, he indicates indirectly that, in agreement with Nietzsche's genealogy of the ascetic ideal, Western human beings would not be able to feel that they could live properly if their being were merely the possibility of no possibility at all. The first, appropriate interruption is thus one in which the assurances and sense of presence that constitute us are put in question by the *Vorlauf* of being to death. This mortal temporality, along with its refusal, are part of who we are. Our existence lives the interruption that Heidegger attempts to reinherit in his description of dasein in *Being and Time*.

dasein's secular and religious rituals must thus be interrupted, and both its questions and answers must undergo the second rupture, that of dasein's truth, its disclosure of being possibly impossible. The second interruption is like that of self-overcoming. The move natural for dasein, given its history, is to find a body of certainties to replace those that have proved to be inadequate. The certainty of Heidegger's 'strict' and careful description of dasein, for example, might give us assurance that we have our meaning in our temporality, or another account might be taken to prove that Heidegger is mistaken and to constitute a more reliable analysis on the basis of which to conduct our lives. But there is a recoil at this point in Heidegger's thought. On the one hand, he is providing an account that he takes to be well-founded and preferable to the metaphysical tradition from which it departs. On the other hand, his account leads him to the truth of dasein, its disclosive mortal temporality, which puts in question the desire for certainty, the neutrality of accurate thought, and the ability of meaningful discourse to circumscribe and express dasein's being. *What* his analysis finds recoils on both the meaning and historical subjectivity of his finding, making it doubtful that his grasp definitively holds the sheer possibility that it designates. Heidegger's thought in *Being and Time* expresses the meaning of dasein's being, which, on its own account, runs ahead and 'possibilizes' outside the circumscriptions of meaning.

As we proceed in the investigation of Heidegger's account of dasein's proper resolve and response to its own being, we are involved in a reflective movement that puts in question its own certainty, its structure of expression, its perceptive reach, and its prescriptive possibility. His word, *Entschlossenheit*, which is translated *resoluteness*, also has the normal meaning of decisiveness or of bringing something to a conclusion or end. The *Ent*, however, can have both an intensifying function or one of opposition, for example, *entkommen* means to escape, *entschlüsseln* means to decode or open up. When the *ent* of *entschliessen* is taken as intensifying, as it usually is, dasein resolves and decides for its being; it makes up its mind. But the ambiguity of *ent* allows Heidegger, in the context of his account of *Being and Time*, to say in effect that dasein unlocks or opens itself to its being in the sense of *erschliessen* but also that it opens to its continuous closing, its mortal temporality. To be resolved in one's being to death provides no ground for concluding anything with certainty and puts in question the appropriateness of the kind of thinking that expects human existence to find its fulfillment on the basis of structures like those of good and evil that are decided by human being or human nature. Although *Being and Time* cannot be read as proposing a historicist position, neither can it be read as finding an enclosed universal basis for normative ethical judgement. Resolution, by opening to dasein's disclosive mortality, interrupts the enclosing structures necessary for traditional systems, concepts, and universal principles. The priority of both judgment and universality is in question by virtue of the mortal temporality that constitutes dasein, its language, and its conceptuality.

The tension that we thus have to work with in *Being and Time*, when we consider dasein's propriety with respect to itself, that is to say, its authenticity, is found in Heidegger's emphasis on dasein's ontological structure as the unifying origin, in the sense of the condition for the possibility of all relative, ontic ways of existing, and in his showing that this ontological structure and its account are in question by virtue of dasein's own disclosure. Dasein's ontological structure provides the basis for raising the question of being, for interpreting its historicity, and for showing how it might exist appropriately with regard to its being. But the basis is more like an abyss than like anything that can be properly called normative. Given our inherited sense of ultimate meaning for reality and the intrinsic value of human existence, this discovery at first appears to be nihilistic. If we have no solid reference to support the values of individual lives, then anything can be justified. But anything *has* been justified in our history by appeal to universal values and meaning, including the most severe repressions, torture, extreme cruelty, wars, and the morbid enslaving and destructive segregation of vast groups of people. The proliferation of 'universal' norms whereby we justify certain values and contend against other values mirrors our fear of what the world would be like if we lacked an adequate basis for justifying our values and realizing the best possibilities of ourselves. The tension in Heidegger's thinking between the search for a normative basis for thought and the discovery of a 'basis' that puts that search in question arises directly out of the fear to which our tradition responds by supporting its ideals and highest hopes with a combination of axioms, authorizing disclosure, and careful judgment, whether through the agency of God, reason, nature, or humanity.

The tension in Heidegger's thinking, we shall see, puts in question the combination of axioms, authorizing disclosure and judgment as well as the belief that with a proper normative basis for our values, we can hope to overcome the destructive proliferation of violently opposing ways of life. The question we are approaching is whether people can find options to grounded normativity as the basis on which they come to be who they 'should' be. Do options to the traditionally ethical ones arise for our language and thought when the tension between ontological grounding and being that cannot be a ground, but is like an *abgrund*, defines the space for thought? Does Heidegger's account of the basis for authenticity twist free of its ethical desire for grounding presence?[2]

Heidegger uses *self* to refer to 'who' dasein is. The term is meant to suggest not universality but the relative activity of a socialized, acculturated individual's making its way in life. The self is a mediating agency who ordinarily chooses on the basis of something other than itself. Even if it chooses itself, it chooses an agency that has been constituted in a history by language and customs that are not selves or like selves. Usually the 'something' that functions normatively is the vague, general, and pervasive image of normalcy that Heidegger calls 'das Man' and that functions as the general, anonymous agency by which we desire, decide, and constitute ourselves within a range of options that define proper identity in our broad culture and specific society. Only if we make our decisions on the basis of our being, Heidegger says, are we who we are as I-myself *(ich selbst)*. Being an authentic self is a modification of our normal, quasi-anonymous identity, a modification that takes place when our way of life makes manifest, and, in that sense, is based on our being, not primarily on selfhood. The self twists free of its inherited way of being by coming to attend to its being, its disclosiveness.

As we have seen, *this* movement of twisting free is not incidental to the authorship of *Being and Time* or to Heidegger's account of resoluteness. One characteristic of our everyday identity is a quality of certainty that seeks universalization in our daily personal and professional disciplines. Most things are already decided and known by virtue of the rules and standards, the assignments of values, the sense of relative urgency and range of applicability that structure and provide meaning and significance in our environment. We are relatively at ease in our communities of value, even with regard to what shocks, horrifies, or inspires us, unless something occurs to interrupt or unavoidably challenge the shared values of our lives. When our ethos is threatened, we naturally bristle and become hostile and resistant.

Heidegger's analysis suggests that our 'natural' identities are formed within complex histories and communities that structure our identities as though the inherited values were absolute. It further suggests that their conceptual structure is based on the assumptions that being is simple and continuing presence, that time is linear and quantifiable, that death is the end point of life, and that human being has a kind of nature that is available to objective discovery. Our everyday, "fallen" lives are thus the basis of traditional metaphysical thought and the manner of evaluating that accompanies it in the name of ethics. He further shows that dasein's ability to be, its ungraspable running ahead in the possibility of no possibility at all, is not only not a clear part of everyday identities, but that our sensibility is formed in a traceable movement away from our being. Just as Nietzsche makes plain that philosophical thought as such, given its lineage, invokes the ascetic ideal, Heidegger shows us that to be who we normally are and to think as we normally think is to live out a history that is adverse to the being that we are.[3] And, analogous to Nietzsche's account of the ascetic priest as giving hope to desperate people by relieving them of the burden of meaninglessness, is Heidegger's account of normal selfhood as providing the benefit of relieving people of the burden of confronting their own being. The middle voice of dasein's being is silenced for all practical purposes in the structures and processes of normal living. Moreover, dasein is relieved of the perplexity of being without reality in the midst of everything that we experience as real, and of being abysmal in the ground of our being as such.

The normal is thus *"uneigentlich"*—improper, not true, not essential—and *"verloren,"* lost. When we hold in mind that the possibility of ethical thought and action is found in traditional 'normalcy' and its history, we see the cutting edge of Heidegger's thought concerning dasein's resolve: as we turn to the possibility of *Eigentlichkeit*, authenticity, we are turning away from ethics as we know it. This turning away is no less than a twisting free of a body of selfhood that is given in its investment in not knowing its being or its propriety vis-à-vis its being. Heidegger's position is far stronger than one that provides only a formal basis for determining what our normative values should be. We shall see that this metaphysical strategy of formal-positive determination is changed by his thought. The question is whether we are able in our normalcy to recognize this new position in the range of our suffering and pleasure, or the meaning of the institutions and disciplines by which and in which we become who we are.

The "voice" of dasein's possibility "calls" in the midst of our involvements. Heidegger uses the experience of conscience, not its contents, as his phenomenal field. In his account, we undergo a calling away from our identities and selves to the possibility of our being. This call is corrupted by religions and moralities to seem as though it were calling to a specific way of life or ethos, and as though it were initiated by a specific violation that arouses guilt in a given individual. But the call itself does not disclose the power of an ethos but the difference of human being, in its being, from traditional ways of life. One undergoes, in the disclosiveness of dasein, a continuous "call" to its propriety, its *eigenste Selbstseinkönnen*, its most appropriate ability to be itself. Dasein's call to itself is like a voice that comes to if in the midst of its traditional life, like an appeal or summons to undergo the difference, in its being, from itself: "It gives dasein to understand" that its being is found in the disclosiveness of its ability to be in its possibility of being no possibility at all, not in its values or in the objects of its religious and philosophical projections. The voice of conscience, as the disclosure of dasein's being in the midst of its everyday values and standards, functions to make those values and standards uncertain and to "call" dasein to its difference from who it is in its efforts to be someone recognizable in its culture.[4]

The wrenching away from dasein's self and the interruption (Heidegger says breaking into) of our identities by the call of conscience are constitutive movements of dasein that put it in touch with itself. Dasein's self, Heidegger says in *Being and Time*, Section 57, is clearly not transparent in the call of conscience, which presents neither a person nor a definitive and definite way of life. Nothing familiar is encountered. In our experience of ourselves, we ordinarily say that we are lost when we find no landmarks or customs to which we can relate with familiarity. But on Heidegger's account, we begin to find ourselves when we are dislocated and displaced by the disclosure of our being that has no standing, no name or heritage in our environment. The wrenching movement and displacement are aspects of the disclosure of being in our everyday world. In this "call," we began to hear the "understanding" that constitutes the *Vorlauf* of our finitude. There is no observer, no judge, no clear definitions or standards. But instead of being lost, we are homing in on our being. This wrenching movement means, in the context of *Being and Time*, that we are being freed from the "lostness" of our familiar world of cultural inheritance and from the surveillance of our identities that make us who we are. To be *eigentlich*—proper to our being—and attuned to our being in our everyday lives, we have to overcome the monopolizing power of valences and exigencies that define who we are.

Heidegger's account of the call on conscience provides for his interpretation the possibility of this overcoming, this twisting free. It further establishes the difference that constitutes our lives and shows that in this difference we, as culturally determined identities, have access to the being whose erasure is part of who we traditionally are. To trust our meanings and values by giving them axiomatic status, to stake our lives on them, and to know ourselves in their mediation is to forget our being and the possibility of living appropriately as the being that we are. Only by the severity of the wrenching, twisting movement out of the surveillance and authority of our normalcy and identity can dasein come into its own.

If the being of dasein were determinant and if it provided immediately a nature to be realized by individual action, ethics would not be put in question. We could in principle find out what our nature is and how to meet its standards. But since dasein, in being called to itself, is called to a being whose meaning is mortal temporality and thus has no intrinsic, determinant meaning at all, the structure of ethics as such is in question. To be in question does not mean that we may hope for a time when ethics will be abolished and we will live a higher life, undistressed by the difference between our being and our cultural lives. The "lostness" of everyday life is not to be lost, on Heidegger's account. It does mean that, as we follow unquestioningly the patterns of our best ideals and values in a state of mind that knows, at least in principle, what is genuinely and universally good and bad, we are lost to our being and to our mortal indeterminacy. We cannot expect that such a life will unconsciously and inevitably override its mortal temporality by, for example, organizing our environments in systems of value that create totalities of meaning that are invested in ignoring both their own being and the meaning of their being for totalizing meanings. In the traditional thought of subjectivity, one expects some type of self-realization consequent to conformity to the reality of the subject—whatever the subject might be—whereas, in *Being and Time*, authenticity means the disclosure of human-being-in-question, rather than the possibility of resolving the question or the problems that follow it. Is it possible that our systems of self-realization and self-sacrifice for higher values inevitably maim a human life that is recognizable only when our best ways of being are profoundly disturbed by the non-presence of our being? Do our axiomatic values at their best constitute a blindness to who we are and what we do? Does the disclosure of our being and its appropriation along with the pain and disruption that constitute it and follow it, make possible a profound and thoroughgoing uncertainty that itself reveals the limits of ethics?

The question of ethics in the context of *Being and Time* is a way of being that is concerned in the world and with other people.

Heidegger's analysis in Part I of *Being and Time* has made clear that dasein is constituted in world relations. Dasein is not a simple thing existing with other single things to which it may or may not relate. Solipsism is an ontological impossibility for dasein, since dasein only occurs in disclosive relations. It happens in language and practice and comes to itself as an individual who is already constituted by relations. The difference between being and everyday existence takes place only in world relations. Hence the emphasis on continuously twisting free of cultural domination *in* cultural life, never outside of it. The terminus is not a life that is withdrawn from culture and history, nor is it found in projected experiences that are ahistorical and purged of corruption. The aim involves an individual's being with others in a specific environment and history, attuned in its relation to the *Vorlauf* of its being without presence. The "perversion" that inevitably occurs in our standards for living is found in their insensitivity to their mortal temporality.

Heidegger articulates his interpretation in the traditional language of being as presence. Existential understanding is "given." Being "presents itself." dasein "comes to itself." His interpretation is no less involved in the wrenching, twisting recoils than in dasein's authentic movements. In association with this articulation, Heidegger shows that as being presents itself, no subject or substance or nature comes forth. The possibility for no possibility comes forth. Mortal disclosure takes place. As dasein comes to itself, no specific course of action is indicated. The given existential understanding—dasein's *Verstehen*—has neither a subject nor an object. Dasein's being does not name anything present, but names, rather, mortal, temporal disclosure that forecasts itself as temporal possibility instead of as a standing nature. The language of presence in this text is thus in a process of twisting free from its own inevitability in the tradition in which it occurs and in which Heidegger thinks. This movement in *Being and Time* articulates dasein's recoiling movement toward the possibility of propriety regarding its being.

The issue of dasein's coming to itself is thus one of allowing its difference in its being vis-'a-vis the status of its life. If an individual can allow and affirm its mortal temporality, in contrast to the invested obfuscation of this same temporality, and can allow also the *question* of the meaning of being in its historical identity, if it can want the 'address' of its being in spite of wanting a sense of continuous and meaningful presence, it can, perhaps, come to appropriate the difference of its own being as it decides its daily issues. This alertness is like a person's affirming or loving another person with a full sense of mortality in the relationship.[5] Or it is like experiencing the validity of a system of values without a sense of certainty or universality. Nothing specific is there to will in dasein's owning its being—hence the anxiety to which Heidegger gives attention. Allowing its being, dasein allows the "calling forth" of its continuous need to take care, given its primordial lack of stasis. This allowing, given the constitution of its identity, is like dasein's unburdening itself of traditional resistances and opening itself to the inevitability of being without foundations. Resoluteness thus cannot be conceived in terms of self-constitution. Rather, self-constitution requires a basis for validation, and authentic experiences falls into question as dasein comes into its own through resoluteness.

The middle voice is particularly important to Heidegger's account of authenticity. His claim that dasein's wanting to have conscience, its affirmation of the difference of its being and the dislocation that this difference makes in its life, is a "Sich-verstehen" (self-understanding) in its most proper *(eigensten)* ability to be. Affirming conscience includes allowing a self-understanding that is "a manner *(weise)* of dasein's disclosure." If, however, self-understanding is taken as a reflexive state or as a self-constituting state, his claim is missed. Understanding and dasein's disclosiveness are immediate to willing to have conscience. We might say that they stand out of the circumscription of action and of will. Self-understanding is to be read as understanding understands (itself) in dasein's ability to be, that is, dasein's ability to be is at once mortal temporal awareness which, in understanding itself, is unmediated and beyond willing. Furthermore, affirming conscience is not circumscribed by an individual's action. Affirming conscience is conscience-in-act, and the (self-) understanding of dasein's ability to be is immediate to it. Although an individual may incline to hear the call of conscience *in* conscience's call, understanding is neither active nor passive on this account. The call of conscience is an occurrence that is constitutive of dasein and that is neither active nor passive in the context of an individual's action. And the occurrence of dasein's ability to be is neither active nor passive. The call of conscience and the ability to be refer to themselves in their occurrence without the mediation of a subject. The middle voice gives articulation to dasein's ability to be, its understanding, and its wanting to have conscience, each of which constitutes a manner or *Weise* of disclosiveness *(Erschlossenheit)* that also is not a subject or object with regard to an action. We are in a position to see that, in resoluteness

(Entschlossenheit) and authenticity *(Eigentlichkeit)*, disclosure discloses and time times, that Heidegger's emphasis is not on self-constituting action or intentional action, but is on the (self-) disclosure of dasein's disclosiveness. In opening to its being and allowing its being, dasein does not constitute itself. It stands outside of the possibility for self-constitution and finds itself in question in all of its reach and stretch. Dasein's disclosiveness is its being. It is being to death, the possibility of no possibility, the *Vorlauf* of no continuing presence that disrupts dasein's presence. Dasein's being is *its* difference from the finite continuity of its identity and its being in the world. In its most proper being, no 'I' controls it. Rather, the I is interrupted and something other than a self takes place.

'I' is always situated in a locality of specific determinants. It does not enjoy the benefits of an ontologically founded ideal that can guide it to right decisions. Decisions are made in the power of the values and possibilities for action that are allowed by the situation. This is not a version of historical relativism, however, since the ontological indeterminacy of the specific situation is made inevitable by dasein's being, not by the control of history. This inevitability is the possibility of no possibility that is heard in dasein's being. The proliferation of values and meanings that characterize our history has its meaning in dasein's being, in its situated ability to be, as we have seen. The I that resolves properly opens to its being in its situation, twists free from the control of predominant standards of judgment by attending resolutely to its being, and makes its judgments and commitments in the loosening of the bonds of the everyday by virtue of concerned and open attunement to its being.

Insofar as the I, as it judges and chooses, is always in the heritage and culture that is invested in turning away from its being, Heidegger's and Foucault's positions are similar in this respect: every decision and involvement is dangerous because of its inevitable everyday drift toward universalization and totalization in defiance of its temporality. Their interpretations of time are different, but both see that distortions of time are distortions of human being and that time does not tell people what specific decisions are right or wrong. The silence of being/time, in Heidegger's terms, regarding how we are to take our stand in life, is a part of dasein's mortality and the close distance of being in our lives. Hearing in this silence is finding oneself in the question of ethics. It is like acting without knowing the necessity of the action. It is like having to be without resolving the question of being. As dasein lets itself be called forth in its most proper being, the I is modified by the non-I of its being. It becomes strange to itself in its clarity of purpose and certainty, and it acts forthrightly in understanding the collapse of clarity in its being. No less situated, no less concerned or committed, the individual's attunements and expectations, its perceptiveness, satisfactions and priorities are conditioned by, as it were, an open door to mortal time and lets in an element different from the presence and totality of value. It acts, but now in the questionableness of the possibility of its actions and in the transgressions of being that mark its living.

To be this way is to be resolved, and to be resolved is to attest to the difference of being in the value-laden situation that one lives in and through. Hearing this difference might well include a pause, an interruption, a standing out of the law of rightness. What can be heard in such a pause? I am persuaded that what can be heard is not predictable by the law of rightness, that an other to rightness and wrongness may be heard, and that in such hearing an obsessiveness regarding both right and justification, an obsessiveness which determines who we are, is given pause in an indeterminacy to which we belong and that is other to us. We stand out in the questionableness of our ethos, knowing less who we are and who we are to be, in silence before the decisions that we have to make. In *Being and Time*, this silence is proper to dasein's being, and it makes dangerous the values by which we give ourselves common lives and establish the rules within which we are constituted and become clear to ourselves.

Notes

1. All references in this section are to Part II, Chapter 2 of *Sein und Zeit*.

2. I take the term *twisting free* from David Krell's translation of *Herausdrehung* and from John Sallis's use of the term in "Twisting Free: Being to an extent Sensible," *Research in Phenomenology*, 17 (1987): 1–21.

3. Does this mean that the being of dasein is a transcendental reality that is independent of its history? I discussed this question in detail in chapter 3 of *The Language of Difference* (Atlantic Highlands, N.J.: Humanities Press, 1986). The short answer is that the being of dasein, as the term is employed in *Being and Time*, must be historically formed and transcendent in its disclosiveness vis-á-vis everyday identities and selfhood. *Being and Time* begins a process whereby the issue of historicity and transcendence and the terms of the debate concerning them are recast and decisively changed by the priority that Heidegger gives to disclosure.

4. We said that in Foucault's account of surveillance the power to observe and judge is also a power to incarcerate. One developing claim in *Discipline/Punish* and toward the end of *The History of Sexuality* trilogy is that the state's manner of enforcing its interests in the welfare of its citizens changes as government changes from regency to forms of democracy. Authority is internalized. Instead of an external state's surveillance, an interior surveillance forms whereby we become incarcerated by a body of values to which we are taught to give voice: the power of conscience in this sense of the word is the power of a hierarchy of values. Genealogy is the approach Foucault uses to break this power in his writing. Instead of a different authority that counteracts the authority of modern conscience—and hence the authority of modern self—genealogy counteracts conscience by means of disclosing the power-interests that invest self and conscience in the context of those values. So, for example, our predisposition to distaste and disgust regarding dissemblance recoils against the dissemblance that constitutes the values of sincerity and non-dissembling honesty, the very values that generate our predisposition to disgust regarding dissemblance. In this way the modern conscience and self are in question in his writing.

Although Heidegger, in contrast to Foucault, uses *conscience* constructively in his analysis, we may also appropriately ask who is looking and judging in the context of his description of conscience. His direct answer is "das Man," the anonymous 'one' of our inherited structures of value. In the function of conscience, however, in its distance from its contingent religious and moral contents, and in the ontological function that Heidegger ascribes to call, language, and guilt, he finds neither a normative self not the priority of meaning and value. He finds the articulation of dasein's difference vis-à-vis its daily and traditional observations. *Conscience* names a movement of dasein that has no surveillance and no judgment, and, by conceiving it that way, one is in a movement of twisting free from the everyday that puts the priority of value-judgment in question. How are we to think outside this priority?

Nietzsche's account of the ascetic ideal claims that philosophical reflection as such originated in an ascetic, priestly contemplation that removed people by its activity from alertness to earthly, fragmented existence. Nietzsche's thought recoils in the strain that it puts on itself as thought and always diminishes itself in the metaphor of will to power and eternal return. Heidegger's thought, in the context of conscience, diminishes no less its own conscience regarding dasein's forgetful and banal life. The contents of everyday conscience, its clarity regarding right and wrong, its fearful guilt, its concern over metaphysical security and peace of mind, its presupposition not to question the axioms for conduct—its forgetful, banal life—are suspended by the recoiling movement whereby it puts itself in question by the values that it holds. This wrenching motion is an aspect of the conscience of *Being and Time*. It is in question in *Being and Time* no less than Nietzsche's philosophical reflection is in question in his reflective account of the ascetic ideal. If the wrenching, recoiling movement is emphasized, rather than the specific and static claims that Heidegger makes regarding the ontological status of conscience, we find the process in which both the subject of the description and the subjectivity of describing are in question.

5. In pathological grief, for example, a person is often traumatized by the interruption of death, and the grief is less over the loss than over the mortality that infuses the other and one's relation with the other.

Chapter 11

Heidegger on Values

Jacques Taminiaux

It is impossible to fully account for Heidegger's meditation on value without investigating how it links with the only pursuit of his long quest of thinking. A pursuit which *Being and Time* identified as the question of the meaning of Being, which the writings dating from the late thirties began to label as the question of the truth of Being, which the last writings finally characterized as the attempt to risk a step beyond metaphysics, into the thinking of Being. My purpose here is to deal successively with the later period of Heidegger's thought, and then retrospectively with his early thought.

I

The themes most likely to be noticed in the output of the last writings, initiated in that very attempt, are now familiar: our age is the one of the end of metaphysics; it is characterized by the planetary reign of technology; technology is, properly speaking, the metaphysics of our times; its field is not limited to the production of more and more sophisticated contraptions, nor to science, which this production always presupposes and presses to new advances, but it encircles our culture as a whole, the fine arts, politics, our entire relationship to things, our entire discourse, the entire human interaction; this reign finally offers nothing to thought other than the way of calculus, for which whatever *is* gets exhausted in its availability for all kinds of manipulations, forms of planning and renewed evaluations. All this accounts for everything, except the step that can be attempted, by retrogressing beneath metaphysics and its completed figure—technology—toward the meditation on Being.

Our age is the age of the end of metaphysics. The end takes place in the reign of technology, which is the reign of values. Nietzsche is the philosopher of that age. To go beyond the rule of values involves in Heidegger the recall of a long history, that of metaphysics precisely.

Metaphysics, from as early as its Platonic beginnings, suffered from an intrinsic equivocality which was relayed throughout its legacy and which, in the long term, gave way to modern technology. In a first approximation, it could be said that this equivocality is determined by the way in which metaphysics, in its beginnings, posed the question of Being. The way metaphysics posed the question from the outset obliterated the scope of the question. In it, the task of thinking Being was absorbed at the outset, almost imperceptibly into saying the truth about beings as such, and about the totality of beings. Trying to express what can universally be said about any being as such, metaphysics inaugurated something like a logic of beings, a theory of their predicates, of their essence, of their beingness, in one word, it became onto-logy. Simultaneously trying to gather the totality of beings, metaphysics likewise set itself to the task of discovering the being which is in the highest possible manner, the supreme being that is the ultimate foundation of all beings. Thus backing beingness with a supreme being, metaphysis inaugurates itself as theo-logy. Since both efforts simultaneously were combined and ended up overlapping each other, one can speak of an onto-theological essence of metaphysics. This essence is paradoxical and circular, since the categories which define the beingness of beings are understood in the light of a supreme being, and the latter is demonstrated with the help of the categories of beingness. As an ontology presupposing a theology, and a theology presupposing an ontology, metaphysics is a circular science, as Hegel liked to stress, who, close to us in time, attempted to bring it to a completed figure. Is this to say that Heidegger on that point does nothing but repeat Hegel? Certainly not. Deeper indeed than the circle of the foundation and of beingness which Hegel discovered and celebrated, there is the circle of Being and beings, which Hegel obliterated no less casually and perhaps more deeply than his predecessors. Regarding this ever obliterated circle, it is purely provisional to say that metaphysics moves within the onto-theological circle.

Let us notice that, by moving circularly between beings and their beingness, between the beingness of beings and the ultimate foundation of the totality of beings, metaphysics as onto-theology reveals that what keeps it alive and in movement is intrinsically differentiated, that its aim and its topic are in keeping with some differentiation. But never does this differentiation, as it is recognized by metaphysics, come to bear on Being itself. Precisely because, in the onto-theological circle, there is room only for differences between beings and beingness, between beingness and the supreme being, the difference is never other than ontical. Never does the difference concern Being itself, in as much as it is neither being(s) nor beingness, nor a supreme being, without, however, being anything other than the Being of what is. It is here that a feature of metaphysics is being touched upon, which is less apparent and provisional than its onto-theological structure, namely, what Heidegger has called the forgetfulness of Being, or more precisely, the forgetfulness of the fact that Being itself is not a being nor the totality of beings, in other words, the forgetfulness of the difference between Being and beings, the forgetfulness of the ontological difference. Here is the deeper circle that is obliterated by the onto-theological circle. It is one and the same thing to say, regarding this deeper circle, that Being is not beings and to say that it *is* beings. But it would be a mistaken view to consider that metaphysics simply fell prey to negligence by forgetting either this difference, which sustains all thinking, whether it wants it or not, or this ontico-ontological circle within which thinking cannot but be immersed. The forgetfulness of Being, of the difference between Being and beings, of their differentiated and differentiating circle, this forgetfulness which reaches its culmination in the reign of technology and values has not been the result of deeds of negligent people, the fault of metaphysicians who, from Plato to Nietzsche and Marx, paved the way to the current reign of values.

At the decisive time when under the spell, to be sure, of his 1933 erring and hallucinating in the midst of one of the most monstrous enterprises—after and before many other ones—of our century, Heidegger started his long meditation on Nietzsche's work in relation to our times and on the history of metaphysics as a whole, the following features imposed themselves on him: metaphysics as the increasing forgetfulness of Being, laying a final stamp on the destiny of the West, and—beyond—to that of the whole planet, far from being external to Being, is the guise under which Being itself destines itself to Western man. He was then writing:

Metaphysics is destiny in this strict sense, the only one considered here: as the fundamental feature of the history of Western Europe, it suspends human things in the midst of beings without ever allowing for the Being of beings to be experienced as the Fold of the two and hence to be known, questioned and positioned in its limits from and by metaphysics, in the truth of metaphysics (VA 77–78).

Because it is a destiny in this strict sense, metaphysics as the forgetfulness of Being and of the fold of Being and beings could in no way be considered throughout the succession of its main epochs as an unfortunate sequence of human, all too human errors. But that very notion of destiny is prone to lead us astray, if it suggests some lasting obstacle, or some evil power that plays with philosophers in spite of their integrity, but which would leave Being itself untouched. That is why Heidegger adds that: ". . . this destiny must be thought in relation to the history of Being." The history of metaphysics, as the lectures on Nietzsche emphasize, is not the history of the bad conceptions about Being which it would be high time to replace with correct notions; it is the very history of Being. Here we are getting closer to the inner equivocality which affects the entire Wester heritage. One must not only say that, by virtue of its onto-theological structure, metaphysics is assigned to oscillate between beingness and supreme being, nor even more deeply that this oscillating obliterates Being and brushes aside the difference between Being and beings, but one must say, even more deeply, that it is Being itself which throughout its historical guises, subtracts itself, forecloses itself, and excludes itself from what it gives to see: beings, entities, foundations. There is an equivocality specific to Being, deeper than metaphysical equivocality, and which helps the latter sustain itself without knowing it. To say that the history of metaphysics is the history of Being amounts to saying that, in each of the metaphysical epochs, Being itself is what advents, what unveils itself under a determined guise, but one under which it holds itself, retreats within itself, since, as Heidegger contends in *Der Satz Vom Grund*, "such is the meaning of the history of Being: Being itself offers itself to us, but in such a way that it hides its true essence."

Thus the questioning recollection of that long history does not aim at repairing the forgetfulness which constitutes its core. Much rather, it aims at experiencing it as an ordeal, in a way that is not accessible to metaphysics, at experiencing it as forgetfulness and in the full strength of its secret.

One knows the support that the oldest words of Greek thought bore to the Heideggerian trial of that secret, starting with the privileged word *aletheia* commonly translated by "truth" but which literally says: unveiling, unconcealing, disclosing. Heidegger stresses in his meditation on the history of Being that this word, before designating a capacity of man or of his discourse, refers to the process in which beings in their totality *(physis)* are brought to the open; moreover, it signals within that process a central ambiguity, the tension between a hiding or a reserve and an unconcealing or a coming out. The fact that in the Saying of the oldest poets and thinkers of the Greek world, vocables such as *aletheia, physis, logos, dike*, could be exchanged and that always in this crisscrossing the ambiguity of reserve and of unconcealing is kept vibrating, suggests that at the dawn of western thinking, Being, unnamed though it might have been, was not conceived but experienced as fully differentiated in the manner of an offering which holds itself back in what is offers, of a presence which subtracts itself within what it presents. This suggests that, at the same time, with Parmenides, the relationship of Thinking and Being is expressly named for the first time, and so we must be extremely careful not to project into that relationship one or the other of the metaphysical versions of the "identity" of the "rational" and the "real," or of the "subject" and the "object." We must instead attempt to decipher in it the sign that thinking means, in the sense of the deepest, opening of oneself to the call of Being in as much as Being keeps itself in the reserve while giving way to unconcealing. There is a correlative finitude of Being, understood as the difference between reserve and unconcealing, and of thought, in as much as the power that the latter bestows upon mortals finds its spring and its limit in a receptivity towards that very difference. There is a fundamental mutual belonging of those two finitudes, in the direction of which pre-Socratic Saying points.

II

Consequently, questioning the current reign of values first means recalling that in which metaphysics, out of which this reign is born, metamorphosed—along successive layers that are as many deviations from that to which pre-Socratic Saying was pointing to—the words of that Saying by erasing more and more their signifying power. Let us here limit ourselves to showing the most important strata of the erasing by following the major mutations brought to bear, along this history, upon the meaning of what the first Greeks called *aletheia*.

The first erasing, to which the history of metaphysics is linked, starts with Plato. Truth as "*aletheia*," that is to say, as the ambiguity of reserve and of concealing at the core of the process in which the totality of beings as a whole *(physis)* does not stop exhibiting itself under multiple guises, this truth is still on the horizon of Platonic dialogues, but these show a tendency to turn a mere consequence of the ambiguous process of *aletheia* into the very essence of it, which is then devoid of its initial ambiguity. For Plato, beings reveal what they are in their Idea. The "*idea*" is a word that designates first of all the look, the aspect, the appearance that things offer as they emerge out of the *physis*. The *idea* is therefore a consequence of the *physis* as the process of unveiling called *aletheia*. But in the Platonic concept of *idea*, the latter, because it has now moved to the forefront of the stage to the detriment of what it originates in, tends to separate itself from the origin. What is more, it acquires a founding and normative status in relation to *physis* itself. The unveiling process becomes the result of the clarity of Ideas. And the very light shining through each of them refracts the clarity of the highest Idea. Such is the birth of onto-theology in it obliterating power. Being, for which *physis* and *aletheia* are other names, is now prone to be obliterated in its polemical essence for the benefit of an ontical hierarchy: the sensible beings, the intelligible entities (the Ideas), the supreme being. The ambiguity inherent in initial *aletheia* conceived of as unconcealing then tends to vanish in the brightness without the shadow of the Idea. From now on, unconcealing—since its initial ambiguity is absorbed in the unadulterated clarity of the Idea—is a matter of correct seeing, of adjustment of the eyes *(omoiosis)*. That in the direction of which the Parmenides's Saying was pointing out, the belonging together of Being and thinking in their communal and reciprocal ambiguity gets levelled down to a univocal correlation, the conformity of the mind, *nous*, to the clarity of the Idea.

Along with that early metamorphosis of *aletheia* into a correct adjustment, an early anticipation of the reduction of Being to a value takes place. Heidegger writes in his *Nietzschebuch:* "The metaphysical thought in terms of values (...) is prepared in its essential features by the beginning of Metaphysics when Plato conceives of *ousia* as *idea* and *idea* as *agathon*" (NII 232). And again in the same context: "At the beginning of Metaphysics, the interpretation of Being as value is foreshadowed. Indeed Plato apprehends Being in terms of the Idea. But the highest of all Ideas—

i.e. at the same time the essence of all—is the *agathon*. For Greek thought the *agathon* is what makes being possible, what makes a being capable to be. Being makes possible, it is a condition of possibility. As Nietzsche says, Being is a value" (NII 221–222). This does not mean, of course, that Nietzsche, who, for Heidegger, is the metaphysician of values *par excellence*, merely repeats Plato, in spite of his violent anti-platonism. This does not mean either that Plato is already some sort of technological thinker. Plato's Metaphysics merely prepares from afar the Metaphysics of values. But the Metaphysics of values is a typically modern and not a Greek phenomenon. It required, in order to be developed, the modern invention of subjectivity. The invention of subjectivity was, after Plato's transformation of *aletheia* into correctness, the second step towards the current unbridling of values.

Let me recall Heidegger's characterization of this second step. The notion of truth, as conformity of the intellect to the beingness of beings with regard to the founding role of the supreme being, historically played a decisive role in medieval thinking in which it was linked to the notion of creation. Truth in the Scholastic sense, as "*adaequatio humani intellectus rei*" was founded indeed upon the deeper "adaequatio rei Dei intellectus." But the decisive shift for the advent of the current reign of values occurred at the dawn of modern times. The recognition of it can be traced in the writings of the founders of modern physics, and in their reappropriation in Descartes's theory of method.

For Aristotle, physical phenomena manifested themselves from the *physis* that brought them to unconcealment, and to acquire the science of these phenomena was to learn to express them such as they exhibited themselves from their own core. The phenomena were the outlooks of things. In that sense, the discourse of the Greek physicist was nothing but faithfulness to experience, that is to say, to the perceptive and sensible acceptance of the looks and face of things. The things of nature revealed their properties, depending on what face they presented. Their mobility, for example, i.e., the spontaneous way that the motions of water, air, stone and fire are exhibited, testifies to our bodily eyes that there are specific differences in nature each time corresponding to the specific appearance of the bodies in motion. It is well known that the invention of modern physics meant the end of all those differences. What is less suspected is that such an abolition presupposed a mutation in the concept of truth. The mutation becomes blatant if one pays attention to the way Galileo introduces the first formulation, still in approximate terms, of what Newton was soon to term the law of inertia. Galileo writes in his *Discorsi*: "I think of a body thrown on a horizontal plane and every obstacle excluded. It results from what has been given a detailed account in another place, that the motion of the body over this plane would be uniform and perpetual if this plane were extended infinitely." In the original Latin text, the sentence begins by the words *"Mente concipio"*: I conceive in my mind. The important matter here is not the replacement of the sensible perception by an intellectual one, but the fact that the phenomenon of inertia requires in order to appear, i.e., in order to be a phenomenon in a new meaning of the word, that the mind of the Ego leap ahead of what is given, give itself a preconception of what motion is, decide and project in advance the condition for phenomenality. In this, the properly modern mutation of truth is revealed, the metamorphosis of it into a conformity that keeps itself in view, that ascertains itself from itself. In the conformity between the intellect and the thing, the stress is not put so much on the thing, but on the intellect itself. The thing of nature from now on manifests its truth, is truly a phenomenon, in as much as it is in conformity with a project emanating from the *mens*. To this project the issue of mathematics in the restricted sense, the organizing of elements according order and measure, will be essential. But modern physics is not born from the fact that people like Copernicus, Kepler, Galileo started to apply measures. This recourse to mathematics is nothing but the consequence of something that runs deeper, namely, of the project by which the *mens* starting from its predetermines the phenomenality of that which is. Deeper than mathematics and at the core of it, *mathesis* is the very project in connection with which Descartes will say, in the *Regulae*, that mathematics is "the cover, rather than the parts." Descartes, here, claims Plato's authority. But from Plato to Descartes, the *mathesis* was deeply transferred. With Plato, it designated at the core of the soul the native familiarity with the Ideas, their remembrance left in each of us. With Descartes, Galileo's heir, it is less a remembrance than a project. A project which decides beforehand what the ideas must be, subjecting them to the rule of a *clara et distincta perceptio*. The confidence in the project is what the *cogito* expresses, no matter how much importance Descartes later assigned to finitude and dependency on the creator. The fact that the *cogito* tenaciously resists doubt signifies that, before any visible thing, before the world in its totality, before mathematics in the restricted sense, even before any clear and distinct idea, it is what posits itself as the unique center for reference, as the compelling basis upon which beings much reveal their Being, the first *hypokeimenon*. Object is now going to designate what is certain for the subject who seeks self-sustaining validity. The things that are, beings, the world, taken as objects, *are* in as much as they submit themselves to the project of *mathesis*. To know is therefore to keep oneself in view, to keep one's power in view, as, each in his own way, the first heralds of modernity—Descartes, Bacon, Hobbes—said it.

Such is the metaphysical birth of reckoning and evaluating reason that is today generalized. In a way, all its features appear together at the outset: the *mathesis* is universal, i.e., it plans for the totality of what is; this planning is both subjectification of all things, since it refers them to the only *cogito*, and objectification as such, since it makes them all equally calculable and controllable; well before the reign of machinery, it conceives of nature as a vast mechanism and projects an intrinsically technological eye upon it.

The further developments of modern philosophy did no more than unravel those features, so that between Descartes, on the one hand, and Nietzsche, on the other, there is no fundamental discontinuity.

There is no heterogeneity between the motto *Scientia propter potentiam* and the Nietzschean notion of will-to-power. The latter find its sway through the Leibnizian concept of the monad as the conjunction of perception and appetite, and in Leibniz's principle of reason. It is confirmed in Kant with the concept of a theoretical reason, which is only capable of knowing what it produces with its categories, and in the concept of a practical reason as condition of possibility. Then with Fichte, with the reinterpretation of Kant's Copernican revolution on the foundation of the pure activity of the Ego. Then with Schelling, who wrote that "there is absolutely no other Being than Will." Then in Hegel's speculative concept of the Absolute as willing its identity with itself throughout its differentiation. No matter how loudly Nietzsche claimed that with him metaphysics was dead, he was carrying subjectivity to its summit, unbridling it at the same time, under the form of an onto-theology of the Will. Is not the will to power, as aiming its own intensification, the beingness of all beings? And what is the eternal return of the same if not the ultimate foundation of that beingness? Even though he despised the age of the last man, and the triviality of engineers and of positivist minds in search of objectivity, one can wonder, Heidegger claims, whether Nietzsche was expressing anything else than the metaphysical essence of modern technology, an essence freed of all obstacles. Does not the will to power, conceived of as the beingness of all beings, bring to its utmost the universal project of objectification and subjectification inherent in *mathesis*? Here the objectification is brought to an extreme because such a will not only turns each being into an ob-ject *(Gegenstand)* but it even compels any object to become a core, a reserve *(Bestand)*, entirely available for any kind of summons. The subjectification is no less extreme since beings are only what will makes them be, since they are reduced to values that the will bestows upon them by means of the calculation through which it keeps in view its own intensification. As the ground of the totality of beings, the Eternal Return of the Same might well express then the essence of modern technology. Heidegger asks: "What is then the essence of the modern machine if not *some* configuration of the Eternal Return of the Same?" One should not conclude that the Eternal Return is to be understood in mechanical terms. The machine is only *one (some)* configuration among many others of a deeper, total, repetitive, endless, circular, frantic machination. This fundamental machination as a perpetual re-evaluating process is what the abysmal thought of the Eternal Return expresses. It says that the will that wants its own intensification is itself willed, that it undergoes the challenge to will itself endlessly. In Nietzsche's words: "Being? (. . .) just a vapor"; i.e., it is just a provisional value.

III

Our age is the age of values. Being is now entirely absorbed in and reduced to the again and again renewed perspectives that the will-to-power constantly projects in order to maintain and increase its power. In the age of values, the will no longer recognizes any other court than its own power and the values are the perspectives it has to project as means to guarantee its power. To the question of Being, the present answer is: the evaluating will-to-power is the essence of what is; the eternal recurrence of such evaluation is the ultimate ground of beings. This is the present version of onto-theology.

Consequently the ontological difference, i.e., the enigmatic withdrawal of Being within beings that the pre-Socratic thinkers meditated upon, is now completely covered up.

Such are the main features of Heidegger's treatment of the notion of value in the framework of his meditation on the history of Being, i.e., the history of Western metaphysics.

Instead of concluding, however, allow me to raise a few questions that intentionally restrict Heidegger's treatment of the problem of values to an internal discussion.

Heidegger's treatment of the problem of values such as I have tried to summarize appeared rather late in his thought. It took place in the late thirties after the so-called *Kehre* or Turn that he talks about in the *Letter on Humanism*. So that the first question to be raised in the framework of an internal discussion of his treatment of the problem of values should obviously be: what about values in Heidegger's philosophy *before* the turn? Moreover, since after the turn his treatment of this problem takes the form of a meditation on a historical process of which Plato marks the beginning, whereas Nietzsche marks the end, our confrontation between Heidegger's treatment of the problem before and after the turn should include questions like: What about Plato in Heidegger's early thought? And what about Nietzsche for the same period?

But as soon as we raise these questions, while keeping in mind the problematic I have recalled so far, we are puzzled. If we look, for example, for an explicit discussion of the problem of values in *Being and Time*, we soon realize that our search is vain. There are only a few dispersed allusions to the notion—twelve allusions if I am correct. To be sure, in those discreet and dispersed allusions, Heidegger often uses the world "value" in quotation marks, which seems to indicate that he does not make the notion his own, more precisely that he does not think in terms of values, and even that he dismisses the relevance of the notion for his own ontological problematic. However, we would be wrong in believing that his distrust towards the notion is based on a dismissal of the modern principle of the priority of subjectivity. To be sure, he distrusts at once the notion of value and the modern concept of the *ego cogito*. But such distrust is less the symptom of a dismissal than the sign of a radicalization. Heidegger at that time agrees with modern philosophy, from Descartes to Husserl, that philosophical investigation has for its only ground the being that we ourselves are. What he disagrees with is not the priority of our own being, but the modern ontological definition of our own being. Modern philosophers were right in affirming the priority of our own being over nature. They were wrong in understanding our own being in terms of consciousness instead of existence and in conceiving of consciousness in the light of the being of nature. When Descartes affirmed "*cogito sum*," his understanding of the word "*sum*" was ontologically deficient. He simply meant under the word *sum* presence-at-hand, *Vorhandenheit*, constant presence, i.e., the way of being of natural entities. Over and against this conception, the right ontological understanding of our priority supposes an ontological distinction between *Vorhandenheit* and existence. Our way of being is existence and not *Vorhandenheit*, and the privilege we give to *Vorhandenheit* is the outcome of a falling away from our own way of being. Likewise when Heidegger in *Being and Time* holds in suspicion the modern distinction between fact and value, the former understood as a natural occurrence, the second understood as a human projection, what he reproaches in the distinction is that it is not radical enough. In a sense, the distinction fact-value suggests the recognition of a radical distinction between *Vorhandenheit* and existence, but the recognition is blurred out right away by the attribution to values of an ontological status, which is nothing else than *Vorhandenheit*. By adding values to facts, do we not tacitly suppose "that these value characters themselves are (. . .) just ontical characteristics of those entities which have the kind of Being possessed by things? Adding on value-predicates cannot tell us anything at all new about the Being of goods, *but would merely presuppose again that goods have pure presence-at-hand as their kind of Being.* Values would then be determinate characteristics which a thing possesses, and they would be *present-at-hand*. They would have their sole ultimate ontological source in our previously laying down the actuality of things as the fundamental stratum" (SZ 99). In other words, what Heidegger holds in suspicion here in the notion of value is the implicit ontological understanding of values based on a higher stratum of presence-at-hand added to a previous stratum of the same. However, he does not reject values; he refers them to an ontological source which is not presence-at-hand but existence. And in *Being and Time*, existence is understood in terms of the entire constellation of notions that Heidegger after the turn criticizes in Nietzsche's philosophy of values: projection of possibilities, interpretation, will. The key phrase, *Das Dasein existiert umwillen seiner*, clearly indicates that Heidegger at that time was far removed from his later critique of subjectivity. The *Dasein* exists towards itself and for the sake of itself. It is in itself that the key for the understanding of the ultimate meanings, the meanings of Being, is to be found.

All this is confirmed by the way Heidegger treats Nietzsche and Plato in the framework of his early project, namely, fundamental ontology.

As far as Nietzsche is concerned, let me just recall the fact that he is quoted by Heidegger in two decisive paragraphs of *Being and Time*, that is to say, in §53 whose topic is the "existential projection of an authentic Being-toward-death," and in §76 whose topic is "the existential source of historiology in Dasein's historicality." In both cases, Nietzsche is referred to without any reservation or discussion and presented as a fellow-traveler. Let me quote §76: "Nietzsche recognized what was essential as to the 'use and abuse of historiology for life' in the second of his studies 'out of season' (1874), and said it unequivocally and penetratingly. He distinguished three kinds of historiology—the monumental, the antiquarian, and the critical—without explicitly pointing out the necessity of this triad or the ground of its unity. The threefold character of historiology is adumbrated in the historicality of Dasein (...) Nietzsche's division is not accidental. The beginning of his study allows us to suppose that he understood more than he has made known to us" (SZ, 396). The above passage amounts to an acknowledgment by Heidegger at that time of a close proximity between Nietzsche and himself. This was discreetly stressed by Heidegger later on when he started criticizing Nietzsche. In the *Gesamtausgabe* version of a course on Nietzsche offered by Heidegger in 1936–1937, we find a footnote which stresses the following: "My debate with Nietzsche is supported by 'the most intimate kinship'" (GA 43, 277). Indeed, in *Being and Time*, there is at least one central topic about which Heidegger is in full agreement with Nietzsche—the topic of truth. He shares with Nietzsche the idea that the mere contemplative adequacy with an objective state of affairs is not the original form of truth but rather the outcome of a relapse from an authentic form of truth which is an active movement of disclosing oriented towards the future possibility of Being of the knowing individual. For Heidegger as well as for Nietzsche, this movement, which is the very impetus of interpreting what is at stake, concerns a *selfwilling*, as opposed to what Nietzsche in the second essay in *Untimely Meditations* calls the *Selbstlosigkeit* that is involved in the condition of an objective mirroring of facts. In other words, what is at issue here in the authentic notion of truth is not at all the mystery of Being, but an *evaluating* process of which the only rule is the utmost and ownmost possibility of the *Self*.

As far as Plato is concerned, I have suggested above that, after the so-called turn, Heidegger claimed that the metaphysical thought in terms of values that blurs out the enigma of Being is prepared by the Platonic theory of Ideas, and by Plato's concept of the *agathon* conceived of as a condition of possibility. In other words, Plato's concept of the *agathon* is the first decisive obliteration of the ontological difference, and Plato is the grand-grand-father of Nietzsche. Now, what do we find about Plato's *agathon* before the turn, let's say in the period of *Being and Time*? As far as I know, there are at least two writings of that period in which Heidegger deals with Plato's concept of the *agathon* as the highest Idea which is *epekeina tes ousias*, beyond Being. Those writings are: the lecture course, *The Metaphysical Foundations of Logic*, given in Marburg in 1928, and the 1929 lecture course, *The Essence of Ground (Vom Wesen des Grundes)*. Consider this citation from the 1928 lecture course:

> What we must, moreover, learn to see in the ἰδέα τοῦ ἀγαθοῦ is the characteristic described by Plato and particularly Aristotle as the οὗ ἕνεκα, the *for-the-sake of-which*, that on account of which something is not, is in this way or that. The ἰδέα τοῦ ἀγαθοῦ, which is even beyond beings and the realm of ideas is the for-the-sake of-which. This means it is the genuine determination that, transcends the entirety of the ideas and at the same time thus organizes them in their totality. As ἐπέκεινα, the for-the-sake of-which excels the ideas, but, in excelling them, it determines and gives them the form of wholeness, κοινωνία, communality. If we thus keep in mind the οὗ ἕνεκα characteristic of the highest idea, the connection between the doctrine of ideas and the concept of world begins to emerge: the basic characteristic of world whereby wholeness attains its specifically transcendental form of organization is the for-the-sake of-which. World, as that to which *Dasein* transcends, is primarily defined by the for-the-sake of-which (MFL 184–85).

It is obvious from this passage that Heidegger here does not at all conceive of Plato's concept of the *agathon* as the first decisive obliteration of the ontological difference. He doesn't stress any gap whatsoever between Plato and his own ontology of *Dasein*. Quite the contrary. Plato's concept of the *agathon—epekeina tes ousias—* is presented as Plato's version of being-in-the-world as a movement of *transcendence* beyond beings towards Being. In other words, Plato's notion of the *agathon* reveals *the ontological difference as that very movement*. In Heidegger's ontology of *Dasein*, Plato's concept of the *agathon*, instead of being held in mistrust by Heidegger, is celebrated and reappropriated by him. In what terms is it reappropriated? In terms of willing. Right after the passage I just quoted, we find the following: "But a for-the-sake of-which, a purposiveness *(Umwillen)* is only possible where there is a willing *(Willen)* (...). To put it briefly Dasein's transcendence and freedom are identical. Freedom provides itself with intrinsic possibility; as being is, as free, necessarily in itself transcending" (MFL 185). In other words, Plato's idea of the *agathon* not only reveals transcendence, and the ontological difference; it also reveals that the ontological difference is a matter of *will*.

This means that, before as well as after the turn, Plato and Nietzsche go together, but they do so for opposite reasons, since before the turn they are both reappropriated and celebrated, whereas after the turn they are both held in suspicion.

But if my presentation is correct, it raises perhaps the suspicion that the later critique of Plato and Nietzsche as metaphysicians of value is first of all a critique of Heidegger by himself.

But then our astonishment rebounds as it were. First, because Heidegger never explicitly said that his work after the turn was a self-criticism. Second, because in a self-criticism which transfers a fate to the history of Being conceived as a destiny, the origin of the flaws in one's own thought can perhaps be suspected of some lack with respect to a sense of responsibility. Isn't it strange that, in Nietzsche's mediation on the history of Being, the very notion of responsibility seems to vanish? This entails a third reason for astonishment. How can one come to terms with the concept of value while avoiding the issue of responsibility? Last question: is it possible to come to terms with the notion of value from a merely ontological viewpoint? Is it right to think that, in the problem of value, Being alone is an issue? After all, we can all experience that, in many discussions on values, what is at stake is human plurality and the way people judge human affairs. It does not seem that these topics have ever been a central concern in Heidegger's meditation.

VI. Reading the *Beiträge*

Chapter 12

Ultimate Double Binds

Reiner Schürmann

(translated by Kathleen Blamey)

> Entering into being-there, its instant and its place: how does this occur in Greek tragedy?
>
> —M. Heidegger[1]

What has Heidegger done with—and to—philosophy? The question is worth asking since he himself seems to claim that he has (a) established philosophy on entirely new grounds, (b) put an end to it, and (c) remained content with merely reading its history. These claims seem rather difficult to hold together.

Philosophers have traditionally assigned themselves the task of securing foundations by which to legitimate laws for thinking, knowing, acting, and making. Arguing one first law determining all regional laws a secondary, they have served as "the functionaries of mankind."[2] In order to glimpse what Heidegger has done with and to philosophy, it is therefore advisable to take one's bearings from his single issue throughout his writings—his attempt to understand being as time—and ask: Does the temporality by which the later Heidegger seeks to understand being in any way function as the law of laws, and, if so, how?

The question can be answered tersely. In moving out of the transcendental subjectivism whose shadows still lingered over *Being and Time*, Heidegger does not exactly move away from the quest for ultimacy that philosophers have pursued since Parmenides; being as time remains, one may say, the ultimate condition of phenomena. But he disrupts in that condition what has been essential to any figure of firstness: simplicity. Representations held to be ultimate impose on phenomena a single bind. If they did not, their multiplicity or complexity would have to be accounted for, which means that they would have to depend in turn on one more fundamental representation and thus could not be ultimate. Now if being is to be though of as time, it will no longer satisfy that principal requirement. 'Being' cannot be listed, then, in the archive of names given to the First more originary than which nothing can be thought. In the later Heidegger, the retrieval of the issue of being has to be placed under an epigraph, not taken from Plato (as in *Being and Time*), but one invoking the tragics (see the line quoted above). The heroes of Attic tragedy suffer indeed *a condition that is originary without being simple*.

Inasmuch as it repeats that condition, being as time obliges one to think ultimacy anew. It obliges one to think of the law of laws as a normative double bind.[3]

The starting point of any philosophy has been a perplexity before one precise phenomenon or region of phenomena. In Plato, it was axiomatic geometry; in Aristotle, substantial change brought about by human know-how. In *Being and Time*, the heuristic experience was everyday involvement with 'stuff'. Now, what struck the later Heidegger as problematical was the global reach of contemporary technicity. He diagnosed it as the apogee of thetic subjectivity exhausting its normative resources. The diagnosis entails that our locus in Western history is bifrontal, as is a line of closure or the face of Janus. In the apogee of hegemonic subjectivity lies the possibility of its perigee; in the most brutally subsumptive *single bind* lies the opportunity of remembering a more ancient *double bind*. To learn how the later Heidegger understand being, one must therefore try to trace the step back by which he moves from that pathology of our historical site to the tragic essence of being *qua* event.

His attempts at retrieving the being event are as diverse as they are unrelenting. They offer various avenues to trace this step backward. I choose to read a few sections from a text written during the years when the contemporary pathos forced itself upon Heidegger with blinding self-evidence (just what sort of blindness will soon become apparent), namely, form the *Beiträge zur Philosophie (Contributions to Philosophy)*.

In starting from the disparate site that is our own, one can say that the *Contributions* succeeds where *Being and Time* failed. A heuristic temporality that is only marginally subjectivist allows Heidegger to step back toward the temporality of being itself: the one and only step for which he had been practicing, as it were, all along. In this temporality of withering subjecto-centrism, the edges of the era instituted by the *cogito* are fraying. The contemporary pathos signifies a non-thetic possible, announcing itself in an ultra-thetical present. This essential discordance of times is what needs most to be retained from the 'closure of metaphysics'—at least, if one wishes to understand Heidegger's suggestion that the end of epochal history may produce the liberation from self-incurred tutelage.[4] The temporality of the possible exit from normative theticism is non-subjectivist in that, unlike the temporal ecstasies, it appears in an epochal constellation, not in some offshoot of the solipsistic ego; and it reveals originary temporality in that such constellations spell out a history of being, not of some collective subject. In the fading of subjectivity as the modern focus for constituting the phenomenality of phenomena, Heidegger reads the self-emptying—the *kenosis*—of all normative representations. The 'loss of standards' that has been happening to the West over the last century and a half is instructive for the being-question as it indicates a hiatus that spatializes and temporalizes from within what philosophers have pursued as ultimate conditions. Indeed, in accordance with the hypothesis of a closure of metaphysics, our historical site is marked by a deferment separating the 'not-there' from the 'there'[5]—a spatial gap which is not the issue here, but which translates the temporality split between the integrative violence of the technological present and the potential for disintegration that is displays. This economy, spaced and deferred from within, sums up the heuristic function of our age for answering the question, What is the temporality of being?

The argument worth considering here is that discordant space-times can be granted only by a *condition in itself discordant*. Heidegger describes this condition as the event of appropriation-expropriation (thereby collapsing the problem of space into that of time).

The fractured condition—the discordance of times *(dissecutio temporum)* which is being—will obviously not remain without repercussion upon beings. It is what makes us mortals. It places the beings that we are within the double bind of birth and death, i.e., within differing pulls (rather than between distant facts). It places us within the double bind of being-through-birth and being-toward-death, or of natality and mortality.[6] Heidegger's entire effort, however, aims at thinking the discordant time of being in its singularity and without the detours, either via our de facto history (which fulfills the merely heuristic function inasmuch as late modernity knows itself to be *bound* by a paralyzing planetary grip apparently beyond solution and, at the same time, *unbound* from the idealities in the name of which, only yesterday, we killed and died), or via the beings that we are (who fulfill a verificatory function, since everyone knows being-toward-death which makes us finite and so *binds* us, as well as being-through-birth from which arise the maximizing impulses that *unbind* us). Originarily discordant time, then, appears as the law in disaccord with itself. To the old question of being *qua* being, the Heidegger who speaks after the fault of 1933–34 answers with this nomic monster: the originary, and in that sense ultimate, disparity of legislation-transgression. This is the tragic double bind.

The Birth of the Law from Tragic Denial

On a wall in Pompeii there is a fresco that represents Agamemnon sacrificing his daughter, Iphigenia. What is remarkable about the picture is that the head of the koricidal faither is veiled.

Agamemnon, Homer wrote, ruled over "many isles and all Argos" (*Iliad* 2, 108). He was the most powerful of the Greek princes. After Paris had carried off Helen, the wife of Menelaos, it fell to Agamemnon, Paris's brother, to lead the punitive expedition against Troy. None other than Zeus ordered the operation. The flotilla was assembled in Aulis, in Boiotia, but Artemis caused adverse winds to blow. It was she who demanded the sacrifice. Agamemnon, therefore, found himself placed at the intersection of two divine commandments. Is this not enough to make one cover one's head?

He also found himself placed at the intersection of two laws. Whence his complaint: "Heavy doom will crush me if I disobey, and heavy doom as well if I slaughter my child, the glory of my house. How could I stain the virgin blood these father's hands and slay my daughter by the altar's side! Is there a choice that does not bring me woe?" The conflict of laws appears more clearly here than with other tragic heroes. For the first among leaders, what law could win out over the obligation to carry through a war ordered by the first among gods? Yet for a father, what law could be stronger than that of preserving his child's life? "Is there a choice that does not bring me woe?" The question is obviously rhetorical. Disaster, indeed, is sure to fall on the father who, in the name of public responsibilities, denies his family ties; but disaster, too, will fall on the leader of the army who, in the name of his bloodline, denies his political duty. Faced with such a nomic conflict, how could one not cover one's head?

Lastly, Agamemnon finds himself placed at the intersection of two transgressions. His brother's hubris in abducting Helen can only end up ruining the city *(polis)*, just as his ancestor's hubris—Atreus's, who had killed his own son—can only end up ruining the household *(oikos)* and the family line. He himself had committed neither of these two faults: neither the one that is now plunging the cities into war, nor the one that is about to destroy his home. They *fall* upon him. "Heavy doom will crush me if I disobey and heavy doom as well is I slaughter my child." Whether he chooses to desert *(liponaus,* 1. 212) his commander's post or to disrupt his lineage, there remains no way out of the situation without incurring guilt. Is it then these two destinies of retribution that intersect under the veil: two ancient kinds of blindness and their sudden differing as it strikes at Aulis?

Now, speaking at Aulis, Agamemnon takes a strange turn. Without transition or pause, he changes tone. From one verse to the next, the conflict of obligations is carried off—as if by favorable winds, effective even before they blow. "It is right and holy that I should desire with exceedingly impassioned passion the sacrifice staying the winds, the maiden's blood" (1. 214 ff.). The either-or, which just an instant ago was so cruel in its two opposing laws, is now *decided*. What is more, the law embraced by Agamemnon is no longer an evil, it is *themis*: right, just, sacred.[7]

With a wave of the hand, one of the laws in conflict—the law of the family—has been erased. This is *tragic denial*.

It amounts to a new hubris, one that will bear its terrible fruit upon the return from Troy. At Aulis, Aeschylus shows this denial enflaming the passions of Agamemnon. Anguish gives way to audacity: "He dared to sacrifice his daugher" (1. 233f.). "He would not hear nor heed the girl's voice plead: 'pity me, father'." The routine of ritual slaughter is applied to her. Her father places her on the altar, "as one hoists a goat for sacrifice" (1. 232). To silence her curses—and to avoid that these fall upon the house—she is gagged. Also as with an animal, a "bit" is placed in her mouth (1. 237). The expression is Agamemnon's. Thus he completes the transformation of his daughter into an animal to be slaughtered.

Thus, more noteworthy still, Agamemnon makes himself into a military leader, released from contrary allegiances. *A tragic denial is necessary if a univocal law is to be born.*

The Pompeiian fresco is then not so difficult to understand. What is it that Agamemnon no longer sees? It is what the chorus sees only too well. Of Iphigenia, the chorus says: "with one last piteous dart her glance struck the sacrificers..." (1. 239). To this human gaze, calling for another human gaze, Agamemnon blinds himself. The painter has depicted this very veil of denial.

Tragedy traces out something like a path of sight. The hero *sees* the laws in conflict. Then—this is the moment of tragic denial—he *blinds himself* toward one of them, keeping his *gaze fixed* on the other. Armies and cities have lived, and continue to live, within the shadow of this blindness. Then follows a catastrophe that *opens his eyes*: this is the moment of tragic truth. The vision of irreconcilable differing *takes his sight away* (even gouges his eyes out, as was the case for Oedipus and in another way for Tiresias), and it singularizes the hero to the point that the city has no room for him any longer. From denial to recognition, blindness is transmuted. His orbits empty, Oedipus sees a normative double bind, i.e., tragic differing.

In the elation of the slaughter, the law of the city asserts itself wantonly against that of the family. Hence the legislative hubris which will cost Agamemnon dearly once back from his expedition.

Now—such is the lesson of Heideggerian *Ereignis* as the differing of appropriation-expropriation—the law is always born from a repression of the transgressive other, just as life sustains itself by repressing death, the other that transgresses it. This conflictuality by which Heidegger understands being stands most in need of elucidation. In the sphere of history, it makes for innumerable constellations of *epechein* (suspension or withholding of originary strife), i.e., for innumerable epochs. In the sphere of the political, it breaks the univocity of the law. One has therefore to ask: What legislation and what transgression are at issue here?

Legislation

To the genealogist of normative representations, philosophical hubris declares itself in legislative, not transgressive, acts. The representations successively phantasized as ultimates to legitimate order in the West have forced themselves upon us through the very terror whose effect sent piteous darts from Iphigenia's eyes. A wantonness comparable only to Agamemnon's has promoted phantasms to the rank of ultimate standards for their epoch. To philosophers, acting in this as mankind's functionaries, has fallen the task of *Urstiftung* as understood by Heidegger: the task of instituting one focal sense of being. If one were to draw up a genealogy of these institutitions, the law of laws would in every instance turn out to arise from this or that finite phenomenon phantasmically maximized into a standard. For this normative theticism alone, Heidegger lumps together as 'humanist' all philosophies of order (a pleonastic phrase, anyway, since, for the genealogy, the very vocation of philosophy is to display things to man, according to an order).

Legislative hubris is to be spoken of, then, in the comparative as well as in the superlative. In the comparative, for if all things manifest have been fixed by man around himself according to one order or another—if he has made himself their measure—this is because he has posited himself, and continues to do so, as worth more. The standardization of beings results from a comparison of valence and of value whereby man validates his hegemony in the constitution of phenomenality. But 'humanist' wantonness reaches the superlative when man sets about to leap over his own shadow and attempts to establish himself on a post-hegemonic terrain; when he makes the post-subjectivist, post-thetic economy his affair within his means. Then, Heidegger asks, "does the hubris of the given standard *(Anmaßung der Maßgabe)* not turn out *even greater* than where [man] remains posited simply as the standard?" (GA 65, 25). Thus the denial of transgressive counter-laws curiously reaches its apex when the loss of norms becomes a common conviction, when there prevails a common resolve to shake ancient and modern fixations, and when it looks good—or even a little old-fashioned already—to hold forth on transgression. There is more impassioned elation still than Agamemnon's. It intoxicates pronouncements stating with no more ado than the commander at Aulis that metaphysics is closed and that its play of normative theses is over.[8] A rabid denial it is. The claim merely adds to the thetic game. It locks itself up for good in the poses and positions struck: in the very theticism it declares out of date.

Yet language itself commits us without escape to generalization and subsumption. We cannot speak 'in singulars'. In every utterance, we obey the law of the common. If, however, in every law a transgressive strategy disrupts the legislative strategy, then this oldest observation about language is not well served by the vocabulary of universals. It is best described in that of phenomenalization, which thematizes *singulars in contexts*. Hence this lesson of legislative hubris: there is a phenomenalizing—regional—violence that cannot be unlearned; and there is a universalizing—trans-regional—violence that the West, while in its throes, has been trying to unlearn for more than a century. Phenomenalization means that things gather in a world. Legislation as Heidegger understands it is entirely regional, as the law of such contextualizing and 'worlding' remains in incessant flux.

It is impossible to escape regional violence: the micro-violence through which a body organ asserts itself, the macro-violence through which a collectivity asserts itself—both 'micro' and 'macro' nourished by language. Indeed, one must not forget that Thebes becomes livable again through the nomotheses of Oedipus the *tyrant*. Life sustains itself through claiming territory after territory. So, too, do the concepts in our languages get serialized. This polymorphous integrative violence results from the phenomenological trait of natality.[9] In other words, it is impossible to get away, without suffering *factual singularization*, from either the *polis* or the concept. Nevertheless, to go through life with one's eyes open means to see tragic denial shape the entire morphological scope of the law. Crossing through our public spheres, in particular the national, with one's eyes open is seeing that they maintain themselves at the cost of obliterating—if necessary, through extreme violence—the counter-law that I shall call below the *singularization to come*.

Another thing entirely is the violence of some trans-regional law, maximized out of one region of experience. Thus normative subjectivity is maximized out of the experience that 'I think'. What late modernity may be striving to get away from is this very univocity. It is a harsh unlearning, marked by relapses of various scales. The *Führer* differs from the Greek *tyrannos* precisely through the nomothetic maximizing of a collective subject, posited as the phantasmic ultimate focus. I have suggested the analogy that likens epochal institutions, from which such hegemonic phantasms are born, to Agamemnon's legislative coup at Aulis. Now in National Socialism, this analogy between a regional referent (such as Solon in the institution of the phenomenal region, democracy) and ultimate referent collapses into identity. From Aulis to Berlin, the political, regional code gets exalted into an ultimate, hegemonic nomothesis. The Heidegger of the *Contributions*, having just come back, as it were, from the properly modern hyperbolic self-assertion of normative subjectivity, now puts all his effort into bringing the counter-law to recollection through which the singular always subverts ultimate foci such as the one he had served.

The lesson teaches the double blind. What would public life be like under the disparate *versions* of uni*ver*salizing principles and of the singular sub*ver*ting them—the version whose functional origin is the 'event turned against itself'? Faced with the apparatus set into place by the univocal law, this tragic knowledge hardly ever has a chance. It may even lack legitimacy in the polity.[10] One may be no more successful in attempting to slip away from underneath ultimate phantasms than in sneaking outside of the *polis*, let alone of the concept. But here is what makes all the difference, setting Heidegger's 'other thinking' apart from 'the one thinking' which has been that of mankind's functionaries: in ultimate phantasms, subjectivity included, there is no denying the denial on which they feed, as Creon and Antigone deny that their respective law feeds on the denial of its other. There is no denying the denial in ultimacy claims since the necrology of past epochs's destitutions is just as recordable as the genealogy of their institutions.

The knowledge of the double bind will, at the very most, act through sporadic, discursive interventions: through 'the other thinking'. It recalls—both remembers and repeals—publicly the hubris of any univocal law, that is, of any collective single bind.

Concerning the law, the other thinking no longer traces the genealogy of epochal nomotheses, but its origin in the event of appropriation-expropriation. From that other viewpoint, the law remains traversed by the nocturnal retraction denied to it by the attraction of diurnal order. As one seeks, not its epochal condition in one focal sense of being, but its originary condition in being as *Ereignis*, the law loses its ordering power. Here, then, is Heidegger at his most radical: in his step back, from the epochal institutions that have held and continue to hold normative power, to the origin of all normativity in the conflictual event. This step leads from a plainly subsumptive Yes to a conflict in which a No enters the Yes, shattering its power of subsumption.

In epochal institutions, Heidegger writes, "the ordinary Yes gets immediately and heedlessly maximized into *that* Yes pure and simple that lends its standard to every No" (GA 65, 246). He distinguishes between two kinds of Yes. One is ordinary, uttered tacitly or vocally before something that is the case: 'yes, she is beautiful'; 'yes, at this moment I am thinking'; 'yes, my country'. By such a constative Yes we give our assent to whatever is. The correlative No, one might add, is its strict constative counterpart: 'no, she is not ugly like her mother'; 'no, I am not now singing'; 'no, I am not American'. The other Yes, or the other kind of Yes, results from an operation more complex than reporting. First, there is but one of that kind: it is the Yes *schlechthin*, he says. Then, correlation to the No changes into determination, since this Yes does something "to every No". The No, for its part, remains manifold, but this Yes passes into the position of ultimate standard for any constative Yes or No. Lastly, what the single Yes does to all No's is to lend them its plain standard.

Such normative institution is a complex operation inasmuch as oneness, ultimate determination, and standardization lack any phenomenal mooring. They are no longer wrested from what shows itself as being the case. The standard-setting Yes (one may call it the norm) results, and this is now the key word, from a maximization starting from an assent to something that does show itself. The standard-setting Yes is *aufgesteigert*. For Heidegger this operation marks the end of all faithfulness to phenomena and the start of speculation. To claim that one can deny—namely, particulars—only after having affirmed—namely a universal—is to state the very mechanics of subsumption. This mechanics produces, as law, some Yes *in relation* to which alone every No is a No. With the No so rendered secondary, being is 'forgotten'.

It is noteworthy that for Heidegger legislative maximizations are never formal in the sense in which they would posit a neutral structure. They always elevate some content. From 'yes, she is beautiful' the operation passes to the fullness of *kalokagathia*; from 'yes, I am thinking' it passes to the thickness of the *cogito*; and from 'yes, my country', to the country *über alles*. . . .

It is just as noteworthy that, in this critique of assertoric maximization, the possibility of a Yes that would be phenomenologically prior to any negation never even arises. For Heidegger, it is precisely a matter of remaining faithful to phenomena; no longer to this or that one among them, nor to this or that region of experience, but to the phenomenon not to be outstripped which is the double bind between being-through-birth and being-toward-death. A Yes that would be an originary word (*Urwort*[11]) remains literally out of the question once the being question takes its starting point in this double bind, which the pathology of global technicity makes increasingly obvious and which alone is originary—and alone neutral—since it is the sole phenomenon truly familiar to everyone. Hence the phenomenological project more ancient than theticism and denial, a project that is neither speculative nor optional, namely, to rehabilitate the No and the Not as *the singular other of being as singular*. "From the singularity of being follows the singularity of the Not belonging to it, and consequently the singularity of the other. The one *and* the other are binding" (GA 65, 267). Rehabilitating a Yes-No of disparate singulars amounts to giving the last word to an originary differing that sets every law against itself (more about which, below).

The origin of the law in the event of appropriation-expropriation disturbs the principles of order such as oneness, ultimate determination, and standardization. It makes them function against—in a nondialectic 'against'—the most efficient mechanics of order: oppositional negation. Heidegger restores to the Yes its correlation to the No, denied by the legislating coup that likens these principles to the law championed by Agamemnon at Aulis. However, such restitution forever ruins any *tranquillitas ordinis*. Before examining this normative double bind restored, one needs to look at the transgression it retains as co-originary.

Transgression

How is one to understand the expropriation in *Ereignis* (event of appropriation-expropiation)? In terms of the law: How is one to understand the transgression in the ultimate (legislative-transgressive) double bind? Two senses of transgression are to be excluded; a third will have to be retained.

a. Heidegger's sarcasm concerning any extra-territoriality posited by mere *fiat*, the target of which was clear in the 1930s, has by no means lost its relevance. It could easily be redirected today. In self-proclaimed avant-garde circles, transgression is made *the* law. Yet this does not guarantee faithfulness to expropriation in the event. If in our day and age such faithfulness is best learned by inquiring into the distant origins of technicity and into the potential it yields, then transgression is not to be taken here in the sense for instance "preluded" to by Michel Foucault.[12] Transgression does not denote here the passage beyond some closure, not some step across the line *(trans lineam)*.

b. Another strategy of *trans*-is more complex. In the part of the *Contributions* titled *The Leap*, one of the sections is headed "Overmeasure in the Essence of Being" (GA 65, 249). By overmeasure *(Übermaß)* is to be understood, Heidegger adds, not a quantitative surplus, but a measure that "refuses to be evaluated and to be measured." The paradox—a standard of measurement beyond all measurement—is ancient. It recalls the step beyond being *(epekeina tes ousias)* as construed by the Alexandrians and their epigones. This paradox, however, pertains to the core of every doctrine of principles. A standard is a principle only if it is not in turn measured by some other standard. Whence the warning: "Overmeasure is not the beyond [that would define] some supra-sensible realm." In other words, it puts out of play any sequence of 'before and after' among intelligibles. It does so as it puts out of play the representation of universals and their hierarchy. Thus overmeasure is "binding" *(Erzwingung)* indeed, but not *simply* so. It cannot, therefore, be modeled after *a priori* constraints as exerted, for instance, by the Greek *agathon* and *hen*. Every principle, every norm and law, is a binding standard—on the condition, however, that it reign *simply*. Now simplicity is just what Heidegger challenges in 'overmeasure'. He undoes the *a priori* by dealing a blow to the prestige of simplicity. Of that blow, anti-subjectivism is but a consequence. One may well fail to see that he tries to think of an ultimacy that would not entail simplicity, for the expressions used have an all too familiar ring: "nothingness alone is of a rank equal to being because it belongs to it." If it is a matter of 'rank' after all, is one not compelled to recall, for instance, the Dionysian *hyper-on*, itself a *hyper-metron*? Such ancestry seems all the more obvious since nothingness is to be understood, he continues, "*as the overmeasure of pure refusal*" (GA 65, 245). In Dionysius, the prefix *hyper-* compounds the distance marked by the more ancient *epekeina*. The prefix removes the term to which it is attached out of reach. It designates an ultimate focusing that refuses to yield to our thinking[13]—a refusal which, to the Neoplatonic mainstream, indicates an excess of simplicity.

Now this precise and venerable lexicon gets diverted here on the very exaltation of simplicity. The overmeasure, Heidegger writes, "opens the *strife* and keeps open the space for every strife" (GA 65, 249). That, then, is how it binds beings. It commits them to discord. Not, to be sure, to the war of all singulars against all others, but to the *polemos* of life and death permeating every singular and singularizing it. The overmeasure stresses the polemical essence of the event. One is far from the doctrine of principles and from its most rigorous argument, where the ascent through negations produces an ultimate focus reachable in excess *(hyperoche)*. How could Heidegger's 'going-beyond', 'rank', etc., lead to a single bind when the event itself is not simple? As he twists inherited thought models out of the mechanics of simple subsumption, they lead rather to a double bind, phrased here as that of being and nothingness.

c. By transgression one is to understand the *co-normativity of the law's disparate other* under the very reign of the law. If being is to be characterized by discordant temporal pulls—an attraction and a retraction within manifestation—then all laws, whether theoretical or practical, natural or positive, are always deferred and spaced from within by their singularizing negation, just as an epochal hegemony is, from its establishment onward, deferred and spaced from within by its decline to come. The decline of an epochal standard occurs when the phantasm endowed with normativity suddenly appears as one commonplace representation among others (just as psychoanalysis is said to be finished when the analyst, no longer phantasmically endowed with maximal knowledge, turns into one professional earning his living like others of his ilk). Such a decline or destitution was suffered by the *natura* of pre-modern 'natural law' when the Scotists detected in it an essential contingency. It is with singularization, then, that a change occurs in an ultimate standard's referential and legislative prestige. In normative theticism, the transgressive pull consists in the *possible singularization at the heart of any actually legislating universal*.

For this disparity of strategies sundering *Ereignis*, I find it difficult to endorse reading that would take Heidegger to vary, yet again, symmetrical contraries. To see the dissymmetry of the double bind, it is enough to recall how the transgressive strategy asserts itself in everydayness, namely, through the pull toward death. Now being-toward-death, or 'mortality', temporalizes phenomena by the loss of their world: by a *possible*, singularizing loss, inscribed in being-in-the-world. Only if one stops one's reading at the words and their symmetry will the contextualizing-decontextualizing strategies oppose one another inside one genus and yield some dualism. Such a reading would amount to jumping over the decontextualizing factor itself: the possible which, in Heidegger, always arises from the future. The possible is therefore also the temporalizing factor. Nor can it be said that, as such, the possible reflects the actual as its antithesis; this now would amount to leaping over the possibilizing factor in the everyday, which is *my* death. For Hegel, death is what makes us all equals and thus properly constitutes the human *genus*. Mineness, on the other hand, disrupts generic equalization. In Heidegger, death as mine temporalizes phenomena because it is absolutely *singular*. But the singular cannot be treated as the determinate negation of the universal; the contrary opposite of the universal is the particular. It takes a neglect of the persistent tie between time and the singular, a tie signified to me by my death, to append these conflictual strategies to the list, long since Antiquity, of terms that are mutually exclusive within a genus and jointly exhaustive of it.

Dissymmetrical otherness best describes tragic conflict, which remains paradigmatic for Heidegger. The law of the household and the law of the city can be construed as opposing one another and sublating each other, only once revised by the dialectic of the objective spirit and under the authority of the modern State. Aeschylus's heroes, for their part, perish from that conflict as they are left without recourse to any covering law. Antigone differs with Creon as her law, and his, lack a common genus. The same is true of the attraction-retraction that splits *Ereignis*. There is nothing new, in philosophy, about claiming that being is not a genus. Yet philosophy has made it its job to block the reasons for this most common claim, i.e., tragic differing.

Transgression by singularization to come deposes *(ent-setzen)* hegemonic referents, takes their 'may'—their might—away and hence provokes dismay *(das Entsetzen)*. Once transgression is retrieved as pertaining to our condition, being-there can come to pass. "This de-posing becomes an event only out of being itself; indeed, being is nothing other than that which de-poses and dis-mays" (GA 65, 482). It is nothing other than legislation-transgression.

With ultimacy pertaining to nomic strife in the event, all univocally binding phantasms—whose reign has culminated in twentieth-century totalitarianism and 'giganticism'—appear as illusions. Their "illusory reign must some day be broken" (GA 65, 336). That breaking up is incumbent upon 'the other thinking' whose critical task consists, then, in laying bare the one enduring interest behind any focal sense of being: the interest in mastery. This interest has not only been served by logic; it has instituted logic, the know-how of subsumption, to being with. Indeed, 'logic' itself is an illusion, though the most necessary illusion that the history of being has known up to now" (GA 65, 461). The enabling conditions for rethinking the political after Heidegger lie in the *agôn*, in the agonistics and the agony of the being-event turned against itself. Such conditions are impossible to institutionalize. They settle institutions (and thereby unsettle them), however, on the same broken foundations that appear in everydayness as 'natality' and 'mortality'.

Since I only seek to understand how the nomic strife within the event frees philosophy from univocally binding phantasms, it remains to be seen in what way the legislative-transgressive double bind is originary.

Legislation-Transgression

How, then, is this other (non-*a priori*) step back to be taken which un-denies the disparate and leads to being as it deposes and dismays—the step which retrieves, in other words, a differing more originary than which nothing can be encountered? The how-to is learned by doing. The step back seals the normative double bind in several ways.

First, in tearing apart referential phantasms, it puts an end to the *contents* that have been endowed with ultimacy. Rehabilitating the No as co-originary with the Yes does not amount to declaring the ugly equal to the beautiful, or thoughtlessness equal to the 'I think'. In this sense, originary differing remains formal and neutral, as I have stated. It works upon everydayness the way a category works upon the empirical—except that everydayness can no more be treated as an empirical given that can the late modern pathology where differing becomes most acute. It would force the received lexicon to call originary differing the 'condition of the possibility of phenomena'; it is, indeed, just as much the 'condition of their impossibility'. Phenomenological phenomena proper do not yield to the same kind of description as this beautiful woman, that act of thinking, or this country; they have rather to be wrested from empirical givens. So it is with differing. If—and as—it works upon phenomena without preceding them as a condition that is formally one, then it can no longer determine and measure them materially (as does the *eidos* that makes beautiful things beautiful; or as does nature, making one's acts natural; etc.). It works upon them in destroying from within the apriorism that posits some eidetic focus. By the same stroke, it destroys maximized contents. The conflict of natality and mortality in everydayness, along with the conflict of positing and letting-be in the epoch of extreme theticism, *reveal* the event turned back against itself:[14] turned back as can only be, against a formal Yes, an equally formal No.

Next, and apparently in a blatant inconsistency, Heidegger declares *the No greater* than the Yes.[15] Phrases to this effect abound. They do indicate that singularization always wins out over the phenomenalization making a world. But how is this to be understood? Received wisdom is one thing, which holds the death always ends by winning out over life. Quite another is the question of conditions: How can the expropriating retraction in the event be said to be "greater" than the appropriating attraction?

One feature at least about the equi-originary, yet unequal, No and Yes is *not* hard to see. Their unequalness prevents their equi-originariness from recycling oppositional figures in which the principle of non-contradiction combines with the principle of the excluded middle to produce a binary division within some genus posited as supreme. But does Heidegger then undertake an inverse secondarization of normative theses, devising a primary No followed by a Yes that would feed upon it and, in turn, confirm it—Yes to No, hence twice No? Such a mephistophelization of being as originary catastrophe would not only be absurd,[16] but it would moreover disjoing once again the tragically equi-originary laws and counterlaws.

To understand the No, greater than the Yes, one has to return to normative maximization. Is it not Heidegger's best known teaching that being differs from beings, that the latter alone are something and that being is, consequently, nothing? The word says it well: 'no-thing', *non-ens*, being is 'not a being'. Now, Heidegger observes, such 'negative' determination of nothingness follows the very type of reifying predications whereby a particular thing is said to possess or not to possess a particular quality. The logic of prediction has little to teach us about the origin of phenomena—about their emergence, *oriri*, or their manifestation, *phainesthai*—where the condition gets fractured. This logic indeed assumes that phenomena be describable as data, that the phenomenal signify the actual, and that being be understood as the actuality of data. Whence the task, he says, of "determining a more originary manner how being and nothingness belong together." The polemic against predicative logic therefore serves to make nothingness problematical, regardless of the ontological difference. The new problematizing is spelled out in a cascade of rhetorical questions[17] pointing to the 'event turned against itself': "What if being itself were what withdraws itself and if refusal were its essential way to be? . . . And what if it were by the force of *this nihilation* of being itself that 'nothingness' is filled with the power out of which arises . . . all 'creation' (by which a being takes on greater being)?" (GA 65, 246). Something else is at stake than the so-called ontological difference. The cascade falls on the other side of a dam sheltering the being question from 'vulgar', describable, maximizable phenomena that are always rushing forth as the sole matters of interest. How is No greater than Yes? Maximizing remains excluded, as this always consists in a Yes endowing some given phenomenon or feature of pheomena (including *ousia*, *entitas* or *ens commune*, *Seiendheit*, 'beingness') with greater being.

All actual phenomena are thus to be dammed up, suspended, bracketed. To grasp the originarily transgressive No in being, one must stop briefly to consider the traditional prestige of the actual over the possible and to detect the interest that speaks through this prestige. Just as normative phantasms become problematical for Heidegger through transcendentalism and hence through Kant, so too, No, Not, and nothingness become problematical through kineticism and hence through Aristotle.

No, Not, and nothingness first became philosophical issues through the analysis of *possible* change, inscribed within *actual* data. Aristotelian kineticism reduces the possible beforehand to what can be rendered actual, just as it reduces being actual to what has been made such, to being fabricated. This twofold reduction of the possible to the makable and of the actual to the made is doubtless among its few pervading presuppositions. A lintel, a column, and a pile of sand are possible from a block of marble, provided that a contract, an architect, a workshop, mallets, chisels, and so on, intervene. If kineticism presupposes this twofold reduction, then moreover it reduces the logic of predication and assent to techno-logy. In Heidegger's words, Yes to the actual denotes the "Yes to 'making'" (GA 65, 246). The phrase indicates both the interest pushing toward normative maximization and an assessment calling for a critique of such maximization.

Maximizing a Yes of 'making' is indeed not without interest. What can be done with things is always what is most interesting about them. A primordial Yes would be full of order, which means in this instance: full of an order to be realized, full of a technical organization to be actualized. This is the technological core of all classical paradigmatism. It implies already the elements for a critique, since when some Yes lays down a univocal law, things (via their representation) alone set the standard; assent (via subsumptive hubris) universalizes the actual; producibles (via a *metabasis eis allo genos*) pass for all beings—and the best made, namely, primordial order, for the best of beings; and finally nothingness (via predicative logic) signifies the negation of beings, a non-thing, the non-actual understood as a non-product. Aristotelian *dynamis* has dictated the proper usage of nothingness in philosophy and has forced out knowledge of a No greater than any Yes.

The age-old variations on the actual and the possible have one trait in common: they treat the possible in the same way as, and following, the actual. The possible can only be equal to, less than, or better than the actual. In other words, it amounts either to the actual itself, which then figures among the possibles (for example, the best of all possible worlds), or to a bad actual because it is not (the unicorn), or, yet again, to a better actual, one that will be (a messianic society).[18]

How then is one to think of nothingness or No as 'the other', not comparable to the equivalences and oppositions put into place by Aristotle's physics? How is one to think of it as the "singularity of the Not," of which Heidegger stated in the lines cited above that it was just as binding as the "singularity of being" (GA 65, 267)?

The other way of thinking the No or the Not will place it neither *vis-à-vis* actual things as their technical negation, nor above the Yes as its catastrophic annihilation.

How is it to be placed? What has to be the place of No? Phenomenologically, it is always *to come*. Nothingness or No is immanent to the world as its possibility, that is, as imminent. The twist Heidegger inflicts on the proper usage of the actual and the possible responds to the de-phenomenalizing pull which always twists in advance any given phenomenal edifice or 'dwelling'. For the sake of responding to the unsame phenomena our vocabularies force into coupling—for the sake of responsiveness and responsibility—one has to begin where their stirrings begin, namely, with the futurity of the possible.

To claim that "the possible stands higher than the actual"[19] amounts already to shattering this old pair. The locus of the possible shifts; it no longer borders in any way on the actual, nor follows from it. Its place is rather the simple opening in which, as we say, anything is possible—not 'any thing', any entitative and representable content, but the gap between my inhabitable world and this same world as undoing itself. Weaned from the realm of entitites, the possible no longer denotes this column or that lintel as latent in the block of marble, awaiting the passage, the choice and hand of the architect, Ichtynos; it no longer denotes *possibles* (in the plural) capable of being turned into actuals. Whence the new link of the possible to futurity, "higher" than actuality, since it is indifferent to things present and absent just as to things actual and eventually actual.

Here, then, is the key point in the argument. So weaned from the actualizable and the feasible, the possible is not simple. The present opening, as opening to the future, breaks the rule of *consecutio temporum*. If 'possible' means 'to come', then possibility consists in a *formal discordance of times*. This is not bipolar as are presence and absence, but disaccordant as the to-come itself. It distracts (literally) the everyday through the traits of natality and mortality, as it distracts the truth through unconcealment and concealment. The possible always pulls in two directions, as attraction *(Bezug)* of Yes and retraction *(Entzug)* of No (GA 65, 183, 293). Does this double pull recycle symmetrical dualities? Only a retina with the most rigid sort of grid would read the strife of attraction-retraction prompted by the possible, yet again in accordance with the geometry of determinate negation. Rather, that strife undoes, once and for all, bipolar mechanics. Heidegger gives a few examples, all of which instantiate dissymmetry: birth is 'toward death'; "the clearing, for concealment" (GA 65, 351); "the groundless is the ground's originary way of being" (GA 65, 379); nothingness, "what is more originary in being" (GA 65, 247); the No, "of an even deeper essence than the Yes" (GA 65, 178) . . . Such prepositions and comparatives as 'for', 'more originary', 'deeper', can hardly be said to pair off contraries. None of the bipolar models received from the tradition would survive were it to be arranged in the form of: 'Yes, *for* No', or: 'No, *deeper* than Yes'. What sense would it make to say (to paraphrase a title by Lévi-Strauss) that microbiological fullness in honey is 'for' the biological No in ashes? Or that ashes are 'deeper', 'more originary' than honey? Their symmetry would be done with—as indeed, with the discordance of time, the symmetry of Yes and No is done with.

There remains the speculative baggage of comparatives. One quite naturally would say: if No is not the determinate contrary facing Yes, and if No does not follow Yes as dependent on it, then No can only precede Yes in the manner of a condition. Thus No would end up rendering Yes secondary after all.

But what is it that can be described according to locations such as above, equal to, beneath? As we have just seen, gradations of this or other orderings always serve to represent beings. As far as the traits traversing the to-come are concerned, the prepositions and comparatives in question can no longer posit any sort of scale. More originary does not mean, then, primordial—'of prime order'— as a first cause is of prime order in relation to second causes. As the paradigm of binary opposites is put out of function, so is the great ladder of a maximal archetype, degraded through stages of ectypes. It is not thinkable that death, concealment, the groundless, nothingness, Not, and No could in any way occupy a primordial place.

What is phenomenologically originary can only pertain to manifestation. There alone does it make sense to speak of a No that is more originary than the Yes. At first sight, this has been all too familiar ever since Heraclitus. A certain No has to determine manifestation, in that manifestation as such can never become manifest. Coming-into-presence likes to retreat, or to retract itself.

A self-hiding of manifestation has been familiar to all persuasions of phenomenology as well. Since visibility must always have been 'intended' prior to any visible content, there seems to be nothing more evident even than just the originary No. Visibility never becomes visible. That evidence is of the kind with which all phenomenology sets out. The attraction of Yes points to appearing. *Yes, there is manifestation* (a statement that holds a double tautology inasmuch as 'yes', 'there is', and 'manifestation' all denote the same phenomenalizing). The contrary statement would assert: No, there is no manifestation; appearing does not occur. No one, to my knowledge, has as yet drawn the curtain on the world in this way. Phenomenologists observe instead: *No, there is no manifestation of manifestation.* Heidegger subscribes to the evidence of this observation. However, if manifestation is constituted, not by enduring self-consciousness, but by precarious contextualization and re-contextualizations, he has to add: *There is a No that debilitates all manifestation.* This statement, which neither denies manifestation nor tautologizes non-manifestation, moves elsewhere. To see where it goes, one must, according to the very project of phenomenology, look not only at how one speaks, but at what one is speaking of.

Here the undertow of No is more familiar and more evident still. Its familiarity and its evidence lie in everydayness, neither in the history of philosophy nor in the method of phenomenology. This undertow is therefore the most decisive for the understanding of being. In what way does the No pull *otherwise* than the Yes? To ask about manifestation and the No, in everydayness, reveals an otherness (which indirectly accounts for both Heraclitus' *kryptesthai philei* and Husserl's intentionality) in which the tragic condition of being is at stake.

Of what is Heidegger speaking when he speaks of *phyein* or manifesting? Always of singulars forming a constellation, that is to say, phenomenalizing themselves as they enter into an economy of presence. This entry into presence, this presencing, was to remain his single and persistent issue. It works upon singulars by regionalizing them. It inscribes them in a context—in a world—and thereby makes them into phenomena. Marcel Duchamp seems to have perfectly understood the strife of phenomenalizing and singularizing when he mounted a bicycle wheel on a stool and exhibited it in a museum. A bicycle wheel is made for turning around an axis, held in a metal fork, and serving the purpose of locomotion. Yes to that object of spikes and a rim as it composes a world, contextualized between the pavement and the traffic through which it allows you to thread your way. That is where it appears, pehnomenalized according to what it is. But a No traverses its phenomenalization as the possibility of being dislodged. In this case, the dislodging exiles and singularizes it on a stool in an exhibition hall. The singularization that is always to-come in phenomena points to the No of their world (their 'own' or 'proper' world, yet one deprived of any appropriating subject and of full possession).

To call a being 'singular in its world', or beings 'singulars in their world', would amount to countersense: a sense over-determined by non-sense. That over-determination *is* the tragic. It is strikingly accused in Rimbaud's line: "We are not in the world."[20] A phenomenon in its world alone has meaning. Singularization is the loss of meaning, but a loss that is always imminent.

Here, then, is how Heidegger remains faithful to the philosopher's ancient quest for conditions while at the same time staying clear of the *a priori*, simplicity, universality, univocal standards, as well as all other corollaries of normative theticism: factual decontextualization—as in Duchamp's 'ready-made' or in my own terminal entropy—can happen only because the decontextualizing No is first of all a trait of being. Singularization, as possible, always disrupts from within any actual phenomenality bestowed by a world. Nothingness has to be more originary than being because *it singularizes being into an event*. Such singularization is the pathetic stakes of the *Contributions to Philosophy*. Each time that Heidegger speaks of the supreme danger, this is what he is speaking of.

Singularization to come is indeed the other belonging to no genus, alienating being in its essential ways, in its *Wesen*. What parity, symmetry, determinate negation, contrariety, contradiction— or what hierarchy of particulars under a universal principle—could couple the singular with the phenomenon? One must let oneself be duped by the *lexical* match when the double bind is described as appropriation-expropriation, unconcealment-concealment, being-nothingness, Yes-No, or, again, legislation-transgression. In each of these pairs that are not pairs at all, the first word designates the phenomenality that a being owes to its world, and the second, its singularization to come.

This singularization spells out a *passibility* in phenomena, namely, that they can suffer expulsion from their world. As an orignary trait, singularization to come means that dispossession is always imminent, that full possession never happens. From the viewpoint of the event that is being, such eviction is called 'expropriation'; from the viewpoint of epochal hegemonies, some normative phantasm's 'destitution'; and from the viewpoint of everydayness, it is called 'death'.

These are but so many retractions instantiating the possible, hence, futurity. Whether Heidegger is speaking of the singular or of time, the same *differing* is at issue: the dissimilar laws in which nomic being always opens up a world, but in which the Not—more originarily nomic in that it singularizes phenomena toward their exit—strips this world, forever and from all time, of its reconciling, consoling, and consolidating foci.

Heidegger's world is therefore not an anomic world. It is doubly nomic. Recess binds and obligates us just as much as process; reclusion, just as much as inclusion. "What closes up on itself opens up as that which holds and binds [us]" (GA 65, 260).

As for the world of the twentieth century, Heidegger doubtless lets himself get carried away a bit when he suggest that today singularization becomes pathological to the point that ours is hardly a world anymore. Things can no longer become phenomena in accordance with what they are. "Machinations are unbound" (*Ungebundenheit der Machenshaften*, (GA 65, 120), he says. The phrase makes sense if it is meant to suggest an extenuation of deictic pertinence in contemporary language, as words get detached from everyday experience. Marked by technicity, life becomes impenetrable to experience to the point that a thick mutism covers the originary condition. If, however, it is meant to suggest that technicity today leaves things under the *single* bind of their *singularization*— if it implies a new worldlessness, this time due not to subjectivist solipsism, but to an enfeeblement of phenomenalization—then the formula cannot but prompt headaches. At least it bespeaks why, according to the *Contributions*, being-there is not yet. It will be, when an age will acknowledge itself in all clarity placed in a given phenomenal economy, without denying in it the singularization to come. This is what *diasozein ta phainomena*, preserving the phenomena would be.

"The one *and* the other are binding," Heidegger said in a passage cited above. We have seen whence every univocal law is born: from the hubris that denies singularizations as if it were not. Idealists of all times have been the model functionaries of order, declaring flatly that the singular has no being. Unlearning this hubris (*Gelassenheit*, as Heidegger would later call it) restores to the law its disparate other and hence the double bind. From beneath tragic denial, it restores tragic truth which always ends by singularizing the hero to the point of silence and ruin.

Such occurs with Agamemnon. At Aulis, his blood-ties singularize him in the phenomenal region constituted by the armies under his command. Conversely, the constraints of arms singularize him in that other phenomenal region, constituted by Clytemnestra and the house of Atreus, at Mycenae. At Aulis, his nomic allegiance to the military economy effaces the singular No pleading with him through the eyes of Iphigenia, bound and gagged. A few years later, he will find himself singularized in quite the same manner, in the net of Aegisthus.

Such occurs also in Michel Foucault: "Only a fiction can make us believe that laws are made to be respected. . . . Illegalism constitutes an absolutely positive element in social functioning, whose role the general strategy of society includes in advance."[21]

When Heidegger says that "the event alone is binding" (GA 65, 416), he is speaking of the tragic event in its disparate pull of appropriation-expropriation. This answers the question of what he does with and to philosophy, namely: he establishes it indeed on new grounds while putting an end to it and also reading its history—all, however, to phase out its traditional charge of securing simple ultimates. In terms of the law: the originary, legislative-transgressive, double bind alone has the force of obligation.

Notes

1. GA 65. An earlier version of the present article was published in the *Graduate Faculty Philosophy Journal* (Spring, 1991). This contribution is fully understandable only in conjunction with three related papers: in K. Harries and C. Jamme, eds., *Martin Heidegger: Politics, Art, and Technology* (New York: Holmes & Meier Pub., 1994); in J. Margolis and T. Rockmore, eds., *The Heidegger Case: On Philosophy and Politics* (Philadelphia: Temple University Press, 1992); and in M. R. Zinman, ed., *Multiculturalism and American Democracy* (Lawrence: The University of Kansas Press, 1998).

2. "We are the functionaries of mankind," Edmund Husserl, *The Crisis of European Sciences and Transcendental Philosophy*, trans. D. Carr (Evanston: Northwestern University Press, 1970), p. 17.

3. The phrase *double bind* was first coined in 1956 by Gregory Bateson, as far as I can tell. I am retaining the three formal traits by which Bateson characterizes this concept (*Steps to an Ecology of Mind*, London 1972, p. 206 ff.): a primary injunction declaring the law; a secondary injunction declaring a counter-law, hence conflicting with the first; and lastly a tertiary injunction "prohibiting the victim from escaping from the field" constituted by the first two injunctions. Obviously, I am not retaining these features as they are used in social psychology.

4. "Enlightenment is man's release from his self-incurred tutelage": I. Kant, "What is Enlightenment? trans. Lewis White Beck, *Kant, On History* (New York: Prentice Hall, 1963), p.3. On Heidegger's view, Kant instituted but another tutelage, viz., under the legislative ego. Heidegger can thus calim to radicalize the Kantian project of enlightenment.

5. According to the *Contributions*, being-there *(Da-sein)* is not yet; cf. GA 65, 90, and elsewhere.

6. In speaking of natality and mortality as phenomenological *traits*, I am following Hannah Arendt in *The Human Condition* (Chicago: The University of Chicago Press, 1958), pp. 9, 177, 247.

7. The abrupt change in Agamemnon's attitude has been underscored most recently by Martha Nussbaum in *The Fragility of Goodness* (Cambridge University Press: New York, 1986), pp. 32–38. For the expression *orgai periorgos epithumein*, which Nussbaum translates as "desire with exceedingly impassioned passion," see the parallel constructs and the commentary in Eduard Fraenkel, *Aeschylus: Agamemnon* (Oxford University Press: Oxford, 1950), v. I, *sub loco*.

8. One of Jacques Derrida's strategies has been "to decide to change terrain, in a discontinuous and irruptive fashion, by brutally placing oneself outside, and by affirming an absolute break"; *Margins—of Philosophy*, trans. A. Bass (Chicago: The University of Chicago Press, 1982), p. 135. This might be read as a description of events in France at the time the essay was finished—"May 12, 1968" (*ib.*, p. 136)—were the proclamation of a future "which breaks absolutely" with the present not a leitmotif in Derrida. (cf. the Exergue to *Of Grammatology*, trans. G. C. Spivak (Baltimore: The Johns Hopkins University Press, 1974), p. 5.

9. Legitimizing specific forms of these regional types of violence would require a doctrine of judgment. Given its subjectivist presupposition, such a doctrine would obviously be incompatible with Heideggerian phenomenology, just as it remains incompatible with other contemporary philosophical projects, for instance, Wittgenstein's.

10. It would be difficult to disagree with the well-known line from William Butler Yeats: "Civilization is hooped together . . . by manifold illusion"; cf. "Meru" in *The Poems of W. B. Yeats*, ed. by R. J. Finneran (New York: Macmillan, 1983), p. 289.

11. According to Franz Rosenzweig, the Yes, in the sense of *sic*, of *amen*, of 'it is good', is the "originary word" (*das Urwort*); cf. Rosenzweig, *The Star of Redemption*, trans. W. Hallo (New York: Holt, Reinhart & Winston, 1970), pp. 27 and 127. The translator renders *Unwort* indiscriminately as "archetypal word" and as "arch-word". Both renderings carry connotations that are too Greek for the context.

12. Michel Foucault, "Preface to Transgression," *Language, Counter-Memory, Practice*, ed. by D. F. Bouchard (Ithaca: Cornell University Press, 1977), pp. 29ff.

13. The two main works by Pseudo-Dionysius Areopagite open with hymns in which the prefix 'over-' *(hyper-)* and the adverb 'above' *(epekeina)* abound. God is "He who is beyond every being" *(ho panton epekeina)*, He is "over-unknowable" *(hyperagnoston)*, "over-most-evident" *(hyperphanestaton)*, etc. . . . (*On Mystical Theology*, I, 1); He is "the non-being cause of every being, beyond being" and "beyond thought" (*The Divine Names*, I, 1), from Pseudo-Dionysius Areopagite, *The Divine Names and Mystical Theology*, trans. John D. Jones (Milwaukee: Marquette University Press, 1980), pp. 109 and 211, translations slightly modified.

Ultimate Double Binds   267

14. Here are some formulations of that (literally) crucial thought: "the event turning within itself", (*das in sich kehrige Ereignis*, GA 65, 185); "the event swinging against itself in itself" (*das in sich gegenschwingende Ereignis*, GA 65, 261); "the turning-against" (*die Widerkehre*, GA 65, 407); "the countering" (*die Ent-gegnung*, GA 65, 470); "the turning-against" (*das Gegenwendige*, GA 65, 247). None of these phrases is to be understood in a dialectical fashion.

15. Cf. GA 65, 246 ff. The apparent inconsistency follows the model of ecstatic temporality in which the to-come is the "primary sense" of existentiality, while on the other hand having-been, being-present, and to-come are said to be all "equi-originary." Cf. *Being and Time*, Sect. 65; trans. J. Macquarrie and E. Robinson (New York: Harper and Row, 1962), pp. 370 ff.

16. A catastrophe is, literally, an overturning. Now for something to be overturned, it must first be. Logically, therefore, a negation cannot be claimed to be originary. Operations such as negating and affirming require a prior Yes as their transitive object. In phenomenological terms, an originary No, making the Yes secondary, would annul the *phainesthai* itself and, hence, the world. As concerns Mephistopheles, Goethe shows himself to be a good theologian when he has this spirit, who always denies (*"ich bin der Geist, der stets verneint"*), state that from time to time he does like to see that old gentleman, God (*"von Zeit zu Zeit seh' ich den Alten gern"*), *Faust*, Part One, lines 1338 and 350.

17. In reading an author, it is useful to have detected the few literary devices by which he sums up his thinking. In Kant, this usually happens in the opening paragraph of a section, a chapter, or even a work; in Heidegger, in rhetorical questions.

18. These various senses of the possible entail various relations to time. The break between entitative time and originary time appears when the possible connotes the future. Thus, when a society-to-come or a democracy-to-come are being announced, some content gets assigned to the possible. 'Classless society' and 'democracy' are descriptions of possible entities. They denote a factual to-come. Heidegger, on the other hand, holds that time originates in the to-come, regardless of contents. Here, the possible is no more describable than is our simple opening to the phenomenal world. It denotes an *originary to-come*.

19. *Being and Time*, § 7; *op. cit.*, p. 63.

20. Arthur Rimbaud, "A Season in Hell: Delirium I"; trans. L. Varèse, *'A Season in Hell' and 'The Drunken Boat'* (New York: New Directions, 1961), p. 37.

21. Michel Foucault, "Des supplices aux cellules," *Le Monde*, February 21, 1975, p. 16.

Chapter 13

Contributions to Life

David Farrell Krell

Heidegger's *Beiträge zur Philosophie* contribute to a thinking of *Ereignis*, not of life. They are contributions to *philosophy*—if one may dream for a moment that philosophy can think the granting of time and being. The granting of time and being to whom? To the mortals, presumably, who for the time being *live*. Heidegger's contributions to philosophy are certainly not made for the sake of life-philosophy, the *Lebensphilosophie* that he abhors. Yet they must in any case be made by the living for the living, not because of some ontic constraint—as though life were an inconvenience that thought has to put up with—but for reasons of the granting itself and as such.

The bulk of the present article appears as chapter 6 of my *Daimon Life* under the title "Paranoetic Thinking."[1] Even though the piece was written in 1990–91, I have allowed most of it to stand—including the insertions concerning Freud's analysis of the Schreber case. Those insertions do not and cannot take the place of a careful, critical interweaving of Heidegger's *ontological* and Freud's *psychoanalytic* discourses. However, the insertions are meant to suggest that these two discourses are much closer to one another than we usually like to think. In brief, what they try to show is that Heidegger's discourse is *paranoetic*—not paranoid, but more desperate still, worse off than the discourse of paranoia. I do not doubt that the "mechanisms" of paranoia, as Freud describes them, fixation, repression, and the return of the repressed, can be traced in Heidegger's thinking of the sending of being. Nor do I doubt that

Freud's tendency to reduce all of love and life to certain well-rehearsed psychoanalytic schemata needs to be blown wide open by Heidegger's thinking of being. As modest—or as irritating—as my interweaving of Freud and Heidegger may be in what follows, it constitutes a start, not a finish. Heidegger is not committed to an asylum, and President Schreber is not celebrated as the new prophet of being. Yet neither is Heidegger enclosed in a tabernacle for worship, and Schreber consigned to the hitherside, the hopeless side, of the ontological difference.

Finally, in order now to begin, a word about the daimonic, and *Daimon Life*. Since completing the book I am all the more convinced that the realm of the daimonic serves as a meeting place for many generations of German thinkers, from Goethe and Novalis to Heidegger and Benjamin. It is also a clearing (*the* clearing?) for contemporary efforts to think such things as the politics of friendship, radical evil, human and animal life, and gender and sexual differences. Because I am unequal to the task of thinking through any one of these themes, the following article touches on them all.

We first find τὸ δαιμόνιον hovering in Heidegger's 1928 logic course in the thicket of transcendence, freedom, temporality, the overpowering, and the holy.[2] The common element of these apparently disparate items proves to be bestrewal, *Streuung*, the root of emphatic *Zer-streuung*, dispersion and distraction. The present article will take up the domain of *life* as the daimonic domain of bestrewal *and* dispersion. It will nevertheless concentrate its forces and focus sharply on two or three pages of a single—and vast—text, a text over five-hundred pages long. We shall examine only two of the 281 sections or aphorisms of Heidegger's 1936–1938 *Beiträge zur Philosophie (Vom Ereignis)*, Part IV, "The Leap," namely, the two aphorisms that treat of "life." We shall let nothing disturb our focus.

Herewith, then, a preliminary reading of sections 153–154 of the *Beiträge*. These sections or aphorisms appear well after the midpoint of "The Leap," perhaps three-quarters of the way through it, at the moment when a leaping animal—say, a deer or a horse—extends its folded forelegs in anticipation of the shock of landing. The animal hopes that it will land on the farther rim of the gap that is to be leapt, trusts that it will not plummet into the abyss. Of the four key words, "the intimation" or "resonance," "the assist" or "interplay," "the leap" or "the fissure," and "the grounding" or "founding" *(der Anklang, das Zuspiel, der Sprung, die Gründung)*, the leap is itself the third of four, on the descending arc, on the *chute*.[3]

At that point in the trajectory of "The Leap," three-quarters of the way through it, something unanticipated, something altogether surprising, rises to meet us. "The Leap" consists of fifty-two aphorisms, most of them, while not familiar (for every leap is full of surprises), at least suggesting a familiar trajectory. The leap of thinking—sustained by its fundamental mood of awe and reticence, propelled by all the variegated energies of a time of transition, a time that subjects its thinkers to a bizarre regime of terror and jubliation—aims to surmount the guiding question of metaphysics (τί τὸ ὄν . . . , what is the being?) in the direction of the fundamental question, the question of the history, truth, or essential unfolding of being (or, as Heidegger now writes it, of "beyng"). "The Essential Unfolding of *Seyn*" constitutes the farther rim of the abyss that the leap of thinking hopes to attain.[4] Thinking thus leaps across an opening in beyng, a yawning cleavage (*die Zerklüftung*, §§127 and 156–159) in what Heidegger in the mid-1930s has begun to call *the earth*. The title *Die Zerklüftung* appears at two different moments of "The Leap," in the first quarter, in order to introduce a discussion of "the nothing," then immediately before the shock of landing on the farther side, the side on which "the grounding" is to commence. There it introduces a discussion of "beyng unto death." Near the conclusion of its leap, which, to repeat, stretches from "the nothing" to "beyng unto death," something uncanny springs from the abyss to meet it. Daniel Paul Schreber's *Denkwürdigkeiten eines Nervenkranken* propels us in two directions at once: back to Johann Georg Hamann's 1759 *Sokratische Denkwürdigkeiten*, and thus back to at least two generations of German Romantic and Idealist thinkers and writers, and forward to Heidegger's reflections on what is worthy of thought, *denkwürdig*. The full title of Hamann's text would propel us forward in any case to Heidegger's 1929–1930 lecture course, the first half of which depicts the fundamental mood of philosophizing as melancholy and profound boredom. Hamann's title is: *Sokratische Denkwürdigkeiten für die lange Weile des Publicums, zusammengetragen von einem Liebhaber der langen Weile*. For the moment, in the present context, the leap and the abyssal cleavage of beyng and of the earth, it will be Schreber over Hamann, not in order to declare Heidegger's *Contributions to Philosophy* demented, schizophrenic, or even paranoid, but in order to probe the limits of a thinking that undergoes what Heidegger in the *Beiträge* calls *Zwang* and *Verrückung*, compulsion and radical displacement.

What is uncanny in the *Contributions to Philosophy (Of Propriation)* is the irruption of the two aphorisms on "life." Section 153 is called "Living," *Leben*. Section 154 is entitled "'Life,'" "*Das Leben*." No other aphorisms among the 281 of the *Beiträge* share these titles—in a meditation that consists almost entirely of repetitions. At each moment of every hour Schreber can feel the miracle that is taking place in his body. Of course, "life" and living are mentioned elsewhere in the *Beiträge*, although almost exclusively as something to be avoided and kept at a distance from thought. "Closeness to life" is the contemptible claim of a besotted and sentimental *Lebensphilosophie*, the wretched legacy of a bankrupt Neokantianism, an inane *Weltanschauungsphilosophie*, and a flaccid *Existenzphilosophie*; life-philosophy is the last palsied offshoot of a moribund Platonism and Idealism, a mere shadow of the regnant technophiliac positivism that is bedazzled by its own machinations and *Er-lebnissen*—both positivism and life-philosophy benumbed by their contrived "lived experiences."[5]

The sheer mass of Heidegger's compelling, repetitive polemics against *Erlebnis* and *Lebensphilosophie*, polemics that are always energetic and passionate, often heavyhanded, at times even sardonic, suggests a kind of compulsion, *Zwang*, which is—I would argue—the shadow side of the responsive and even docile Heideggerian thinking of pious acceptance of the dispensation of being. Sarcasm and contumely are the obverse of an unresisting acquiescence that feels itself seized, transported, and delivered over to what is to be thought. We shall have to ponder this odd alternating current of piety and polemic in what I will call Heidegger's *paranoetic* thinking. Not *paranoid* thinking, inasmuch as here there is no being, no *Seiendes*, that is to be feared and hated. For Heidegger's "other" thinking, there can be no being—no thing or person—that is available for the mechanisms or strategies of fixation, repression by reversal, return of the repressed, and reconstruction ("I love him," "He loves me but I hate him," "He hates me and persecutes me," "Behold my wretchedly reconstructed universe"). Not paranoid thinking, to repeat, inasmuch as in Heidegger's case there is no being that can be sought out and blamed for the unspeakable catastrophe that is about to advene—or that has always already advened from the beginning. Schreber senses that the end of the world is at hand, a Stoic ἐκπύρωσις, a *Weltuntergang*: the final 212 years of the 14,000-year cosmic cycle have run out. He is the only human being left. Not paranoid, but *paranoetic*, a thinking that must surrender every noematic correlate, every conceivable being, and all guiding questions concerning beings and their grounding. It is a thinking, not even of ontological difference, but of beyng, which has never shown its face, which has no face.

However, there are one or two moments in the earlier parts of the *Beiträge* where living and "life" command thought in potentially more positive ways. First, in a discussion of truth in the "Preliminary View" (71), Heidegger refers to the "sheltering" or "salvaging" *(Bergung)* of "stone, plant, animal, and human being," both the "inanimate and the animate," which are to be "taken back into the self-occluding earth." The earth, first introduced in the 1935–1936 lectures on the "Origin of the Work of Art," appears in the "The Leap" immediately before and just after discussion of "life" and the living. Earth is therefore designated in proximity to "the nothing," "the cleavage of beyng," and "beyng unto death." Second, in the context of a detailed discussion of the history of being (or beyng) from Platonism through German Idealism (see sphorism 110), Heidegger relates Plato's "one," the ἕν, through κοινωνία, to the unifying thought of γένη, the "genus" and "species" of all classification of *"Gattungen"*; the unifying being beyond beings is thus, according to Heidegger, the source of human felicity, εὐδαιμονία (two of the rare appearances of this word in Heidegger's thinking occur here, in aphorism 110); thus the Platonic ἀγαθόν, "the good," "the fitting," *das Taugliche*, is a "condition of 'life,' of the soul, and thereby of the essence of life and the soul as such"; the soul, in Platonism, yearns for the good and the beautiful, and such yearning is ἔρως. "Because the essence of beings is gathered in ψυχή, the ψυχή itself is the ἀρχή ζωῆς [i.e., the dominant principle of life], and life is the fundamental figure [*Grundgestalt*] of beings" (210; cf. 214 and 221–22). In these pages of the *Beiträge*, Heidegger sketches the trajectory for a history of being that has more to do with reproduction than production; more to do with life than technicity; more to do with organism than the organon. His sketch identifies τὸ ὄν with ζωή, beings as a whole with life. Not until his 1943–1944 lectures on the early Greek thinkers, especially Heraclitus, will he return to this lightly limned yet never fully fleshed out sketch.

These two sets of remarks invite us to ask whether the principal plot of the history or sending of being—the captation of truth in the ἰδέα and its subjugation under the yoke (ζυγόν) of correctness, the ancient model of production eventually leading to the hegemony of technology in the epoch of representation—does not neglect the equally fundamental figure of being(ness) as life and generation. Is not the Platonic Demiurge both craftsman and father? Does not the Demiurge go to meet, if only in fear and trembling, the mighty Ἀνάγκη? Is not τέχνη always and everywhere haunted and hounded by τίκτειν, production by reproduction?[6] The essential step toward the mission of redemption, according to Schreber, is that the savior undergo metamorphosis into a woman, *die Verwandlung zum Weibe*. Freud suspects that the savior's passion, the entire mission of redemption, in fact, flows from his desire for such a metamorphosis, and that such homosexual desire underlies all paranoia as such. Heidegger insists that thinking be receptive and responsive. Schreber retorts that personally he would far rather retain the honorific status that his life as a male guarantees him than risk transfiguration. Yet he realizes that no thinker thinks by personal preference. Ultimately, Schreber too submits to receptivity and responsibility. Are not the organon and all the ergics and energics of organism accompanied surreptitiously by an orgiastics, with craving (ὄρεξις) as its fundamental mood (ὀργή)? Schreber knows that every soothsayer must surrender the dignity of Κάλχας for the blind insight of Τειρεσίας.

In response to Heidegger's sketch of the history of the oblivion of being in modernity, one could ask: Does German Idealism simply peter out into positivism and "philosophy of life"? Or does not Schelling, for example, think being as willing, willing as the will of love, love as languor and longing, and languor and longing as the divine body of woman?[7] Schreber stands before the mirror. Costume jewelry and ribbons bedeck his naked torso. Beneath the soft skin of the hollow between his breasts he can feel a woman's voluptuosity-nerves. He knows that these used to be the nerves of God. Whatever excesses a Ludwig Klages (Robert Musil's "Meingast") may have perpetrated in and against life-philosophy, is there not a *history of beyng as life* that has to be traced as meticulously as Heidegger has traced the history of beyng as "truth"? Just as Heidegger concedes that *Being and Time* is less a refutation than a culmination of modern metaphysical subjectivity, must he not concede that life, "'life' as the totality of the living, and at the same time as human 'life'" (221), is the culminating point in the history of metaphysics? (It is number 27 in his 27-point anaylsis.) The fact that this culminating point is decried as degenerate *Er-lebnis* and *Lebensphilosophie* is an indication, not that life is without importance for the history of beyng, but that it remains to be positively confronted and appropriated—better, propriated—at the "other commencement" of thinking. Is not *Seynsverlassenheit*, the abandonment of beings by beyng, as much a "family romance" as a tale of technics and forgetfulness? Like Newton, Schreber believes that after He performed the work of creation, God withdrew from the world, abandoning it, growing utterly remote. One is tempted to say of Heidegger what he says of Nietzsche in *Being and Time* (§76, 396), namely, that he knew more than he let on—even if what Heidegger knows can be thought only within unrelieved anxiety, only paranoetically.

Be all that as it may, the sudden upsurgence of living and of "life" three-quarters of the way through "The Leap" remains unnerving. Especially if we recall that in the meta-ontology of 1928 something like a "primal leap" *(Ursprung)* first initiates Dasein to embodiment and sexuality.[8] These brief and enigmatic invocations of life in the *Beiträge* serve to mediate the discussion of the essential unfolding of beyng (which discussion they interrupt) and to introduce for a second time the cleavage *(die Zerklüftung)* of beyng.

The cleft of beyng releases beings but occludes itself. That the essential unfolding of beyng occurs as radical cleavage and sundering is perhaps the very essence of the leap—"*der Sprung* erspringt *die Zerklüftung des Seyns.*" Indeed, the more one thinks *Zerklüftung* the less certain one becomes of "the leap." For *der Sprung* is also (or perhaps eminently and in the first place) the crack, rent, or fissure in beyng. One does not get over it, even and especially through the leap inspired by Kierkegaard.   At one time, according to Schreber, Flechsig's (i.e., God's) soul showed forty to sixty cleavages *(Abspaltungen)*, as though all beyng were irreparably cloven.   Just as Heidegger radicalizes *Kluft, Klüftung*, and *erklüftende* by means of the emphatic prefix *Zer-* (GA 65, 103, f.b.; 231, 1, 10 f.b.), so we must think every *Erspringen* as a *Zerspringen*, not as a brave leap of faith or thought, but as a shattering, cracking, or cleaving, a *Riß* or rift. Is it an accident that throughout the *Beiträge*, we read again and again of ecstatic *Entrückung, Berückung*, and *Verrückung*—rapture, transport, and radical derangement? One might well wish that the leap—if it is a leap—pursued clearly defined *steps* or *stages*. Yet the overdetermined gaping of the truth of beyng shows none.

In this time of transition to the other beginning we must think that cleft or cleavage of beyng as the ontological difference. Such difference itself dissolves into sundry differences and relationships *sans rapport*, among them: (1) the difference between *Sein* (as *Seiendheit*) and *Seienden*; (2) the difference between *Sein* and *Seyn* as the essential unfolding of the truth and history of beyng, *die Wesung*; (3) the difference between *Sein* and *Da-sein* as the "instantaneous place" of the leap; (4) the difference within the clearing, as *die verbergende Lichtung*, between the self-obfuscation of beyng and the *showing* of such obfuscation, as well as between concealment *(Sichverbergen, Verborgenheit)* and sheltering, shepherding, or salvaging *(Bergung)*; and finally, (5) difference as the striving of earth and world, the agon wherein gods and daimons come to be, struggle, pass by, and pass away.

If we were to fall into the abyss of the cleavage, we would confront, as we hurtled by, all the strata of the Kantian and post-Kantian modalities, where the possible and the necessary affront one another (75). We would descry something very much like death (283: *Der Zusammenstoß von Notwendigkeit und Möglichkeit*; see §§160–63 on being-toward-death). In the abyssal *Zerklüftung*, modalities proliferate beyond necessity and possibility, engendering what Heidegger calls singularity, rarity, instantaneity, contingency and seizure, reticence and freedom, preservation and need (118: *Einzigkeit, Seltenheit, Augenblicklichkeit, Zufall und Anfall, Verhaltenheit und Freiheit, Verwahrung und Notwendigkeit*); or, as another list has it, refusal and default, seizure and contingency, reticence and transfiguration, freedom and compulsion (280: *Verweigerung und Ausbleib, Anfall und Zufall, Verhaltenheit und Verklärung* Flechsig's rays have destroyed Schreber's stomach and intestines, lanced his lungs, split his esophagus, burst his bladder, fractured his ribs, *Freiheit und Verzwingung* and yet Schreber submits utterly to the compulsion to think, accepts *Denkzwang*, because every time he pauses, God (Flechsig) believes that he (Schreber) has lost his (Schreber's) mind. Somewhat after the manner of Descartes). Furthermore, the play of space and time occurs in the cleavage of beyng itself (103: *Das* Zeit-raumhafte *der Entscheidung als aufbrechende Klüftung des Seyns selbst*). Indeed, *Zerklüftung* gapes in the turing of propriation as such (231: Im anderen Anfang *gilt es den Sprung in die erklüftende Mitte der Kehre des Ereignisses*). In short, what looks like a leap *over* the gorge is instead a plunge *into* its midst—*Zerklüftung* is the fission of propriation (235–39). Thus, finally and most mysteriously, *Zerklüftung* is the trembling of the godhead in conception and nativity (239: *die Erzitterung des Götterns*), the very unfolding and flexing of the godhead. Schreber senses that there are gaps or cleavages in the cosmic order, such that God's flexibility is threatened, his perfection flawed, his species endangered. The shudder of the godhead in struggle and decision (244: *das Entscheidungsreich für den Kampf der Götter..., in welchem Kampf die Götter erst göttern und ihren Gott zur Entscheidung stellen*) marks both the coming-to-be and the passing-by (as passing-away) of the last god. In the verb *Göttern* we may hear the "gathering" of godhead in ἀγαθόν, in *gattern, be-gatten*, and *Gattung*—once again the untold tale of the history of beyng as ἔρως. Trembling at birth, but also in refusal and flight (244: *Götterung [Verweigerung]*), quivering in excessive refusal (245), the godhead eventually goes to meet a violent end in the net-work of space and time:

Das Er-eignis und seine Erfügung in der Abgründigkeit des Zeit-Raumes ist das Netz, in das der letzte Gott sich selbst hängt, um es zu zerreißen und in seiner Einzigkeit enden zu lassen, göttlich und seltsam und das Fremdeste in allem Seienden.

Das plötzliche Verlöschen des großen Feuers... (263).

Propriation and the enjoining of propriation in the abyssal character of time-space is the net in which the last god hangs itself, rending the net, letting itself come to an end in its singularity, godlike and rare and the strangest thing among all beings.

Sudden extinguishing of the conflagration...

The death of the shivering godhead marks the end of an era, the era that commenced with Hölderlin's *Empedocles*. Or, as President Schreber puts it, "I emerge as victor from the apparently unequal struggle of a single weak human being against God Himself, albeit after much bitter suffering and deprivation, because the order of the cosmos is on my side." Perhaps it is the end of ontotheology, of the history of beyng as we (fail to) know it. The death of the last god, portrayed in the two brief concluding sections of the *Beiträge*, is both the most terrifying and the most jubilant event of propriation, inasmuch as death is the supreme witness of beyng (230; 284). Thus, "the most frightful jubilation must be the dying of a god," and, reading the proposition as a speculative proposition, "the dying of a god must be the most frightful jubilation" (230: *Der furchtbarste Jubel muß das Sterben eines Gottes sein*). What others will have called *la jouissance de Dieu*.

No sensible reader of Heidegger's *Beiträge* will want to fall into such an abyss, unless he or she is compelled to do so; unless the fissure opens beneath one's own feet or below our leaping bodies. For if we did fall, then Heidegger's "tepid paganism" (Lévinas) would become the whiteheat of "solar extravagance" (Bataille), and Heidegger's theodicy a journey quite beyond compulsive polemics into a realm where the masters are few and most of them shut away. If we did fall into Heidegger's cleft of beyng and earth, we would have to reopen the entire discussion of a *politics* of life and of friendship. We would have to ask why, when "the futural ones" find their god, they become a *Volk*. Further, we would have to ask why this people's last god gets caught up in questions of *Geschlecht*, a word and an issue of troubling complexity, as Derrida has taught us in his recent texts. One of many passages in Heidegger's oeuvre that Derrida would have to add to his repertory is the following one on "the essence of the people *[Volk]* and Da-sein":

> The essence of the people is grounded in the historicity of those who belong to *themselves* on the *basis* of their belonging to the god. From the propriation in which such belonging is historically grounded there originates first of all the grounds as to why "life" and the body, sexual reproduction and *Geschlecht*, lineage and—to say it by way of a fundamental word—the earth, belong to history.... (GA 65, 399)

We cannot doubt that the nexus of god and *Geschlecht*, life and the body, sex and reproduction is a cultural, if not *völkisch*, nexus. Surely, Foucault and Irigaray have taught us at least that. Yet the daimonic node is as tightly drawn as it is hopelessly amorphous in Heidegger's thought.

Let us now allow the daimon that is called variously "life" and "living" to interrupt the leap or fissure of thinking, beyng, and the earth. It all begins innocently enough with a recollection of the gradations, stages, or hierarchies that traditional metaphysical systems (from Plato's *Republic*, through Philo and Plotinus, to Christian theology and ontology generally) express in and as the great chain of being—*die Stufen des Seyns*. Heidegger refers to the relation in Leibniz's *Monadology* of the "central monad" (God) to the "sleeping monads" on the periphery.

In his 1928 logic course, Heidegger had invoked the central monad and the preestablished harmony that pervades every monad, "each according the stage *[Stufe]* of its wakefulness" (GA 26, 119). Such vigilance or alertness, which has fascinated Heidegger early on in his career, even during the early Freiburg period, and the very impulse *(Drang)* of *vis primitiva*, imply that the monad, "as a force, is something living" (112: *etwas Lebendiges*). As a living pulsion, the atomic monad is ecstatic. It seems to explode, expending its energies to the point where inside and outside become indistinguishable, as though the monad were limitlessly vast and imperceptibly small at one and the same time, the incalculable *aleph* of all space. (As Hans Castorp muses on a moonlit night in Thomas Mann's *Der Zauberberg*, "The atom was an energy-laden cosmic system. In it, celestial bodies raced in rotation about a sunlike center. Through its ethereal space comets flew with the speed of light, compelled in their eccentric orbits by the force which the central body exerted.")[9] Leibniz's monadological metaphysics returns to Heidegger's own deliberations on transcendence, temporality, and the source of the world in what he calls the *nihil originarium* (GA 26, 271ff.). If one thinks of the dark side of those stages of wakefulness, as Heidegger soon will, one may recall what Leibniz calls "a prolonged state of unconsciousness *[étourdissement]*," or "the profound and dreamless sleep" into which a soul may "swoon," the soul being "stunned" or "dazed" by myriad *petites perceptions*, which cause it to suffer both vertigo and—at least in the case of animals—something approximating death.[10]

In the 1936–1938 *Beiträge*, Heidegger's own question, set in spaced type or italics, is as follows: *"Are there, from the vantagepoint of the question concerning the truth of being as propriation, gradations of this kind at all; are there even gradations of beyng?"* To be sure, such a hierarchy would no longer be a great chain of being(s), descending from the Supreme Being by analogy or emanation to monstrous fish at the bottom of the muddy sea. It would be a hierarchy of the force of truth *(Wahrheitskraft)*, a graded originality in the salvaging of beyng *(Bergungsurprünglichkeit)*, or an order of rank in the essential unfolding of propriation itself *(Erwesung des Ereignisses)*. However, Heidegger will soon deny that, properly speaking, there can be such a hierarchy. In later essays he will insist on the "unified field" of φύσις.[11] Yet the question remains as to how "the living, how 'nature' and nature's inanimate components, such as equipment, machination, work, deed, and sacrifice... are to be ordered *[zu ordnen sind]*" (GA 65, 274). The very frontier between animate and inanimate nature—between, as it were, the astral and the maternal Earth—seems to be as uncertain in this new universe of thought as it was in the old. (Hans Castorp continues, "Was it improper to think that certain planets of the atomic solar system—of these throngs, these milky ways of solar systems that constituted matter—that one or other of these innercosmic celestial bodies found itself in a condition that corresponded to the condition of the Earth when it became the dwelling place of *life*?") Heidegger feels compelled to risk such an ordering of disclosive power, even though he rightly fears the family tree of all such hierarchies:

> Nevertheless, does there not still remain a way, at least provisionally, of creating a spectrum within the projection of being *[einen Gesichtskreis des seinsmäßigen Entwurfs zu schaffen]*,

after the manner of "ontologies" of the various "realms" (nature, history), so that we can experience these realms afresh? Such a thing can become necessary as a *transition*. Yet it remains an embroglio, because it is easy to slip from such a spectrum into the systematics of an earlier style. (GA 65, 274)

Heidegger will soon give us occasion to remember the dangers of the slippage to which philosophies of life—whether in Leibniz, Schelling, or Scheler—are prone. For the moment, he tries to think order as enjoining *(Fügung)* and as the striving of world and earth *(die Bestreitung des Streites von Welt und Erde)*, in recollection of (what will become) "The Anaximander Fragment" and (what has by that time become) "The Origin of the Work of Art."

I shall forego all comment on the notion of *Fug* and *sich fügen* in "The Anaximander Fragment" in order to recall briefly the striving and the strife of world and earth in "The Origin of the Work of Art" (UK, 41–45). Perhaps that striving can best be recollected by means of a certain rift in the image of earth that Heidegger himself invokes; it is an architectural image of a work that does a great deal of work in Heidegger's text—the Greek temple. The Greek temple is supported by the earth, more specifically, by a cliff, more specifically still, by a cloven earth of cliff and cleft. The temple "simply stands there in the midst of the cloven vale of rock," *inmitten des zerklüfteten Felsentales*. If the temple stands there in relief as something inconcussible, something that resists all shattering *(Das Unerschütterte des Werkes steht ab)*, the earth itself is the memory of rendings and strivings, the memory, we might say, of what Heidegger in 1936–1938 calls *die Zerklüftung des Seyns*. In "The Origin," Heidegger does not invoke such a terrestrial memory; he emphasizes the solidity and support of the earth. Yet the hewn stone of the temple columns itself recalls the cleavage of earth and of beyng. *Out of that cleavage arise life and living.* Among the beings that the temple gathers into presencing are the god, the holy, birth and death, disaster and blessing, victory and disgrace, perdurance and decrepitude; also, as Heidegger adduces, the raging storm, the grace of the sun, the light of day (a second invocation of birth, at least in the language of Homer), the expanse of the sky, the gloom of night, and the swelling sea. Then Heidegger says this: "Tree and grass, eagle and bull, snake and cricket first enter into their configured relief *[gehen erst in ihre abgehobene Gestalt ein]* and thus come to the fore as they are." Such advent and upsurgence, he concludes, are what the Greeks long ago called φύσις.

I shall truncate Heidegger's meditation on the work of art here by posing a question. With the upsurgence of *the living* into the clearing, can it be merely a matter of yet another configuration and relief? Do the (living) beings that come to the fore in beyng constitute a *tableau mort*? Or must not φύσις, onto which the cloven earth too opens, embrace the coming-to-presence *of* (whereby the *of* is now to be taken as a *genitivus subjectivus*, that is to say, as the multiple and varied presencings of *and to*) what are called cricket and snake, bull and eagle, and, yes, even the rooted tree and the leaves of grass? To put it negatively: Could these (living) things be disclosed and assume their proper shapes if they themselves are deprived of all disclosure? If they themselves assumed the figure of cadavers? Or is not the question of an order and rank in disclosive power, of gradations in beyng, however dangerous it may be, absolutely essential to a meditation on φύσις?—However, let me truncate the truncation and return now to the *Beiträge*.

For the moment, Heidegger does not seem to be worried about an absolutely classic distinction that slips into this own thinking directly from the pages of the *Monadology* (§49), to wit, that of activity and passivity: earth is proclaimed "in one respect *more original* than nature," because it is "related to history." The passive voice of *geschichtsbezogen* conceals the essential *activity* of human history, which raises earth above the sheer impassivity of what Leibniz and Hegel (and, on occasion, Heidegger) think as a "swooning" nature.   Schreber believes that the hyperactive Flechsig will never withdraw from him, will never abandon him again, and that like Kierkegaard he is condemned forever to adopt a feminine position before Him. Freud believes that if he does not analyze Schreber's *Denkwürdigkeiten* he will be in the ridiculous position of the man Kant portrays in his *Critique of Pure Reason*, the same man Socrates portrays elsewhere, who bends to hold the sieve while his mate milks the billygoat.   Further, *world* is proclaimed "higher" than both nature and earth, inasmuch as world is *"formative of history* [geschichtsbildend] and thus closest to propriation" (GA 65, 275). Recall that in the remarks on theoretical biology in 1929–1930, Heidegger had distinguished between the passivity of brute *Benommenheit* and the activity of a *weltbildenden* humankind. He neglected at that time to indicate that in *Being and Time* he had used the word *benommen* to designate both a passive Dasein enamored of the world and a vigilant Dasein stunned by its radical individuation in anxiety. A dazed Dasein, while not yet resolutely open, not yet fully present to its own mortality, poises on the verge of anxiety proper.[12] By 1929–1930, Dasein has found its feet, assuming a braver stance toward beings. It holds and keeps itself *(verhält sich)* in the openness of being, while the animal ostensibly remains ensnared in the closed ring of what both Leibniz and Scheler call disinhibitions (GA 26, 103, ll. 10–14: *Enthemmungen*), at least until *something like death* shatters that ring. In 1936–1938 Heidegger is worried about the technologized animal called man, who can neither shape a world nor be stunned by his own mortality: "Is technology the historical path toward *the end, to the regression of the last man to the technologized animal, the animal that loses even the original animality of the integral animal* [die ursprüngliche Tierheit des eingefügten Tieres]; *or can it, if taken ahead of time as salvaging* [Bergung], *be integrated* [eingefügt werden] *into the grounding of Da-sein?*" (GA 65, 275; cf. 98). If the animal called *man* cannot be so enjoined, it is destined to be, not the "as yet undetermined animal" of Nietzsche's reflections, not *das noch nicht festgestellte Tier*, but the already distorted animality of the "rational animal." Early in the *Beiträge* (28) Heidegger asks whether "the beginning of the last man drives humanity into distorted animality *[verstellte Tierheit]* and denies historical humanity its last god." Heidegger's hope is that the essence of technology can be enjoined to the world of man as the animal is enjoined in its world—the world that it has in not having it (in 1929–1930), and which, as Heidegger later argues, it may not have at all (in 1936–1938 and throughout the 1950s).

Aphorism 153, *Leben*, without quotation-marks, rejects the reduction of life to organism, of organism to the realm of the corporeal *(das Leibliche)*, of the corporeal to mass *(der Körper)*, and of mass to Galilean–Newtonian mechanics. That rejection appears to be a constant in Heidegger's thought, whether in 1927, 1929–1930, 1936–1938, or the 1950s. What now occupies him is the question of a fundamental relation to the living *(Grundverhältnis zum Lebendigen)*. What *are* plants and animals, once we cease using them to feed and entertain the lives of the regressive, technologized animals?[13] Heidegger's first reply to the question is as unforeseen as everything must be on a leap that in fact is a fissuring of the very gap to be leapt. He wonders whether once we have stepped back from machination, in which everything is laborious *(das Mühsame)*, we will finally be able to descry the living as the effortless *(das Mühelose)*. That reply is surprising, because in 1930 he quoted both Paul and the apocryphal Book of Esra in order to suggest that the ways of life, reflected in the longing gaze of all creation's creatures, are laborious *(mühselig)*. That was one of the rare moments in Heidegger's theoretical biology when the fundamental mood of philosophizing (discussed throughout the first half of the 1929–1930 course) spread its veil of melancholy over the whole; it was one of the rare moments when it seemed at least possible to integrate the difficult problem and invaluable touchstone of *death* into the discussion of life (GA 29/30, 270–71, 387, 396). Now, in 1936–1938, as all the world darkens, life appears to be "effortless."

As long as he remains a male, Schreber will not be mortal at all. Only after he has mothered a new breed of humanity, a new *Geschlecht*, will he die a natural death and be assumed, bodies and soul, into heaven.   Be that as it may, the fundamental relation of Dasein to the living is anything but effortless: the *Beiträge* resound with echoes of a problem unresolved in *Being and Time*, to wit, the way in which the living is to become "the other reverberation of Da-sein" (GA 65, 276: *zum anderen Widerklang des Daseins*). "Life" runs and hides from ontology as well as from biology, precisely in the way that beyng withdraws from the thinker (293). Concerning reticent "life," in quotation-marks, Heidegger writes the following in his *Contributions to Philosophy*:

154. *"Das Leben"*

a "mode" of the beingness (beyng) of beings. The incipient opening of beings to it *[beginnliche Eröffnung des Seienden auf es zu]* in the safe-keeping of the self. The first darkening *[Erdunkelung]* in the safe-keeping of the self is grounded in the benumbment of the living, in which all stimulation and excitation run their course, along with the sundry stages of the dark and its unfolding.

"Life" in Heidegger's view is the strife of opening and closing, of a brightening and darkening, as Schelling long ago affirmed. "Life" is some sort of opening to beings: the words *auf es zu* suggest the ecstatic futurity of Dasein, which runs ahead by letting what-is-to-come approach it, approach its ecstatic "self." "Life," at some stage (for the gradients or stages of being will have to be preserved for beyng in order to fend off the dark, no matter how grave the danger that we may slip into the abysses of past systems), safeguards and keeps the self.   Schreber is willing to wait centuries. At some point, finally unmanned, he will bear divine fruit. Freud says his wish-fulfillment is asymptotic.   "Life" at some stage (but at which stage?) safeguards and secures the ecstatic self that is outside itself, the "self" that perdures and reemerges in section 64 of *Being and Time*, having withstood as though by magic the "destruction" of all personhood, subjectivity, humanism, psychic interiority, and spiritualism, as well as the dismantling of the meaning of being as perdurant presence *(beständige Anwesenheit)*. Nothing is more problematic in *Being and Time*, where everything is problematic, than a certain stubborn atavism of the "self," the selfsame self of past metaphysical systems that foists itself on "life" once again in the *Beiträge*.

However, after the very first sentence on "life" in the *Beiträge*, "life" as incipient opening, the perspective is suddenly reversed: as quickly as one might slip into a gully, Heidegger writes of a first darkening *(Erdunkelung)*. Barely safeguarded, the neophyte self now regresses to the benumbment of the (merely) living. Barely in the ascendant, "life" regresses. It succumbs to raw stimulation and excitation, which, as Freud showed in the 1895 "Project" and throughout his metapsychological writings, are always incitements to death. Schreber's overexcited nerves jangle so wildly that even divinity is distracted; Flechsig deviates, descends, invades from behind; Schreber sometimes wishes that the cosmic order had left excitability to the animal stage of being. The sundry steps or stages of the living proceed *downward*, as steps of a ladder descending into the great dark. Yet from what Archimedian point do they proceed downward? From the *summum ens*? From the *animal rationale*? From *homo techno-habilis*? Can these beings be distinguished by an animal that is no longer enjoined even to its own brutishness? And which is the graver danger to life—slipping into the abyss-of-essence that ostensibly separates Dasein from the animal, or slipping into the unthought of metaphysics, slipping into systems that always prided themselves on making distinction after distinction—inside from outside, activity from passivity,
Freud finds Schreber's *Denkwürdigkeiten* to be full of "hair-splitting" distinctions, "as in all theodicies," speech from writing, presence from absence—as though in order to rescue human beings from (other forms of) life? Would not the desire to separate animality from Dasein be the metaphysical desire to preserve intact the full presence of an "inside" from the death that invades from the "outside"? No matter how minute such an "inside" may become, or how monstrously vast an "outside"? (Hans Castorp, still perched on the *Magic Mountain*, muses as follows: "The 'minuteness' of the innercosmic stellar bodies would be an altogether invalid objection, for the standard that measured large and small had slipped through our fingers by the time the cosmic nature of the 'smallest' particles of matter revealed itself. Likewise, the concepts of outside and inside had suffered a blow to their stability. The world of the atom

was an outside, just as the planet Earth on which we dwelled was in all probability, from an organic point of view, a profound inside.") But let us continue our descent into 154. *"Das Leben"*:

> *Darkening* and the essence of *instinct*. The *safe-keeping* of the self and the *preeminence of the "species,"* which does not recognize any "individual" as selflike.

Here we have a reminiscence of "life" in the Hegelian system, in which the respective *Gattung* is preeminent over each *Einzelnes*, the latter containing within its "self" both the seed of death and the universal impotence of all merely "natural" species. From the ashes of such life, Phoenix-like, spirit as such must rise (see Hegel's *Enzyklopädie*, §§367–76). The safeguarding and securing of the self cannot occur in animal life, Hegel teaches, and Heidegger presumably concurs.

Does Heidegger simply accent the Hegelian preeminence of *Gattung*, or is there here a faint intimation, a living *Widerklang*, of the untold history of beyng as ζωή, ἀγαθόν, and ἔρως, the erotic gathering of life? Does Heidegger simply repeat the identification of instinct and occlusion, the life of drives as fundamental passivity, as *weg! sein*, that is to say, a form of being that is always already bygone? Or does he affirm precisely in Da-sein a *being away*, an ecstatic *Weg-sein*, as the very opening of disclosure in the direction of death, *Seyn zum Tode*?[14] Is what seems effortlessly alive—precisely in its vulnerability and transiency, precisely in its being-away-toward-death—the site of disclosure? Is such disclosure εὐδαιμονία, the blessedness of "life"? Schreber believes that he is called upon to redeem the world, to restore its vanished happiness, felicity, or blessedness, *Seligkeit*. He would affirm what another has written of such daimonic felicity: "Blessed are they who dare to belong to the unblessedness of [the] cleavage" (GA 65, 416), that is to say, to the cleavage of beyng.

Let us fall still farther into "life":

> Darkening *[Erdunkelung]* and *worldlessness*. (Earlier as *world poverty*! Misleading. The stone not even worldless, because it is altogether without darkening.)

Here Heidegger revises—tentatively, telegraphically—his earlier theses (from the 1929–1930 biology lectures) that the stone is worldless and the animal poor in world. Both realms of being, both animate and inanimate nature, are dropped down a peg, as it were, in the order of disclosure. Dropped down a peg, reduced in rank—in spite of the fact that the ultimate darkening of death is what grants all "life" its aperture on beings. It now appears to be the case that the stone is less than worldless (although what could be less than least, lower than last?), and that the animal is no longer merely destitute, no longer having-in-not-having, but absolutely, stonily deprived of world. Perhaps in this absolute deprivation the animal finds its lapidary ease? Perhaps Heidegger has here signed a temporary truce with Rilke—before the final outbreak of hostilities against Rilke's animals in 1943? At all events, we are now approaching the end of the aphorism, the very bottom of the *Zerklüftung* of "life":

> Petrifaction and regression of life from the incipient opening. Accordingly, no occlusion either *[Demgemäß auch keine Verschließung]*, as long as the living is not in accompaniment—"earth" (stone, plant, animal). Stone and stream not without plant, animal. How does the decision to "life" stand and fall? Meditation on "the biological."

Does a second reversal stir here, in favor of "life"? "Life" on the upswing? Upsurgent φύσις as plenipotence (190: "φύσις is so overpowering")? It is difficult to say. The aphorism ends, clipped and cryptic, yet also gaping, calling for an extended meditation on "the biological," which the *Beiträge* has rejected all along.[15]

"Life," scarcely begun, falls back, turns to stone, is paralyzed and petrified. Yet in that very regression and occlusion a kind of reversal seems to occur. Heidegger concedes that there can be no closure, *keine Verschließung*, unless "life" accompanies, *mitzugenommen wird*. "Life" is essential to the *earth* that the thinking of beyng and propriation tries to think. Earth, as the self-occlusion that juts forth and shows itself, is the supportive site not only of stone but also of *plant* and *animal*. Hölderlin's stone and stream—not without lizard, lichen, and fish. As though every being and all beyng were precisely as an earlier system of metaphysics and an earlier regional ontology of nature portrayed them. Leibniz, *Monadology*, §§66–69:

> 66. Whence we see that there is a world of creatures, of living beings, of animals, of entelechies, of souls, in the smallest particle of matter.
> 67. Each portion of matter may be conceived of as a garden full of plants, a pond full of fishes. Yet each branch of

the plant, each member of the animal, each drop of its humors is also such a garden or pond.

68. And although the earth and air which lie between the plants of the garden, or the water between the fish of the pond, is neither plant nor fish, they yet contain more of them, but for the most part so tiny as to be imperceptible to us.

69. Therefore there is nothing fallow, nothing sterile, nothing dead in the universe, no chaos, no confusion, except in appearance; somewhat as a pond would appear from a distance, in which we might see the confused movement and swarming, so to speak, of the fishes in the pond, without discerning the fish themselves.[16]

All of which leads Leibniz to say that "all bodies are, like rivers, in perpetual flux, and parts are entering into them and departing from them continually" (§71), so that "there is strictly speaking neither absolute birth nor complete death..." (§72). "What we call *birth*," concludes the thinker of the regressive stages or infinitesimal links in the great chain of being, "is development or growth, as what we call *death* is envelopment and diminution" (§73). Life fatal is life natal, in a universe where large and small, dark and bright, wave and particle, organic and anorganic, self and other are impossible to distinguish once and for all. Hans Castorp, for his final appearance under the moon:

Had not one bold and visionary researcher spoken of "milky way animals," cosmic monsters whose flesh, bone, and brain were constructed of solar systems? Yet if that were so, concluded Hans Castorp, then the moment you thought you'd come to the edge, the whole thing would start all over again! Perhaps the youthful Hans Castorp was hiding once again in the innermost recesses of his own self, a hundred times over, huddled warmly on his balcony with a view of mountain crags in the moonlight of a frosty night, where, frozen of finger and flushed of face, enthralled by the humanistic science of medicine, he studied the life of bodies?

Heidegger's *Beiträge zur Philosophie* does not take up the near "end" of Dasein as birth or birthing, *gebürtig*, alluded to so cryptically in section 72 of *Being and Time*. However, precisely now, precisely when Heidegger returns to the cleavage of beyng, he does take up the far end of death, "the supreme and uttermost testimony of beyng" (GA 65, 230 and 284). Such testimony the gods too must render. Their dying is joined to beyng-toward-death as such by "the shortest route" (282, 414: *die kürzeste Bahn*). Daimonic testimony therefore only confirms the experience of mortals, rendering evidence, moreover, not of nihilism but of affirmation (284: *Bejahbarkeit*) and creative yes-saying (246 and 266–7: *das wesentliche, "schaffende" Jasagen*). If the human being's bodily kinship with animals is, as the "Letter on Humanism" says, abyssal and abysmal, *ab-gründig*,[17] it is because Da-sein senses the *abgründigen Grund* (GA 65, 286), the abyss that envelops both of the stages of beyng that we call *the human* and *the animal*, though not to forget *the vegetable*, stages that are not stages at all but infinite differencings of infinitesimal life. Or of "life." "Life" being the kind of thing Max Scheler once saw and felt as he watched a film about plants. On March 3, 1926, during the period of his final cosmological and anth(rop)ological musings, he wrote the following to Märit Furtwängler:

> I saw a film on plant life, a film in which twenty-four hours of life were reduced to a few seconds. It was wonderful! You could see the plants breathing, burgeoning, and dying. The natural impression we all have—that plants possess no soul—vanished altogether. You could see the entire drama of life, all its unheard-of exertions. The most beautiful thing was to see the creepers that were planted near little four-runged trellises. Their turbulent "search" for a hold, the "satisfaction" when they found the rungs of the trellis, their frustrated attempts (often one tendril tried to find a hold in the tendrils of another plant, which was in as precarious a position as the first, so that they both collapsed), and, above all, the following phenomenon—when they reached the fourth rung they would cast about in "desperation," searching and searching, until (incredibly!) after repeated failures they would return to the fourth rung. It agitated me so *[erschütterte mich so]*, that it was all I could do to hold back tears. Oh, life is everywhere of the same sweetness, everywhere enchanting, everywhere painful. . . . And all of it, all of life, is one.[18]

In the end, as at the beginning, of course, life does have as much to do with birth as with death, with flourishing as with decay. In his discussion of "the cleavage and the 'modalities'" (281), Heidegger discusses possibility and necessity as the two "horns" of actuality or ἐνέργεια. He pauses in order to sketch in a few lines "the kernal of Aristotle's 'ontology'." If actuality is thought on the basis of a dynamic yet undeveloped φύσις, then it is conceived in the light of change, turnabout, or overturning, μεταβολή. In other words, it is thought ecstatically. Such ecstatic metabolism seems to be the counterpart or the foil to what we take to be prototypically Aristotelian being, namely, constancy and presence, especially when μεταβολή takes the form of φορά. φορά means gestation, carrying, and bearing; it means a being borne or swept along in rapid motion, as a planet is swept along in its orbit; it means a rush, pulse, pulsion, or impulse. Aristotelian being as οὐσία, permanence of presence, would thus be in tension with metabolic life, and a restive life could only cleave (to) such being.

Must not such a tension—between permanence of presence and the ephemeral modalities of metabolism—be thought paranoetically? That is to say, without recourse to a being that one could blame? Must it not be thought within what might be called the proto-ontological difference, whereby life would be a matter of being *(Sein)* as such, and not merely of beings *(Seiendem)*? Such a thinking is not paranoid: its situation is more dire than that. For as we have seen, there is no being that has conspired to engineer beyng's abandonment of beings, no being to be excoriated by the thrown project(ion) of insane hatred. Not even an oblivious humanity can be blamed, so that vituperative polemic is all in vain, and must succumb to the piety that it energizes. Paranoetic thinking finds no noematic correlate on which to pin its hopes or project its phobias. The last god is unavailable for sacrifice, for it *is* merely as passing by, *Vorbeigang*, a passing by that is a passing away, a passing away into the absolute past of everything that is *Vorbei!* The last daimonic god signals in withdrawal, forever out of reach, and tantalizes thought.   During the lengthy process of his puri-fication, Schreber learns a new language: his speech no longer projects Jehovah-rays and Zoroaster-beams, but sparkles with the idiom spoken by God Himself. Schreber speaks *die Grundsprache*, "a somewhat archaic yet quite forceful German," notes Freud, "particularly remarkable for the wealth of euphemisms it contains."   The fundamental attunement of paranoetic thinking, responding to the daimon's ultimate withdrawal, is the cacophony of piety mixed with scurrilous sarcasm; it produces a grating sound, the *Mißton*, as Heidegger calls it in one of his essays on Nietzsche, of a quietism constantly interrupted by the compulsive polemical screech. Occasionally the *Beiträge* succeeds in integrating the two modes, the result being a parody of Zarathustra's parody of the Biblical idiom: *"Denn all dieses hasset der letzte Gott zuerst"* (406).

What Heidegger *wishes* to think, what he *must* think, is an οὐσία that would no longer be counterposed to μεταβολή and φορά. The forgotten beyng, the beyng that has abandoned beings such as ourselves like a gigolo, is the object of his dreams and the demon of his nightmares in the apocalypse of "the other commencement." *Such beyng, as disclosure, is not without life; the very story of revealing and concealing, the story of the truth of beyng, is a life-story.* The story of propriation, *Ereignis*, is a tale of the granting of time and being to those beings—whether gods or mortals or the mortal godhead—who can be cultivated and used, if only for a finite time.   God suffered from the fact that in accord with the very order of things He enjoyed social intercourse only with cadavers. It was never granted Him to know a living human being. No wonder He was so awkward with Schreber.
Daimon life would name that region of beings for which revealing and concealing, growth and decline, faith and treachery, would come to the fore and into question. And, beyond question, into anxious heed. It would no longer be a *region* of beings at all but what Heidegger elsewhere calls *the dimension.*

Amid the overwrought, distraught polemics, amid the outcries against the publicists, pundits, and Babbits of modern life-philosophy, against the nihilists and know-it-alls of positivism, Bolshevism, biologism, and racism, of pragmatism, value-philosophy, and Weltanschauungen, Heidegger hears the raucous sound of the jubilant dying god, the expiring god suddenly passing by, the last god croaking like a real toad in imaginary Leibnizian gardens: if the word *Erdunkelung* is cloven otherwise, cloven as *Erd-unkelung*, then it is not (only) darkening but (also) the throaty song of the earth. *Erdunkelung* is (also) *Erdunkelung*, which is to say, *das Unken der Erde. Die Unke* is a toad; figuratively, a croaker, a Jeremiah. Though not, as the dictionaries say, a grouse.

Notes

1. D. F. Krell, *Daimon Life: Heidegger and Life Philosophy* (Bloomington: Indiana University Press, 1992), pp. 197–214.

2. Martin Heidegger, *Metaphysische Anfangsgründe der Logik im Ausgang von Leibniz*, Martin Heidegger Gesamtausgabe Band 26 (Frankfurt am Main: V. Klostermann, 1978), p. 211 n. 3.

3. See Martin Heidegger, *Beiträge zur Philosophie (Vom Ereignis)*, Martin Heidegger Gesamtausgabe Band 65 (Frankfurt am Main: V.

Klostermann, 1989), pp. 9 and 64, for the *four*, as opposed to the *six*, key words. Yet I would be the last to deny a place to the two final key words, "the futural ones" and "the last god," *die Zukünftigen* and *der letzte Gott*, which undoubtedly have everything to do with the daimonic. Note that the section that now appears as section eight of the book, "Das Seyn," does not belong where the editor has placed it: Heidegger no doubt intended that the two brief, apocalyptic sections *("Die Zukünftigen," "Der letzte Gott")* should close the book. I shall cite the work either by aphorism (§) or by volume and page in the body of my text.

4. See aphorisms no. 130, 133, 135, 139–142, 147, and 164.

5. See GA 65, at the following pages, for a few samples of Heidegger's polemic against "lived experience," biologism, and "philosophy of life": 19, 38, 40–41, 53, 68, 74, 102–103, 109, 112, 114, 123–124, 127–134 passim, including the diagrams, 173–174, 182, 203, 213, 218, 227, 229, and 259; after "The Leap," see 315, 337–338, 362, 365, 406.

6. See chap. 1 of D. F. Krell, *Archeticture* (Albany: State University of New York Press, 1997).

7. I have discussed this in "The Crisis of Reason in the Nineteenth Century: Schelling's Treatise on Human Freedom (1809)," in John Sallis, Giuseppina Moneta, and Jacques Taminiaux, eds., *The Collegium Phaenomenologicum: The First Ten Years* (Dordrecht: Kluwer Academic Publications, 1988), pp. 13–32.

8. See GA 26, 171–74 (§10); and Jacques Derrida, "Geschlecht [1]: différence sexuelle, différence ontologique," in *Psyché: Inventions de l'autre* (Paris: Galilée, 1987), 395–414. English translation in *Research in Phenomenology*, vol. XIII, 1983, 65–84.

9. Thomas Mann, *Der Zauberberg* (Frankfurt am Main: Fischer Taschenbuch, 1980), pp. 300–301, for this and the following quotations.

10. Leibniz, *Monadologie* §§14, 20–21, 23–24 etc. I cite *Die philosophische Schriften von G. W. Leibniz*, ed. C. J. Gerhardt (Hildesheim: G. Olms, 1961), vol. 6. We shall soon hear more about bedazzlement, and we will have to wonder whether the entire discussion of *Benommenheit* in the 1929–1930 lectures rises directly from the pages of the *Monadologie*, perhaps through the mediation of Max Scheler.

11. On the unified field of *physis*, see Krell, *Daimon Life*, the Introduction and chap. 6.

12. See chapter 6 of D. F. Krell, *Of Memory, Reminiscence, and Writing: On the Verge* (Bloomington: Indiana University Press, 1990), esp. pp. 248–52.

13. Such questions compel thinking today: see John Llewelyn's excellent book, *The Middle Voice of Ecological Conscience: A Chiasmic Reading of Responsibility in the Neighbourhood of Emmanuel Levinas, Martin Heidegger and Others* (London: Macmillan, 1992).

14. See GA 65, 301, 323–25. *Nota bene*: not *der Weg*, but *DAS Weg!* *Weg* as gone, bygone, and even "get gone!" See the use of *weg* in this descriptive-imperative sense with regard to animal behavior, particularly sexual and alimentary behavior: GA 29/30, 363–364. One would have to

trace quite carefully the parallel between *Benommensein* (cf., for example, 65, 410) and *Wegsein*. Both designate that undecidable moment when everything is to be decided: the moment of absolute degradation of humankind in inappropriateness *and* of elevation into the rapture of instantaneous being-toward-death. Both designate the absolute ambivalence of Heidegger's thought from beginning to end. Perhaps a more fitting motto for the Gesamtaugabe, at least in the perspective of "life," would have been: *Weg!—nicht Werke!*

15. See GA 65, 50–53, 173, 182, 203, and 221–222; but cf. 71–72, on the "gathering back" of stone, plant, animal, and man into the self-occluding earth—a reference cited earlier in the article.

16. Leibniz, in the Gerhardt ed., 6, 618–619; for the English translation, see Leibniz, *Selections*, ed. Philip P. Wiener (New York: Charles Scribner's, 1951), pp. 547–548.

17. Martin Heidegger, *Wegmarken* (Frankfurt am Main: V. Klostermann, 1967), p. 157.

18. Quoted by Wilhelm Mader in *Max Scheler* (Reinbeck bei Hamburg: Rowohlt, 1980), pp. 117–118.

VII. Thinking the "Da" of Dasein

Chapter 14

Empty Time and Indifference to Being

Michel Haar

(translated by Douglas Brick)

"If only we could: get along without being."[1]

Existence is never neutral. No moment is insignificant or lacking in tonality.[2] Each one can shine with a singular light, vibrate intensely, and suddenly can seem to unveil the ultimate depth of things. Leaden grey is, after all, a color of the sky just as much as turquoise—and yet, how many monotonous, atonal moments, their singularity flown, are reduced to nothing! How many moments become colorless, their music silent! Has the call of Being deserted us then? From what sphere does this *uncanny* indifference descend upon us with all its weight? Where does this uncanniness itself come from?

The tonality of each moment, that resonance which is never twice the same, which Heidegger calls *Stimmung*, reveals—need I even repeat—neither a purely interior "state of mind," nor a matter of fact, but rather a manner in which the world gives itself. *Stimmung* informs us of the air of things, their tone, their style, their modulation. We discover it along with things or beings themselves: a sad street, a likeable face, a peaceful or disquieting countryside, a happy or severe room. . . . Emotions are inscribed in the texture of the world. It is not a matter of the subject's projection onto objects, nor of a determination of interior by exterior, but of a bidirectional correspondence, which can be felt as "accord" or "discord." To verify this phenomenological truth, it is sufficient to note that, luckily for us, neither grey nor blue skies invariably plunge us into depression or exaltation. The same "objective" atmospheric color gives Hölderlin the ecstasy of "adorable blue," and awakens in Mallarmé the terror of the obsessional "eternal azure."

Apparently *Stimmungen* never leave us. They are as old, stubborn, vivid and continuous throughout their temporal fluctua-tions as the presence of the world: "*From the ontological point of view* we must as a general principle <grudsätzlich> leave the primary discovery of the world to 'bare mood' <Stimmung>."[3] "The fact that moods <Stimmungen> can deteriorate [verdorben werden] and change over means simply that in every case Dasein always has some mood [gestimmt ist]."[4] To be rid of a tonality, whether it be passing whim or something more lasting, is possible only by passing to another one: "When we master a mood, we do so by way of a counter-mood; we are never free of moods."[5]

If this is the case, how can we ever become indifferent? Why are there indifferent, flavorless moments? When we feel what is called "dead time" or "vagueness of the soul"—a lessened interest in what normally fascinates or occupies us—could this be something like an absence of *Stimmung*? Is indifference a *Stimmung*, or is it the absence of all tonality? Is it so shot through with disinterest that we suspend our relation with time and, consequently, with being? When "nothing interests us any more," at the height of boredom and melancholy, are we situated *outside of being*? Boredom, by making us deaf to solicitation, insensible to attachment, and strangers to the world, is not like anxiety, a call and revelation of being, but "suspends claims, especially that of being," Jean-Luc Marion writes in a brilliant analysis.[6] "Nothing makes any difference any more, not even the ontological difference."[7] "Boredom, by disengaging itself from the ontological difference, detaches beings from their beingness, abolishes the very name of beings."[8] Can this interpretation be defended? Can man be indifferent to being?

It would be necessary to show that boredom *(ennui)*—why do we insist on that word, so overdetermined with Pascalian, and then Romantic, Symbolist, and pessimist resonances, why not simply say 'indifference'?.... It would be necessary to show that boredom, if you will, excludes us from every situation, destroys and decomposes us absolutely, and—even more than mystical ecstasy—depersonalizes us, delivers us from our identity, throws us into nothing and nowhere. In boredom there is undoubtedly something like an inverted ecstasy (think of Sartre who spoke of Nausea as a "horrible ecstasy"); but is this not an ecstasy *of time*, rather than a passage to some neutral dimension, neither temporal nor eternal? The fact that time begins to weigh horribly on us and slows to almost nothing, does not authorize the supposition of the annulement of time and, consequently, the suspension of our understanding of being. Besides, if we could close ourselves off from being-in-the-world, get out of the clearing, how could we return to it again? We are held *(tenus)* in being, and, no matter how tenuous *(ténu)* the thread attaching us to presence—for example, in fainting or dreamless sleep—we are never, as long as we *are*, released into pure nothingness, *nihil negativum*. When somebody says he is "bored to death," he is not thinking of a *factual* disappearance, but rather of the despairing feeling, so perfectly described by Kierkegaard, of "being unable to die." The frightening monotony of a time that irregularly drags out its own old age, the impression of stagnation and *regression* (temporal succession inverted and opened onto a monstrously enlarged past) can certainly swell to the point of being *close* to nothing, like Baudelaire's spleen:

> Nothing equals the length of limping days
> When, under the heavy flakes of snowy years,
> Boredom, fruit of drab incuriousity,
> Takes the proportions of immortality.[9]

But that gigantic inversion of the eternal does not disinterest us from being, does not subtract us from time. Once again, as long as we *are*, our interest—our "inter-esse," as Lévinas says—may well fade out, our Care diminish radically; but we can never reduce it to *nothing*. Mallarmé is saddened as not being able to attain "the insensibility of the azure and of stones,"[10] and in the poem *L'Azur*, he despairs of finding in nature the adequate symbolization of his "dear Boredom." The appearance of the Azure, breaking through the clouds, always turns sadness, once again, into bitter derision. The *Stimmung* of insensibility never rises to pure detachment, to the serenity of the eternal Azure, but suffers from being mocked, by what—outside, in the world—is in disharmony with it. Boredom is never without fault, never perfectly satisfied with itself, and that is undoubtedly why it does not fall out of being. It is all too obsessed and overcome by its situation in the world to truly distance it or to be held by it at a distance from all. Is it possible to imagine an indifference lacking all disquietude, even if merely latent? Is there a happy boredom? Isn't "deafness" to being secretly worked over by it sown negativity? Doesn't boredom communicate with anxiety?

The 1929 lecture *What Is Metaphysics?* already attributed to boredom the same power of ontological revelation as to anxiety.

> Profound boredom, drifting here and there in the abysses of our existence like a muffling fog, removes all things and men and oneself along with it into a remarkable indifference. This boredom reveals beings as a whole.[11]

There is the same atmosphere of *Unheimlichkeit*, the same dissolution of preliminarily recognized identities, the same monstrous proportions of universality. Most importantly, anxiety and boredom have the same power to strike the totality of beings with indetermination, insignificance, and thus to reveal the *being* of the world, *as such*. Whereas anxiety leaves one without *a voice, cuts speech short* ("in the face of anxiety all utterance of the 'is' falls silent"),[12] boredom is marked by the *silence* of that "fog," which is the metaphor of the indifferentiation that invades and drowns all things. But anxiety seems to retain a phenomenological privilege, even if only by the detail and length of analyses dedicated to it, both in this passage and, earlier, in section 40 of *Being and Time*. Yet a belatedly published course from Winter Semester 1929–1930,[13] leaves no doubt as to the equally primordial nature of boredom for *Dasein*. One can no longer say, as did Bollnow, that "Heidegger's entire philosophical edifice rests on the narrow base of a single affective tonality."[14] In his expansion of the citation from *What Is Metaphysics?* (explicitly alluded to several times),[15] the ontological significance of that *Grundstimmung* is analyzed at great length: more than 170 pages on boredom! This quantity alone is sufficiently rare in Heidegger's work—in relation to a single theme—to indicate a possible reversal of priority.

Is not boredom, precisely because of its *everydayness*, more revealing than anxiety? In boredom (German, *Lange-weile*, 'longwhile') isn't there a more primal and perhaps more fundamental rapport with temporality? And yet, isn't boredom necessarily inauthentic, alienating, impotent, an evil to be avoided? If, however, we compare *Sein und Zeit* and the *The Basic Problems of Metaphysics*, it appears that Heidegger tried to reduce the pejorative or "inauthentic" side of that *Stimmung*, which has the rare and precious quality of revealing the temporal constitution of *Dasein*. It is not inept and empty, as common sense would have it. One must not simply flee boredom, repress it, dissipate it with whatever "pastime" happens along. Paradoxically, it is necessary to know how to welcome it. Then superficial, passing boredom can be understood in its essence, experienced as "profound boredom," as the resonance of time itself in the depths of *Dasein*. This happens if we are not simply against it, if we don't immediately react, in order to be safe; if, instead, we give it room. This is what we must first learn: *not to immediately stand against [it], but to let [it] oscillate freely.*[16]

This patience with the *Stimmung*, this attitude of listening to a voice (*Stimmung* is always the flip side of a *Stimme*), a voice that is in us without belonging to us, already corresponds completely with the availability (*Verfügbarkeit*) and letting-be of the late Heidegger. Is such a move totally foreign to *Sein und Zeit*?

Indifference and Inauthenticity

Let us first note that in *Being and Time* there is no mention of boredom, but simply of *indifference (Gleichgültigkeit)*. The analysis of this *Stimmung*, which occurs late in the text (section 68b, "The temporality of state-of-mind"), is rapid and apparently the antithesis of the analysis of anxiety. Whereas anxiety brings *Dasein* closer to its own "authentic" presence, calling it to being-in-the-world as such; indifference disperses *Dasein*, throwing it back into the They, turning it over to the forgetfulness of its situation.

But first, let us cite this essential passage:

[T]he pallid lack of mood—indifference—which is addicted to nothing and has no urge for anything, and which abandons itself to whatever the day may bring, yet in so doing takes everything along with it in a certain manner, demonstrates *most penetratingly* the power of forgetting in the everyday mode of that concern which is closest to us. Just living along [Das Dahinleben] in a way which 'lets' everything 'be' as it is, is based on forgetting and abandoning oneself to one's thrownness. It has the ecstatical meaning of an inauthentic way of having been.[17]

This is not a matter of intellectual indifference, the indifference of judgment belonging to scepticism, nor the indifference of a phlegmatic temperament. Instead, it is a climate of apathy, an absence of connectedness with every decision or with anything whatsoever, an abandonment of oneself that constitutes a sort of low-water mark for completely "fallen" being-in-the-world—that is, a being-in-the-world identical with its factual existence. It is noteworthy that indisposition (a more literal translation of *Ungestimmtheit*, the fact of being disposed toward nothing, carried toward nothing, interested in nothing) is not an absence of *Stimmung*. The bond with the past, which is one of the characteristics of indifference, is designated as an "ekstatic" rapport—that is, as one that puts a certain comprehension of being into play. To believe that basically "there is nothing new under the sun," that "I've already seen it all," that "I've read all the books," and so on, is obviously a determinate way of understanding being. It is perfectly correct to say, as does Jean-Luc Marion, that "the gaze of melancholy sees beings in terms of their nonbeing" (191). But that cannot mean, as he says of boredom, that it "finally dissolves given beings themselves and undoes itself from what gives given beings: being . . ." (170). By understanding beings as annulled by their own empty repetition, as "carrying nothing," as "without the least interest," boredom perceives them as what they are *and* what they are not. In the eyes of a bored person, things *are as if* they were not. But this negation doesn't express any absolute annihilation, any pure emptiness, any escape from being: beings *are*, but as if in a *fog*. They float in being. They become unreal, uncertain. It is as if they had been given over to pure, indeterminate being. Their meaning is erased, searching for itself, redesigning itself. How could the vague, the inconsistent, escape from Being?

But the first and principal trait of indifference is *forgetting*. Heidegger says that forgetting *penetrates* and *dominates* the *Stimmung* of indifference, as well as the other *everyday Stimmungen*, with its power. But forgetting doesn't simply let *Dasein* err in a neutral dimension, without any relation to being. Instead, in being-there, forgetting evasively attaches *Dasein* to being, which is always in question. Doesn't all erring, as long as it remains qualifiable as erring, relate to truth? The power of forgetting is *"positive"* insofar as it relates *Dasein* (however obscurely) to its past, its "having-been" *(Gewesen)*—that is, to being *(Wesen)*. Heidegger emphasizes this several pages earlier:

> This forgetting is not nothing, nor is it just a failure to remember; it is rather a 'positive' ecstatical mode of one's having been. . . . *Having forgotten* [Vergessenheit] as an inauthentic way of having been, is thus related to that thrown *Being* which is one's own; it is the temporal meaning of that Being in accordance with which I *am* proximally and for the most part as-having-been.[18]

Forgetting, as the opposite of authentic having-been, which renders *Dasein* capable of a *repetition* of the possibilities of existence appropriated by it, does not suppress having-been. It gives *Dasein* an "inauthentic" understanding, that is, a floating, irresolute understanding of its possibilities, but it doesn't throw *Dasein* out of being. Forgetting is the background, the horizon of all memory, and not the simple negation of remembering. On the contrary, all remembering must reverse the first movement of occultation and opacity that constitutes temporality. But remembering doesn't restore being to the past. To say that forgetting puts *Dasein* out of being would be just as ridiculous as saying, in regard to the history of being, that the forgetting of being abolishes or suspends being. For Heidegger, forgetting is "consubstantial" with being, just as negativity is with Spirit for Hegel.

According to this text, the second ontological trait of indifference is the degradation of existence by its reduction to *life*. Indifferent, *Dasein no longer exists, it lives*. It lets itself live. It is the *Dahinleben* of "just living along." For Heidegger, life is a subsisting-being that encounters itself in the world. Strictly speaking, *Dasein* cannot reduce itself to the purely natural dimension of living being. There is no relationship between Heidegger's "pallid lack of mood" and Sartre's Nausea, the distaste for the "ensnarement" of consciousness in the in-itself. For, in *Being and Time*, facticity is not the being of fact, the objectively natural side of man (an aspect that Heidegger refuses as being the substantialization of *Dasein* in the animality of the rational animal). Facticity, inasmuch as it carries a certain comprehension of thrownness, is always taken up again in existence, in *Dasein*'s project *(Entwurf)*. Nonetheless, "to live" is to identify with subsistent-being, with natural things. To live is to forget one's transcendence. For Heidegger, man is a being outside of nature who can never define himself as simple physical or biological vitality. To assimilate oneself with that is still a project, a comprehension of being, and not an objective fall into natural in-itself, as Sartre thinks. Indifference is an existence seduced by the life of nature, seemingly spared from making choices, and forgetting that it is still a project.—How far does that Heideggerian position imply a refusal or negation of nature, a refusal of any power of nature over *Dasein*? This question itself would take a long time to examine. For Heidegger, "There is no nature-time...."[19] and the factual succession of day and night doesn't intervene in temporality. Indifference rests on a (necessarily illusory) abandonment to a vague universal vitality. Heidegger shows that even everyday existence still carries with it a derived and fallen ekstatic temporality, which is in no way a return to natural simplicity.

The third trait of indifference is *Dasein*'s submission to a temporality nominated by the past. This may seem surprising—why the past instead of a dissipated present? Why does Heidegger say that the tomorrow of indifference is the "eternal yesterday?"[20] In fact, everyday existence, which passes from one immediate preoccupation to another and *passively* awaits events, has no tradition, no continuity; just as it has no future. By not supporting any projection into time, it appears to be reduced to the present, simply dispersed in the present. But this dispersion is precisely *not* the immobilization of time that characterizes indifference. Apparently, inauthenticity is not indifferent, preoccupied, "keeping things moving," captured by the *Betrieb*; it is inhabited by a solely *latent* emptiness. Admittedly, agitation, idle talk, curiosity, all the figures of an existence "fallen" into its present[21] refer to a nothing that "nothing is happening." "Idle talk and the most ingenious curiosity keep 'things moving', where, in an everyday manner, everything (and at bottom nothing) is happening."[22] But the "whirlwind" that characterizes the agitation of "keeping things moving" obtains for *Dasein* a "tranquilized supposition that it possesses everything."[23] The nothing comes close, but is immediately covered up by keeping-things-moving's pretension to dominate everything by the rapid circulation that creates the illusory equivalence of everything and nothing.—Only when the "pallid lack of mood" announces itself does a slippage or regression toward the past appear. Toward what past? Certainly not the "personal" past of the feeling-of-the-situation, but rather the immemorial and impersonal past of *Geworfenheit*, of thrownness, which includes all the unchosen possibilities that *Dasein* receives from the world. Remember that thrownness or facticity is not the being of fact, a determination by nature or life. Facticity—birth, for example—never falls behind *Dasein*, like an event that came to it and went away from it. The past, factical being (the tie with natural beings), is always included in *Dasein*'s own being.[24] Facticity is always "taken back" into existence. If every project is "thrown," then, conversely, that "thrown" character is in turn pro-jected.[25] But not without a remainder. Ordinarily *Stimmung* reveals being-in-the-world's constant relationship with a past that is both personal and impersonal. *Stimmung* reveals or masks the past. "For the most part ... [*Dasein*'s] mood *(Stimmung)* is such that its thrownness gets *closed off*."[26] Whereas anxiety authentically opens *Dasein* to its past in the world, indifference reattaches it in an obscure, closed way. Indifference is therefore closely linked with a facticity that is nothing but *closure* toward thrownness. To be indifferent is to understand one's own presence in the world as always having been. Anxiety is the authentic feeling of thrownness; indifference is its inauthentic, yet nonetheless *"ecstatic"* counterpart.

Finally, indifference, by way of facticity, plays an indirect role in the constitution of "public" time, the objective time of the world. In fact, neutral, calendar time, the time to be filled and administered, is not originally based on physics, clocks, quantification, but on the depossession of true time, and accomplished by the transference of *Dasein*'s finite temporality onto the indefinite or infinite time of things. Inauthentic temporality is profoundly indifferent. It makes possible public time, which is for everyone and belongs to no one. Only insofar as indifference is possible can objective, anonymous time consolidate itself and conserve the straight, perfectly uniform line of completely equal and identical moments.

The Three Circles of Boredom

In his 1929–1930 course, Heidegger successively describes three forms of boredom—from the most superficial to the most profound—which are like three concentric circles of tormented temporality. Paradoxically, the more *Dasein* has the feeling of *absolutely* wasting its time, the closer it is to regaining a plenitude of time.

1. Something bores us: we find a book or play to be "empty"; a person, "without interest"; a wait, tiring. What is "boring" is found to be an irritating property of certain objects in the world.

2. We get bored with ourselves. We have the feeling that the emptiness of things comes from us. We can no longer find ourselves, although the occasion is of our own projection. For example, time passes slowly during a dinner engagement. We have the painful feeling of wasting time, even though we were prepared to pass our time in that precise situation.

3. We feel boredom as existing outside of every situation that relates to us. It is a universal, neutral boredom, which comes without reason, from nothing in particular. It seems objective, yet it is indeterminate; it soaks into the atmosphere, as when, for example, on a Sunday afternoon we wander through the streets of a large city. But that example, says Heidegger (it is his example), is a bad one, since it is too logical: it seems to explain the impression of boredom by idleness, those abandoned "instruments": business-center streets, closed cafés, and so on. In fact, there is no "example" of this boredom. It puts one out of the world. It is not linked with an exterior cause, nor with our lack of interest, but it has the same

function and power as anxiety: it reveals beings, in their totality, as disappearing, sinking into indifference. It is neither the accidental "that bores me," nor the "I am bored," but rather the "it is boring" *(es ist einem langweilig)* that characterizes "profound boredom." However, through the empty time of such a boredom, the possibility of another time reveals itself, the possibility of time reappropriated.

But how is the relationship with time characterized in each of these three forms? In the first, time drags, but only because things in themselves, by their slowness, delay you; there is impatience and irritation. In the second, time seems to be suspended for us and leave us hanging. Hence the melancholy. In the third, time feels disarticulated and imprisoning: in the face of a monstrously enlarged present, the past and future become phantom-like. But this frozen or dismembered time in which we float attaches us even more strongly to time and forces us to *decide* in regard to our time. Through boredom, *Dasein* is returned to its most essential possibility. The more it suffers from time, from nothing but time, the closer it comes to a mutation and rehabilitation of time.

Heidegger's description brings out numerous correlations and oppositions between these three degrees of boredom. Thus, in relation to the search for remedies to boredom, or "pastimes," we can (in the first form) *flee* boring things, people, and situations. Something arbitrary delivers us from an equally arbitrary cause of boredom. But that flight engenders an uncanny agitation, a confused way of running after "distractions," in which we become entangled and find boredom once again. When we know that we ourselves cause the boredom (second form), we again flee definite situations: we don't want to let ourselves be bored; we search for occasions to actualize our real self. Finally, in the third form, we can no longer flee boredom; no pastime is appropriate to what is without cause. We are then forced to listen to what boredom makes manifest in our *Dasein*. We are then *suspended* in time by boredom. This forces us to recognize and pass through empty time.

This "suspension" (*Hingehaltenheit*—literally, the fact of being stopped or held back) is the first and fundamental structure of boredom, no matter what its degree of profundity. The second structural moment brought forward in this analysis of each of the three levels constitutes the most obvious, most commonly observed and described trait of that *Stimmung*: *Leergelassenheit*, being-left-empty or "emptying." There is no "emptying" of things, of oneself, of the world, except when their temporality is somehow held-back *(hinhalten)*, retracted, suspended. The "suspension" of time is the suspension of true temporality. This suspension gives one the irritating or disheartening feeling of wasting time. The emptiness felt in things, or thrown back on us, or discovered as the universal emptiness of beings that have become indifferent in their totality—that emptiness comes from the withdrawal of true temporality. Here, just as in *Sein und Zeit*, time supports the very being of *Dasein*; we might say, its *ultima ratio*, if we forgot the abyssal, unfounded nature of that foundation.

Heidegger tries to show that the level of "it is boring" carries with it, above all and essentially a "suspension" of time, which, far from being a loss of the temporal horizon, constitutes a sort of replenishment or renewal of time, a revivification of time, and finally allows for a change of boredom into absolute interest. There is no phenomenological answer to the question, How does this suspension of time come about? Suspension can be described only as the essence of boredom. To explain why (why we don't have enough time, why it disintegrates and gives way, like the ground under our feet) would be a metaphysical step, a step that Pascal or Schopenhauer took. For them, boredom can be explained by man's nature: "the misery of man without God," or satiety of the will to live. But we must ask whether Heidegger in turn does not engage in a metaphysical process when he makes boredom the principle of a rediscovery of time and what seems to be a total autoappropriation of *Dasein*.

In boredom, time is suspended, stopped, to such a point that *Dasein* is "bewitched." Boredom is time itself as "bewitching" (*bannende*, fascinating, captivating). This spell (*Bann*) holds us at a distance from ourselves: first from our own possibilities (of action, of thinking), which are given, but unattractive and powerless; and then, at a distance from our past and future; and finally, from time itself, which changes from familiar to strange, slightly uncanny. There truly is a spell, for, no matter how obsessed or overwhelmed we are by boredom, we are fascinated by emptiness, to the point that we don't even try to be distracted from it, nor do we want to be. Nothing happens, or everything that happens leads back to nothing. And yet, this nothing holds us, stops us, attaches us, despite it all, to that unknown time. What fascinates us is the time that doesn't change, that unfolds and grows without direction, without horizons. This time is different from time. It is reduced to a monstrously dilated, distended, and unbounded present. This present leads to nothing but a repetition of the same present. This present is different from the present. Memories and projects become distant, depthless. Completely in the present, but without any contact with the life of the present, we are not really deprived of the past or future. We feel those dimensions dissolve in a vague stagnation. This amorphous, thick, opaque pseudo-presence, this captive time, "heavy, suffocating time," the "pure time," of which Mallarmé speaks in his astonishing evocations of Igitur's boredom, seem to be the fearsome, terrifying actualization of the metaphysical nostalgia for permanent presence ("the illness of ideality"). In boredom, Igitur feels "as if he were menaced by the torture of being eternal," and experiences "a terrifying sensation of eternity," accompanied by "the horror of that eternity."[27] Learning narcissistically over his nothing, Igitur is divided between fascination and horror at his own evanescent image, glimpsed in the emptiness of a mirror, "a horribly null mirror," itself the image of time's devouring emptiness. In this case the spell is clearly anxiety producing: boredom does not exclude anxiety. Mallarmé's boredom slips toward anxiety when, for Igitur, arrested time seems to faint away, "leaving him not even the boredom that he implores and dreams." The emptiness of boredom seems to present itself as a relatively ideal state that is more desirable than the fall into nothing.

Anxiety, Revelation of Being; Boredom, Revelation of Time

The emptiness of boredom is not the nothingness of anxiety. Beings don't just disappear; they present themselves heavily and insistently, deprived of any interest. The emptiness doesn't come from a withdrawal that annihilates the pragmatic solidity of beings, but from a devalorization that hesitates to affirm itself. In "profound boredom," *we don't even know* if anything has any value: "everything is worth both much and little."[28] The value of things simultaneously affirms and hides itself. If thought that conforms to values must, for Heidegger, necessarily come to that universal pseudo-equivalence, it is undoubtedly because that thought carries nihilism within itself. But boredom doesn't arise from a metaphysics articulated in propositions, or judgments of values. It is like a spontaneous metaphysics, a pre-predicative valorization and devalorization, and not a construction: this reduction to equivalence—which, though leading back to the similar, does not reduce to zero—rests on a simple *Stimmung*. It becomes impossible for us to inventory or evaluate things so as to declare them worthless or nearly so, or to estimate that they still retain some small worth for us. This equivalence strikes our habitual comportment so essentially that we lose our identity (not to mention our vocation or social standing); it subtracts us from every determinate *situation*. It has a power and a *generality* that would be impossible merely on the basis of a sum of judgments and values. "It is with a single stroke *(mit einem Schlag),*" Heidegger says, "that each and everything becomes indifferent":

> This indifference does not first spring from one thing to another, as with a fire, in order to consume it; rather, in a single instant, everything is grasped and held by this indifference.[29]

The same thing is true of anxiety—as of all *Stimmungen*. Every *Stimmung* puts us in a preconceptual relation with the totality of beings. But anxiety and boredom have this particular trait in common: they both refer to a *totality in suspense*. Anxiety reveals, entirely, the total structure of the world; boredom reveals, decomposed, the total structure of time. "In anxiety what is environmentally ready-to-hand sinks away."[30] "The totality of involvements of the ready-to-hand and the present-at-hand ... is ... of no consequence; it collapses into itself."[31] Instrumental paths and firm identities lose their significance. Nevertheless, the global structure of the world remains intact as a purely formal, neutral possibility. "What oppresses us is not this or that ... it is rather the *possibility* of the ready-to-hand in general; that is to say, it is the world itself."[32] What makes anxiety anxious is the nothing that is the pure structure of the world as such. The difference between anxiety and boredom is that the first does not primally and exclusively bring the relationship with time into question. Admittedly, as section 68b takes great pains to show, anxiety refers back to both the authentic past and future: it allows *Dasein* to return to its essential possibilities so as to "repeat" them; it is the disposition that supports every true resolution. But only boredom—in its most profound form—takes apart the synthesis of time. Time appears to be unreasonably *long*. All of duration is ready-to-hand, but inert and disarticulated. Time no longer flows; it stagnates. It seems to have come off its hinges, to have come off its essential articulation in the apparently incontrovertible law of three dimensions and the succession of before and after. *Dasein* feels itself to be projected out of time's flow and, simultaneously, exposed to a paradoxical and indefinite duration.

Whereas in anxiety there remains the possibility of the world as a pure contentless synthesis, in boredom we experience a disintegrating totality, a synthesis at the point of disappearing. The nothing of anxiety reaffirms *Dasein*. Beyond the retreat of beings, it again teaches *Dasein* the solidity of being-in-the-world. The emptiness of boredom does not seem to reveal time as such, but a deformed, caricatural time, both lengthened and shortened. Emptiness sets *Dasein* adrift. The "superiority" of anxiety is that it provides access to a beginning of certitude. But boredom isn't purely destructive: apparently it can both suspend *and* reanimate the ordinary, everyday feeling of time. As Heidegger says, if we know how to listen to it, boredom introduces a regeneration of time. This movement of regeneration resembles that which later characterized the relationship with Technology: proceeding from the danger of extreme loss, to a return that saves. Here, time is so exhausted, so disarticulated, so intolerable, that, in itself, it calls for and provokes a transformation. Boredom not only puts us in relation with the possibility of the world, but it introduces a more or less painful tension between that possibility and a time that takes it takes it even farther from us. Boredom reveals the pure possibility of the world as submitted to time: the collapse of the world, itself collapsed into time.

The Replenishment of Time at the Depths of Its Own Abyss

But, at this degree, we have already left superficial boredom, which is always animated by what Nietzsche would have called "resentment against time." That resentment must first explode, unleash itself, against "objects," then detach itself from them, returning toward the self, only to swerve away once again, finally dissipating itself and changing into affirmation. How is that? How can a feeling of hate[33] toward time lead to a regeneration of temporality as such? Because there is an ambivalence in resentment itself. In boredom, even the most superficial—for example, when I am upset at having to wait, or irritated by an obstacle holding up a certain project—I am "furious about wasting my time." My boredom/irritation would be meaningless if it didn't have the explicit or implicit opposing idea of time better spent. In the same way, when boredom drives us to change our occupation or center of interest, or simply to seek some diversion; isn't this to *change the time*, to somehow find time anew? To find it, not to reconquer it. The project of *voluntary reappropriation*—of substituting one time for another—seems doomed to failure. Isn't the attempt to grasp time just as illusory as the attempt to grasp being? To what extent, however, does this illusion exist in the early Heidegger? It is very clear that for him, resentment as such must cede to listening. In several places, Heidegger insists on the necessity of knowing how to listen to boredom, to let it express itself, expose itself, oscillate-freely *(ausschwingenlasen)*.

> The remarkable contentlessness of what actually makes *Dasein* possible should not disturb us; that is, we should not set aside the disquieting nature of the countentlessness that belongs to the 'it is boring,' if we are at all capable of letting its *Stimmung* oscillate in us at its full amplitude.[34]

Such a boredom contains a "call" *(Anrufen)* to an "authentic possibility." In order to perceive it, resentment must be broken. In short, it is time that must be reborn in us, rather than it being up to us to rejuvenate time. Only profound boredom which feels resentment by revealing that there is no real reason to be bored, reestablishes the link with time itself. All the causes of boredom must be experienced as exterior and inessential. We discover that no situation can bore, irritate, or sadden us, if we are of sufficiently happy distortion. The only possible reason for boredom is time's own lengthening. The long time presents itself as the only reason, but it is without reason. For, how does it happen that time lengthens and empties itself? Because we are no longer interested in anything? But why do we lack interest? We have no idea. We have nothing but the growing feeling that everything has slipped into the past before having been present, that we have already seen it, already heard it, and so on: "I've read all the books." The keen edge of time has been dulled.

People who are superficially bored live with their eye on the clock. They think they can conquer time by counting the minutes: "only fifteen minutes to wait." Those who are profoundly bored don't even care what time it is. They know that they can't fool time by cutting it into pieces. They know that it will be just as boring "after" as it was "before." Those who are bored to this point exclaim, "*It's* boring!" In that situation their feeling of responsibility, and even their subjective identity, shrinks. They don't even really know *who* is bored. It's boring. Nothing in particular is boring. No one is really the subject of that boredom. The more boredom gains control, the less we feel that we are really the ones who are bored. In boredom the "subject" feels itself to be stripped of its attributes and reference points, carried back to the abstract nudity of pure being-there. "Name, state, profession, role, age, and destiny—as yours or mine—fall away from us."[35] But we are not detached into pure emptiness. Instead, we are attached in a different way to the power that governs us in our furthest depths, more intimate than our intimacy. We rediscover all *possible* time.

In this way boredom forces *Dasein* to be what it *can* be. But how can time's bewitchment turn in to a replenishment of time? At this point Heidegger appears to pass from descriptive to normative. Only an event of time can break the spell of time. *Dasein* can rejoin fully open time only by turning dispersion into the unity of an "instant" *(Augenblick)*. That instant is not the simple present: it is the glance *(coup d'oeil)*, as rapid as a lightening flash, in which past-present-future are seen as one, suspended in their ekstatic unity. Heidegger tries to show that boredom calls up the decisive moment, the moment of a mutation of time. The long time calls up an extreme shortening. But in order for that brief "flash" of new time to erupt, outside of all resentment, time had to be allowed to deploy itself in all its length. The painful lengthening of duration has enlarged the temporal horizon. That enlargement is overwhelming, disquieting, because it is disorienting, decentering. The "point" of existence disappears, but the essential possibility, time, far from disappearing, imposes itself with force. It becomes more indeterminate, but not less pressing. Time itself leaves us empty and holds us in suspense. These two traits, emptiness and suspense, create a constraint, a pressure. The absence of constraint in emptiness and boredom is itself constraining. Time is pressing. Boredom reveals the time at the depths of *Dasein* to be essentially pressing, as distress and constraint *(Not)*. This constraint to decide has nothing to do with a should-be. It is not "normative." In fact, Heidegger emphasizes that the decision that reassembles time is the flip side of temporality's bewitching enlargement. When boredom opens the entire length of the horizon, if forces "resolution." The length of the boredom is proportional to the amplitude of the "being-resolved." The two are one and the same thing: "we are not simply blindly abandoned to that bewitchment," nor are we capable of capturing the instant by ourselves; rather, both refusal and grace are given to us together. As in Corneille: "or let a great despair aid him." "Being-resolved" is not free-will, the free mastery of self, based solely on the power of subjectivity.

> The point of the instant is neither chosen as such, nor is it thought or considered. It opens itself to us as the original possibility, and yet it remains foreseen only in the bewitched-being of the temporal horizon, foreseen as what *could* and should be freely given in *Dasein's* own essence as its inmost

possibility, but which, in *Dasein's* bewitchment, is not now [given].[36]

Paradoxically, bewitching time both suppresses and gives "the point of the instant." When Heidegger says that *Dasein* resolves *(entschliesst)* itself to itself, this means that it radically opens *(erschliesst)* itself to itself—that is, to its temporal depths. Taking charge of oneself is not to appropriate time; it is to submit to it.

The mutation of time, the "instant," the salutary decision, is therefore not a heroic effort of *Dasein*. There is no conversion worthy of the name that has not first ripened in the secret of time, and which is the effect of a single moment. Besides, the true instant recapitulates time. It is the unity, the junction of the past that projects itself into the future. Time transforms itself and transforms us. Time itself places us in the impasse and induces us to leave—as long as we know how to wait for it and hear it.

But is this mutation an infallible consequence of boredom? Heidegger doesn't consider the case where boredom never dissipates, where time continues to disintegrate indefinitely, bogging down without ever contracting. What about those who continue to be bored their entire life, who never learn anything from their boredom? Nor does Heidegger consider the hypothesis of a psychopathological emptiness of time, the emptiness of melancholy. For him there is undoubtedly a necessary link between accomplishing an extreme degree and passing beyond its limit.

This is true for metaphysics, which, being achieved, is, if not "overcome," at least left behind itself. This necessity is truly *"eschatological,"* which means logic of the ultimate, but also *assembling (logos) of the extreme*. Everything that is extreme assembles and reinforces itself, for it has run into its own limit, and thus sees into it—and beyond. Eschatology is the thinking of the dawn within twilight and *beyond*.

In fact, and in capital letters, the same is true for epochal time or the history of being. Isn't the relationship between the "danger" of technology and "salvation" the same as that between empty time and the instant? It does seem that with the advent of technology, indifference to being is completely entrenched, and yet that extreme indifference is particularly capable of abruptly changing into its opposite. It is as if being were indifferent to human indifference, strangely shielded, immune. But indifference has nothing to do with boredom. As a *fundamental* tonality, indifference doesn't reveal the depths of *Dasein*, but those of the epoch. The epoch is not ignorant of its own time, but of destiny, "historial"[37] time. It seems as if there is more boredom nor *Stimmung* in general, except through what used to be justly called the "mal du siécle," and what is now a new form of indifference. Heidegger suggests, without making an absolute statement, that private tonalities must in some way be subsumed under the fundamental tonality of the historial times. But what happens when the entire epoch comes to know the experience of emptiness?

Indifference to Being in the Technological "Mechanism"

In truth, the epoch of technology is not fundamentally dominated by boredom, but by a very particular, neutral *Stimmung* that Heidegger calls "the absence of distress." One of the primary requirements of the essence of technology is that it be able to efficiently deal with any problem without "being emotional." Corresponding to the mechanism that plans the exploitation and devastation of the earth, to the will to will that ceaselessly builds the "reserves" of stockpiled energy, is a climate of coldness and insensitivity. Calculating thought doesn't necessarily demand cynicism, but it imposes a sort of dulling and repression of moods in which being is shaken or manifested in its finitude. "It almost seems as if the being of pain were cut off from man under the dominance of the will, similarly the being of joy."[38] The untiring activism of the will to will promotes an unrestrained "movement of business" *(Betrieb)*, which, at least for business, is not at all boring or monotonous, despite its repetitive aspect, but which rests upon a deliberately *extreme* indifference to being. The absence of distress is the way to hide the "emptiness of being" under the richness and variety of technological productions. The organization and ordering of generalized consumption serves to mask the emptiness—that is, the purposelessness of a Machine that turns upon itself. And finally, the absence of distress manifests itself in the growing number of "security" programs. We no longer wish to be assured of progress, as in the nineteenth century, but of the power, efficiency, and "perfection" of technology, no matter what its field of application. The flip side and counterpart of that "security" is found in the illusion of total power and the refusal of any reflection on the origin and metaphysical significance of technology: "Lack of need consists in believing that one has reality and what is real in one's grip and knows what truth is, without needing to know in what truth *presences (west)*."³⁹

Indifference to being expresses itself through many regularly noted symptoms, principally in economic and political life. Thus the choice offered to consumers in industrial societies tends both to multiply and to annul itself, in that the nuances that they present are insignificant, nearing zero, or vaguely absurd. Consider, for example, the recent add for *sterilized* milk that praised "the real taste"! Or again, the false familiarity of the television image, which suppresses the close or distant, tragic or ordinary nature of events. Who can watch the daily tides of images crying out unhappiness, misery, ruin, despair, famine, war, and catastrophe, tranquilly curled up on the sofa, without shutting off his heart, without arming himself with indifference? The world becomes a spectacle for which we feel nothing more than neutral, conventional emotions; and about which we think nothing but the cliches dictated by the "media": that contemporary form of the They. Or again, the difference between war and peace⁴⁰ is effaced in the universal climate of aggression and provocation, leading to small sporadic wars now that the menace of an atomic war has disappeared. No international convention will ever be able to abolish the fact that technology has acquired the ability to destroy the planet. Everyday, technology universalizes the constant ready-to-handness of beings, independent of differences of time, of place, of people. No computer will ever know *where* it is, *who* is operating it and much less *why*. Become accustomed to having the movement of buttons, keys, and levers under hand; to living symbolically with the foot on the accelerator or the brake; how could we not lose our feeling for being, for what escapes from our graspings and does not obey our commands and programs?

"Unidirectional," calculating thought closes itself off to understanding the enigma of the withdrawal of being. It can listen only to itself. It has no exterior. It doesn't understand lack, poverty, anguish. It necessarily is ignorant of mourning as well as joy. It doesn't understand its own plentitude because it knows nothing of distress. In order to develop, it needs uniformity and apathy, the absence of all memory of finitude.

But what is the meaning of this *extreme* indifference to being? Does such an indifference indicate that man is outside of all relation to being? Is technology's own absence of distress radically different from the forgetting of being?—In a certain way, the extreme indifference of the technological epoch is nothing but that forgetting. It is the simple continuation and result of the forgetting of being that has reigned since the very beginning of metaphysics. The forgetting of being is the first in-difference, in that it is the forgetting of the difference between being and beings. Metaphysics, by thinking the being of beings as a first or universal being, by understanding the relationship between the first of the beings and the other beings as a causal relationship, prefigures and prepares the reign of calculating thought. But even extreme indifference cannot signify that man is rejected *outside of being*. Even if he leaves being unthought, "out of his guardianship," without relation to history, being nonetheless has power over him. Even if man does not "guard" being, being maintains, utilizes, "concerns" *(regarde)* him. "Enframing is, though veiled, still glance, and no blind destiny in the sense of a completely ordained fate."[41] The *extreme* ontological indifference of technology also has a double nature. On the one hand it signifies a more absolute domination and determination by metaphysics than in any previous epoch.

"Extreme" therefore refers to the eschatological thought of a final, ultimate sending of being. Extreme then signifies the unlimited and apparently unshakeable installation of accomplished metaphysics, and thus an extreme forgetting, but it also signifies the limit and end of that forgetting. The *turning* can occur at no other epoch, the *turning* of indifference into attention and faithfulness to being. At no other epoch can metaphysics attain its limit. The epoch of technology is the only one in which extreme blindness and the obscure hope for a completely different destiny can live together, where "the irresistibility of ordering and the restraint of the saving power draw past each other [like the paths of two stars in the course of the heavens]."[42] Neighborhood of extremes: tearing apart of the epoch in two faces in which latent despair is just as present, powerful, and true, as latent hope.

In the end, why is extreme indifference to being called merely a "danger"? Just as the forgetting of being doesn't "ruin" being, indifference—which forbids awakening to the ontological difference, which dissimulates the meaning of the epoch and closes things off to the play of the world—cannot *destroy* being and the world. In the ultimate metamorphosis of its essence, the initial Greek truth of *alêtheia* is confronted with the "shunting aside of essence" *(Wesenbeseitigung)* "not an annihilation" *(nicht Vernichtung)*.[43] To what point is being vulnerable or invulnerable? Can being be completely eclipsed? Apparently not any mre than we can be eclipsed from being. Indifference obscures the light of being and hides the space of the world. But, like the forgetting of being, it remains an event of being, maintained in being. It remains powerless in the face of the power that brings the world to its appearing.

When Heidegger explains the last word of metaphysics, technological nihilism, as the moment in the reign of the unrestrained will to produce and "machine" when "the last reverberations of any intimation of *alêtheia* fade,"[44] the era of "completed absurdity" and the "perfect absence of meaning," the epoch when all the metaphysical distinctions fall into indifference, the epoch that is too feeble even for despair or violence, the most indigent of epochs, "no longer sensing its indigence," the relationship with being reinscribes and reestablishes itself of its own accord, in a buried and smothered way, admittedly, but in a simple and sensible way: insensitivity to *Stimmungen* is still a *Stimmung*, a sensitivity, a correspondence between being and the technological world. The unthought is still a thought. Between the two there is solely the relationship of the implicit and the explicit. We can never "get along without being." In the "night of the world" where we are, *it* never stops attuning us to it, giving us the tone. We are neither forgotten nor abandoned.

Such is the elementary, groping assurance that founds the uncertain expectation of a mutation of the epoch.[45]

Notes

1. A translation of Michel Haar's "Le temps vide et l'indifférence à l'être," *Exercices de la patience* 2 (1986): 17–36. Epigraph from GA 29/30, 515: "Wenn wir das nur könnten: ohne das Sein auskommen." Following Albert Hofstadter and Michael Heim (translators of Heidegger's *The Basic Problems of Phenomenology* and *The Metaphysical Foundations of Logic* respectively), *l'être* (the nominal use of the infinitive 'to be'; Heidegger's 'das Sein') will be translated as 'being'; and *étant* (the present participle of *être*; Heidegger's 'das Seiende') as 'beings' or, when the context demands the singular, as 'a ... being' (as in 'a subsisting-being' or 'a first or universal being')—Trans.

2. Haar uses 'tone' or 'tonality' to echo (if not to translate) Heidegger's *Stimmung*, emphasizing the musical overtones ('attunement' or 'accord'); cf. BT, 172, n. 3: "The noun 'Stimmung' originally means the tuning of a musical instrument, but it has taken on several other meanings and is the usual word for one's mood or humor. We shall usually translate it as 'mood' ... thought sometimes ... we prefer to call attention to the root metaphor of 'Gestimmtsein' by writing 'Being-attuned', etc."—Trans.

3. SZ 138; BT 177 [since Macquarrie and Robinson use both square brackets and parentheses in their translation, I will insert Harr's paren-

theses in diamond brackets < >; note, however, that, strictly speaking, *Stimmung* is not parenthetical since Harr does not translate it—Trans].
  4. SZ 134; BT 173.
  5. SZ 136; BT 175.
  6. Jean-Luc Marion, *Dieu sans l'être* (Paris: Fayard, 1982), p. 169.
  7. Marion, p. 170.
  8. Marion, p. 172.
  9. Rien n'égale en longueur les boiteuses journées
     Quand sous les lourds flocons de neigeuses années
     L'ennui, fruit de la morne incuriosité,
     Prend les proportions de l'immortalité.

Baudelaire, 69 (poem 76 of *Flowers of Evil*, second of the four poems entitled "Spleen").
  10. Stéphane Mallarmé, *Oeuvres Complétes* (Paris: Gallimard, Pléiade, 1945), p. 37.
  11. BW 101.
  12. BW 103.
  13. *Die Grundbegriffe der Metaphysik: Welt—Endlichkeit—Einsamkeit, GA* 29/30, published in 1983.
  14. Otto Bollnow, *Les tonalités affectives* (Neuchatel: La Baconnière, 1953), p. 65.
  15. GA 29/30, 115, 119.
  16. "wenn wir ihr nur nicht entegegen sind, wenn wir nicht immer gleich reagieren, um uns in Schutz zu bringen, wenn wir ihr vielmehr Raum geben. Dies ist es, was wir erst lernen müssen, dieses *Nicht-alsogleich-Widerstehen*, sondern *Ausschwingenlassen*." GA 29/30, 122.
  17. SZ 345; BT 396 (Heidegger's italics).
  18. SZ 339; BT 388.
  19. BP 262.
  20. SZ 371; ST 422.
  21. SZ sections 35–38.
  22. SZ 174; BT 219.
  23. SZ 178; BT 223.
  24. Different from Sartre, there is no "ensnarement" *(engluement)*, no fall into natural in-itself.
  25. In English, the play on 'thrown' (Fr. jeté, Ger. geworfen) and 'projected' (Fr. pro-jeté, Ger. ent-worfen) does not translate—Trans.
  26. SZ 276; BT 321.
  27. Mallarmé, *Igitur*, 440–441.
  28. "*Alles gleigh viel und gleich wenig gilt*," GA 29/30, 207.
  29. "Diese Gleichgültigkeit springt nicht erst von einem Ding auf das andere über wie ein Feuer, um es zu verzehren, sondern mit einem Mal ist alles von dieser Gleichgültigkeit umfangen und umhalten." GA 29/30, 208.
  30. SZ 187; BT 232.
  31. SZ 186; BT 231.

32. SZ 187; BT 231.
33. Certain etymologists refer the French word 'ennui' to the Latin expression *in odio esse*.
34. "Diese merkwürdige Inhaltslosigkeit dessen, was eigentlich das Dasein ermöglicht, darf uns nicht stören, bzw. Das Beunruhigende dieser Inhaltslosigkeit, das zu diesem ›es ist einem langweilig‹ gehört, dürfen wir nicht beseitigen, wenn wir überhaupt imstande sind, diese Stimmung ›es ist einem langweilig‹ in ihren ganzen Sehwingungsweite in uns ausschwingen zu lassen." GA 29/30, 216.
35. "Name, Stand, Beruf, Rolle, Alter und Geschick als das Meinige und Deinige fällt von uns ab." GA 29/30, 203.
36. "Die Spitze des Augenblickes wird weder als solche gewählt noch überlegt und gewußt. Sie offenbart sich uns als das eigentlich Ermöglichende, das dabei als dieses nur im Bebanntsein in den Zeithorizont und von da her geahnt bleibt, als das, was im eigenen Wesen des Daseins als dessen innerste Ermöglichung freigegeben sein könnte und sollte, aber jetzt im Bann des Daseins nicht ist." GA 23/30 227.
37. French translation of *geschichtlich* versus *historisch* (historical as factual).
38. "Overcoming Metaphysics" *The End of Philosophy*, trans. Joan Stambaugh (NY: Harper & Row, 1973), p. 110.
39. *The End of Philosophy*, p. 102.
40. *The End of Philosophy*, p. 104–106.
41. "The Turning," QT 47. [A subtle play on the French *regarde* which can mean 'gaze' (as in this quotation the French translation of *der Blick*) or, as a verb, either 'to gaze' or 'to be a concern for' (as in the passage just before this quotation, where I have taken it to mean primarily 'concern,' but where it obviously also refers to Heidegger's *Blick*, as well as his *wahren* 'to guard')—Trans.].
42. "Question Concerning Technology" QT, p. 33.
43. Heidegger, "Eternal Recurrence of the Same...." *Nietzsche* III, trans. David F. Krell (NY: Harper & Row, 1987), p. 173.
44. Heidegger, *Nietzsche* III, p. 173.
45. For further considerations on these reflections, especially the question of nature in Heidegger, see the author's *Le change de la Terre* and *Heidegger et l'essence de l'homme*.

Chapter 15

Heimat:
Heidegger on the Threshold

Will McNeill

Die Schwelle ist der Grundbalken, der das Tor im ganzen trägt. Er hält die Mitte, in der die Zwei, das Draußen und das Drinnen, einander durchgehen, aus. Die Schwelle trägt das Zwischen.

The threshold is the foundational beam that carries the doorway as a whole. It sustains the middle in which the two, the outside and the inside, traverse one another. The threshold carries the between.[1]

The following reflections, which are barely more than a string of notes on what I believe to be a crucial stream of Heidegger's thought, arose some time ago and were really spurred by two events. The first was a paper I was working on at the time on the subject of violence and the question of politics in Heidegger's 1935 course, *Introduction to Metaphysics*.[2] The second was a series of conversations with David Wood about the notions of fate, destiny, and historicality in *Being and Time*, conversations pervaded and punctuated by worries concerning the extent to which Heidegger's thinking of history, and indeed his thought in general, might be magnetised by the desire for a kind of peasant rootedness in the soil, by the summons of a Swabian, Black Forest homeland, in sum: by the belief in a soil-like rootedness of the identity of the German people. The temptation to unthinkingly affirm such a tendency in Heidegger, and, further, to straightforwardly identify it with the discourse of National Socialism and to use it as an "explanation" of his erstwhile support for that movement could not be greater. It happens everywhere. What I would like to do in these remarks is simply to problematize any such summary dismissal of "the Heidegger case"—not by offering an apology for Heidegger, but by pointing to what I take to be a real matter or issue for thinking here. This issue may be posed in the question: How does Heidegger understand the "national"? More precisely: What is the homeland for Heidegger? How does Heidegger think the nature or essence of the home? What is meant by the home in Heidegger's work? That is to say: What calls for the home? What is the call of the home? In German: *Was heißt Heimat*?

My remarks here do not mean to resolve this question—which would in any case be fatal for thinking—but to point toward the threshold of the very question. Accordingly, what follows may go under the title: *Heidegger on the Threshold*. The threshold, that is, of the *home*: Heidegger on the doorstep, as it were.

What is the home in Heidegger? It would be possible to show, I think, that the question of the home is second to none in Heidegger's work, not even to the question of being. At any rate, it is the essence of the home that provides the *first* answer to the question of the meaning of being in *Being and Time* (1927). More specifically, it provides the first answer to the meaning of Dasein's being: Dasein, that entity which we ourselves in each case are, and which is ontologically furthest from itself (though preontologically "not foreign," *nicht fremd*: SZ 16), is nevertheless alongside *(bei)* things in the world in the manner of dwelling, *wohnen*. Yet Dasein's dwelling, its being "in" the world, is not like the "insideness" or *Inwendigkeit* (SZ 56) pertaining to beings other than Dasein:

> "*in*" is derived from *innan-*, to dwell, *habitare*, to reside; "*an*" signifies: I am in the habit of *[gewohnt]*, familiar or intimate with *[vertraut mit]*, I look after something; it has the signification of *colo* in the sense of *habito* and *diligo*. We characterized this being, to which being-in in this signification belongs, as the being that I myself in each case am *(bin)*. The expression "*bin*" is connected with "*bei*"; "*Ich bin*," "I am," means in turn: I dwell, reside alongside . . . the world as that which is familiar in such and such a way. Being as infinitive of the "I am" [. . .] signifies dwelling alongside . . . , being familiar with. . . . (SZ 54)

Dasein's being is accordingly thought as *habitare, wohnen, gewohntsein*: being used to or in the habit of. . . . Yet this (in-)habitation of Dasein does not mean being enclosed in a "housing" *(Gehäuse)* in the sense of an inner sphere or capsule to be transcended (SZ 60–62). Rather, Dasein dwells in the intimacy of already being among things. Its "inside," its home or dwelling place in which it has taken up residence, is "outside," out "there" among things, alongside and with other beings in the disclosedness of what will prove to be constituted as Dasein's existential spatiality and temporality. Even more originarily, this disclosedness proves to be the movement of Dasein's historicality *(Geschichtlichkeit)*, a historicality which, as always already "thrown" and bound up with the world of others, also unfolds as the destiny *(Geschick)* of a community or of a people *(Volk)* (SZ 383–84).

And yet, there belongs to Dasein's ownmost being the extreme possibility of unhomeliness, *Unheimlichkeit* (usually translated as uncanniness[3]), which manifests itself in the attunement of anxiety. In anxiety, it is not you or me or this or that Dasein that is unhomely, but "it is unhomely for one," *es ist einem unheimlich*: this "one" being the "one" of *das Man*. Unhomeliness is thought here as "not being at home," *das Un-zuhause*: the "at home" *(Zuhause)* is identified with the average, everyday disclosedness of the public realm, with the world as it initially appears to be for the most part, with the discourse and interpretedness belonging to "one" (SZ 188–89). This extreme possibility of unhomeliness does *not*, then, simply belong to Dasein's ownmost being: it is rather the opening up of the very possibility of ownness, of selfhood, of mineness. That is to say, of the possibility of *identity*: of the identity of an individual or of a people or nation, in short: of any belonging or non-belonging whatsoever. This is why Heidegger says that it first opens or makes manifest the existentiell possibilities of authenticity and inauthenticity, *Eigentlichkeit* and *Uneigentlichkeit*, as possibilities (SZ 191). The *Unheimlichkeit* of Dasein thereby implicitly exceeds the order of the proper.

In its average everydayness, governed by the anonymity and dominant interpretations furnished by the "one," Dasein implicitly understands that it itself is not the things to which it relates; it understands a distinction between itself and intraworldly beings. And yet, it understands itself predominantly in terms of or from out of the things themselves, in terms of what it does, its comportment toward intraworldly beings. This is why, when it comes to explicitly interpret itself, it does so as though it, too, were a thing, as in the classic paradigm of modernity: the *res cogitans* versus *res extensa*. Now, Heidegger in *Being and Time* sets out to problematize this distinction via a radical posing of the problem of transcendence.

If Dasein is indeed not the (intraworldly) things themselves, if it is neither itself a thing, nor *in* things themselves, it is nevertheless alongside *(bei)* things in the manner of dwelling. The realm of this being alongside..., the place of this dwelling, Heidegger calls *world*. World is also always equiprimordially a being with *(mit)* others who have the same kind of being.[4] The being of Dasein is being-in-the-world, where this "in" does not mean spatial enclosure in a container, but, if anything, the opposite: a radical openness to beings as a whole that ultimately proves to be nothing other than the temporality of Dasein, the ekstasis of its "there." Yet how does world, the place of this dwelling, become visible as such? Strangely enough, through the unhomeliness of anxiety; the latter, says Heidegger, *"discloses world as world"* (SZ 188). Unhomeliness is disclosed in one's anxiety in the face of *(vor)* and about *(um)* being-in-the-world as such. The uncanny unhomeliness of anxiety thus stands at the threshold, at the threshold of the home.

A crucial problem running through *Being and Time* is that of hermeneutic *access* to world as the place of our dwelling. In that treatise, Heidegger appeals to the phenomena of death and conscience as ways in which disclosive anxiety can awaken. In the 1927 course, *The Basic Problems of Phenomenology*, which continues the project of *Being and Time*, Heidegger states: "The elucidation of the concept of world is one of the most central tasks of philosophy. The concept of world and the phenomenon it designates is something that has never yet been recognized in philosophy at all. You will think that that is a bold and presumptuous assertion. How can it be that world has never yet been seen in philosophy?" (GA 24, 234).

Nevertheless, it is an assertion that Heidegger stands by. And here—already in 1927—he appeals to the *poetic* word to point to the phenomenon at issue (allow me, following Heidegger, to quote at length here):

> Poetry is nothing other than the elementary coming to word, that is, uncovering of existence as being-in-the-world. With what is spoken the world first becomes visible for the others, who before this were blind. As testimony to this we may listen to a quotation from Rainer Maria Rilke taken from the *Notebooks of Malte Laurids Brigge*:
>
> Will people believe that there are such houses? No, people will say, I'm falsifying. This time it's the truth, nothing omitted, and of course nothing added either. Where should I get it

from? People know that I'm poor. People know it. Houses? But, to be exact, they were houses that were no longer there. Houses that had been demolished from top to bottom. What was there were the other houses which had stood beside them, tall neighbouring houses. Evidently they were in danger of collapsing, since people had taken away everything that had been next to them; for a whole framework of long, tarred poles was rammed at an angle between the ground of the square full of rubble and the exposed wall. I don't know if I've already said that I mean this wall. But it was, so to speak, not the first wall of the houses before me (as people would surely have thought), but the last wall of the previous ones. One could see its interior side. On the various floor levels one saw the walls of rooms with the wallpaper still sticking to them, here and there the beginning of the floor or the ceiling. Beside the room walls a dirty-white space remained along the whole wall, and through this space crept, in unspeakably nauseating movements, soft like those of a digesting worm, the open, rusty channel of the toilet pipe. The paths that the gas for lighting had taken left behind grey, dusty tracks along the edge of the ceilings, and here and there, quite unexpectedly, they bent right round and ran into the painted wall and into a dark hole that had ruthlessly been torn out. The most unforgettable thing, however, was the walls themselves. The tenacious life of these rooms had refused to let itself be stamped out. It was still there, it hung onto the remaining nails, it stood on the remains of the floor the width of your hand, it had crept together where the corners began, where there was still a tiny bit of interior space. One could see that it was in the paint, which it had slowly transformed year by year: blue into mouldy green, green into grey, and yellow into an old, decayed white that was now rotting away. But it was in the fresher places too that had remained preserved behind mirrors, pictures and cupboards; for it had drawn their outlines and redrawn them and, with spiders and dust, had been in these hidden places too that now lay bare. It was in every strip that had been ground down, it was in the damp blisters on the lower edges of the wallpaper, it swayed in the torn-off shreds, and it sweated out of the ugly stains that had been made a long time ago. And from these walls once blue, green, and yellow which were framed by the tracks of the fractures of the intersecting walls that had been demolished, the breath of this life stood out, the tenacious, sluggish, musty air that no wind had yet dispersed. There stood the noondays and the illnesses, and what had been exhaled and the smoke of years ago and the sweat that breaks out under the armpits and makes the clothes heavy, and the stale breath of mouths and the fusel oil smell of fermenting feet. There stood the pungency of urine and the burning of soot and grey reek of potatoes and the strong, oily stench of decaying grease. The sweet, lingering aroma of neglected suckling infants was there and the anguished odor of children going to school and the sultriness from beds of pubescent boys. And much that had come from below had joined this company, evaporating upward from the abyss of the alley, and other things had seeped down with the rain, which is not clean above cities. And the domestic winds, weak and grown tame, which always stay in the same street, had brought much along with them, and there was much else there whose origin one didn't know. I did indeed say, didn't I, that all the walls had been demolished, right down to this last one—? Well, I've been talking all this time about this wall. People will say, I must have stood before it for a long time; but I will swear an oath that I began to run as soon as I recognized the wall. For that's what's terrifying—that I recognized it. I recognize everything here, and that's why it goes right into me: it is at home in me *[es ist zu Hause in mir]* (GA 24, 244–46).

Faced with the last wall of our previous dwellings, pervaded by the sudden intimacy of what is at home in us, world lights up in its uncanny unhomeliness, the terrifying *(das Schreckliche)* strikes into our hearts in the very moment of recognition.

Anxiety as the attunement of unhomeliness—as was already indicated by *Being and Time*—is essentially anxiety in the face of death as the "Nothing of the possible impossibility" of existence (SZ 266). This theme is taken up again in the inaugural Freiburg address of 1929, "What Is Metaphysics?", where the unhomeliness of anxiety is said to manifest the Nothing in the withdrawal or slipping away of beings as a whole. At the same time, Heidegger there intimates that in this unhomeliness that "one" experiences, "anxiety strikes us speechless": *Die Angst verschlägt uns das Wort* (GA 9, 112). Unhomeliness is speechlessness, is withdrawal of the word, is the poverty of the poet. The experience of un-homeliness marks, as it did already in *Being and Time*, the very threshold of language.[5] The home therefore stands in a relation to the word, to language. To language—i.e., to that which might, above all, seem to be the ultimate court of appeal guaranteeing the gathering or belonging together of a people, of a nation, or of the "spirit" of a community. When Heidegger, as is well known, in 1935 asserts a privileging of the Greek and German languages, "the most powerful and spirited" *(mächtigsten und geistigsten)* with respect to their possibilities for thinking (EM 43), can this be anything other than a spirited power-wielding form of nationalism, a metaphysics of spirit?[6] This might be the case. But what of unhomeliness?

Metaphysical nationalism is a charge implicitly denied by Heidegger in the "Letter on 'Humanism'" (1946). It is here that Heidegger coins a saying that has long since become a meaningless catch-phrase: "Language is the house of being *[das Haus des Seins]*. In its housing *[Behausung]* man dwells. The thinkers and poets are the guardians of this housing" (GA 9, 313). By contrast, the public, the "one," *das Man*, says Heidegger, appears as the very institution of dictatorship *(Diktatur)*. In the era of subjectivity, language falls into the "dictatorship of the public." This dictatorship is associated with everything becoming accessible in identical form *(gleichförmig)* (GA 9, 317). Referring to his address of 1943 on Hölderlin's elegy "Homecoming" *(Heimkunft)*,[7] Heidegger states that the "there" or *Da* of Dasein as the nearness "of" being is thought "in terms of *Being and Time* ... and named the 'home,' *Heimat*, in the light of the experience of the forgottenness of being." The German word *Heimat* means 'home,' but also 'home town' or 'homeland,' depending on context; like the English word *home*, its signification is distinctly indeterminate, yet invokes a powerful sense of belonging. Now this word *Heimat*, Heidegger continues,

> is here thought in an essential sense, not patriotically, not nationalistically, but in terms of the history of being. The essence of the home, however, is at the same time named with the intention of thinking the homelessness *[Heimatlosigkeit]* of modern human beings from out of the essence of the history of being. (GA 9, 338)

Hölderlin, says Heidegger in the "Letter," is concerned that the German people discover their essence. Yet:

> The "German" *[das "Deutsche"]* is not spoken to the world so that it can convalesce in the German essence, but is spoken to the Germans so that they may become world-historical in their destinal belonging to other peoples and with these. [...] The home of this historical dwelling is nearness to being. (Ibid.)

The essence of a people is to be thought in their belonging to the destiny of the West—the West likewise not thought in opposition to the East, nor merely as Europe, but world-historically. All nationalism, we are told, is metaphysically an anthropologism and, as such, subjectivism. It cannot be overcome simply by internationalism. Homelessness has become a world-destiny that was already experienced by Marx and Nietzsche (GA 9, 338–42). And Heidegger confirms: the essence of being-in-the-world, as already thought in *Being and Time*, is dwelling:

> The talk of the house of being is not some transfer of the image of the "house" onto being; rather, from out of the essence of being thought appropriately we will instead one day be able to think what "house" and "dwelling" are. [. . .] Language is at once the house [*Haus*] of being and the housing [*Behausung*] of the human essence. Only because language houses the human essence can historical humankind and human beings not be at home in their language, so that it becomes the capsule [*Gehäuse*] of their machinations. (GA 9, 358–61)

Language as such is *geheimnisvoll*, mysterious. Language? "Language is the language of being like the clouds are the clouds of the heavens" (GA 9, 364). House "of" being, language "of" being, clouds "of" the heavens: subjective or objective genitive? Or is this question itself perhaps inappropriate to the issue to be thought here? Ought we to hear in this genitive something more akin to the middle voice: a voice coming from the middle or midst, a voice from the threshold? But what would that mean?

The theme of dwelling as the fundamental trait of being (VA 155) is continued in "Building, Dwelling, Thinking" (1951), and in the lecture on Hölderlin's "Poetically Man Dwells . . ." of the same year. "Building, Dwelling, Thinking" again confirms the essence of dwelling as being alongside things (VA 145). This dwelling is now thought in terms of the dwelling of mortals with one another on the earth. On the earth in itself means under the heavens and before the gods. The singular fold of the fourfold of earth and heavens, gods and mortals is the place of mortal dwelling. Dwelling means protecting the fourfold, saving the earth and heavens in letting them be. The singular fold of the fourfold gives mortals their directive *(Weisung)* (VA 153), i.e., shows them their ēthos. And yet, in order to dwell, there is a need for dwellings. However the proper need *(die eigentliche Not)* of dwelling does not simply consist in a lack of dwellings:

> The proper need of dwelling consists in the fact that mortals must always seek, time and again, the essence of dwelling, that they *must first learn how to dwell*. What if the homelessness of human beings consisted in the fact that humans do not yet at all ponder the *proper* [eigentliche] need of dwelling *as the* need? . . . homelessness *[Heimatlosigkeit]* . . . is the singular address *[der einzige Zuspruch]* that *calls* [ruft] mortals into dwelling. (VA 156)

Mortals, it seems, are initially homeless, not at home: to all appearances, this is a reversal of the hermeneutic order of *Being and Time* that situates Dasein initially "at home" in *das Man*. Yet one should perhaps not be too quick to identify homelessness with unhomeliness. What if the task of dwelling were precisely to become "at home" in unhomeliness? What if *Unheimlichkeit* were the proper *Heimat* of mortals? What if, more precisely, our seeking of *Heimat* were our being *unheimlich*?

And yet, for all this insistence on the preoccupation of his thought with what we might call a "quasi-metaphysical" dwelling and home, the suspicion remains that a naive or nostalgic appeal to the ontic soil of the Black Forest sometimes enters Heidegger's discourse. Consider, for example, the discourse of "*Gelassenheit*," a speech given in his home town Meßkirch some four years later. The first lines open: "The first word I may say in public in my home town can only be a word of thanks. . . . I thank my home *[Heimat]* for everything it has given me with me on a long journey *[für alles, was sie mir auf einen langen Weg mitgegeben hat]*." (The reference to something *mitgegeben*—a Hölderlinian word—is not unimportant, as we shall see in a moment.) A few pages later: "We note that from our home soil *[Boden der Heimat]* a work of art has flourished. If we ponder this simple fact then we must at once recall that the Swabian soil has produced great poets and thinkers in the previous two centuries" (G 14). Need we go on? Can anyone mistake the tone here? Yet not too fast! For there is a guest present at this speech; a guest that was in fact introduced a little earlier in the speech, but whom we forgot to mention. A very special guest, but by no means a rare one:

> Let us have no illusions. All of us, including those who think in the course of their profession as it were, we are all often

enough poor in thought; all of us are all too readily thoughtless. Thoughtlessness is an unhomely guest *[ein unheimlicher Gast]* that moves in and out *[aus- und eingeht]* everywhere in the contemporary world. (G 11)

Moving in and out, this guest haunts the threshold of our contemporary dwelling in the technological world. In view of our unhomely and uncanny guest—a guest already recognized by Nietzsche[8]—we might wish to read through this speech in a somewhat different light. Are we hearing an appeal to a merely "ontic" rootedness in this address? Or is the rootedness referred to already beyond the ontic/ontological distinction, a distinction no longer tenable for an appropriate response to the technological world? A cursory reading of this text certainly encounters the emphasis on the Swabian home soil, yet this emphasis must also be considered in the context of the overall theme of this address: the question concerning the relation of human beings and their finitude to the technological world. The emphasis on the factical situatedness, the "here and now"—"here, on this patch of home ground *[auf diesem Fleck Heimaterde]*; now, in the present hour of world history *[in der gegenwärtigen Weltstunde]*" (G 14)—stresses the finitude and thrownness, the particularity of always existing in a specific place and time, in relation to and dependent upon the presence of particular, tangible things around us. It stresses this in contrast to the uprooting, alienating nature of formalizing, technological thinking in which the unsubstitutable particularity of individuals and things is drawn into a system of infinite substitutability and formalization, thus leading us to overlook the dependent and fragile finitude of our situatedness. The references to *Heimat* here, far from indicating some kind of nostalgia for a past way of existence, might just as well be read as a sobering reminder concerning the future of an increasingly technological world, a reminder about the "concrete" world that approaches us. Indeed, one could show that it is the very futuricity projected by technological thinking that uproots and unbinds us from our thrownness. The theme of *Heimat* here is perhaps not so much concerned with any metaphysical or quasimetaphysical prioritizing of the Swabian soil as with our very relation to particularly as such. Indeed, is not the very *worry* concerning any emphasis on the significance of particularity already indicative of a (quasi-)metaphysical or technological thinking, a thinking that is already persuaded of the priority of a universalizing, formalizing interpretation of the world?[9]

But we must interrupt here. For we have already gone too fast, too fast forward. It is time to rewind. To 1933, precisely, and to the decade following that year. It is there, after all, that the appeal to the soil appears, in retrospect, most ominous. In his notorious reflection, "Why do we remain in the Province" (1933), for example, Heidegger states: "The inner belonging of our own work to the Black Forest and its people comes from a century-long Alemannic-Swabian rootedness *[Bodenständigkeit]* that is irreplaceable" (D 10). And yet, this rootedness, as Heidegger proceeds to indicate, is to be thought not as physical or geographical locatedness, but in terms of solitude, *Einsamkeit*, which is something other than being alone or on one's own, and experiences the extending of a "nearness to the presencing *[Wesen]* of all things" (D 11). Here, too, we must not be too quick to conclude.

Solitude recalls, among other things, the 1929/30 lecture course, *The Fundamental Concepts of Metaphysics*, subtitled: *World, Finitude, Solitude*. The entire lecture course is concerned with delimiting the place of human beings in the midst of beings as a whole and the manifestness of such beings, i.e., world. Solitude is to be thought in one with world and with mortal finitude. The course begins with Heidegger approvingly citing Novalis in identifying homesickness, *Heimweh*, as the fundamental attunement of all philosophizing. For Novalis, philosophy is really homesickness, the desire to be at home everywhere, i.e., among beings as a whole. Philosophy, notes Heidegger, can be such a thing only if we who are philosophizing are not at home *(nicht zu Hause)* everywhere. Yet, "What does that mean—to be at home everywhere?" (GA 29/30, 7).

In his search for the home, Heidegger, as we have noted, finds himself accompanied by Hölderlin. He lectures in 1934/35 on Hölderlin's hymns, "Germania" and "The Rhine." For Hölderlin, human beings dwell poetically upon this earth: being is dwelling, poetry the essence of language, and language man's protection against the gods. The fundamental attunement of poetizing is a "holy mourning" "with" the "homely waters of the earth." Yet what does "homely" mean here? What is the poetic call of the home? Home, *Heimat*, is *"the power of the earth* [die Macht der Erde]" (GA 39, 88). The waters of the homely earth are the rivers of Hölderlin's poems; the river for Hölderlin is that which "violently *[gewaltsam]* creates paths and limits on the originally pathless earth" (GA 39, 93). A people, a *Volk*, says Heidegger, must be thought in terms of their originally historical time, the time of the creators: "at issue is a world destiny of the homely earth" (GA 39, 96). Yet what of the

German people? Who are "the Germans"? Does Hölderlin mean the Germans of 1801? "Or do the Germans of 1934 also belong to these? Or does Hölderlin mean the Germans of 1980?" In response, Heidegger cites Hölderlin's poem "To the Germans," whose last two verses read:

> Wohl ist enge begränzt unsere Lebenszeit,
> Unserer Jahre Zahl sehen und zählen wir,
> Doch die Jahre der Völker,
> Sah ein sterbliches Auge sie?
>
> Wenn die Seele dir auch über die eigne Zeit
> Sich die sehnende schwingt, trauernd verweilst du
> Dann am kalten Gestade
> Bei den Deinen und kennst sie nie.

In translation:

> Our lifetime, it seems, is narrowly spanned,
> We see and count the numbers of our years,
> But the years of the peoples,
> Has ever a mortal eye seen them?
>
> If your soul too beyond your own time
> Transports you in its longing, mournful you tarry
> Then on the cold shores
> Alongside your own and never know them. (GA 39, 49–50)

If the poet, himself a mortal, does not know the time of his own people, it is not because he stands somewhere outside or beyond them in the sense of having a privileged perspective or vantage point, but because, existing in their midst, he does not know his own time, but is transported beyond that which is his own, beyond the calculable time of "today." We do not know our own historical time, says Heidegger, "The hour of world history of our people *[Die Weltstunde unseres Volkes]* is concealed from us. We do not know who we are when we ask concerning our being as properly temporal" (GA 39, 50). This poet leads us to the threshold: we stand, says Heidegger,

> before the closed doorway *[dem verschlossenen Tor]* to what the poet names the "most forbidden fruit," which "each shall taste last": "the fatherland." For the poet this means neither some dubious greatness of an even more dubious patriotism

full of noise. He means the "land of the fathers," he means us, this people of this earth as historical, in their historical being. Such being, however, is founded poetically, ordered in thinking, and put into knowing, and is rooted in the activity of the founders of the state, who belong to the earth, and in historical space. This historical being of the people, the fatherland, is sealed in a mystery *[Geheimnis]*, and indeed essentially and forever. (GA 39, 120)

What is the fatherland? Being *(Seyn)* itself, says Heidegger (GA 39, 121). Yet for Hölderlin this fatherland is divine, at once exposed to the gods, "the heavenly," and reaching into the earth. The path to the fatherland must first be poetized, and such poetizing is poetizing of the mystery, of something essentially concealed: the midst *(Mitte)* of being.

The poet Hölderlin thinks the rivers as demigods. What, Heidegger asks, gives rise to and compels this thinking of the demigods? "The poet has his place standing at the threshold of the home *[an der Grenze der Heimat]*. From there his sense is carried into the distance, and from out of this turning away he is unsuspectingly called back to the homely earth *[züruckgerufen auf die heimatliche Erde]*. The need of the homely earth is what generates the nature and direction of his thinking, which is concerned with the singular task of finding the truth of his people *[die Wahrheit des Volkes]* (GA 39, 226). Yet *this* "truth of the *Volk*" is not that of the dominant political discourse of the time, where "everything is dripping with *Volkstum* and *Blut und Boden*," remarks Heidegger sarcastically (GA 39, 254). The thinking of the rivers as demigods is the thinking of "a destiny" *(Schicksal)*, of a single destiny and dialogue *(Gespräch)* in its uniqueness or singularity *(Einzigkeit)*. The way in which those who are singular are together, their world, is solitude *(Einsamkeit)*. The latter

> does not close off or exclude, but carries out into that originary unity that no community *[Gemeinschaft]* ever reaches. . . . The singularity of historical Dasein is destiny. This the poet thinks in his poem "The Rhine." Being as destiny is the unhomely, *das Unheimliche*. . . . (GA 39, 228–29)

The lecture course finishes by reappraising its singular thematic: the metaphysical place of Hölderlin's poetry. The poet of the Germania must hold out in the midst of being *(Seyn)*, so as to receive the encounters with the gods at this place and thus to found the dwelling of humans on the earth, their history. Yet history, says Heidegger, is always singular, "the singular history of each respective people, in this case of the people of this poet, the history of Germania" (GA 39, 288). What the poet of this people must name in order to reach the midst (or "middle": *die Mitte*) of being is, on the one hand, "the mother, the earth itself"; but also, in this very naming, "the gods of the past," together with the divinity of the future. Only from these two (namely, past and future) does history arise, does Dasein attain "the midst of time *[Mitte der Zeit]*—a true counter-turning *[Gegenwendigkeit]*" (GA 39, 289). Yet this midst of time can be attained only in the struggle for the *freedom* of the German essence. And precisely the insistent struggle for this freedom, as Hölderlin himself attests in a letter to Böhlendorff, is what is most difficult: "to make free use of the national" (GA 39, 290–91). The historical determination of the national is always to transform what a people is endowed with *(das Mitgegebene)*, namely, "the national," into what is given up to them as a task *(das Aufgegebene)*, that is, the free use of "one's own," of the national, that allows them to create a free relation to the national, a space in which the national can freely become history. This, however, is what is most difficult. The Germans, states Heidegger, must achieve this most difficult task, find what is historically their own, in encounter and confrontation *[Auseinandersetzung*[10]*]* with the Greeks, who were endowed with a "rousing nearness to the fire of the heavens, being struck by the violence of being *[die Gewalt des Seyns*[11]*]*" (GA 39, 292). Precisely this is what the Germans must find as their task. Yet how? Heidegger's conclusion is cautious:

> The hour of our history has struck. We must first accept and purely preserve our endowment, but only in order to comprehend and take hold of our task, i.e., to question our way toward and through it. If we are to be able to grasp it, the violence of being *[die Gewalt des Seyns]* must first and really become a question again. (GA 39, 294)

The "violence of being" becomes a question for Heidegger elsewhere in the very same semester of 1935, in his *Introduction to Metaphysics*. At the core of this course is his interpretation of the first chorus of Sophocles' *Antigone*, which sings the essence of the human being as the one who is superlatively *deinon*. Heidegger translates this Greek word with *das Un-heimliche*, the un-homely, understood as that which casts us out of the homely, the habitual, the ordinary and familiar. Yet human beings are not merely uncanny, unhomely; they are the most uncanny of all that is uncanny, the most unhomely of the unhomely (*das Unheimlichste des Unheimlichen*: EM 114). The essence of this most unhomely one that the human being is lies in the counter-turning *(Gegenwendigkeit)* between *deinon* understood as the violent, overwhelming prevailing of the being of beings as a whole (identified with *dike*), and *deinon* as the violent activity or *techne* of the human being. In their active violence human beings cut their way through beings as a whole; they are *pantoporos*, "everywhere underway" in their breaking out into the midst of the prevailing of sea, earth, and animal life (in short, of *phusis*). At the same time they become *aporos*, "without way out" in the face of the "Nothing" of death, in the face of their essential thrownness. The site of their essential being is named as the *polis*, in which they dwell as *hupsipolis apolis*: towering high in the place of history, yet at the same time without site, unhomely and solitary, essentially "lone-some ones" *(Ein-same)* insofar as they are confronted with the overwhelming violence of being through their constant exposure to death. The realm of the "political," the "there" of Da-sein as the site *(Stätte)* of human historicality, thus finds its limit in the unhomely. The human being is without any way out in the face of death not at the point where he or she comes to die, but "constantly and essentially," "insofar as the human being *is*." Thus Da-sein is uncanniness itself, "the very occurrence of un-homeliness *[die geschehende Un-heimlichkeit selbst]*" (EM 121). For death is "that uncanny thing *[dieses Unheimliche]*" that "exceeds the limit of every limit," the threshold of every threshold, casting us definitively beyond all that is homely, that against which the violent activity of human *techne* shatters, exposing the human being to "the uncanniness of language *[das Unheimliche der Sprache]*" and of the passions (EM 120), the uncanniness that is normally concealed amid the apparent familiarity of human activity. The human being's exposure to death as that which exceeds every limit *at once* marks the limit against which all human activity shatters in running up against its limit, a limitation set for it and that exceeds it in overwhelming it, *and* that step over the threshold of the homely into the midst of the overwhelming and the unhomely:

> We understand *das Un-heimliche* as that which casts us out of the *"Heimlichen,"* i.e., the homely *[Heimischen]*, the habitual, the ordinary, the unendangered. The unhomely does not let us be at home *[Das Unheimische läßt uns nicht einheimisch sein]*.

Therein lies the excess of its overwhelming character *[das Über-wältigende]*. Yet the human being is the most uncanny one *[das Unheimlischste]* because he not only prevails in his essence in the midst of the un-homely *[des Un-heimlichen]* thus understood, but because he steps out *[heraustritt]*, departs, from what are for him initially and for the most part the habitual limits of the homely, because as the actively violent one he steps over the limit of the homely *[die Grenze des Heimischen überschreitet]* and does so precisely in the direction of the uncanny *[das Unheimische]* in the sense of the overwhelming. (EM 115–16)

Seven years later, in 1942—a seven-year hiatus bearing the name "Nietzsche"[12]—we see a renewed attempt to determine the free use of the national, again in the context of a Hölderlin interpretation: the course on Hölderlin's hymn "The Ister." The Ister hymn reads:

Jezt komme, Feuer!
Begierig sind wir
Zu schauen den Tag,
Und wenn die Prüfung
Ist durch die Knie gegangen,
Mag einer spüren das Waldgeschrei.
Wir singen aber vom Indus her
Fernangekommen und
Vom Alpheus, lange haben
Das Schikliche wir gesucht,
Nicht ohne Schwingen mag
Zum nächsten einer greifen
Geradezu
Und kommen auf die andere Seite.
Hier aber wollen wir bauen.
Denn Ströme machen urbar
Das Land. Wenn nemlich Kräuter wachsen
Und an denselben gehn
Im Sommer zu trinken die Thiere,
So gehn auch Menschen daran.

Man nennet aber diesen den Ister.
Schön wohnt er. Es brennet der Säulen Laub,
Und reget sich. Wild stehn
Sie aufgerichtet, untereinander; darob
Ein zweites Maas, springt vor

Von Felsen das Dach. So wundert
Mich nicht, dass er
Den Herkules zu Gaste geladen,
Fernglänzend, am Olympos drunten,
Da der, sich Schatten zu suchen
Vom heissen Isthmos kam,
Denn voll des Muthes waren
Daselbst sie, es bedarf aber, der Geister wegen,
Der Kühlung auch. Darum zog jener lieber
An die Wasserquellen hieher und gelben Ufer,
Hoch duftend oben, und schwarz
Vom Fichtenwald, wo in den Tiefen
Ein Jäger gern lustwandelt
Mittags, und Wachstum hörbar ist
An harzigen Bäumen des Isters,

Der scheinet aber fast
Rükwärts zu gehen und
Ich mein, er müsse kommen
Von Osten.
Vieles wäre
Zu sagen davon. Und warum hängt er
An den Bergen gerad? Der andre
Der Rhein ist seitwärts
Hinweggegangen. Umsonst nicht gehn
Im Troknen die Ströme. Aber wie? Sie sollen nemlich
Zur Sprache seyn. Ein Zeichen braucht es,
Nichts anderes, schlecht und recht, damit es Sonn'
Und Mond trag' im Gemüth', untrennbar,
Und fortgeh, Tag und Nacht auch, und
Die Himmlischen warm sich fühlen aneinander.
Darum sind jene auch
Die Freude des Höchsten. Denn wie käm er sonst
Herunter? Und wie Hertha grün,
Sind sie die Kinder des Himmels. Aber allzugedultig
Scheint der mir, nicht
Freier, und fast zu spotten. Nemlich wenn

Angehen soll der Tag
In der Jugend, wo er zu wachsen
Anfängt, es treibet ein anderer da
Hoch schon die Pracht, und Füllen gleich
In den Zaum knirscht er, und weithin hören

Das Treiben die Lüfte,
Ist der betrübt;
Es brauchet aber Stiche der Fels
Und Furchen die Erd',
Unwirthbar wär es, ohne Weile;
Was aber jener thuet der Strom,
Weis niemand.

In translation:

Now come, fire!
Eager are we
To see the day,
And when the trial
Has passed through our knees,
May someone sense the forest's cry.
We, however, sing from the Indus
Arrived from afar and
From Alpheus, long have
We sought what is fitting,
Not without pinions may
Some one grasp at what is nearest
Directly
And reach the other side.
Here, however, we wish to build.
For rivers make arable
The land. Whenever plants grow
And there in summer
The animals go to drink,
So humans go there too.

This one, however, is named the Ister.
Beautiful he dwells. The foliage of the columns burns
And stirs. Wild they stand
Erect among one another; above
A second measure, from rocks
The roof juts out. Thus it surprises
Me not, that he
Invited Hercules as guest,
Gleaming from afar, down there by Olympus,
When he in search of shade
From the sultry Isthmus came,
For full of courage were

They even there, yet there was need, for the spirits' sake,
Of cooling too. Whence that one preferred to travel
To the water's sources here and yellow banks,
Their scent wafting high above, and black
With the forest of firs, within whose depths
A hunter likes to roam
At midday, and growth can be heard
In the resinous trees of the Ister,

He appears, however, almost
To go backwards and
I presume he must come
From the East.
There would be
Much to tell of this. And why does he precisely
Cling to the mountains? The other
The Rhine has departed
Sideways. Not in vain do
Rivers run in the dry. Yet how? Namely, they are
To be to language. A sign is needed,
Nothing else, plain and simple, so that sun
And moon may be borne in mind, inseparable,
And pass on, day and night too, and
The heavenly feel themselves warm by one another.
Whence those ones too
Are the joy of the Highest. For how else would he
Descend? And like Hertha green,
They are the children of the heavens. Yet all too patient
He appears to me, not
Free, and almost to mock. Namely, when

The day is to commence
In his youth, where he begins
To grow, another there already
Drives high his splendor, and like colts
He grinds at the bit, and far away the breezes
Hear his activity,
He is saddened;
The rock, however, has need of cuts
And of furrows the earth,
Inhospitable it would be, without while;
Yet what that one does, that river,
No one knows.

"The Ister" is the Greco-Roman name for the lower *Donau*, the river Danube. The river once more names the site of human dwelling *(Wohnstatt)* on this earth, the locality *(Ortschaft)* where human beings are intimate and at home *(heimisch)*, and thus brought into that which is their own *(ins Eigene)* (GA 53, 23). Yet the river is itself also a journeying *(Wanderschaft)*. It *is* the locality of dwelling only as the journeying of a becoming homely, *(Heimischwerden)* (GA 53, 39). Hölderlin's poetry is concerned with becoming homely in what is one's own, i.e., here, in "what belongs to the fatherland of the Germans. What belongs to the fatherland is itself homely *(heimisch)* alongside *(bei)* mother earth. This *becoming* homely in one's own entails that humans are at first and for a long time and at times forever not at home" (GA 53, 60). Their becoming homely, which is the encounter or *Auseinandersetzung* between what is one's own and what is foreign *(fremd)*, is the fundamental truth and law of history. Why? And what are we to understand when, in this context, we read the following?:

> We know today that the Anglo-Saxon world of Americanism has resolved to annihilate Europe, that is, the homeland *[die Heimat]*, and that means: the commencement of the Western world. Whatever has the character of commencement is indestructible. America's entry into this planetary war is not its entry into history; rather it is already the ultimate American act of American ahistoricality and self-devastation. For this act is the renunciation of commencement, and a decision in favor of that which is without commencement. The concealed spirit of the commencement in the West *[Der verborgene Geist des Anfänglichen im Abendland]* will not even have the look of contempt for this trial of self-devastation without commencement, but will await its stellar hour from out of the releasement and tranquillity that belong to the commencement ... (GA 53, 68)

Here, *Heimat* is identified with "Europe," understood as "the commencement *[Anfang]* of the Western world." But is the *Auseinandersetzung* between one's own and the foreign, as Heidegger sees it, being played out concretely in the planetary war taking place before his very eyes? Is *Heimat* "one's own" here, "the German" as opposed to the foreign? Clearly not. Or at least, it is not that which initially appears to be "the German," the dominant and prevalent everyday understanding of "the German," that which one initially thinks is "one's own." For one thing, *Heimat*, as Heidegger explicates it in this course, is never something simply given, but comes about only in the journeying of becoming unhomely; it only *is* as an *Auseinandersetzung between* the foreign and one's own. But more importantly, *Heimat* exists only as this encounter or confrontation between *historical* human beings, which in the present instance (the interpretation of Hölderlin's dialogue with Sophocles) means between the Greeks and the Germans. Any relation to the commencement entails a relation to the Greeks, "for in the Greek world something having the character of a commencement once occurred *[hat sich ereignet],* and that which has the character of a commencement alone grounds history" (GA 53, 69).

America's entry into the war, by contrast, is a sign of "ahistoricality" *(Geschichtslosigkeit).*[13] Heidegger's remarks here (which one would have to quote and comment on at greater length than we can do here, particularly in regard to technology), while they may have the tone of anti-American polemic, do not in principle exclude America from the possibility of entering history; after all, America or Americanism (assuming for now that one may equate these) is, according to Heidegger's later remarks, not altogether excluded from the historical, but, as unhistorical, stands in a relation (albeit a "catastrophic" one) to the commencement and is possible only on the basis of this commencement. Its entry into history, its becoming historical, would presumably entail its entering into dialogue and *Auseinandersetzung* with the foreign of its own, i.e., once more with the Greeks and with the "spirit" of the Greek commencement. On the other hand, if Americanism is precisely the concealment of this commencement, i.e., of *Heimat*, then the resolve to annihilate it cannot be a *knowing* resolve on the part of America. America's intervention is implicated in a blindness to the commencement and thereby to its own historicality, a blindness that Heidegger appears to associate (though this would have to be shown in all its complexity) with the spirit of unrestrained technologism. Yet the issue is complex, because it was certainly clear to Heidegger by this point that the dominant forces of National Socialism were under the sway of essentially the same technologism (even if it was being deployed for different ends).

Yet why must becoming homely be understood as the encounter or *Auseinandersetzung* between what is one's own and what is foreign? Without some relation to the other, the foreign, there can be no understanding of one's own. And if the other, and one's own, are understood in each case as a way of thinking borne by the "spirit" of a language, then explicitly understanding (i.e., appropriating) the spirit of one's own language at any given moment entails a dialogue with the spirit of the foreign, insofar as the latter, in a concealed or inexplicit manner for the most part, defines what is one's own. But must one not already know one's own in order even to know of "the foreign"? Is what one thinks to be the foreign merely the foreign *of* one's own, and thus not the foreign *as foreign*? Where is the "spirit" of a language to begin with? Neither in "its own," nor in "the foreign," but somewhere between the two, somewhere else, already history, even if it does not know it? The mystery or *Geheimnis* (GA 53, 69) of becoming homely, Heidegger argues, concerns the site of *translation*, the *threshold* at which one can make the transition (or "step over": *Überschritt*[14]) from the spirit of one language into that of another (GA 53, 75).

Heidegger discusses this in the context of a renewed interpretation of *deinon* in the *Antigone* chorus, a discussion that comprises the second of the three parts of the Ister lecture course, and precisely at that point where he turns the accusation of a violent (*gewaltsam*) translation of *deinon* against himself (GA 53, 74). Philologically, Heidegger admits, the translation of *deinon* as *das Unheimliche* is "false." But what is translation? All translation is already interpretation. And conversely, all interpretation is a translating. Translation therefore does not only occur between two different languages, but within one and the same language. All understanding needs translation. Insofar as we are necessarily compelled to interpret works in our own language, this indicates

> that a historical people is not of its own accord, i.e., not without its own intervention, at home *[beheimatet]* in its own language. It may therefore be that we indeed speak "German," but talk entirely "American." ... If becoming homely belongs essentially to historicality, then a historical people can never come to satisfy its essence of its own accord or directly within its own language. A historical people *is* only from the dialogue *[Zwiesprache]* between its language and foreign languages. (GA 53, 80)

Note that Heidegger here speaks of foreign *languages*, in the plural, thereby implying that it is not simply a matter of an exclusive dialogue with one, "privileged" language. But presumably a dialogue with "the Greek" is what is most pressing, most urgently needed in our time, if we are to understand the grounds of our own historicality.

Thought historically, translation is the encounter, the exchange and confrontation (*Auseinandersetzung*) with a foreign language for the sake of the appropriation *(Aneignung)* of one's own language. Yet this implies already that one does not appropriate "one's own" from within one's own, the very task of appropriation entailing that one can never simply *be* "at home" in one's own. All of which means, says Heidegger, echoing Hölderlin, that we first have to *learn* our own language (i.e., not merely acquire it). For Hölderlin, as for Heidegger, such learning is to happen, at least in the first instance, in confrontation with the language of the Greeks. Yet, as we have noted, Heidegger in the above citation speaks of a dialogue with foreign *languages*, in the plural, and not merely with a particular "privileged" language. The privilege or priority of the Greek lies for Hölderlin in the fact that what is proper to the Greeks ("the fire from the heavens," or, as Heidegger puts it, their "being struck by the violence of being": GA 39, 292) is precisely what is foreign to the Germans, who have made "the clarity of presentation" their own. And vice-versa: what is proper to the Germans is what was foreign to the Greeks. Yet the appropriation of the clarity of presentation on the part of the Germans has occurred—this appears to be Heidegger's underlying "thesis"—in the spirit of what he would elsewhere call the "'technical' interpretation of thinking,"[15] which, among other things, entails a domestication of a radical excess and heterogeneity intrinsic to the foreign fire experienced by the Greeks. This spirit of appropriation or domestication of the other in its radical otherness of course begins already in Greek thought, with the beginning of philosophy and the ascendant domination of *techne* (although this domination is precisely concealed in the beginning, i.e., not understood as such). But this symmetry, which is only an *apparent* symmetry, between the Greek and the German—"the Greek" and "the German" here meaning only "that which is [initially] given one as an endowment" *(das Mitgegebene)* in each case— would presumably also hold precisely, indeed even more so, between "the Greek" and "the Anglo-American," insofar as the latter is, if anything, even more dominated by the spirit of an appropriative *techne*, a spirit concretely manifest in the technological "supremacy" that was already becoming evident in America's entry into the war. An openness for, and dialogue with the foreign, one that could perhaps let the foreign be as it is, would be preserved as long as there still were German thinkers and poets who could be open for the *question* of the foreign (and thereby of one's own). Precisely such openness to the radical heterogeneity bestowed by (because latent in) the commencement would be foreclosed or concealed by the "unhistoricality" of Americanism. The Anglo-American world becoming historical would entail its entering into thoughtful dialogue with its own limits, those of the dominant foreignness concealed within it, i.e., its entering into dialogue with the Greeks.

Now Heidegger does not say all of this explicitly, and much more would need to be said concerning the issue of *techne* in this lecture course and in Heidegger's thought of this period. Yet do we find in this 1942 course any traces of what I am calling a "radical heterogeneity" of the commencement?

What is meant by becoming homely? Becoming homely happens only in and as being unhomely, *Unheimischsein*. Being unhomely is to be thought as dwelling in the *polis* in being exposed to *tolma*, risk. Being exposed to the risk of being *apolis* in their dwelling in the site of history entails that in their comportment toward beings, humans "can be mistaken, and at times, i.e., continually within the most extreme realms of this site, must be mistaken within being. . . ." (GA 53, 108). What if, asks Heidegger, "that which is most intrinsically unhomely, thus most remote from all that is homely, were that which in itself simultaneously preserved the most intimate *[innigste]* belonging to the homely?" (GA 53, 129).

The unhomely becoming homely of humans on this earth is "poetical." Meditating on this, Heidegger turns back to Hölderlin's question of the free use of the national, of what is one's own. A fragment of Hölderlin's reads:

> *nemlich zu Hauss ist der Geist,*
> *nicht im Anfang, nicht an der Quell. Ihn zehret die Heimath.*
> *Kolonie liebt, und tapfer Vergessen der Geist.*
> *Unsere Blumen erfreun und die Schatten unserer Wälder*
> *den Verschmachteten. Fast wäre der Beseeler verbrandt.*

> namely at home is spirit
> not in the commencement, not at the source. The home
>   consumes it.
> Colony, and bold forgetting spirit loves.
> Our flowers and the shadows of our woods gladden
> The one who languishes. The besouler would almost be
>   scorched.

Spirit, according to Heidegger, is for Hölderlin always communal spirit *(gemeinsamer Geist)*. Interpreted in terms of the metaphysics of German Idealism, this means that in thinking, spirit thinks what which is common to the being of all beings. For this metaphysics, thinking constitutes the being of spirit; spirit truly *is* itself only when, in thinking the being of beings, it thinks itself as thinking and thus is "alongside" or "with" *(bei)* itself. Yet Hölderlin's poetizing does not, Heidegger argues, poetize this metaphysical determination of spirit. According to the fragment, spirit is to begin with not at home *(zu Hauss)*, i.e., not at the source.[16] But why not? Because, on Heidegger's reading, the home itself *(die Heimat selbst)*, "left purely to itself," eats away at spirit and threatens to consume it (GA 53, 163). The home itself, that which is one's own, has yet to be freed and appropriated as such, in a free relationality.

Yet what kind of "appropriation" *(Aneignung)* does Hölderlin poetize? For German Idealism, as noted, spirit has the desire or longing to appropriate itself in its own essence (in Hegel, for example, to think itself in the truth of the concept). And this on account of its not being at home to begin with, in the beginning. But does spirit in Hölderlin appropriate itself in overcoming its not being at home, so as then to be at home? Or does it appropriate itself precisely *as* not being at home, i.e., as being unhomely, so to be definitively at home in its being unhomely? Heidegger's reading might seem to imply the latter when he writes: "Spirit is only essentially unhomely when, for the sake of what is its own, out of the desire for its essence, it desires the unhomely *[das Unheimische]*, the foreign" (GA 53, 164). However, if we read this statement in the manner suggested, the journey of spirit would essentially be no different from the way it is thought in German Idealism, where negativity sanctions the infinite self-appropriation of spirit. Heidegger's reading, by contrast, finds in Hölderlin something else. What is "essential" or "of the essence" is not necessarily that which is one's own, or that which appears to be one's own. For spirit's "love" of colony, according to Heidegger, as "the essential will for what is of the essence," is not the love of a son (the river) for a daughter of the *fatherland* (i.e., the home as "one's own"); rather, "colony" means "the land of the daughter that is related and drawn back to the motherland. Spirit 'loves' colony; in the foreign it essentially desires the mother *[er will im Fremden wesentlich die Mutter]*. . . ." (GA 53, 164). For the fatherland, as noted earlier, is homely alongside or with *(bei)* "mother earth." And the mother, as Heidegger recalls from Hölderlin's hymn, "The Journey" *(Die Wanderung)*, is "difficult to attain, the closed one *[die Verschlossene]*." In his first Hölderlin course, Heidegger had characterized this "concealed one" who "carries the abyss" (as the hymn "Germania" poetizes her) as "concealment itself, the closed reserve of the womb that leaves things immersed *[die versinken lassende Verschlossenheit des Schoßes]*" (GA 39, 242).

In spirit's love of colony, this love *(Liebe)* is thus not, on Heidegger's reading, an appropriative love directed back toward the possibility of one's own. Love is the desire that the beloved remain the one that it is, in its otherness. "Bold forgetting," in the foreign, "gives thought to" *(bedenkt)* one's own, and yet in such a way that it is a "deferral" *(hintanstellen)* of one's own; it is a peculiar *(eigentümliches) non-thinking* about the home, so as to experience the unhomely, in which experience, however, the "spell of the home" remains preserved (GA 53, 165–66). "Our" flowers and the shadows of "our" woods name the homely, i.e., that which belongs to the Germans. The shadows bring coolness and protect against the excessively intense glow of the foreign fire; the flowers bring soft illumination, protecting against its excessive brightness (GA 53, 167). The flowers and shadows of the homely protect the one who languishes in the heat from the threat of being consumed in the foreign fire. Here the "besouler," the one who brings soul to things, that is, the poet himself, must recognize the flowers and shadows as that which gladden. Heidegger states:

> This experience now becomes a way of learning how to freely use what is one's own. . . . The journeying into the unhomely must go "almost" to the threshold *[Grenze]* of being annihilated in the fire, in order for the locality of the homely to bestow that which gladdens and saves. (GA 53, 167)

This journeying toward the locality of the homely is, Heidegger asserts, "for the singular history of the Germans," the law of becoming homely in being unhomely (GA 53, 168). Dwelling itself, being homely on the earth, is a journeying, "the becoming homely of a being unhomely" *(das Heimischwerden eines Unheimischseins)* (GA 53, 171).

This journeying is itself the flow of the river that is poetized as (and not merely in) Hölderlin's hymn. Thus we can begin to understand the words in the second strophe of "The Ister" that read:

So wundert
Mich nicht, dass er
Den Herkules zu Gaste geladen,
Fernglänzend, am Olympos drunten,
Da der, sich Schatten zu suchen
Vom heissen Isthmos kam,
Denn voll des Muthes waren
Daselbst sie, es bedarf aber, der Geister wegen,
Der Kühlung auch.

> Thus it surprises
> Me not, that he [the Ister]
> Invited Hercules as guest,
> Gleaming from afar, down there by Olympus,
> When he in search of shade
> From the sultry Isthmus came,
> For full of courage were
> They even there, yet there was need, for the spirits' sake,
> Of cooling too.

The Ister has invited Hercules as a guest from the land of the foreign fire. What does it mean to be a guest? Heidegger remarks: "A guest is that foreigner [or stranger: *Fremde*] who for a time becomes homely in a homely place foreign to them, and thus themselves bring what is homely for them into the homely of the foreign and are received by the homely of the foreign." Yet a guest does not come uninvited: "In guest-friendship, however, there also lies the resolve not to mix what is one's own, as one's own, with the foreign, but to let the foreigner be the one he is" (GA 53, 175–76). The hospitality of the Ister toward the foreign demigod is only one form of spirit's love of colony, namely that form according to which—and this is essential—spirit must still love colony even when it has journeyed back to the homely that is its own. The guest is the presence *(Gegenwart)* of the foreign fire, of the unhomely in the midst of the homely. The appropriation of one's own, Heidegger states,

> *is* only as the encounter *[Auseinandersetzung]* and guest-like dialogue *[Zwiesprache]* with the foreign. Being a locality, being the essential locale of the homely, is a journeying into that which is not directly bestowed upon one's own essence, but must be learnt in journeying.... The river "is" the locality and the journeying at once... (GA 53, 177–78)

In what way and in what locality does the Ister journey? Hölderlin says of it:

> Der scheinet aber fast
> Rükwärts zu gehen und
> Ich mein, er müsse kommen
> Von Osten.
> Vieles wäre
> Zu sagen davon....

> He appears, however, almost
> To go backwards and
> I presume he must come
> From the East.
> There would be
> Much to tell of this. . . .

It seems "almost" as though the Ister flows backwards, does not flow away from its source, because there must be something like a mysterious counterflow *(eine geheime Gegenströmung)* that pushes in the opposite direction already in its springing from the source. In the hesitant flow of the Ister the poet, says Heidegger, has an intimation of *(ahnt)* the mysterious concealment *(die geheimnisvolle Verborgenheit)* of the way in which the relations to the foreign and to one's own intertwine: "The Ister *is* that river in which the foreign is already present as a guest at its source, that river in whose flowing there constantly speaks the dialogue between one's own and the foreign" (GA 53, 182).

This hesitant, intimative flow of the Ister thus poetizes a different relation to the source from that poetized by "The Rhine," the river alluded to in the closing lines of "The Ister" as "that river." For the Rhine, according to the hymn, "The Journey" *(Die Wanderung)*, wished, as Heidegger puts it, "to plunge directly to the heart of the mother of the home" (GA 53, 201):

> Von ihrer Söhnen einer, der Rhein,
> Mit Gewalt wollt er ans Herz ihr stürzen und schwand
> Der Zurückgestoßene, niemand weiß, wohin in die Ferne.

> One of her sons, the Rhine,
> Wished to rush to her heart with force and vanished
> The rejected one, no one knows whereto, into the distance.

Far from coming to know itself and its own determination, the river that wishes to appropriate with violence or force *(Gewalt)* its own origin takes an unknown direction, vanishing into a distance that is truly, i.e., unknowingly uncanny, unhomely, for it is a distance that is excluded from an intimative openness to the mystery *(Geheimnis)* of the earth.[17] Such intimative knowing is, Heidegger's reading suggests, poetized in the flow of the Ister, "the properly homely river of this poet" (GA 52, 185).

But we must interrupt here, though there would be much more to tell. We have touched upon only a few of the many issues

Heimat: Heidegger on the Threshold 347

that gather around this great theme of the home in Heidegger.[18] Our remarks have been made with the sole intention of making us attentive to the extent to which, on the journey of his own thought, including that of the 1930s and 40s, the home for Heidegger has always returned as a *question*, perhaps even *the* question.

What the essence of the home is we may begin to think in listening again to the opening lines of the hymn, "The Ister." The poem begins with a call that is an invitation. The first word names a threshold: the time of an invitation, of an openness. The ones who call thereby announce their readiness to receive the guest. They can be ready only because they themselves are in turn called by the guest, called upon to listen. The poem begins:

> Jezt komme, Feuer!
> Begierig sind wir
> Zu schauen den Tag,
> . . .
>
> Now come, fire!
> Eager are we
> To see the day,
> . . . [19]

Notes

1. Heidegger, *"Die Sprache"* (1950). In *Unterwegs zur Sprache* (Pfullingen: Neske, 1979), p. 26.

2. "Porosity: Violence and the Question of Politics in Heidegger's *Introduction to Metaphysics.*" *Graduate Faculty Philosophy Journal* (New School for Social Research), Volume 14, Number 2–Volume 15, Number 1 (1991), 183–212.

3. One must hear both resonances in the German word, and I shall vary the translation in this essay according to context. Heidegger, as we shall see, places special emphasis on the root *heim*, "home," as central to the sense of *Unheimlichkeit*. Freud's essay *"Das Unheimliche"* ("The Uncanny") provides a useful overview of the traditional resonances of the word *unheimlich*. Particularly important for Heidegger is the connection of *heimlich* with concealment, secret, and mystery *(Geheimnis)*. Cf. Schelling's definition of *unheimlich*, cited by Freud: "One names *unheimlich* everything that ought to have remained a mystery, concealed *[im Geheimnis, im Verborgenen]*, and that has come to the fore." (Freud, *Studienausgabe* Bd. IV, 248)

4. Heidegger emphasizes this equiprimordiality even more strongly in Section 20 of *The Basic Problems of Phenomenology* (GA 24).

5. Cf. the entire analysis of conscience *(Gewissen)* in *Being and Time*, in particular Section 60, where Heidegger remarks that the "voice" *(Stimme)* of conscience, as mode of discourse *(Rede)*, calls in the attunement *(Stimmung)* of *Unheimlichkeit*, and does so in *silence*: "Conscience calls only in silence; that is to say, the call comes from out of the soundlessness of *Unheimlichkeit*, and calls the Dasein that is summoned back into the stillness of itself, such that it is to become still." The keeping silent of this silence "withdraws" *(entzieht)* the word from *das Man* (SZ, 296). A careful and extensive analysis would be required to compare this call of conscience with Heidegger's much later interpretation of the "call" poetized in Hölderlin's hymn, "The Ister" (see below).

6. On this question, see Jacques Derrida, *De l'esprit* (Paris: Éditions Galilée, 1987).

7. See *Erläuterungen zu Hölderlins Dichtung* (Frankfurt: Klostermann, 1981), 9–31.

8. Cf. *"Zur Seinsfrage,"* GA 9, 387.

9. I say "(quasi-)" metaphysical here because modern technological thinking is not, properly speaking, metaphysical (it operates beyond, or outside of, the ontological difference), although it is a transformation—if Heidegger is right, the *last* essential transformation—of metaphysical thought.

10. The word *Auseinandersetzung*, which conveys the sense of a setting out or apart from one another, is particularly difficult to translate. It is often rendered as "confrontation," and undoubtedly carries something of this "polemical" tone in the first Hölderlin course. In the last, 1942 Hölderlin course to which we shall turn in a moment, however, the term *Auseinandersetzung* seems less "polemical" and, I would argue, carries more the sense of a mutual encounter than that of confrontation. Accordingly, I shall interweave these different translations depending on the context, indicating the German term where helpful.

For a reading of Heidegger's use of *Auseinandersetzung* in another context, see my "Traces of Discordance: Heidegger—Nietzsche," in *Nietzsche: A Critical Reader*, ed. Peter Sedgwick (Oxford: Blackwell, 1995).

11. The translation of *Gewalt* as "violence" is not unproblematic. It might alternatively be rendered as "might," "power," or even "force." "Power" and "force," however, correlate more closely with *Macht* and *Kraft* respectively. *Gewalt* carries for Heidegger the sense of a powerful prevailing or overwhelming power, a dominant holding sway. The English word "violence" is closer to the sense of *Gewaltsamkeit* or *Gewalttätigkeit* (the latter in this essay being rendered "active violence" or "violent activity" to convey the sense of *Tätigkeit*). In none of these instances should "violence" be taken in the sense of arbitrary acts of wantonness or willfulness, but must be thought as an irruption into *phusis* that occurs at the site of human *techne*. For a further discussion of Heidegger's understanding of *Gewalt*, see my remarks on these terms in "Porosity . . ." (op. cit.).

12. On Nietzsche in relation to Hölderlin and the theme of *Heimat*, see the 1944/45 course, *"Denken und Dichten,"* now published in GA 50 (Frankfurt: Klostermann, 1990).

13. Presumably, Heidegger meant "unhistoricality" *(Ungeschichtlichkeit)*, for he later attributes the latter to "Americanism," reserving "ahistoricality" *(Geschichtslosigkeit)* for "nature." See GA 53, 179.

14. In the previous Hölderlin course, on the hymn "*Andenken*," Heidegger had explicitly identified the place of such stepping over as the threshold: "The threshold means the place where one steps from one realm over into another *[Die Schwelle meint die Stelle des Überschritts von einem Bezirk in den anderen]*" (GA 52, 37). Note that the term *Überschritt* is used earlier in *The Metaphysical Foundations of Logic* (1928) to characterize the temporal *ekstasis* of Dasein as transcendence: "Dasein itself is the *Überschritt*," remarked Heidegger in that course; it is the "passage across," as Michael Heim translates it (GA 26, 211).

15. See "Letter on 'Humanism,'" GA 9, 314.

16. Heidegger here reads *Anfang* as meaning *Beginn*, beginning. For Heidegger's own thought, by contrast, *Anfang*, normally translated as "commencement" or "inception," is precisely distinguished from *Beginn*. Heidegger explains the distinction at the outset of the first Hölderlin lecture course in 1934/35 as follows (I cite his remarks here because they are particularly relevant to our discussion of the political and spiritual context of the 1942 course): "Beginning *[Beginn]* is that with which something starts; commencement *[Anfang]* is that from which something originates *[entspringt]*. The world war had its commencement centuries ago in the spiritual-political history of the Western world *[in der geistig-politischen Geschichte des Abendlandes]*. The world war began with skirmishes in the outposts. The beginning is at once left behind, it disappears as events proceed. The commencement, the origin, by contrast first comes to appear in the course of events and is fully there only when the course of events ends. Often, whoever begins lots of things never reaches the commencement. Of course, we human beings can never commence with the commencement—only a god can do that—but must begin, i.e., start, with something that first leads to the origin or points toward it . . ." (GA 39, 3–4).

17. Elsewhere, I have suggested that "The Rhine" poetizes the journey of Western *techne* that seeks to appropriate all otherness in its desire of self-determination. See "The Telling of a Destiny: Hölderlin's *Der Rhein*." In *Poetizing the Political*, by Helen Chapman, Will McNeill, and Anthony Phelan (published by the Centre for Research in Philosophy and Literature: University of Warwick, England, 1993). On the relation between "The Ister," "The Rhine," and "Germania," see GA 53, 202.

18. For a more extended discussion of some of these issues, cf. Michel Haar, *Le chant de la terre* (Paris: Éditions de l'Herne, 1985), in particular the last chapter, "L'habitation ekstatique. . . ." Translated by Reginald Lilly as *The Song of the Earth* (Bloomington: Indiana University Press, 1993).

19. Revised version of a paper first presented at a seminar in Warwick, England, 1989, at the invitation of David Wood. My thanks to David Wood for his invitation and hospitality.

BIBLIOGRAPHY

Adorno, Theodor W. *Negative Dialektik*. Frankfurt: Suhrkamp Verlag, 1970.

Arendt, Hannah. *The Human Condition*. Chicago: The University of Chicago Press, 1958.

Baudelaire, Charles. *Oeuvres Complètes*. Paris: Gallimard, 1961.

Baudrillard, Jean. *In the Shadows of the Silent Majorities*. Translated by Foss, Johnston and Patton. New York: Semiotext(e), 1983.

Beck, Lewis W. *Kant, On History*. New York: Prentice-Hall, 1963.

Benjamin, W. *Gesammelte Schriften*. Frankfurt: Suhrkamp, 1980.

Bernasconi, R. *The Question of Language in Heidegger's History of Being*. Atlantic Highlands: Humanities Press, 1985.

———. *Heidegger in Question: The Art of Existing*. Atlantic Highlands: Humanities Press, 1993.

Bernstein, Jay. "Aesthetic Alienation: Heidegger, Adorno and Truth at the End of Art." *Life after Postmodernism*. Edited by John Fekete. New York: St. Martin's Press, 1987.

Bloch, Ernst. *The Utopian Function of Art and Literature*. Translated by Zipes and Mecklenburg. Cambridge: The MIT Press, 1989.

Blumenberg, Hans. *Work on Myth*. Translated by Robert M. Wallace. Cambridge: The MIT Press, 1985.

Bruns, Gerald L. *Heidegger's Estrangements*. New Haven: Yale University Press, 1989.

Buchner, Harmut. "Fragmentarisches." *Erinnerung an Martin Heidegger*. Edited by Günther Neske. Pfullingen: Neske, 1977.

Bollnow, Otto. *Les tonalités affectives*. Neuchâtel: La Baconnière, 1953.

Beaufret, Jean. "Kant et la notion de *Darstellung*." *Dialogue avec Heidegger II*. Paris: E. de Minuit, 1973.

Descartes, René. *Meditations On First Philosophy*. Translated by J. Cottingham, R. Stoothoff, and D. Murdoch. Cambridge: Cambridge University Press, 1984.

Derrida, Jacques. *Margins Of Philosophy*. Translated by A. Bass. Chicago: The University of Chicago Press, 1982.

———. *Of Grammatology*. Translated by G. C. Spivak. Baltimore: The Johns Hopkins University Press, 1974.

Farias, Victor. *Heidegger and Nazism*. Edited by J. Margolis and T. Rockmore. Philadelphia: Temple University Press, 1989.

Fichte, J. G. *Wissenschaftslehre*. Berlin: de Gruyter, 1971.

Fóti, Véronique M. *Heidegger and the Poets*. Atlantic Highlands: Humanities Press, 1991.

Foucault, Michel. "Preface to transgression." *Language, Counter-Memory, Practice*. Edited by D. F. Bouchard. Ithaca: Cornell University Press, 1977.

———. "Des supplices aux cellules." *Le monde*. February 21, 1975.

Fraenkel, Eduard. *Aeschylus: Agamemnon*. Oxford: Oxford University Press, 1950.

Franzen, Winifried. "Die Sehnsucht nach Härte und Schwere." *Heidegger und Praktische Philosophie*. Edited by Otto Pöggeler and A. Gethmann-Siefert. Frankfurt: Suhrkamp, 1988.

Gadamer, Hans-Georg. *Kleine Schriften I*. Tübingen: Niemeyer, 1967.

———. "Zur Einfuhrung." *Der Ursprung des Kunstwerkes*. Stuttgart: Reclam, 1967.

Gay, Peter. "Burckhardt: The Poet of Truth." *Style in History*. New York: Basic Books, 1974.

George, Stefan. "Kein Ding sei wo das Wort gebricht." *Das Neue Reich*. Berlin: Georg Bondi, 1919.

Grossman, Andreas. "Hegel, Heidegger, and the Question of Art Today." *Research in Phenomenology* 20 (1990): 112–135.

Haar, Michel, (ed.). *cahier de l'Herne "Heidegger."* Paris: L'Herne, 1983.

———. *Le Chant de la Terre: Heidegger et les assises de l'histoire de l'être*. Paris: L'Herne, 1985.

Habermas, Jürgen. "Work and Weltanschauung: The Heidegger Controversy from a German Perspective." Translated by John McCumber. *Critical Inquiry* 15 (1989).

Haverkamp, Anselm. "Error in Mourning—A Crux in Hölderlin: 'dem gleich fehlet die Trauer' ('Mnemosyne')." *The Lesson of Paul de Man*. Translated by Vernon Chadwick. New Haven and London: Yale University Press, 1985.

Hegel, G. W. F. *Vorlesungen über die Ästhetik*. Werke in zwanzig Bänden. Frankfurt: Suhrkamp, 1970.

———. *Aesthetics*. Translated by T. M. Knox. Oxford: Oxford University Press, 1975.

Heidegger, Martin. *The End of Philosophy*. Translated by Joan Stambaugh. New York: Harper and Row, 1973.

———. "Die Herkunft der Kunst und die Bestimmung des Denkens." *Distanz und Nähe*. Edited by Peter Jaeger and Rudolf Lüthe. Würzburg: Königshausen and Neumann, 1983.

———. *The Metaphysical Foundations of Logic*. Translated by Michael Heim. Bloomington: Indiana University Press, 1984.

———. "'Only A God Can Save Us': The *Spiegel* Interview (1966)." Translated by William J. Richardson, S. J. *Heidegger: The Man and the Thinker*. Edited by Thomas Sheehan. Chicago: Precedent Publishing, 1981.

———. "Technik und Kunst-Gestell." *Kunst und Technik*. Edited by Walter Beimel and Friedrich-Wilhelm von Hermann. Frankfurt: Klostermann, 1989.

———. *Ontologie: Hermeneutik der Faktizität*. Gesamtausgabe vol. 63. Edited by Käte Bröcker-Oltmanns. Frankfurt: Klostermann, 1988.

———. *Zur Bestimmung der Philosophie*. Gesamtausgabe vols. 56–57. Edited by Bernd Heimbüchel. Frankfurt: Klostermann, 1987.

———. *Zur Sache des Denkens*. Tübingen: Max Niemeyer, 1969.

Hölderlin, Friedrich. *Hölderlin Sämtliche Werke*. Edited by Friedrich Beissner. Stuttgart: W. Kohlhammer Verlag, 1954.

———. *Poems and Fragments*. Translated by Michael Hamburger. Ann Arbor: University of Michigan Press, 1968.

———. *Friedrich Hölderlin: Essays and Letters on Theory*. Translated by Thomas Pfau. Albany: SUNY Press, 1988.

Husserl, Edmund. *The Crisis of European Sciences and Transcendental Philosophy*. Translated by D. Carr. Evanston: Northwestern University Press, 1970.

Krell, David Farrell. "Daimon Life, Nearness and Abyss: An Introduction to Zaology." *Research in Phenomenology*, 27 (1987).

———. *Of Memory, Reminiscence, and Writing: On the Verge*. Bloomington: Indiana University Press, 1990).

Kristeller, Paul. "The Modern System of the Arts." *Renaissance Thought and the Arts*. Princeton: Princeton University Press, 1980.

Kolb, David. *The Critique of Pure Modernity*. Chicago: University of Chicago Press, 1986.

Kundera, Milos. *The Unbearable Lightness of Being*. Translated by M. H. Heim. New York: Harper & Row, 1984.

Lacoue-Labarthe, Phillippe. *Heidegger, Art, and Politics*. Translated by Chris Turner. Oxford: Basil Blackwell, 1990.

———. *La ficition du politique*. Paris: Christian Bourgois, 1987.

———. *L'imitation des modernes: Typographies II*. Paris: Galilée, 1986.

Le Rider, Jacques. "Le Dossier D'un Nazi 'Ordinaire'" *Le Monde* (October 13–19, 1988).

Levinas, Emmanuel. *Time and the Other*. Translated by Richard A. Cohen. Pittsburgh: Duquesne University Press, 1987.

Llewelyn, John. *The Middle Voice of Ecological Conscience: A Chiasmic Reading of Responsibility in the Neighbourhood of Emmanuel Levinas, Martin Heidegger, and Others*. London: Macmillan, 1992.

Mallarmé, Stéphane. *Oeuvres Complètes*. Paris: Gallimard, Pléiade, 1945.

Marion, Jean-Luc. *Dieu sans l'être*. Paris: Fayard, 1982.

McNeill, Will. "Traces of Discordance: Heidegger—Nietzsche." *Nietzsche: A Critical Reader*. Edited by Peter Sedgwick. Oxford: Blackwell, 1995.

Nietzsche, Friedrich. *Der Wille zur Macht*. Edited by Peter Gast and Elizabeth Förster-Nietzsche. Stuttgart: Alfred Kröner, 1959.

———. *Thus Spoke Zarathustra*. Translated by Walter Kaufmann. New York: Viking Press, 1968.

Nussbaum, Martha. *The Fragility of Goodness*. New York: Cambridge University Press, 1986.

Ott, Hugo. *Martin Heidegger: Unterwegs zu Seiner Biographie*. Frankfurt: Campus Verlag, 1988.

Pöggeler, Otto. "Heideggers politisches Selbstverständnis." *Heidegger und die praktische Philosophie*. Edited by Annemarie Gethmann-Siefert and Otto Pöggeler. Frankfurt: Suhrkamp, 1988.

———. *Martin Heidegger's Path of Thinking*. Translated by D. Magurshak and S. Barner. Atlantic Highlands: Humanities Press, 1987.

Press, Gerald A. *The Development of the Idea of History in Antiquity*. Montreal: McGill-Queen's University Press, 1982.

Reich, Wilhelm. *Listen, Little Man!*. Translated by Ralph Manheim. New York: Farrer, Straus and Giroux, 1974.

Reinhardt, Karl. *Sophokles*. Frankfurt: 1947.

Rimbaud, Arthur. "A Season in Hell: Delirium I." *A Season in Hell and The Drunken Boat*. Translated by L. Varèse. New York: New Directions, 1961.

Rosenzweig, Franz. *Star of Redemption*. Translated by W. Hallo. New York: Holt, Rinehart & Winston, 1970.

Sallis, John. "Deformatives: Essentially Other Than Truth," *Reading Heidegger*. Bloomington: Indiana University Press, 1991.

———. *Delimitations: Phenomenology and the End of Metaphysics*. Bloomington: Indiana University Press, 1986.

———. "Flight of Spirit." *Diacritics*. 19.3–4. (1989): 25–37.

Schirmacher, Wolfgang. *Technik und Gelassenheit*. Freiburg: Alber, 1983.

Schmidt, Dennis J. *The Ubiquity of the Finite*. Cambridge: MIT Press, 1988.

———. "Economies of Production: Heidegger and Aristotle on *Physis* and *Technë*." *Crises in Continental Philosophy*. Edited by A. Dallery and C. Scott. Albany: SUNY Press, 1990.

Schoeller-von Haslingern, Karin. "Was ist Grosse?" *Heidegger Studies* 3/4 (1987): 15–23.

Schürmann, Reiner. *Heidegger on Being and Acting: From Principles to Anarchy*. Translated by C. M. Gros. Bloomington: Indiana University Press, 1987.

———. "Ultimate Double Binds." *Graduate Faculty Philosophy Journal* 14:2–15.1 (1991): 213–236.

Scott, Charles. *The Language of Difference*. Atlantic Highlands: Humanities Press, 1986.

Sheehan, Thomas. "Heidegger and the Nazis." *The New York Review of Books*. June, 16, 1988.

Spengler, Oswald. *The Decline of the West*. Translated by Charles F. Atkinson. New York: Knopf, 1928.

Szondi, Peter. "The Notion of the Tragic in Schelling, Hölderlin, and Hegel." *On Textual Understanding, and Other Essays*. Translated by Harvey Mendelsohn. Minneapolis: University of Minnesota Press, 1986.

Taminiaux, Jacques. "Le dépassement Heideggérien de l'esthétique et l'héritage de Hegel." *Recoupements*. Brussels: Ousia, 1982.

———. "The Origin of the Work of Art." *Poetics, Speculation, and Judgment: The Shadow of the Work of Art from Kant to Phenomenology.* Translated by Michael Gendre. Albany: SUNY Press, 1993.

Tatarkiewicz, W. "Classification of Arts in Antiquity." *Journal of the History of Ideas* 24 (1963): 231–240.

Taylor, Mark C. *Altarity.* Chicago: University of Chicago Press, 1987.

Unger, Roberto M. *False Necessity.* Cambridge: Cambridge University Press, 1987.

Willett, Cynthia. "Hegel, Antigone, and the Possibility of Ecstatic Dialectic." *Philosophy and Literature.* 1990.

Yeats, William Butler. "Meru." *The Poems.* Edited by R. J. Finneran. New York: Macmillan, 1983.

Zimmerman, Michael E. *Heidegger's Confrontation with Modernity: Technology, Politics, Art.* Bloomington: Indiana University Press, 1990.

NOTES ON CONTRIBUTORS

Robert Bernasconi is Moss Professor of Philosophy at the University of Memphis. He is the author of *The Question of Language in Heidegger's History of Being* and *Heidegger in Question: The Art of Existing*. He is the editor of a collection of essays on Gadamer's aesthetics, *The Relevance of the Beautiful and Other Essays*. He is also editor, with David Wood, of *Derrida and Difference*, and with Simon Critchley, *Re-Reading Levinas*.

John D. Caputo is David R. Cook Professor of Philosophy at Villanova University. His publications include *Demythologizing Heidegger, Against Ethics, Radical Hermeneutics,* and *Heidegger and Aquinas*. He recently served as executive co-director of the Society for Phenomenology and Existential Philosophy.

Françoise Dastur is Professor of Philosophy at the University of Paris XII. She has published numerous articles in French, English and German on Husserl, Heidegger, and Merleau-Ponty and other representatives of the phenomenological movement. She is the author of *Heidegger et la question du temps, Hölderlin: Tragédie et modernité, Dire le temps: Esquisse d'une chronologie phénoménologie, La Mort: Essai sur la finitude,* and *Husserl: Des mathématiques à l'histoire*.

Véronique M. Fóti is Associate Professor of Philosophy at Pennsylvania State University. She has published extensively on Heidegger, Hölderlin, Celan, Merleau-Ponty, and continental Rationalism, as well as in the area of Greek philosophy. She is the author of *Heidegger and the Poets: Poiēsis, Sophia, Technē*.

Hans-Georg Gadamer is Professor Emeritus at Universität Heidelberg in Germany. His major work, *Wahrheit und Methode*, has established him as the leading figure in hermeneutic theory in contemporary philosophy. He has just completed his *Gesammelte Werke*, which comprises ten volumes on topics ranging from his work on Greek philosophy to his work on hermeneutics, with essays on aesthetics and commentaries on Heidegger's philosophy.

Rodolphe Gasché is Professor of Comparative Literature at the State University of New York at Buffalo. He is the author of *The Tain of the Mirror: Derrida and the Philosophy of Reflection* and, most recently, *Inventions of Difference: On Jacques Derrida*.

Michel Haar is Professor of the History of Contemporary Philosophy at the University of Paris—I (Panthéon-Sorbonne). Two of his books have recently been translated into English: *The Song of the Earth* and *Heidegger and the Essence of Man*. He is also the author of *Nietzsche et la métaphysique* and *La Fracture de l'Historie*.

David Farrell Krell is Professor of Philosophy at De Paul University in Chicago. In addition to his two Heidegger books *Daimon Life* and *Intimations of Mortality*, he has written *Infectious Nietzsche, Lunar Voices: Of Tragedy, Poetry, Fiction and Thought*, and *The Good European: Nietzsche's Work Sites in Word and Image*. He has forthcoming from University of Chicago Press *The Purest of Bastards: Derrida on the Work of Mourning, Art, and Affirmation*.

Will McNeill is Associate Professor of Philosophy at DePaul University. He has published papers on Heidegger and contintental thought. He is the translator of Martin Heidegger's *The Concept of Time*, and he is co-translator of Martin Heidegger's *The Fundamental Concepts of Metaphysics* and of Heidegger's lectures on *Hölderlin's Hymn "The Ister."* He recently completed a book on Heidegger, *The Glance of the Eye*.

John Sallis is Liberal Arts Professor of Philosophy at Pennsylvania State University. He is the author of *Double Truth, Stone, Echoes: After Heidegger, Crossings, Being and Logos, The Gathering of Reason, Deliminations,* and *Spacings*. He is the editor of *Reading Heidegger: Commemorations* and founding editor of the journal *Research in Phenomenology*.

Dennis J. Schmidt is Professor of Philosophy at Villanova University. He is the author of *The Ubiquity of the Finite*. He is the author of numerous articles in 19th and 20th century continental philosophy, especially on the work of Hegel, Heidegger and Hölderlin. He is the translator of Ernst Bloch's *Natural Law and Human Dignity*, and editor of the SUNY Press series in Continental Philosophy.

Reiner Schürmann is the author of *Heidegger on Being and Acting: From Principles to Anarchy* and *Meister Eckhart: Mystic and Philosopher*. Before his death he was Professor of Philosophy at the Graduate Faculty of the New School for Social Research.

Contributors

Charles E. Scott is the Edwin Earle Sparks Professor of Philosophy at The Pennsylvania State University. He is the author of *The Language of Difference, The Question of Ethics*, and *On the Advantage and Disadvantge of Ethics and Politics*. He served as executive co-director of the Society for Phenomenology and Existential Philosophy from 1986 to 1989.

Jacques Taminiaux is Professor of Philosophy at Boston College and at the University of Louvain-la-Neuve, where he is the Director of the Center for Phenomenological Studies. He is the author of *Dialectic and Difference, Heidegger and the Project of Fundamental Ontology* and, more recently, *Poetics, Speculation, and Judgment*.

Wilhelm S. Wurzer is Professor of Philosophy at Duquesnes University, and has written extensively in the area of 19th and 20th century continental philosophy. He is the author of *Nietzsche und Spinoza* and *Filming and Judgment*.

Index

aesthetics, 102, 137, 192
Agamemnon, 246, 248
Agathon, 237–238
aletheia, 44, 47, 48, 131, 148, 149, 150, 151. *See* truth
anxiety, 307
  as attunement of unhomeliness, 324
Aristotle, 100, 101, 147, 149, 231, 244, 288
art, 5, 96, 99, 134, 193, 202
  great, 95–96, 99, 100, 105–106, 108, 136
  Hegel and, 100–101, 105, 108, 125
  and the past, 124–126
  metaphysical conception of, 134–138
  modern, 126
  and representation, 121, 126
  and truth, 104–105, 123, 131–134
  two essential features of, 126–128
  work of, 121–128, 138. *See* "The Origin of the Work of Art"
artist, 121
attunement (*Stimmung*), 43, 47, 295

Being
  and beings, 228
  history of, 228

  singularity of, 259
  truth of, 4–5
  unconcealment of, 136
  and value, 231
  withdrawal of, 46
Being and Time, 1, 20, 97, 103, 120, 128, 129, 132, 194, 211, 236, 244, 274, 281, 283, 298
  and the analysis of truth, 26–29
  and the twisting free of selfhood, 215
  and the question of ethics, 218
being unhomely, 342–345
Beiträge, 269, 270, 277, 281
biologism, 290
boredom, 271, 297–298, 309
  and anxiety, 306–308
  three circles of, 303–306

community, 82, 150, 203
Celan, Paul, 151, 160
comprehension, 122
conscience, 223
  call of, 217, 220
Creon, 170, 175

Dasein, 2, 26, 27, 60, 64, 120, 124, 132, 211, 281, 284, 302, 320
  and authenticity, 220
  and boredom, 310
  truth of, 213, 300
  and uncanniness, 333–334
Derrida, Jacques, 277

Descartes, Rene, 177, 232, 235
deinon, 65–66, 87, 167, 168, 171, 172, 332. *See* Sophocles
  as uncanny, 65
destiny, 60, 71, 85, 86, 228, 239, 319, 331
  essential, 70, 82
  historical, 60, 83
dike, 65, 87, 168, 172
Duchamp, Marcel, 262–263
dwelling, 236–327

existence, 295
Ereignis, 138, 171, 203, 253, 289

Farias Victor, 57
fate, 89, 319
forgetting, 300
Foucault, Michel, 221, 223, 253, 265, 278
fourfold, 141
freedom, 270
  and Dasein's transcendence, 238
  essence of, 43
Freud, Sigmund, 269–270, 283, 284, 289

Gadamer, Hans-Georg, 98
Galileo, 231–232
George, Stefan, 202
German
  nation, 62
  spirit, 59
  people, 106, 114
Greeks, the, 69, 75, 80, 87, 101
Guardini, Romano, 152

Hegel, G.W.F., 76, 166, 226, 255, 285
Heidegger, Martin
  and history, 76–78
  and the history of metaphysics, 19–20
  and the issue of the turn (*Kehre*), 2–4
  and National Socialism, 6
  his reading of *Antigone*, 165, 172–175, 178
  and the work of art, 5
Heraclitus, 62, 67, 82, 102, 150, 261, 273
hermeneutical situation, 122
historicality (*Geschichtlichkeit*), 319, 321
history
  Heidegger's sense of, 85–89
  of ontology, 96
  truth of, 78
Hölderlin, 64, 65, 87, 91, 104, 107, 110, 113, 130, 145, 151–161, 163, 171, 181, 189, 286, 296, 325, 329, 330, 331, 341, 342, 343
  Andenken, 151, 155–158
  Germanien, 188, 190–191, 204, 205
  Heidegger's view on, 152
  Hyperion, 205
  Der Ister, 334–337
homecoming, 170–177
Homer, 246, 280
Husserl, Edmund, 1, 24, 25

indifference, 299–303
  to being, 313. *See* boredom

Jünger, Ernst, 65

kairos, 170
Kant, Immanuel, 126
Kehre, 3, 203, 235
Kierkegaard, Soren, 275, 297
Klee, Paul, 126
Kundera, Milan, 59

language, 78, 151, 160, 187, 187–188, 194–198, 249, 324, 325–326
  of presence, 219
  spirit of, 339–340
Leibniz, 233, 278, 279
  Monadology, 286–287

legislation, 248–253
Levinas, Emmanuel, 70, 297
life, 270, 271–273, 283, 288
   and indifference, 301
logos, 147, 195–196

Mallarmé, 296, 297, 306
Marion, Jean-Luc, 300
Marxism, 61, 203
metaphysics, 226
   beginning of, 314
   history of, 19, 20, 113, 192, 199, 234, 274
Musil, Robert, 274
mystery, 46

National Socialism, 5, 6, 53, 58, 68–69, 71, 112, 163, 250, 319, 339. *See* Nazis
   historical uniqueness of, 84
   "inner truth and greatness of the movement," 84, 95
   philosophy of, 95
Nazis, 58, 59, 67, 111. *See* National Socialism
Newton, Issac, 231
Nietzsche, Friedrich, 61, 88, 99, 100, 163, 198, 212, 226, 227, 236, 274, 289, 308, 321, 328, 334
   and the ascetic ideal, 216
Novalis, 329

Oedipus, 175, 248
ontological difference, 234, 258, 270, 272, 296
"The Origin of the Work of Art," 97–99, 112, 168
   different versions of, 97, 105, 110, 119–120
Ott, Hugo, 5, 57, 68, 71

painting, 111–112
Parmenides, 129, 150, 230, 243
phenomena
   faithfulness to, 252

philosophy, 243
   as absolute science, 141
   and common sense, 31–32
   and poetry, 187
   and questioning, 55–56, 60
Plato, 83, 100, 101, 230, 237, 239, 244, 273
   and his doctrine of truth, 164
   Seventh Letter, 151
poetry
   and thinking, 148
   as other language, 187
polis, 62, 75, 82, 83, 91, 175, 176, 180, 181, 342
polemos and aboriginal struggle, 62–63
pragmatism, 290
presence (*Anwesenheit*), 164

Rectoral Address, 106

Sartre, Jean-Paul, 296
scepticism, 299
Schelling Friedrich, 169, 280
Schreiber, Daniel Paul, 271–276, 281, 283, 284, 289, 290
selfhood, 212
sigetics, 199–200
singularization, 181
Socrates, 281
Sophocles, 54, 61, 64, 66, 67, 71, 103, 165
   Antigone, 65, 87, 167, 169–170, 171, 332
sublime, 142

techne, 83, 85, 168–170, 172, 178, 342
technology
   essence of, 312
temporality, 169, 218, 219, 243, 245, 270, 298, 301, 308
   and indifference, 302–303
thinking, 320
   of Being, 225
   and the discordant time, 246
   leap of, 271

thinking *(continued)*
  and poetry, 195
  technological, 328
tragedy, 183, 248
tragic denial, 247
transgression, 253–256
truth, 229, 273
  as accordance, 31–38, 42
  as *aletheia*, 47, 230–231
  and attunement, 43
  as correctness, 19, 22, 42
  and dissymmetry, 47
  essence of, 40–41, 133
  force of, 278
  and freedom, 38–40, 42
  happening of, 107–108
  inner, 54, 95
  material, 33
  originary phenomenon of, 26
  traditional concept of, 22, 27, 31
  and untruth, 21, 29–30, 46, 132

uncanny, 171
unconcealment, 146

Van Gogh, Vincent, 104–105, 111

will to power, 233
word
  truth of the, 146, 147, 150
world and earth, 128, 133, 134
  strife/striving of, 135, 275